Engaging Social Justice: Critical Studies of
21st Century Social Transformation

Studies in
Critical Social Sciences

VOLUME 13

Engaging Social Justice: Critical Studies of 21st Century Social Transformation

Edited by

David Fasenfest

BRILL

LEIDEN • BOSTON
2009

Cover design: Wim Goedhart

This book is printed on acid-free paper.

Library of Congress Cataloging-in-Publication Data

Engaging social justice: critical studies of 21st century social transformation / edited by David Fasenfest.
    p. cm.—(Studies in critical social sciences; v. 13)
    Includes bibliographical references and index.
    ISBN 978-90-04-17654-6 (hardback : alk. paper)
1. Social justice. 2. Social change. 3. Capitalism. I. Fasenfest, David. II. Title. III. Series.

HM671.E54 2009
303.3'72—dc22

2009013822

ISSN 1573-4234
ISBN 978 90 04 17654 6

Copyright 2009 by Koninklijke Brill NV, Leiden, The Netherlands.
Koninklijke Brill NV incorporates the imprints Brill, Hotei Publishing,
IDC Publishers, Martinus Nijhoff Publishers and VSP.

PRINTED IN THE NETHERLANDS

CONTENTS

TOWARDS A PROGRESSIVE FUTURE

David Fasenfest

The 2008 Presidential elections was cast as a competition of change from past practices, both with regard domestic policy and foreign affairs, or a continuation of the same kind of leadership offered by the outgoing administration of George W. Bush. The people had become tired of an unpopular war, the local economy seemed to be stalled for most as the top 1 percent of households earned 20 percent of all income, and the standing of this government in the world's eyes reflected the unrepentant use of torture and unjust imprisonment. Just as the election was drawing near the US, followed in lock step by Europe and then the rest of the world, experienced a massive economic meltdown. As a result, a young African-American was elected President, and in effect promised a new world order. While this has been viewed both internally and internationally as a breath of fresh air, serious questions remain about what is possible, and can this kind of change be made from above. Early days in this new administration reveals that institutions and organizations, as well the political leadership, may be too entrenched reflecting established social and political relationships born of the last half of the 20th Century. Indeed, change may not be possible from the top—at least not the fundamental change that will alter how people in this country and the rest of the world experience this capitalist system.

Marx informs us that while we make our own futures, we do so under conditions we have little control over. As a result, it is imperative that we understand the historical context in which we now try to map out a progressive future. History sets out for us a repertoire of past efforts to promote change, and identifies the transformation of material conditions which define or at least describe the opportunities and possibilities for change—and also show us the obstacles and locus of resistance to change. What is that history and how might we understand the limitations and potential for a progressive future?

It is worth revisiting, if only briefly, the last half of the 20th Century for an understanding of how and why we find ourselves at this juncture. Much has been made about the period following the Second World

War, the period of anti-colonial struggle, the Fordist labor accord, and the rising prosperity in the US. Newly independent nations discovered that there was more than nominal political independence, workers in the US and then in a resurgent Europe and Japan experienced improvements in their standard of living even as the rest of the world's workers languished in poverty. Our social theories all posited a model of development that called for patience on the road to modernization, promoted the kinds of stages of growth that mimicked European economic history, and international organizations blossomed to manage and organize an orderly transition from colony to full partner in the new industrial world.

This image of life had limitations that soon became very apparent. By the early 1960s cracks appeared as the labor accord failed to provide all that was promised. Political unrest throughout the US and Europe at the end of the decade, a growing dissatisfaction with the state of economic and social theory, and a rising sense that the rest of the world was not making any headway towards this goal of economic development led to serious questions about existing models. Scholars began postulating theories that challenged the status quo, arguing that the current state of academia was at best apologetic about, and at worst designed to obscure and reproduce, rampant global inequality—especially true for those sociologists forming the Sociology Liberation Movement and economists forming the Union for Radical Economics. As the decade of the 1980s began, student protest a decade early led to the formation of a number of centers and departments devoted to studies of race, gender and class. Scholars now offered a counterweight to theories of modernization by showing that capitalism in the core was promoting poverty in the rest of the world. Economic growth in the center was in large part a result of dependent development in the rest of the world. A series of repressive regimes supported by Western governments, externally instigated coups and the overthrow of legitimate governments, and the suppression of workers and native peoples throughout Latin America, Africa and Asia revealed the true colors of so-called democratic initiatives of the developed world.

The 1980s also revealed cracks in this Fordist accord in the US, Europe and Japan, with talk about post-Fordist arrangements, discussions about the deindustrialization of old industrial regions, a growing awareness of the loss of manufacturing jobs, and a period of concerted assault against organized labor (more successful in the US, but challenges were mounted in all industrial countries). As the century drew to a close, years of reactionary and center-right governments in the developed world heralded the domination of finance capital and facilitated the emergence of global cities to oversee an increasing global economy. To organize the world's economies neoliberal policies challenged, and to some degree dismantled, the remnants of the Fordist social safety nets in the core and spread its ideology and practices to the rest of the world. What had been the efforts of international corporations spreading its operations globally for 50 years became new social and economic arrangements driven by international organizations like the World Bank and the International Monetary Fund. It is perhaps fitting that the current economic crisis has been caused by the moral and economic bankruptcy of financial capital.

This social engineering and the reshaping of the global economy were not unopposed. For many years non-governmental organizations struggled to counter the relentless assault against working people, ameliorate the effects of absent social services, and speak for the millions of disenfranchised and oppressed around the world. Various organizations tried to mount world-wide efforts to coordinate services or bring attention to what was happening. At times there were minor successes. But for the most part these were insufficient to change the tide of despair and decline that was washing over the world's poor nations. In response to the growing cooperation and coordination of economic power, the Alter-globalization (alternate globalization, alter-mundialization or simply the global justice) movement emerged to promote democratic globalization and cooperation, but resist economic globalization and neoliberalism. Its goals were environmental protection, ensuring economic justice, advocating fair wages and labor practices, protecting indigenous cultures and securing human rights.

In 2001 various non-governmental organizations, individuals, and community representatives met in Porto Alegre, Brazil at the first World Social Forum (WSF) dedicated to providing a non-governmental non-partisan space to stimulate discussion and encourage debate in a decentralized manner. The goal was to create an arena where reflection on the issues could take place, proposals for change might emerge, sharing of experiences would provide new tactics, and as a result promote alliances among movements and organizations struggling for a more democratic and fair world. The World Social Forum was in direct opposition to the World Economic Forum bringing together so-called captains of the economy and leaders of governments for the purpose of mapping out the new economic future. Instead, the WSF is a voice of opposition, seeking to present an alternative and better vision for what is possible.

This volume is another step in trying to understand how we go about making change, and more importantly, how that change occurs in opposition to dominant ideology and cultural practices born of globalization and capitalist social relations. If the point of Marx's observation is that we are somehow limited if we do not study our own history, the authors in this book tackle the question of how we might—aware of our histories—bring to bear new strategies, build upon existing successes, and mobilize people all for the purpose of creating a progressive future.

The first section of this volume introduces us to the range of actions we can take to achieve such a mobilization. The article by Bush and Little make a simple and even obvious, but long ignored, point. We must teach young people to care about a just world, or not be surprised that this sentiment is absent as they grow into young adults. Political activism among young people requires that they encounter ideas about social activism, justice and equality not just as topics in the classroom but as values to inform their everyday life. They outline the difficulties of overcoming conventional wisdom and the actions of governments to negate or minimize oppositional views, and stress the importance to instill a repertoire of action, a sense of public engagement and an awareness of social injustice to create the change agents of the future.

Langman uses Hegelian-Marxian dialectics to pose analytically separable, but related crises that follow from globalization. He emphasizes the transformation of social identities leading to "project identities" and provides for us an understanding of the conditions and opportunities for so many forms of oppositional action through the emergence of global justice movements, non-governmental organizations, international organizations and social movement organizations. It is in these organizational forms that social change can be possible.

One of the "wonders" of the election of Barack Obama was the effective use of "new technology" to reach "new voters"—to wit, connecting with younger voters using the Internet. One of the main vehicles building support for Obama in the early days was MoveOn.org and Carty illustrates both the strengths and weakness of New Social Movement theories to understand the impact of new information technologies on political activism. If the Internet is a tool that facilitates global control over production and the transfer and management of financial capital, Carty shows its power to be used to organize opposition on a mass scale.

Her paper is a call for us to reconsider what is meant by participatory democracy, raises questions about what constitutes public space, and asks that we understand public discourse in relation to the collective identity formed by these networks creating new forms of communicative action.

The first section ends with an examination of NGO experiences on the ground, in this instance in the fight against the spread of HIV/AIDS in the newly formed country of the Ukraine. Gutnik details the constantly shifting political and cultural environment that alters the way governments deal with issues like public health, how NGOs must adapt and often rely on international support, and how the mission and focus of NGOs will change whether or not they are aware of those changes. His is a cautionary tale pointing out that the corruption and misdirection of governments and societies can infect NGOs as well. They cannot be counted upon individually to effect long term change, but rather we should look to wider social forces to connect these efforts and provide support to ensure social justice outcomes.

The middle section of the volumes raises the sorts of questions implicit in Gutnik's account of NGOs in the Ukraine. How will an informal association of individuals, organizations and parties from around the world turn into a global political force for real change? The first paper, by Chase-Dunn and Kaneshiro, is an analysis of how and whether disparate organizations and movements associated with the various WSFs form coherent and consistent networks around organizational form, message, and tactics. The authors find that indeed there is what they call a global movement of social movements. Nonetheless, they also identify organizing differences across the locations of the World Social Forums even as the note the centrality of the human rights discourse underlying all the networks uncovered.

The last two papers, by Gautney and Hopewell, cover similar terrain from different points of departure. Gautney asks how do protest movements coalesce into political agendas, paying particular attention to the decision-making processes designed to both channel proposals into action steps while at the same time ensuring democratic processes that discourage control by a central organizational authority. Much as Weber cautions the downside of bureaucracy is the loss of democracy, so Gautney cautions that openness defined as structureless decision-making can do more to limit than enable democracy, resulting in informal hierarchies and disproportionate allocation of power within these loosely defined associations. As an alternative Gautney offers us examples of participatory coordinated organizations that are effective in countering the organizations like the World Bank and promoting local efforts around community-focused projects.

Using the "Battle of Seattle" as her point of departure, Hopewell focuses specifically on how mass opposition to the World Trade Organization (WTO) forms to counter the WTO's hegemony over trade, investment, intellectual property and services—all critical in determining labor market conditions, public health and the overall level of poverty in developing countries. International opposition to these powers led to mass social protest during a meeting of ministers in Seattle in 1999 and highlighted the emerging social movements against these neoliberal policies. The reaction to the increasingly technocratic WTO has resulted—when effective—in advocacy groups adopting equally technocratic forms of opposition. That is, as the WTO changes in reaction to opposition, the transnational advocacy organizations must change if they hope to be (or remain) effective. The danger, however, as Hopewell shows us, is that these advocacy organizations can reinforce the same rules that direct the operations of the WTO.

The struggles of Latin America over recent decades have evolved into a veritable laboratory for social transformation. In many ways, it was the first experimental site for the neoliberal model where it was initially installed at gunpoint and later consolidated by way of the "Washington Consensus." So perhaps it should come as little surprise that the region would eventually lead the way to anti-neoliberal resistance. The six articles that make up the final section of this volume explore the hegemonic power relations that persist in the Western hemisphere, examine some of structural sources and varied forms of recent "hotspots" of social protest in the region, along with new forms of praxis that seek to transform the established order.

The chapter by De la Barra and Dello Buono set out to provide a panorama of social movement resistance along with recent instances of where emancipatory projects have become consolidated in Latin America. They discuss how social movements have worked towards transforming legal structures in challenging economic dependency, restoring sovereignty over natural resources, and confronting military and ideological hegemony over the region. Their essay concludes by exploring the important role being played by new forms of regional integration that have emerged to challenge hegemonic or elite-driven regional entities.

Figueroa's piece turns our attention to the issue of labor migration and offers a rigorous Marxist analysis of this contradictory phenomenon. Building off of the original work of Marx in *Capital*, Figueroa dissects inconsistencies contained in this 19th century formulation of "surplus-population" and proposes some theoretical fixes in the light of contemporary historical developments. In the end, he illustrates how the asymmetrical social relations shaping contemporary migration in the region directly reflect the power relations embodied in capitalist accumulation, evolving into a structurally-delimited source of political resistance.

Kennedy, Leiva and Tilly shifts our attention to the political contours of an important tendency within the region's progressive forces that they categorize as the "Third Left." This refers to leftist movements that seek to build autonomy from the state instead of capturing state power, using grassroots, "bottom-up" strategies to empower exploited sectors and exert popular control over more localized terrains. The authors show why this kind of transformation strategy requires new institutional forms and specific illustrative cases that are then explored in greater detail in the following three chapters.

In the first of these, Collin Harguindeguy examines the explosive dynamics of crisis-ridden Argentina as the backdrop to the workers occupation of factories and the subsequent establishment of self-managed firms. She carefully describes how the workers involved in "recuperating" shut-down or abandoned enterprises were driven by practical concerns rooted in the crisis, rather than ideological concerns based in leftist doctrine. Still, she argues, the movement embodies a leftist orientation in practice and constitutes a popular learning process that is autonomous from and more horizontal than the traditional left. While many of the enterprises may eventually collapse, the author suggests that the imprint made upon popular consciousness is likely to endure and nurture future struggles.

Achetenberg in turn focuses on the transformational role being played by neighborhood councils in Bolivia, both prior to and following the election of the Movement towards Socialism (MAS) government led by the Evo Morales. She shows how a grassroots and urban-based community organization played an important protagonist role in the uprising against neoliberal rule. With their focus on basic neighborhood services delivery, the councils drew upon a hybrid form of organization based in traditional indigenous community structures and radicalized

trade unionist tactics to build themselves into a powerful social movement. The struggle of the councils to maintain a constructive autonomy
from the progressive state and advance a popular agenda of progressive
social change provides a fascinating case study of power and resistance.
The volume ends with Cerullo's analysis of autonomy as it plays out
among the Zapatistas in Mexico. Influential in their call for opposition
to the global forces impoverishing indigenous peoples, the Zapatistas
offer new models of social opposition, creating a space where multiple
identities are possible and where consensus builds to strengthen the
oppositional movements against neoliberalism.

PART ONE

MOBILIZATION FOR CHANGE

TEACHING TOWARD PRAXIS AND POLITICAL ENGAGEMENT*

Melanie E. L. Bush and Deborah L. Little

Introduction

Increased interest in the political sphere on the part of young people has been noted in a wide range of popular and scholarly arenas. Headlines of a recent Higher Education Research Institute (HERI) press release report that "More College Freshmen [are] Committed to Social and Civic Responsibility" (Engle 2006: 1) claiming that in 2005 more freshmen expressed that it is important to help those in need than in over 25 years. They assert that this translates to higher practical and intellectual level skills (Engle 2006: 2). HERI also reports that students express a significant increase (11.6% percent) in their desire to "help promote racial understanding," "help others who are in difficulty," and "influence social values" between their freshman and senior year (Hurtado, Sax, Saenz, Harper, and others 2007: 24). In June 2007, a poll by the *New York Times*, CBS News, and MTV reported that "Young Americans Are Leaning Left" (Nagourney and Thee 2007). These authors state that young people are more likely than the general public to favor universal health care (62 percent versus 47 percent), inclusive immigration policy (30 percent versus 24 percent) and gay marriage (44 percent versus 28 percent). Young people believe that their generation can make a difference and they are taking greater interest in the political and social world (Nagourney and Thee 2007).

While these findings speak to increased concern about social issues, they do not necessarily reflect only one perspective. HERI's report on national norms of the American Freshman for Fall 2006, indicates that:

* This paper is a wholly collaborative effort between both authors. We also want to recognize and thank the students whose words we share in this paper and whose commitment to social justice inspires us. Those students are: Lindsay Rhae Beecher, Dianne Bosquet, Lauren Brickman, Victoria Broadhurst, Brittany Consigli, Alessandra Leigh Esposito, Radha Hettiarachchi, Joannie Rodriguez, and Amy Williams.

> Not only is the percentage of students identifying as 'liberal' at the highest
> level since 1975 (30.7 percent), but the percentage identifying as 'con-
> servative' is also at the highest point in the history of the Cooperative
> Institutional Research Program (CIRP) Freshman Survey. This suggests
> that freshmen are "moving away from a moderate position in their politi-
> cal viewpoints". (Pryor, Hurtado, Saenz, Korn and others 2006: 3)

Students' views indicate heightened concern about the social world,
though they may have different ways to explain current realities or
solve social problems.

Despite this evidence:

> ...the expanded leadership for civic learning about diversity and democ-
> racy still remains on the margins rather than at the center of undergradu-
> ate learning in the American academy...civic learning remains optional
> rather than essential for the majority of faculty, students, and employers.
> (Schneider 2007: 1–2)

While there are millions of people in the US,

> ...especially young people who are trying to 'make a difference,' largely
> through volunteering, there remains an inchoate yet palpable sense
> among most people that what they do matters little when it comes to the
> civic life and health of their communities, states, or the country overall.
> (Gibson 2006: 4)

This is not surprising in a nation where government officials dismiss 10
million people around the globe demonstrating against military intervention in Iraq as marginal and irrelevant and state that these actions
would not impact foreign policy decisions (Simonson 2003: 17).

In addition, educators concerned with issues of justice and equality
face challenges such as an ideology that views politically contextualized
education as motivated by "special interests." Since 2002, legislative
attempts have been made in 19 states to create and enforce governmental monitors to "balance" curricular offerings, hiring and campus
programming. Bill proponents see this as offsetting the "left-leaning"
slant of academia. (Bush 2005: 16–19) These trends and realities speak
to the complexity of the task; however, this is a moment of particular historical possibility. This article examines the potential for more
actively engaged pedagogy and scholarship within sociology, particularly
related to political activism, describes two examples where this has been
attempted and concludes with the implications of this for academia
and society at large.

In his recent call for a stronger "public sociology," Burawoy (2004,
2005) challenges sociologists to enrich and expand our engagement

with the multiple publics outside the academy. Public sociology, in his view, is a sociology that promotes dialog beyond the discipline and academy about the critical issues facing our society, the world, and our planet. Burawoy challenges us to take sociology into the "trenches of civil society," ranging from community and civic groups to social movements (Burawoy, Gamson, Ryan, Pfohl and others 2004: 104). Nonetheless, he notes that our first public is our undergraduate students, who enter our classrooms as a public "steeped in the common sense of the dominant culture." (Pfohl in Burawoy et al. 2004: 113). Many others have written insightfully on classroom engagement to challenge this common sense understanding of the world. In this paper we look outside the classroom to possible forms of academic civic engagement with our undergraduate public.

We argue that academic sociologists can and should make social justice and political engagement a central part of sociological pedagogy, not only within the classroom but in the larger university environment. In particular, we suggest that connecting our students to the lived experiences of those involved in contemporary social justice activism and social movements is a core task of public sociology. We discuss here experiences engaging undergraduate students (sociology majors and others) in two types of connection with social justice action and social movements. With institutional support, we attended the US Social Forum in 2007 with 6 Adelphi students. They participated in wide-ranging dialogues about oppression, voice, change, values, and the place of the US in the world and thereby experienced "reflexive knowledge" (Burawoy 2005: 11). The question "Is Another World Possible?" was made real in their confrontation with others' participation in global social movements. On an institutional level, we have facilitated two university-wide collaboration projects in which students participated in events focused on work for social justice. These projects involved many students in civic or political engagement, in forms other than traditional service learning. We suggest that these forms of pedagogy open up students' understandings of and feelings about the possibilities for social transformation.

"If there currently is an officially sanctioned space in schools for social change, it likely is limited to a perceived politics of the possible" (Abendroth 2008: 41). The combined evidence of increased civic and political awareness of young people, the experience we had at the Social Forum, the call for expanding a "public sociology" and infusing discussion of and possibilities for political and civic engagement in the classroom and the university underscore a potential in this historical moment to engage young people in having an impact in the social world. As "education is never neutral with respect to the power of empire" (Abendroth 2008: 41), there are consequences to taking these possibilities seriously or not. Academia in general, and sociology in particular, would be well served to expand opportunities for students to be exposed to and involved in political processes and social activism in both curricular and co-curricular venues.

Sociology and Social Justice

While many disciplines involve students in community work, usually in the form of service learning/community service, sociology has a unique ability and obligation to educate for political engagement. Sociological research reveals two aspects of our social worlds: the material distribution of goods, services, and statuses *and* the social relations that create, maintain, challenge, and alter those material distributions. As Mills (1959) reminded us more than 50 years ago, a sociological imagination allows us to perceive the link between history and biography. This imagination enables the understanding of social structure necessary to realize the possibility of social change. The diversity of sociological research, the fact that no aspect of social life is off limits for study, makes sociology unique in its ability to help us understand the social world and relations of inequality and oppression.

What are we to do with this understanding? Mainstream sociology, with its emphasis on value-free objective science, provides one answer. Sociologists provide the data and theories necessary for others to understand and shape their world. The value of sociological research lies in its rigor and quality. This is what Burawoy (2005), somewhat uncritically,[1] calls "professional" sociology and it has been the core of the discipline for a century. Alongside this sociology have been "counterstreams" (Feagin 2001), moments in which sociologists have challenged professional sociology with calls to social justice and activism. We agree with Feagin (2001) that sociology must return to

---

[1] Feagin and Vera (2008: 33) offer an extended discussion of Burawoy's surprising lack of critical attention to the products and mission of "professional" sociology, noting that this type of sociology reflects an "instrumental positivism" that does not seek to challenge the status quo or the "often oppressive needs of the nation-state."

its roots of social justice activism combined with sociological research and that a central location for such action is teaching.

Sociology is well suited to education for democratic and political engagement. However, the role of sociologists as teachers is insufficiently examined in the discussions of public sociology, even though teaching is a prominent activity among the academic sociologists who "produce" the 25,000 undergraduate sociology majors each year (Burawoy 2005) and teach as many as 60,000 students each year (Gans 1989). Instead, most commentators focus on the role of sociologists as researchers. While research is central to the discipline and the academic community, our teaching may more directly impact the actions of future leaders and members of society. Sociology undergraduate majors are, as Burawoy (2005) notes, the "public" that is always there.

In general, sociology departments have followed a "weak" model of engagement with this public. However, a "strong" model is needed, one which makes social justice and political engagement a central part of sociological pedagogy. There are myriad examples from sociology's past; in fact, many of the founders of American sociology actively combined social justice activism with sociological research. Feagin (2001) noted the work of Harriet Martineau who wrote of social "things" 50 years before Durkheim's writing on social "facts" and who combined empirical observation of life in the United States with feminist activism and anti-slavery work. The earliest sociology practitioners in the US included the activist women of Hull House and the other settlement houses in late 19th century Chicago. (Lengermann and Niebrugge-Brantley 1998; Grant, Stalp, and Ward 2002). While settlement house workers have long been considered founders of *social work*, Jane Addams was offered a position at the University of Chicago and pursued a career of sociological research and publishing in the pre-eminent sociology journals of the day (Deegan 1988; Lengermann and Niebrugge-Brantley 2002). She chose to work out of a settlement house where she pursued a social justice agenda, linking her research and her activism in efforts to better the conditions of those in her community. Most of these early sociologists strove to educate the public about injustices in America, believing that this type of public sociology would incite reforms. However, settlement house members like Addams were also activists themselves in movements to ameliorate the conditions of the people they studied and lived among (Dale and Kalob 2006).

Early students of race in America, like W. E. B. Du Bois and Ida Barnett-Wells, also combined sociological research with social justice activism. Du Bois believed initially that rigorous research and dissemination of findings would inspire the public to reform. However, he became increasingly involved in political activism, inaugurating a number of black social and civil rights movements during the 20th century (Lewis 2000). Ida B. Wells, well-known as a journalist and activist, published work that combined sociological insights with calls for justice (Grant, Stalp, and Ward 2002).

Sociology's turn away from social justice work as a disciplinary project is well known. As sociology moved into universities, as it struggled to prove its worth, and as it came to rely on foundation and government dollars to fund research, practitioners called for an "objective value-neutral science" that would mirror the natural sciences (Burawoy 2004; Dale and Kalob 2006; Feagin 2001). An "instrumental-positivist" approach dominated and the social activism of early sociologists was downplayed (Feagin 2001). Nonetheless, "counterstreams" like critical sociology, critical race theory, feminism, and humanist sociology, in which sociology was called to critical engagement with pressing social issues, persisted. Some researchers moved to research that directly engaged the public as more or less equal participants in the development of research questions. Applied sociology, clinical sociology and participant action research all potentially bring sociologists to engagement with social change (Dale and Kalob 2006).

Recent presidents of the American Sociological Association have explicitly called for a more meaningful engagement with our students and with the social justice issues that threaten life on the planet. Gans (1989) called for the teaching of a sociological analysis of American institutions and society rather than a teaching of sociological *concepts* peppered with examples from American life. He challenged sociologists to determine who we actually serve, who we help, and who we harm, whether directly or indirectly, intentionally or unintentionally. Gans did not refer to the intertwining of research and activism that shaped the founding of American sociology, but he did criticize a sociology that resides in positivist empiricism rather than engaging the crucial social issues confronting the lay public.

Feagin (2001) issued a stronger challenge, stating:

> In everyday practice all sociology is a moral activity, whether this is recognized or not.... All social science perspectives have an underlying view of what the world ought to be.... In practice, social scientists can accept the prevailing nation-state or bureaucratic-capitalistic morality or they can resist this morality by making a commitment to social justice and human rights. (2001: 12).

In *Liberation Sociology*, Feagin and Vera (2008) reject the claim that sociology cannot be both scientific and committed to work for democracy and social justice. They offer a range of examples of sociologists who use their empirical skills in the service of social justice. This text offers a crucial perspective on sociology to students and some strategies for more engaged dialogue to teachers. However, the authors focus more on critical understanding of the social world and less on the mechanisms for teaching students skills for civic and political engagement.

Burawoy (2004: 1608) compares what he calls *traditional* teaching with *organic* teaching. In traditional teaching the professor lectures, filling "blank slates" with sociological concepts and theories. In organic teaching, however, the professor engages a student, who enters with her own lived experience, in a dialogue that leads both to knowledge. He calls "service learning" a specific engagement in which such dialog occurs. The prominence of service learning is undeniable, with more than half of all high schools and a vast number of colleges and universities offering service learning components within their curriculums (Butin 2003). What is less clear, however, are the mechanisms through which a meaningful dialogue would occur that both builds a sociological imagination and teaches the tools and understanding for social change.

Opportunities and Calls to Action

In analyzing the significance and implications of these trends, this paper draws from our experience as faculty of a Sociology Department at a liberal arts college on the East Coast in attending the United States Social Forum (Atlanta, Georgia/June 2007) with 6 undergraduate students. The travel and participation were fully supported by the administration and student government association of our university. Five of the students had just completed their freshman year; they had taken their first year seminar entitled "Democracy, Diversity and Dreams of a Better Tomorrow" with Melanie Bush and had read about the World Social Forum movement. The sixth was entering her senior year and came highly recommended by the Student Government Association for her active role on campus. Of these students, two had taken other courses with us (American Ethnicity/Bush, Law and Social Inequality/Little). All are female aged 18–22; their ethnic heritage is as follows: European (2), Haitian, European/Korean, Puerto Rican, and Sri Lankan. Three are native born; three came to the US before elementary school. We prepared before the trip by discussing the Social Forum movement and establishing both individual and collective goals. While in Atlanta we met as a group several times each day to facilitate planning, assessment, debriefing and reflection. Upon our return to New York each member summarized their thoughts about their participation in the Social Forum, and committed to organizing the "campus report-back" held in October and carrying out related activities in the campus and broader community.

Our experience falls directly in line with Michael Burawoy's 2004 challenge to reinvigorate a "public sociology." Co-curricular activities that provide students with the means to actually experience theories and concepts they learned in the classroom have long been understood as a means of "deep learning". In this case, the US Social Forum provided these students the opportunity to learn firsthand about social movements and critiques of social, racial, gender, and economic inequality. They were continuously educated both about process and content as organizers of the 4 day event openly dialogued in ways that reflected principles of inclusion, representation and diversity. Students were immersed in discussions of "social problems" from multiple perspectives and had the chance to meet and speak with personally and politically engaged individuals and communities. This experience was entirely in the realm of public sociology both in form and content.

Another call to action is embodied in the Carnegie Foundation's Political Engagement Project's assertion that while students are encouraged to be involved in community and volunteer service projects, most schools do not offer opportunities for developing political skills through education and engagement. While "colleges are well positioned to promote democratic competencies and participation, and to prepare students to be thoughtful, responsible, creative citizens" they do not do so consistently and, thus, lose critical opportunities to engage the democratic arts and strengthen the political process locally, nationally and globally (Colby, Beaumont, Ehrlich, and Corngold 2007: 5). Efforts to promote civic engagement have been called a "movement;" however, challenges remain both in making this engagement a central, rather than elective, aspect of education, and in persuading students that this form of education is a crucial component of their college lives (Schneider 2005).

What would an education for civic and political engagement look like? As sociologists and scholar activists our work is framed and centered in the integration of theory and practice; engaging and reinforcing student learning in the classroom through applied and experiential activities. Our scholarship in publication, teaching and service draws primarily from critical race and feminist theorists and is grounded in principles of the "pedagogy of the oppressed." This paper articulates our belief that "without practice there's no knowledge," as the great Brazilian educator, Paulo Freire once said. (Bell, Gaventa and Peters 1990: 98) Our analytic framework is grounded by an interest in seeking new ways of teaching that "bridge academic learning and life experience." This perspective is exemplified by the work of scholars (particularly women and scholars of color) who offer critiques of traditional ways of "knowing" as rooted in euro-centric and patriarchal orientations and maintaining the status quo. (Kirk and Okazawa-Rey 2007: 1–27) We deeply subscribe to and practice the belief that the social world is intrinsically political, and that ideas both emanate from and are generalized through their material existence. We agree with the call of the Carnegie Foundation and others in the sense of the urgency about the need for faculty/student involvement with political and not solely community service engagement. "Strengthening the preparation of active citizens is important first and foremost because the future health of our democracy depends upon it." (Hollister, Wilson and Levine 2008: 18)

University educators, especially in the field of sociology need to more consistently introduce students to the possibilities of structural social justice work so that students can recognize this form of engagement as an option. "All students need to have opportunities for civic and political participation and...opportunities and space for deliberation on public issues" (Kiesa, Orlowski, Levine, Both, and others 2007: 32). This exposure, in fact, has implications for their development of critical thinking skills, social responsibility and active participation in society. Without such mentoring students remain largely unable to cross the bridge between volunteer and community service projects (with which they are often familiar) and deeper political engagement. While service learning often involves a reflection component, a more focused discussion of the social structures that produce a need for volunteer work is necessary.

A Continuum of Engagement

Academic civic engagement occurs along a continuum from voluntarism to social movement participation. Volunteer work is promoted in many high schools and colleges. There has been a steady increase in the number of students volunteering in high school and college, although the vast majority of this work is done on an episodic, rather than regular, basis. This activity is often viewed as important to the college application process. Young people in the 15–25 year old age group primarily volunteer for youth, civic or religious organizations, while a limited number volunteer for political or environmental organizations. Those who volunteer with the latter groups often do so as a result of some form of outreach from those organizations, while youth are most likely to contact youth, civic or religious organizations on their own (Lopez and Marcello 2007). This speaks to a relative lack of awareness about opportunities to pursue political engagement. Volunteer work is a form of engagement promoted at all levels of US society—think "1000 points of light." While this work remains necessary, particularly during this period of extreme national and global inequality, volunteer work without a connection to social change often sustains, rather than challenging, existing structural inequalities.

Service learning is "a form of experiential education where learning occurs through a cycle of action and reflection as students work with others through a process of applying what they are learning to community problems and, at the same time, reflecting upon their experience as they seek to achieve real objectives for the community and deeper understanding and skills for themselves." (Eyler and Giles 1999) Service learning connects traditional academic coursework with volunteerism, adding the essential component of student reflection upon their experience. It is the most popular method of promoting civic engagement by college students and is widely reported to lead to a sense of personal efficacy among students (O'Connor 2006). As O'Connor notes, however, connecting this personal effectiveness to broader political engagement still remains a challenge.

While service learning can promote greater political engagement in democratic processes and through institutionalized political channels (Hepburn, Niemi, and Chapman 2000), the vast majority of students who participate in service learning do so in education, health/human services, and local neighborhoods/environments (Gray, Ondaatje, and Zakaras 1999). While service learning in non-political forums may lead to greater political engagement (see Eyler, Giles, and Braxton 1997, cited in Hepburn, Niemi, and Chapman 2000), focused political engagement, in the form of service learning or college and university clubs and organizations, seems to involve only a few students. These students gain tremendous education in the political process (Colby, Ehrlich, Beaumont, and Stephens 2003: 248). However, the conscious education of students for engagement in democratic political process is only a small part of the work of colleges and universities. Indeed, it has been reported that some universities and colleges shy away from service in politics, fearing that it can lead to partisanship and politicization (Hepburn, Niemi, and Chapman 2000). These authors quote Alexander Astin, who wrote: "If higher education does not start giving citizenship and democracy much greater priority, then who will? Corporate business? The news media? Politics? How can we ever expect the democratic dream to develop unless education changes its priorities?" (1999: 44) (Hepburn, Niemi, and Chapman 2000: 621)

Participation in something like the US Social Forum introduces students to another form of political engagement, one that exists outside the walls of the institutionalized political process. The social forum movement introduces students to collective action "with some degree of organization and continuity" working "outside of institutional channels for the purpose of promoting or resisting change in the group, society or world order of which it is a part." (McAdam and Snow 1997: xviii) While most of the work on civic engagement does not speak to the issues of intentional engagement of students in the world of social movements, the history of social movements in the US alone with their records of struggles for democracy (the vote), equality (the Civil Rights Movement, the Women's Movement, the Disability Rights Movement, the Gay and Lesbian Rights Movement, etc.), social welfare (the Townsend Movement, the Poor People's Movement, etc.), and other social and environmental justice issues certainly places social movements squarely within the realm of liberal education and civic engagement.

Yet just as universities and colleges seem to shy away from attention to engagement in institutionalized political channels, they avoid engagement with social movements. Astin's comment is, again, strikingly apt. Students are not often encouraged to become politically active and may be unsure of how even to do so. Political participation may be perceived as boring or irrelevant or only for some people. It may be seen as something that one can engage in once a clear perspective is formulated. (Colby 2008: 4). However,

> Learning about political institutions, issues, contexts, and practices should be an integral part of that enterprise (liberal arts education). College

graduates cannot make sense of their environment and their place in it if they are politically ignorant, unskilled, and lacking in a sense of civic agency, the sense that they can work with others to solve problems that concern them—in their communities, workplaces. (Colby 2008: 8)

Making Connections through Praxis

In a short intense period, like those few days in June 2007 it is only possible to get a glimpse of the potential for engagement and motivation to do political work. In this section we share some of the students' insights and reflections about their participation. Despite the brief time span, it is apparent that they experienced many aspects of participation discussed by Colby (2007) who writes:

> Young people are recruited to participate in civic or political institutions and processes for many different reasons, including incentives that may have little to do with intrinsic motivation. Then, in the course of participating, they develop relationships that inspire and make demands on them, gain satisfactions that they could not foresee, and begin to expand and reshape the values and goals that led them to participate, often shifting their sense of identity in the process. (Colby 2007)

This was largely true for the students who went with us to the US Social Forum. When asked why they wanted to attend, they spoke of desires to meet new people and learn about social justice and democracy. In the course of participation, despite the short period, the women began to talk about how they were developing relationships, gaining unexpected satisfactions, reshaping values, and shifting their own sense of identity. Below we share comments and reflections from students Amy, Brittany, Radha, Dianne, Joannie, and Alessandra.

All of us worked as volunteers for several hours on the third day of the Forum. This was structured into the event and encouraged by the organizers. Most of the students expressed that this was their favorite day. In part, *doing work* was a respite from the overload they experienced as they came face to face with thousands of "outspoken" activists (Radha) who "openly expressed their thoughts" (Amy). The exposure to people engaged in various issues and forms of organizing related to the social world made it evident that even "today" many different kinds of people are actively working for social change. The diversity of Forum participants coupled with their unified commitment to making a better world was exhilarating but also overwhelming. Thus Joannie noted the range of activists, writing: "From old to young, hippie to hip hop, different faces, colors, styles, and languages it was just incredible to see so many people come together with different causes but the same purpose—making a better world possible."

Because most of these students had never been to this kind of activity (protest, mobilization, community forum), they wondered, "How did these people get here? Where are they going?" Amy wrote of drawing back from approaching some tables because she worried that she was one of the "only partially active group of people who are swayed by the media or whatever information they hear." Rejecting this identity, she wondered, "Am I already changing? I don't necessarily want to be a radical, but more of a <u>well</u> educated person who forms her opinions through experience and knowledge."

Helping do the work of the forum enabled the students to both make personal connections and reshape their understanding of the social world. Radha talked about meeting a man who had lived in Thailand for 8 years, a Californian activist, and a fellow New Yorker. What struck her was the fact that "we were all here for different purposes, shared no common background, but shared a feeling that the US has issues to be resolved." Joannie found that speaking with people who were very different from her as she distributed flyers about the Forum's media center showed her that "we had more similarities than meets the eye."

Through their volunteer work, the students came to different understandings of social relations and how things happen because people make them happen. Dianne discovered "just how much one volunteer can make a difference in the Forum. I was able to spread the word about the media center and how it could help people get involved." Brittany wrote:

> What we ended up doing was packing the complementary bags each person attending the forum received upon registration. It was a simple task really. However, it got my wheels turning. When I first arrived to the forum and got all registered, I didn't even think about all the work that people did in order to make this event possible. I just expected things to be and come to me fully formed. The fact of the matter is 'things need to be put in bags.' My term for nothing comes to fruition without some form of labor and hopefully care involved in the process. This speaks to the sense of the interconnectedness of all of our lives. For example, you're on vacation and staying at a hotel and you go out for a day of sightseeing. I used to expect the room to be cleaned and the beds made up by the time I returned. But now I realize the full extent of the task. It's not just human labor, and nothing just happens, we all must work

together in order for our objectives and goals to be successful regardless of what those goals are.

Most of the students found that assumptions and sense of self were challenged by things they heard and people they met. This experience was sometimes joyful, but at other times very painful. Radha discovered the feminist truth that the personal is political as an immigrant listening to a plenary on the challenges faced by immigrants. Both she and Dianne learned about the structures of immigration—the push/pull factors, the process of becoming legal, and the importance of being an "asset" to the country you seek to enter. Dianne was led to think about the lack of justice in the world. Ali struggled with her resistance to much of what she was hearing and noted, "I am ashamed to admit that I must be a product of American society; someone with moral and ethical but <u>individualistic</u> concerns about social change." Amy and Brittany summed up their feelings when together they wrote:

> What struck a bunch of us is the fact that many American society "values" are deeply ingrained in our minds and unless we make ourselves conscious of that way of thinking, we're going to be counterproductive in our striving for another world. In the same vein, sometimes it's difficult to approach some of the tables because of the fear of being judged for how we look in comparison to our comrades. In reality, we are all here for one over-arching purpose: to gain the tools we need in order to start perpetuating a change in each of our communities for the better.

In contrast to these feelings of discomfort, Joannie wrote of her profound feelings of affirmation:

> I have to say that the last plenary we attended about sexuality rights and the drive behind feminism was one of the most life changing experiences I have ever taken part in. It was incredible that within two hours, a panel of speakers could have the power to confirm so many things that I had been feeling my whole life. It was one of those Aha moments that just grips you by your insides and jolts every emotion you're capable of. It seems that words aren't even able to explain such an experience.

The Limitations of Service Learning

[W]e must enable students to move beyond direct service and to understand its limitations. We must enable them to develop not just the values and commitment but also the knowledge, skills, and efficacy to address the complex web of social issues that underlie the need for the service they provide. (Jacoby 2006: 31)

Research indicates that service learning courses have a positive impact on students' awareness of and sensitivity to social issues. They

> are thus associated with three post-college outcomes: civic leadership, charitable giving, and overall political engagement, this is particularly mediated by the use of reflective discussions of the service experience (Astin, Vogelgesang, Misa, Anderson, and others 2006: 7).

Analysis and critique help to contextualize the effort as different from charity because it is connected to the structure of society (Astin et al. 2006). However, the service or experiential learning model, while potentially valuable, has not generally been sufficient to engage and prepare students to confront the problems of the 21st century. This is because service learning does not usually draw from the strengths of disciplines that offer social structural analyses of the issues confronting the communities with which they engage.

Service learning, despite its best intentions, often offers an individualistic charity model of education (Eby 1998; Lewis 2004). It puts students face to face with the lived experiences of the inequalities they learn about, but it does not necessarily present them with models for contextualizing the inequality or for social change. Some critics even charge that service learning can result in a "voyeuristic exploitation of the cultural other" (Butin 2003: 1675). In philosophy and in practice, service learning often promotes a model in which the privileged with high levels of cultural capital provide free/volunteer services to the less privileged in order to improve the conditions of the latter. The evidence suggests that the volunteers/interns benefit from such activity, but it is less clear that the recipients gain long-term benefit (Butin 2003: 1679). Part of the reason, Butin suggests, is that service learning is grounded in a radical notion of autonomy and individualism.

Service learning models certainly attempt to bridge this privilege divide through embedding students in contexts in which cultural diversity and respect for others are encouraged. As Butin notes, however, this model assumes that the diversity within the placement site mediates between individual self-knowledge and social responsibility (2003: 1681). It is true that some service learning programs are more explicitly political, encouraging the kinds of interaction in which participants question and work against hegemonic systems of power within their communities. However, the risk is that students may walk away blaming victims and following individual deficit theories, rather than understanding structures of power or participating in real social change within the communities where service learning occurs (2003: 1682). As

Butin concludes, service learning that increases civic engagement does not necessarily lead to a stronger democracy (2003: 1683). Thus, we need a pedagogy that explicitly bridges the gaps between certain lived experiences and the theoretical explanations for those experiences. We cannot assume that the mere experience of different contexts, as in service learning, will mediate between the self-knowledge of the student and commitment to social responsibility.

Education as Praxis: Exposure, Potential and Working for Social Justice

"In a society that doesn't always live up to its ideals, how can we encourage students to live publicly involved, culturally aware lives? The answer is to offer students an "extensive education in the democratic arts... voice, critical judgment, empathy, reciprocity, commitment, and action." (Guarasci 2001: 1). Education clearly plays a major role in shaping beliefs and attitudes about society and provides (or does not provide) the means for intellectual exploration of the concerns and experiences that influence students' perspectives about significant issues in their lives. Students need opportunities to learn in environments that allow for critical analysis of their daily experiences as well as the application of theory learned in the classroom to their everyday world. Without opportunities for both experiential and theoretical growth, ideas remain abstract and do not bear the true power of knowledge. Ideas and facts can be forgotten after an exam or turning in a paper if they have not been integrated into an individual's life. At the same time, exposure to diversity and interactions with people from different groups without opportunities to theorize the causes or significance of inequality or difference is easily personalized without any grappling with the meaning of democracy, diversity, power, or civic duty. This contact, then, is seen as an individual interaction with a nice person who may or may not be "like the rest of 'them'".

As Guarasci (2001) aptly asserts, co-curricular involvement must be inseparable from curricular training in the pursuit of the broad intellectual mission, particularly of higher education. It is central, not marginal; it is where ideas may be tested and experiences understood without concern for grades or retribution. Without this opportunity, it is difficult to achieve the true value of education. Students need space for intellectual engagement where the social context is discussed and personal experiences may be understood. The argument for this type of engagement within the Social Sciences, and Sociology in particular, has been made above.

The greatest possibilities for utilizing education as a force for social change lies in the connection between the agency of individuals and their ability to understand structure and system, between the application of theory and the theorizing of application. There is a synergy in this learning process. Theoretical discussions or analyses about structural inequality generally do not adequately convey the consequences or causes as they impact personal and daily life. Positive interchanges are only personal interactions unless and until they are understood within a framework that can reckon with the structural and institutional forces of inequality that mitigate against those very interchanges. This is the link between exposure and agency. This teaching goes beyond the everyday contact that occurs while interacting in a classroom or on a train, to a method that encourages and supports thorough exploration of the structures, the history and the systems of assumptions, biases, and ideological presumptions about how society functions. (Bush 2004: 244–248)

The most effective strategy in supporting diversity and concern for the common good as a core component of the academic mission involves comprehensive and multi-layered initiatives that enhance the many different structural elements. A positive campus climate, diverse staffing, inclusive curriculum, and support for students from underrepresented groups improve access and success as well as the quality of education provided. In this way, we can draw upon what has been described as "Academics of the Heart," a vision with philosophical underpinnings in Aztec culture. This academics looks for the education of the whole person and a balance of reason and spirit (Rendon 2000: 3–5).

> While other institutions in society are also fostering diversity, higher education is uniquely positioned, by its mission, values and dedication to learning, to foster and nourish the habits of heart and mind that Americans need to make diversity work in daily life as a value and a public good. (Schneider 1995: xvi)

Knowledge that emanates from daily experience and is then theorized, as well as political and economic theory applied to everyday living, has the power to transform individuals and, in turn, society.

Academic Pedagogy, Structures and Strategies

A more radical pedagogy?

The need for an education in the democratic arts and civic engagement is clear. However, most colleges and universities do not yet integrate their mission and curriculum in ways that would facilitate such an education (Colby, Ehrlich, Beaumont and others 2003). Instead, this type of education happens piecemeal on many campuses, in individual classrooms but not in a unified way across the college or university. In institutions that have not made civic engagement and democratic arts an explicit aspect of their mission, faculty find themselves struggling to pursue this type of education in their individual classrooms.

Pedagogy that links structure to individual experiences and knowledge is crucial and can certainly be done by individual faculty. This can be done in service learning courses *if* there is a conscious effort to tie the personal reflections and sense of efficacy gained by students to education that contextualizes the needs which are met by these services. Faculty need to describe the social structures and forces creating these needs and the privilege and presumptions that accompany such structures. In addition to creating opportunities for service learning, however, we suggest that students need exposure to activists, to social movements, to cross-constituency work, and to explicit political activity. We are calling for institutional commitments to *social justice* or *systemic social change* (the latter term is suggested by Colby et al. 2003: 65–66) to avoid the "left-of-center" connotations of the term social justice). Indeed Colby and her colleagues call for education about political engagement that includes:

> ...activities intended to influence social and political institutions, beliefs, and practices and to affect processes and policies relating to community welfare, whether that community is local state, national or international. Political engagement may include working informally with others to solve a community problem; serving in neighborhood organizations, political interest groups , or political organizations; participating in public forums on social issues, discussing political issues with family and friends, and trying to influence others' political opinions; working on a campaign for a candidate or issue; writing letters, signing petitions, and participating in other forms of policy advocacy and lobbying; raising public awareness about social issues and mobilizing others to get involved or take action; attending rallies and protests and participating in boycotts; and of course voting in local or national elections. (2003: 18–19)

In other words, students need curriculum that introduces them to the broad range of actions that people actually pursue in efforts to change and improve public policy and corporate policy. In addition, they need introductions to people who are politically engaged in the present moment.

Faculty can invite such organizations and individuals to their classrooms to talk about work they are doing to change the status quo. They can introduce films about issues that not only describe the problem in individual and structural contexts, but also show the ways in which people are struggling to change the structure. One example might be pairing a showing of the film *Life and Debt* with the film *This is What Democracy Looks Like*. Or they can show the more typical film describing a form of inequality or oppression and then have students seek out information about groups that are working to challenge this injustice. Students can then explore the types of political engagement being done in the present moment and discuss issues of policy, responsibility, goals, and efficacy. For example, the work of Walda Katz-Fishman and Jerome Scott (2005) for a "public sociology" links sociology (in research and teaching) to the sociology being done outside the academy, in the bottom-up struggles of contemporary social movements.

Colby et al. (2003) describe the intentional work of 12 colleges and universities to bring *moral and civic engagement* to their curriculum on an institutional level. Arguing that students are always already introduced to certain moral values, especially values of instrumental individualism and materialism (values that are presented to students in "hidden" curriculums, see, e.g. Colby et al. 2003: 11–12), they call for intentional campus-wide deliberations on common values followed by infusion of those values into curriculum and programs campus-wide. If institutions of higher education agree that one focus should be preparing students for participation in a democratic system, then this implies, according to Colby et al., teaching the moral values of "mutual respect and tolerance, concern for the rights and welfare of individuals and of the community, recognition that each person is part of a larger social fabric, critical self-reflection, commitment to civil and rational discourse" and commitment to the good of the polity as well as competence in judging how that good should be advanced (2003: 13) On campuses that have not explicitly established such common moral values, individual faculty can challenge dominant US values by presenting concepts like "no one has seconds until everyone has firsts." This type of moral value challenges students to deliberate about how resources *should* fairly be distributed and can be extended into discussions of public policy and political engagement.

Bringing in the "Trojan Horse"?

A more powerful way to bring this learning to a wider range of students is to integrate curricular and extracurricular events so that students engage in campus life in a way that builds awareness of the need for political engagement and skills for challenging social injustice. As Colby et al. (2003: 220) explain, most campuses have a division between teaching and student affairs so that faculty don't encourage participation in extracurricular events or even see student affairs as their responsibility, while student affairs staff are cut off from faculty and issues of teaching and curriculum. While evidence shows that students learn most from extracurricular activities that they themselves choose, much more can be done to integrate these two domains, particularly in developing understanding and skills for political engagement.

Here we describe initiatives at our own university over the past two years, initiatives that have come from faculty, staff and students and have received deep administrative support. The 2007 participation of our students and faculty in the US Social Forum engaged them directly in political engagement from the bottom up as they listened to and talked with a wide range of individuals involved in activism for social justice and systemic social change. In March 2008, following the bringing back of lessons from the USSF, the administration supported the participation of a small number of students and faculty in the IMPACT National Student Conference on Service, Advocacy, and Social Action. This conference brought students from diverse campuses together to share information about social justice work on their campuses and in their communities.

While these actions bring the university and a small number of its members into direct contact with a broad range of social change initiatives, more radical efforts have included two "collaboration projects" at our university. Both authors worked to consciously integrate curricular and extracurricular events with a focus on political engagement in collaborations that worked "vertically" (involving administration, faculty, staff and students) and "horizontally" (across disciplines, colleges, and administrative offices).

In October and November 2007, we participated in a campus-wide initiative entitled the *Women Peace and Justice* project (aka WPJ) that unfolded from the idea of having the posters of the 1000 Women for the Nobel Peace Prize displayed on campus. Through an active, inclusive process, members of the university community, as well as high school classes and others from the local community shaped an effort that included intellectual engagement, cultural expression, celebrations, remembrances and the spirit of service, accountability, and even social change community building.

We articulated our goals as: engaging the community in an educational and reflective series of activities that bring to light the particular role that women historically and globally have played in struggles for peace and justice; raising awareness about ways that structures, institutions and constructs related to race, class, gender, ability, age and sexuality frame and marginalize the role that various constituencies have played in these struggles; reflecting inclusive, representative and diverse university constituencies through the process and activities; and connecting talk with action so that the project involves dialogue and activities that apply ideas in real settings within the broader community. Operating on principles of inclusion, representation and mutual respect have allowed for the efforts of many to be a transformative force on our campus.

It is instructive to read from the program for a production of the play, "My Name is Rachel Corrie," presented on October 31, 2007 as part of the WPJ project. Students worked on this production all semester, creating a piece written for one person but presented by 5 actresses while educating themselves about the life of this young woman who became a peace activist in Palestine. These students came face to face with the experience of social change through the medium of theater. Each described her developing awareness in the program written for the performance. For example, Lauren Brickman, the director, wrote:

> I feel Rachel's story is one that needs to be told over and over again and to different audiences, not because of it political message, but because of the spirit of humanity that existed within Rachel and in the passion she lived by. While I disagree with many of Rachel's political beliefs I respect her because she was a young woman able to take the path less traveled...I am interested in the durability of the human spirit in the face of opposition. The issue I am most passionate about is defeating apathy. I believe that apathy is my generation's greatest challenge to overcome and I hope that the message you walk away with from this production is that our time on earth is limited, we must, each of us, use our voices to the best of out abilities.

Actress Lindsay Rhae Beecher wrote:

> I feel by doing this play and others like it, we will continue to do what Rachael wanted, to help spread the word about the things that are going on outside our little boxes. There should be more outreach to those less fortunate, or those who are in the midst of a civil war with nowhere to live, nothing to eat, no clean water to drink. This is what theater is about, to evoke emotion, to evoke change, and to empower people.

Fellow actress, Victoria Broadhurst added:

> This has been a truly eye-opening experience. I've been aware that terrible things have been happening overseas, but for the first time I was opened to more specific details. Some of the things are hard to believe. I don't know if I would ever find myself doing what she did. But then I wonder; if it was for something I was passionate about, how far would I go? How far would you go? Rachel was passionate about human rights-for every human. Although she was stationed in a Palestinian home that does not mean she was biased toward the Israeli people. She was protecting a family…Let her story inspire you, if you so choose, to find your own way of making this world a little bit better.

Indeed, in a meeting between our university president and students in spring 2008, when asked what had been most meaningful during their time in college, Lauren Brickman replied that her participation in *My Name is Rachel Corrie* had been transformative in developing her awareness of the necessity and possibilities of working for a better world.

The 2008 Collaboration Project, ICAN (Imagine Change, Act Now!) focuses on issues of social justice and human rights. It follows the model established with WPJ in bringing together all divisions of the university and the wider community to integrate curricular and extracurricular learning. The participation of classes in events is facilitated by direct outreach from the ICAN steering committee and event organizers to classes that are studying issues covered by the event. Faculty not directly participating in ICAN are, nonetheless, bringing their classes to events and/or encouraging student participation through assignments and extra credit. Higher levels of student learning are facilitated through a process that allows students to choose which of the many events are most interesting to them. In an effort to involve students more deeply and widely, these projects do much of the organizational work in the spring and present events in the fall. In this way students are encouraged to think of their engagement in annual rather than semester long terms. The cooperation of multiple clubs and groups is also facilitated by ICAN steering committee members who introduce those proposing events or activities to others across the campus who might want to work with them. For example, our NAACP club is joining together with another club, Latino Students United, and an administratively-led initiative to get out the vote (VOTER) to produce a series of activities about historical struggles for the vote on Black Solidarity Day, the day before the presidential election. In addition, ICAN is offering workshops that introduce students to a diverse set of possibilities for political engagement. The titles of the workshops indicate their breadth: "World Hunger and the World Hunger Banquet;" "art that matter;" "Nonviolent Communication: An Ethical Practice;" and "Environmental Activism, Environmental Justice." The breadth is not only evident in the substantive focus, but also in the wide range of departments whose students will participate in these events. Students are "mixing it up" as they come from commonly isolated disciplines. The School of Education, the School of Social Work, Performing Arts, the College of Arts and Sciences—all have students who are actively participating in multiple events and in these training workshops. These types of collaboration projects bring moral and civic engagement to the campus in a sort of "Trojan horse." They are driven by the passion of people all across the university to engage in a broad education for systemic social change. They do not require the university to formally compel such a mission (although we agree with Colby et al. (2003) and others who call for such missions), but develop "organically" and "from the bottom up" by engaging the passions and values of a very diverse community.

The Urgency of Now

If, as sociologists, we recognize that social transformations occur most particularly as a reflection of the confluence of historical, social, political and economic forces, it behooves us to consider the particularities of this historical juncture in making an argument for expanding opportunities for students to be politically engaged, particularly as linked to social movements. This is a moment of opportunity when what we do particularly matters. Our responses to the global political, economic and social crises begin to lay the foundations for the world we create. This paper focuses on understanding the ways in which existing systems/structures have created profound inequalities and how we can engage the implications of this reality. Teaching our students about the possibility of acting for social change/social justice exposes them not only to the idea that individuals and groups can make a difference through service, but that systems and structures can and do change. Political engagement offers the potential for that to occur.

Immanuel Wallerstein (2006) and others have articulated analyses of the current period as a "twilight time" for historical world capitalism, white supremacy and US hegemony. These systems and ideologies emerged, developed and flourished as interwoven realities. This means that to understand nationalism, internationalism, citizenship and belonging, globalization, inequality, or even notions about what kind of world we envision for the future, we need to consider the state of these three systems in the ways that they frame and contextualize the material, ideological, theoretical and practical realities for all peoples. This history provided the foundation for where we find ourselves today with those three systems operating hand in hand in organizing everyday life for all peoples around the globe.

At a time now when in fact all three (US hegemony, white supremacy, world capitalism) are weakened, there is a heightened potential for real change, largely thanks to the struggle and resistance in so many forms within the Global South. This transition period is not certain as it is not in our control to shift the rapports de force in ways that will lead to a sufficiently humane future. However when we, in the United States examine the many changes that are underway in society (nationally and globally), there is potential for change. What we do does matter. How we, within the academy support and are part of the struggle for that humane future can help provide leverage—but only by recognizing ourselves in service more so than in leadership. The dismantling, reconstruction, revolution, and re-visioning relations between people, groups, and nations that have been so framed by white supremacy, world capitalism and US hegemony needs to be guided by the wisdom of those who have faced the deepest consequences of those systems.

It is true that what comes next is uncertain. The French historian Fernand Braudel (1972) and others such as Anibal Quijano (1992, 2000) speak about the importance of "temporality" in our understanding of the social world. While we often think of the 1960s as notable for its revolutionary character, in fact contained within was the seeding of the conservative trend we've witnessed over the last several decades. In retrospect, it was not a time of ultimate crisis for any of the organizing systems of the globe. To understand this it is important that we have some understanding of temporalities and the plurality of social times. Braudel argued that time is a social creation and it is of the utmost importance to understand the multiple forms of social time. We need to understand the immediacy of the time of the events, the middle run cyclical natures such of economic expansion and contraction but most importantly we need to frame our understandings in the long term or *longue durée*. (Bush, forthcoming 2009) It is in this view of historical moments that we as observers of the social world can pay attention to the enduring structures (economic, cultural, and structural) that over the long term frame the context for our collective behaviors, our civilizational patterns and organizing principles and institutions of the reigning world system. We must understand the cyclical functioning of these structures as they have a definite life span.

This is all to say that capitalism (and white supremacy and US hegemony) has to this point provided equilibrium within the world system. However, secular trends cannot go on forever, because they hit walls. Once this happens, it is no longer possible for the cyclical rhythms to bring the system back into equilibrium, and this is when a system gets into trouble. It then enters into its terminal crisis, and bifurcates— that is, it finds itself before two (or more) alternative routes to a new structure. But which of the two alternative routes the system will take, that is, what kind of new system will be established, is intrinsically not possible to determine in advance, since it is a function of a multitude of choices that are not systemically constrained. This is what is happening now in the capitalist world-economy and this is why human agency is so important today. (Bush, forthcoming 2009)

Ironically, the great demographic shifts from the South to the North have heightened the polarization and crises within the pan-European world. The fundamentally inegalitarian nature of historical capitalism led to and entered a period of structural crisis during which human agency will determine the direction of transformation of the system. Immanuel Wallerstein gives capitalism roughly 50 years (2006)....what comes next is yet to be determined. In this light, our argument takes on significant urgency. Young people educated both about the realities of the social world they live in and its historical roots AND about the possibility and means toward real change are a powerful force to reckon with.

Conclusion

Social change occurs as a result of the intersection between historical legacies, current predicaments and dreams of tomorrow. It exists in the crossroad between what was done before and what has yet to be done.

Broad social change comes about because the juncture between social forces that are shaped by the before—institutions, structures, systems and patterns—and the power of individuals and groups to make choices that shift those forces. Education that involves not only teaching about structure but structural change and civic involvement related to issues of justice and equality can be extraordinarily powerful.

Social scientists, sociologists and people who are concerned about our future have much at stake. Listening to the voices of the young women with us at the United States Social Forum, participating in a world social movement, calling out that "A Better World is Possible, Another US is Necessary" we affirm the call for engaged scholarship AND teaching and for the contextualization of service and volunteering within a deep civic engagement that has to do with democracy that emanates from the base. Women, communities of color, and all communities marginalized and underrepresented within the current social structure have the skills and the power to lead. Especially given diverse perspectives, constituencies, goals and disciplinary foci, we can and need to come together in projects related to the politics of society, engaging the ideas, principles and practices of justice and democracy.

ANOTHER WORLD IS POSSIBLE:
MOBILIZING FOR GLOBAL JUSTICE

Lauren Langman, Ph.D.

Introduction: The Dialect of Globalization

For a number of reasons, following WWII, the US, whose economy flourished, whose industrial capacity grew, assumed domination of the "free" world. Following various agreements established at the 1944 Bretton Woods conference, the foundations were laid for an unprecedented expansion of capitalist markets and their integration. Given the encouragement, investment capital and expertise of the US, as nations recovered from the consequences of the war, between the development of new technologies of production, as well as the new information technologies, there was a greater integration of national economies. While multi national corporations had a long history as essential agents in the modern world system, with expanded trade came more and more globally dispersed factories, distribution centers and/or financial centers. With such expanded trade, these enterprise began to lose their national moorings and identities and a trans national capitalist system of global corporations. As the economic power of capital grew, its intellectuals began to argue that various governmental restriction, the public ownerships of common resources and various entitlement programs thwarted economic growth. The Keynesian framework was increasingly under attack. But the time of Thatcher and Reagan, the economics of Smith and Ricardo, as resurrected by Milton Friedman, assumed hegemony. This was often combined with right wing politics, if not military dictatorships.

As neo-liberalism transformed the nature of international markets, as its intellectuals promised, it would promote rapid economic growth, and, as they say, the rest is history. Transnational capitalist corporations now dominate the world economy; transnational regulatory agencies, beholden to capital, regulate and control trade and investment. But globalization, as a force of 'creative destruction' has not only created vast profits and transformed the nature of contemporary life but has created major social disruptions, stresses, strains, and hardships starting with declining wages for industrial workers and many service workers in the advanced countries. The forces of globalization have led to massive social dislocations and migrations as destitute and often landless peasants have flocked from rural hinterlands to big cities—only to find unemployment, underemployment, and the impersonality and anonymity of the city. Many people from poorer countries have migrated, often illegally, to the richer countries and find the conditions of the poor slums, barrios, favelas, banlieues, and ghettoes filled with hardship, crime, violence, and despair. Environmental despoliation has not just become rampant, but the proliferation of toxic waste, global warming, species depletion, and desertification threaten the very viability of human life. The problems generated by globalization transcend national boundaries and cannot be addressed by national actors; therefore, new kinds of global social movements are necessary to meet the new kinds of challenges (Cf. Bennett 2003).

Part I: Global Justice Mobilizations

A. Crisis Tendencies of Global Capital

The dialectical understanding of society, rooted in a Hegelian-Marxist framework, rests on the concept of negation, understood as the inherent nature of contradiction that would seek to resolve itself; the 'power of negativity' would seek the 'negation of negation' to overcome contradictions. As such, negativity fosters change. But how does contradiction foster its resolution. In terms of political economy, the contradiction of class domination fosters crises and, in turn, disposes changes/challenges that would transform class relations to overcome crises tendencies based on those inherent contradictions. Such crises evoke emotional reactions that in turn impel actions. Systems of domination foster pain and suffering, as well as various ways that neutralize, control, or deflect efforts at change. Sociologically, social mobilizations become one means of mediating between structural and/or ideological domination/contradictions and overcoming these contradictions that are experienced as crises. Various collective stresses and strains may be individually and collectively experienced as anxiety, anger, shame, humiliation, etc. But how do crises and contradictions, and in turn personal and/or collective distress then foster social mobilization? Habermas (1975) formulated a comprehensive theory of legitimacy crises fostering social mobilizations. His analysis can yet be useful for understanding Global Justice Movements.[1]

As has been suggested, the globalized production of goods, services and entertainment that provides vast corporate profits has had onerous social consequences for many people, beginning with the vast disparities of wealth, power, and lifestyles of the elites of the transnational capitalist class and the vast multitudes. Notwithstanding the "joys of shopping" gleaned through the consumer identities based on goods that provide the "good life" for the few, the clothes, toys, tschoschkes, electronics, etc. of consumerism, are often produced in inhumane "satanic mills"—the third world sweatshops by exploited and oppressed women workers, often in toxic environments. While to be sure large numbers of people have moved from poverty to a better life, for the majority, conditions are worse. Meanwhile, power stations, factories, and transportation systems billow forth vast amounts of CO_2 and SO_4. Global warming remains unabated. For analytic purposes, five such contradictions of neo-liberal globalization foster various kinds of system and subsystem contradictions and crises, though in practice these often overlap (Cf. Buechler 2000). For example, young women may be sexually exploited to gain/keep a job in a polluting enterprise without rights or political recourse. Following Habermas (1975), crisis tendencies occur when a society fails to provide for economic/material needs, the government fails to secure legitimacy, the integration of the society becomes problematic, and finally identity and motivation withdraw from the dominant order. This suggests multiple crises:

1. *Economic/Material:* Globalization in its current neo-liberal form has generated massive amounts of wealth, as well as massive redistributions of wealth from the poor to the rich, as 'corporations now rule the world' (Korten 2001; Perucci and Wysong 2002; Stieglitz 2002). Privatization has raised water, electricity and health care costs while the race to the bottom has contracted most incomes, while the incomes and wealth of the elites has skyrocketed. Between desertification and direct appropriation, many peasants have been displaced or have lost their lands. Moreover, the mass production of goods has created

---

[1] While economic crises may well foster social movements, this does not mean embracing either classical economic reductionism, or ignoring a plurality of identities other than the proletarian—often a conservative element. Thus issues like gay rights or environmentalism are not working class struggles.

various externalities, not the least of which is massive pollution of air, land, and sea. Various extractive industries produce vast quantities of toxic wastes going into the atmosphere and/waterways. In turn, global warming threatens rising sea levels.

2. *Political:* Globalization has led to an erosion of the autonomy of individual State policy, self-determination within clearly demarked boundaries has defined the modern state. Transnational firms and agencies dedicated to regulating global capital (World Trade Organization, International Monetary Fund, World Bank) are increasingly dictating trade policies, tariff rates, investment laws, copyrights, labor conditions, etc. With the invisibility of many global policies, there is little citizen awareness and in turn, citizens have little voice in the policies that impact them. Various crises of legitimacy have fostered fundamentalisms and/or reactionary nationalisms as well as retreats for political economy into mass culture.

3. *Socio-cultural:* There has been a growing concentration of the means of communication, a universalization of homogenized popular culture and transformation of news into entertainment (Bagdikian 1997; McChesney 2000). Media-fostered consumerism increasingly serves the political and economic interests of globalization by providing media spectacles and forms of subjectivity and cultural identification apart from political economy (Langman 1992).

4. *Environmental:* There has been vast environmental despoliation, destruction of ecosystems, deforestation, the loss of many species, and the definition of genetically modified organisms as a social problem (Foster 2002; Kovel 2002).

5. *Human/Labor Rights:* Many types of human/worker rights based global social justice movements have arisen since the sixties with greater awareness of oppression, torture, and even murder as a State-sponsored or State-tolerated practice in non-democratic societies.[2] In many places, governments repress, if not murder, union organizers or civil libertarians. Race, gender, and gender preference-based oppressions, ranging

---

[2] It was only when digital photos of the abuses of Abu Ghraib went out over the Internet that these practices became well known outside of human rights organizations.

from genocide in Sudan, female genital mutilation, or rape as punishment, endure. Meanwhile a mass sex trade has flourished, often involving children. Some of the pornography of the Internet is dependent on coercive practices of the global sex trade. These issues of social justice have complex interactions with class, State polities, national cultures, and religion. Insofar as these problems now cross national boundaries, so too must and have various NGOs and associated social movements taken a transnational course.

6. *Culture, Identity and Motivation:* The dysfunctions, contradictions, and crises at the structural levels and the ideological, where the promises of freedom and prosperity become domination and poverty, foster crises of legitimacy at both collective and experiential levels. In face of the structural crises, contradictions and dislocations due to globalization, there is often a migration from the political economic to cultural/collective identity and emotional realms. Customary identities regarding work, gender, gender orientation, religion, etc. face economic and/or cultural challenges and crises that, in turn, impact identities and cause emotional distress to actors. Thus we have a long history showing how financial crises often lead to self-blame, anger, anxiety, depression, etc. I shall return to this important, but often ignored, point.

B. *Identity, Stability, and Change: Hegemony and its Contestation*

For Foucault, power and domination work through the inscription and control of identity through various disciplinary/discursive practices. (Cf. Buechler 2000). Gramsci's notion of cultural hegemony depends on mediation though identity to naturalize the historical (Langman 2000). Thus a crucial aspect for certain contemporary social movements is rejection or refashioning of identities/values to influence the future directions a society.[3] From what has been said, collective identity can be seen as a contested terrain in struggles for hegemony. The historic blocs in power defend their power and privilege by fostering identities in which subjugation is cloaked and most people accept their domination (ruling bloc interests) as 'normal,' 'common sense,' and 'in their

---

[3] While the present analysis is sympathetic to the notions of the discursive production of hegemonic identities as LaClau and Mouffe (1985) argue, they completely lose sight of the larger political economy—which in terms of the present analysis, is neo-liberal globalization.

best interests.' In other words, the production of identities is a part of hegemonic processes that sustain structures of domination at the level of the person. The acceptance and performances of those identities is not without certain emotional gratifications for most people most of the time. The extent to which such identities are embraced without question and reproduced in performance over time sustains the continuity of the society. This has been the essential nature of the structuration process for Giddens and the nature of the *habitus* for Bourdieu. Most notions of identity locate the person/group within certain structures of hierarchy and domination. This may be racial or ethnic. Colonizers impose subaltern identities upon on the colonized, the acceptance of which empowers the colonizer, even if the colonized turns violence on his/her self (Fanon 1986). Women have been socialized to be subordinate to men, but as Simone de Beauvior noted, the suffering of women as Other, what Freidan called the illness without a name, has impelled the feminist movement. Gays have long suppressed their identities-and now proudly assert queer identities.

Nevertheless, at certain times, to paraphrase Marx, the maintenance of 'typical' and earlier identities becomes a problem for both the society and the people and must be discarded. At times of social change, often due to material factors from technological innovation, people must attenuate certain identities and embrace new ones.[4] But this is a long term process. Crises are often very sudden, and, as such, there come times in a society, where for various reasons, the typical identities become problematic in face of crisis. Further, and unless there are emotional consequences to macro structural crises and/or official policies, most people do not interrogate their identities or values. Various social movements that are often the vanguard of would-be historic blocs typically seek new cultural understanding and identities that would result in political economic transformations that might shape the values and directions of a society. Collective identities can be thought of as loci where a number of material and ideological influences converge to control the culture in ways to sustain the power of a particular historic bloc despite various challenges and contestations.[5]

---

[4] As will be noted, many fundamentalist or nationalist movements today can be seen as attempts to maintain values and identities under besiege by global forces. Progressive activists would say, you can't go back, we must fashion a new kind of society.

[5] For Althusser, the subject is "interpellated" (constructed/hailed) by Ideological State Apparatus, and his/her sense of agency is an illusion. While his is half right

Following Castells (1997), network society fosters four types of collective identities: 1) *Legitimizing identities*. Typically include patriotic, religious, or consumerist orientations sustain the stability of the social order. Such identities are the most typical in any society. 2) *Resistance identities* attempt to reconstruct or restore waning identities-as such, they typically oppose globalization and its impacts. For example, the fragmentation of community, often tied to economic decline, leads some people to turn away from the global and embrace reactionary movements from nationalisms to fundamentalisms that would restore a mythical lost world or 'Golden Age' of strong communities of the past and defend a particular cultural framework that would secure heretofore privileged, traditional identities. In some cases, there may be progressive forms of resistance, albeit romantic, anarchic, and so individualistic, they are unlikely to foster mobilizations. One could add 3) *ludic identities* tied to the consumption mass culture that privilege privatized hedonistic indulgence and mass mediated forms of escapism and/or simulated contestations that allow subcultural withdrawal of self and identity from the larger society, what has been called "retreatism."[6] Alternative subcultures of style and 'transgressive' identities such Goths, punks, metalheads, etc. allow a "withdrawal" from the dominant order through the embrace of a seeminly 'oppositional' culture. 4) For our purposes, the most important, if often least frequent pattern are the *project identities* that challenge the hegemony of the dominant class at several levels, not the least of which is proposing alternative identities that valorize democracy, self determination and fulfillment, and equality. Such identities typically resist rationalization and/or commodification and consumerism. These project identities whether green or gay, feminist or human rights, pose fundamental challenges to late capitalist modernity in which rational technologies, as forms of domination, colonize the life world and insinuate collective identity, child-rearing, family life, work, organizational spheres, and even the pursuit of pleasure (Giddens 1991; Habermas 1975; Hochschild 1997).

---

in that schools, media, churches and families socialize identities that sustain a social order, his New Social Movements perspective argues that indeed it is the agency of the actor that enables social transformation, and that is the constriction upon agency that can impel action.

  [6] Castells did not use this term.

These attempts to re-negotiate and/or fashion new forms of tolerant democratic identities that embrace alternative futures act to impel progressive social transformations.[7] Such people seek to transform people and society in terms greater equality, freedom, and democracy. However, these project identities are emergent in the interaction of struggle; they are neither *a priori* nor clearly envisioned as goals. But as is clear in a number of social movements, gay pride, feminism, etc., the negation and articulation of new identities, as projects to be attained, as ways in which particular aspects of self hood become realized, can be found in many social movements whether progressive, reactionary or reformist (Cf. Reger 2008). But for the various Global Justice Movements these identities are typically progressive, democratic and inclusive.

The articulation of certain identities/social goals by one group necessarily conflicts with those of other groups. Those who seek social transformation buck up against entrenched power that has already secured cultural and psychosocial hegemony and richly rewards those who so conform. The embrace of fundamentalism puts its followers in ideological conflict with secularists. Feminists must challenge both patriarchy and the many women whose identities and values sustain patriarchy and subjugation. Thus, as will be seen, an intrinsic aspect of mobilization is the articulation of new identities that challenge the status quo and offer new forms of identity.

C. *From Crisis to Action—Mediated Thru Identity*

How do structural crises and contradictions impel social mobilizations? The global market has now colonized the life worlds of most human actors. Crises and contradictions, stresses and strains at the structural level thus contextualize and impact the everyday life worlds and experiences of actors.[8] Jobs are lost, new ones found, communities change, immigration/emigration become salient. I would suggest that the emotional reactions to crisis are the initial moment of social mobilization. This is not to revert to the 'irrational mob' theories of LeBon/Freud

---

[7] Such identities might also include contemporary instantiations of progressive trade unionists, anti-war activists, and human rights activists.

[8] This is not to assume that most people understand how global finances work or see how their life styles impact the environment. But when the dollar falls, losing almost ½ its value since 2000, people feel how imported goods are more expensive.

but rather is an appeal to 'bring emotions back in' (Goodwin, Jasper, and Polletta 2000; Goodwin et al. 2001).[9]

Human beings have a number of fundamental needs/desires tied to their emotional life and affect system.[10] People are fundamentally social. They need attachments and ties to others, not only for their very survival but sociality, intersubjective relations, for their own sake. The pleasure of friendship and company is sought in every society, just as isolation, abandonment, and loss of attachments that evoke fear, anxiety and/or depression are unpleasant and avoided. People seek recognition of self, they seek, a degree of self esteem and dignity, and conversely most people would avoid shame and/or degradation. It is almost a sociological truism that systems of domination depend on hegemonic ideologies that denigrate subalterns or critics—while believers and supporters are valorized. People would seek to assert agency, they seek to have some impact on others and on the world; people would avoid powerlessness.[11] For most progressive social movements, a collective, political identity is one of major moments for gaining empowerment, establishing boundaries of inclusion, and providing frameworks of understanding, meaning and values.[12] Finally, most people need to find their life meaningful, lest they suffer anxiety, despair, and worthlessness. When macro structural crises adversely impinge on people's lives, directly as victims or indirectly through value based empathy, people respond with strong emotional reactions, such as fear, anger, or shame. Others may be angered and outraged by famines, human rights/labor rights/animal rights abuses, pollution, genocide, torture, rape, illness,

---

[9] Reactionaries, fascists and fundamentalists have long understood the relations of emotion, identity and social mobilization. They have no problem manipulating fear, revenge and outrage. Progressives and liberals who appeal to either reason or logic and/or the "good will of people", always lose in struggles.

[10] While essentialism may be disdained by postmodernists, and the nature of what is human and human desire are socially constructed, given the universality of the human body, and its innate affect system which has been the product of evolution, there are some general tendencies of all people. There are of course many variations, for example psychopathology.

[11] The need for community/attachment, recognition/esteem, agency/empowerment can be found in Marx's critique of alienated labor that rendered people powerless to outside forced, fragmented community and truncated his/her humanity, s/he was little different from a pack animal.

[12] There is a major literature on the role of identity and agency in social movements, see for example, the Reger (2008) collection, especially the Reger and Bernstein contributions.

or the sex trade, much of which is often based on social policies ame-
nable to change. Similarly, as Scheff (1994) argued, repressed shame
can foster rage and violent nationalisms. I would suggest that emotional
reactions to crises, tragedies, and contradictions, directly or indirectly
experienced, refracted [understood] through a person's identity, impel
actions that would hopefully alleviate the adversity through social
transformation. Consider the case of Hamas leader Dr. Abdel Aziz al-
Rantissi, who was assassinated by Israel in April of 2004. Rantissi took
over Hamas after its founder, Sheik Ahmed Yassin, was assassinated
by the Israelis in March of that year. Rantissi was born in what is now
Israel and driven from his home in 1948 during the war that established
the Jewish state. He, along with more than 700,000 other Palestinian
refugees, grew up in squalid camps. As a small boy he watched the
Israeli army enter and occupy the camp of Khan Younis in 1956 when
Israel invaded Gaza. The Israeli soldiers lined up dozens of men and
boys, including some of Rantissi's relatives, and executed them. The
memory of the executions marked his life. It fed his lifelong refusal to
trust Israel and stoked the rage and collective humiliation that drove
him into the arms of the Muslim Brotherhood and later Hamas. He was
not alone. Several of those who founded the most militant Palestinian
organizations witnessed the executions in Gaza carried out by Israel in
1956 that left hundreds dead.[13] Surely, in view of Israel's more recent
2008–2009 attack on Gaza, another generation of activists will emerge
seeking freedom and self determination.

For various reasons, some people that are either directly and adversely
impacted by dysfunctions and hardships, or have awareness and
empathy with 'distant' Others who face adversities. They are likely to
seek out means of amelioration. In still other cases, people in certain
structural locations are more likely to be exposed to certain information and/or experiences. What is being suggested is that a fundamental
factor for many mobilizations, at least the Global Justice Movements
is the alienation of actor(s). Otherwise said, a degree of alienation is
a precondition for seeing and understanding things in slightly different way. Much as Simmel described the [alienated] 'stranger' as both
'within' and 'without' and thus a more acute observer, the 'alienated'
can see and/or be open to seeing what most might ignore. Alienation

---

[13] See Chris Hedges, Lessons of Violence http://www.truthdig.com/report/item/
20080121_the_lessons_of_violence/.

may come from his/her structural location or conflicting locations, especially if s/he is both emotionally impacted; s/he feels powerless and seeks to foster change.[14] I am not necessarily talking about the powerlessness of class position; indeed many educated affluent people feel a need to assert agency and foster ameliorative transformation.[15] How do we now move from feelings to action?

Part II: Explaining Social Mobilization

Perhaps the most vile and despicable social movement in history was the rise of Fascism. That said, there were important lessons learned about social movements that have been slowly forgotten. The fascist mobilizations consisted of much more than mesmerized crowds at midnight rallies or berserker brown shirts running amok on *Krystallnacht*. While surely the crises of world capital in the 1930s made people fearful, anxious, angry, and desperate, the 'mass psychology of fascism' was not simply about jobs and benefits. It was concerned with creating a valorized identity tied to an imaginary *volk* that appealed to needs to submit to authority, restoring national pride and seeking "revenge" against enemies from without, and even from within, "impure" Jews and treasonous leftists.

Fascism was not simply an attempt to control inflation, provide jobs or increase wages. It created a mythical community and valorized identity of Aryan supermen and women who were born in Valhalla and were now resurrected and destined to rule for 1,000 years—if only the despicable Jews could be eliminated and Bolshevik's defeated. In much the same way, the Global Justice Movements of today are different than the more traditional interest based, instrumental movements of workers struggling over wages, working conditions, or organizing unions. Similarly, anti slavery, Prohibition, suffrage, or civil rights movements were concerned interests in preserving or gaining status

---

[14] Fromm (1941) argued over 60 years ago that the feelings of powerlessness that came from social change disposed an anxiety and in turn a submission to authority via a new collective identity—in the 16th century, it was Protestantism, in the 20th, Nazism.

[15] A central premise of New Social Movement theory argues that these movements are not class based as in classical Marxist theory. But at the same time, in many movements, workers/peasants may well be the most powerful factions, cf., the PT in Brazil or the Korean Federation of Trade Unions.

and/or privileges. The changing nature of societies and its contentious mobilizations, dealing with more individual/personal factors, such as the colonization of the life world and private sphere, the colonization of consciousness, etc., marked a move toward issues of culture, hegemony, legitimacy, and even identity.[16] Thus identity, emotions, experiences including at times sexuality, become central concerns. As Giddens (1991) noted, for the emerging lifestyle politics, new forms of valorized identity and recognition were central for feminist women, racial ethnic minorities, gays, etc. Such movements are more concerned with creating and/or gaining 'recognition' of newly empowered 'collective identities' than material benefits.[17] These mobilizations do not really fit the classical models of strain and irrational response, nor are they the rational pursuits of knowing actors who rationally pursue self interests that may be mobilized by 'social movement entrepreneurs.' Rather, I would suggest that for [some] Global Justice Movements, the concerns with culture and identity are more salient, and indeed such pursuits may be detrimental to the material gains of its members. As such, Global Justice Movements are a particular kind of New Social Movement. For Melucci (1989), structural theories may explain why a movement begins but fail to specify how structural factors impel actual actors, while resource mobilization may explain the processes of how movements may emerge but not why.

Social crises, stresses, and strains at economic, political, cultural, or motivation—identity levels can and do migrate from one realm to another. Contradictions and crises produce victims who find their plight disconcerting and feel anger, rage, shame, etc. Some distant others may identify with concrete victims or more abstract notions of justice and/or experience emotions as a result of information mediated through locally situated interpersonal networks. When people saw bulldogs attacking civil rights advocates or Buddhist monks immolating themselves, many were quite upset. While the directions of chains of influence are variable, in most cases, crises in political or economic spheres have differential impact on people at given social locations and within that location. Variations in identity that are associated with gender, in some

---

[16] The work of Habermas, Offe, LeClau and Mouffe, and Marcuse can now be seen as important precursors to the New Social Movement perspective.

[17] In many ways, various reactionary/fundamentalist movements follow the same model. This was anticipated in Lipset's analyses of 'status anxiety' in the conservatism of the '50's, especially McCarthyism.

cases race/ethnicity, and individual psychological differences impact the consequences of events and their understandings. Identity-motivation has a crucial role in social mobilization; for example, an economic or political change, or anticipated change, may bring some people advantages and other people losses that might impel them to organize and act. Those potentially advantaged would tend to support the status quo, while those burdened might 1) passively accept a new status, especially if understood through a hegemonic ideology, 2) they might seek to retreat or withdraw from the adverse circumstances, or, finally, 3) they might come together, discuss their plight, attempt to understand their circumstances, and attempt transformation.[18]

At this point the fundamental theoretical question asks how crises at multiple levels of global capitalist structure and its neo-liberal ideology foster social mobilizations that recruit, socialize, organize, and mobilize actors.[19] If we understand society as consisting of groups in conflict over material or symbolic resources (recognition/honor), we can understand how social movements consist of communities of actors engaged in the contested terrains of the public spheres, who seek to influence the political to refashion the larger society in terms of their identities, goals/visions (Melucci 1989). The mediations between structural contradictions, injustices, and adversities, which are often far removed from personal experience, nevertheless lead to actual participation in a concrete social movements. This depends on a number of factors; as noted above, the antecedent factors include emotions and a personal disposition, structural location, or circumstances that allow one a critical stance to the status quo.[20] That said, mobilization then depends on: 1) access to information and the way an issue or crisis is framed, 2) a personal identity/emotional constitution that is receptive to this information that may be discrepant from the 'received' wisdom, 3) a structural location or position conducive to activism, and 4) establishing linkages or ties with 'embedded networks' of social actors with similar

---

[18] In some ways, this typology is somewhat like Merton's classical model of conformity, innovation, ritualism, retreatism, and rebellion.

[19] Neo-liberalism becomes a material force when resources or government services are privatized and structural adjustment is implemented and when land is confiscated for World Bank projects, etc.

[20] Thus someone who was adversely affected by political policies, e.g., the relative of someone who died in combat, someone who is denied an insurance claim or whoever experiences first-hand how the "system" operates, which is often quite discrepant from it public presentations.

concerns and goals that join together.[21] This is not sequential; it can often work in many directions. For example, activists, those with more flexible work schedules that are typically more educated, are more likely to be exposed to certain information not often part of local circles or mainstream media. Conversely, activists are likely to get information most people either don't get or have an interest. How then are actors recruited, how do actors foster social change?

A. New Social Movements

We have argued that hegemony include the production of identities, and therefore, counter hegemonic struggles must target the nature of identity (Cf. LaClau and Mouffe 1985; Langman 2005). Moreover, emotions play a central role, not only in prompting the actor to action, but membership in communities provide various joys and emotional gratifications, not the least of which are attachments to a group, recognition by others, and finding meaning as part of 'movement.'[22] Further, contemporary Global Justice Movements tend to be more open, fluid, and democratic; 'leaders' are more like cheerleaders than directors or movement entrepreneurs. Finally, the tendency for transnational advocacy networks, social movement organizations and international non-governmental organizations, often located in different continents, to exchange information, alternative frameworks, and strategies and even forge alliances is unprecedented and must be theorized.

The New Social Movement perspective emphasizes the cultural nature of the new movements and views them as struggles by active agents seeking control over the production of meanings/values and the constitution of new collective identities. It stresses the expressive aspects of social movements and places them exclusively in the terrain of civil society, as opposed to the State. This approach also emphasizes discontinuity by highlighting the differences between the new move-

---

[21] With all due respect to Tilly and Tarrow, the political opportunity structure also plays a role in social mobilization, but the present concern focuses on identity/emotion following a New Social Movements perspective.

[22] For sake of full disclosure, the author has been a member of many activist organizations. Members of such organizations see each other as "movement" people, sort of a valorized "we" vs. a "them" that includes the nefarious evil elites as well as the bulk of people indifferent to the political/cultural struggles beyond voicing opinions.

ments and traditional collective actors.[23] New Social Movement theories specifically address the conditions for the construction and emergence of collective identity formation and collective action of the Global Justice Movements in the contemporary world. These theories have emerged in response to changes in the goals, strategies, and constituencies of social movements that have emerged as a result of neo-liberal globalization. Although social movements may still pursue political and social gains, for the New Social Movements there is greater stress on the construction and legitimating of collective identities for solidarity, meaning, and to articulate resistance.

New Social Movements often carry out organization and resistance on symbolic or cultural grounds—more so than through traditional political channels. Further, in modern societies in which power is dispersed and expressed in various signs and symbols, New Social Movements often challenge those signs and symbols. The organizing base of New Social Movements has been theorized as more dispersed, diverse, fluid, and complex in structure than the more defined and fixed structures of previous movement organizations (e.g., labor movements). Further, New Social Movements generally value autonomous reflexive individuals who engage in participatory democratic relations with decentralized forms of organization (Castells 1997; Melucci 1989; Melucci 1996); these factors combine to create more informal submerged networks than those of past movements or 'vanguard' parties.

Following Touraine (1985), we can suggest that New Social Movements, be seen as groups that struggle over historicity—the ability of society to 'act upon itself' and develop new values, goals, and lifestyles to shape social life. Social movements seek to change the future directions of post-industrial society. Touraine suggests there are three main components of social movements. They seek to **1)** *assert a collective identity 'I'* (self-definition and self-understanding) in face of social fragmentation in general. These struggles take place in the public sphere. **2)** They *challenge opposition and adversaries 'O'* (e.g., the crises and contradictions of neo-liberal globalization). Finally, **3)** *the struggles seek control the future and outcome of the social totality "T."*

---

[23] Resource mobilization theory, in contrast, stresses the political nature of the new movements and interprets them as conflicts over the allocation of goods in the political market. Hence, it focuses on the strategic-instrumental aspects of action and places social movements, simultaneously, at the levels of civil society and the state. It also places emphasis on continuity between the new and the old collective actors.

Some movements are attempts to assert a reactionary agenda based on a mythical return to a utopian past, what Castells called 'resistance identities' as evident for example in the upsurge of nationalisms and/or fundamentalisms which can be seen as attempts to 'restore' a 'Golden age' of a community now fragmented by globalization and cast adrift in 'liquid modernity' (Beck 2006; Langman 2008). Thus it is not surprising that the lower middle classes, lumpenproletariat, and waning segments of the elites, are most likely to embrace reactionary movements that secure a valorized self, rooted in restoring what has been lost. Conversely, others seek more progressive, alternative collective identity, project identities from feminisms and gay rights to ecology and social justice. Others seek alternative futures for those adversely affected by its neo-liberal policies. Progressives more likely come from proletarian or upper middle/professional classes. In either case, one central aspect of mobilization is the crafting of a collective identity within a struggle. As Bartholomew and Mayer (1992) note in their review of Melucci:

> In attempting to grasp how individuals get involved in collective action, Melucci stresses the concept of collective identity as the crucial mediating variable missing in much exiting work on social movements. 'Collective identity' is not equivalent to 'mobilizing interests' (as in Resource Mobilization's market conception of interests and benefits), but is precisely a constructivist concept, which can appear only outside the assumptions and framework of (pluralist or elite) liberal theory. It requires an intermediate level of analysis which brings into relief how individuals come to decide that they share certain orientations and decide to act collectively. Many approaches to social movements have been bedeviled by the problem of bridging the gap between the structural foundations for action and the collective action itself (P. 144).

As Melucci pointed out:

> Collective identity is an interactive, shared definition produced by several individuals (or groups at a more complex level)...that must be conceived as a process because it is constructed and negotiated by repeated activation of the relationships that link individuals (or groups) [to the movement].' While activists may realize their identities and values in their political/cultural activities, they are at the same time, involved in the submerged networks of everyday life, networks of meanings they produce and reproduce (1989: 71).

The network and communities of everyday life are identities which are continually fashioned and negotiated. It is important to note that for the Global Justice Movements, and many other movements as well, identity is not so much given as the product of interaction and negotiation that are part of struggles. Following Simmel, and, in turn, Coser, in situation of conflict, identities are created, negotiated, and consolidated. That said, emergent identities depend on the kinds of concrete performances that secure recognition and confirmations of identity that comes though participation in a social movement. To be sure, as any activist knows, much [most?] of the activity consists of long boring meetings. As Weber ([1918] 1946) pointed out, "Politics is a strong and slow boring of hard boards. It takes both passion and perspective." While activism includes demonstrations, actions, protests, lobbying, handing out literature, and collecting signatures, canvassing, etc., it is important to note that such activities, and we might even note repressions, arrests, and often violence, take place among groups more or less defined by a commitment to social transformation. Again, as Bartholomew and Mayer (1992) point out:

> In order to pursue the level of analysis necessary to analyze contemporary movements as composite action systems, Melucci attends to the networks which constitute the submerged reality of the movements before, during, and after [visible] events' (1988: 338). Networks are the small groups, submerged in everyday life, which require a personal involvement and produce 'alternative frameworks of meaning' (1989: 70). They *are* 'networks of meaning' or signs (1989: 58) which put into practice the alternative meanings which they produce and reproduce (1989: 71). The form of the movement is thus *itself* a message (1989: 60) (Pp. 145–6).

That meaning may well come from the shared ideology that would foster struggles, challenges, and political action/change to so transform the self-production of society to make the world a 'better' place. But different groups might have different notions of what is 'better' from the embrace of Jesus, to stopping abortions, the restoration of the Caliphate, ending patriarchy, neo-liberalism or abolishing of capital. For Melucci (1996: 350), a key element in the ideology of a movement is the "negation of the gap between expectations and reality. The birth of a movement is marked by a 'moment of madness' when all things seem possible…Ideology thus overcomes the inadequacy of action" (P. 133).

B. *Global Justice as a New Social Movement*

Today the life worlds of everyone have been radically changed by neo-liberal capital. If the mediations between the crises and contradictions of globalization are 1) framed though ideology, 2) mediated through an emergent collective identity as locus of action and meaning, 3) impact actors emotionally, and 4) counter hegemonic struggles are often over culture, identity, and lifestyles, it should now be obvious that New Social Movement theory, while rooted in the new social movements of the '70s and '80s, helps us understand the various Global Justice Movements of today. The emergent Internetworked Social Movements share many of these characteristics; however, the influence of new technology on mediation has created a new type of movement that requires new theoretical examination. Today the major differences are: 1) the global context of crises, contradictions, and adversities; 2) a part of that context it should be noted, that many of the activists in these movements were first 'called' to activism in those earlier movements, and I use the term 'called' in much the way that Weber ([1918] 1946) saw politics as a "calling, an expression of an inner determination." "Only he has the calling for politics who is sure that he shall not crumble when the world from his point of view is too stupid or too base for what he wants to offer. Only he who in the face of all this can say 'In spite of all!' has the calling for politics."

To understand contemporary Global Justice Movements, it is necessary to have a social movement model that connects identity, ideology, and network formation to understand how collective action may be mobilized. The New Social Movements were grounded in the resistance of the middle class to the rationalizing forces of modernity, social fragmentation, injustices, identity and the importance of recognition. New Social Movement theory speaks to the cultural critiques of Critical Theory (Habermas and Offe) and, in turn, post structuralism (Foucault and LeClau and Mouffe). Then moving to New Social Movement theories of Tourraine and Melucci, we can see that social movements provide communities with intersubjectively meaningful ties, relationships and realms of sociality. Such communities provide the individual with a number of personal gratifications, as well as a sense of meaning through the attempt to shape the future. Thus, the social movements are thought of as identity granting/recognizing, interacting/socializing communities of meaning devoted to fostering political and/or cultural changes. Thus, for example, the environmentalist movements are not simply concerned with installing scrubbers on smokestacks, detoxifying industrial wastes or saving polar bears. They are seeking to promote lifestyles and values that reject consumerism in general and more specifically dangerous forms, such as fossil fuel based energy, transportation, or products, as well as, say, fast food which requires vast factory farms that may cause massive deforestation, etc. More specifically, the contemporary Global Justice Movements follow much the same patterns and dynamics as the earlier movements studied by New Social Movement students. The major differences are 1) the global nature of the problems and 2) the role of computer mediated communication.

As Sassen (1998) pointed out, most of the activity of the global economy is financial and most of that takes place in the 27,000 or so private networks. Further, the various command, coordination, and control of transnational corporations whether financial, manufacturing, or services, as well as the many transnational regulatory agencies, are all dependent on the Internet. However, the rise and proliferation of the Internet has introduced fundamental changes in the way that information is freely available and the way people/groups can communicate across great distances. The consequences of neo-liberal globalization—growing global inequality, labor injustices from child labor to the sex trade, various kinds of trafficking, the exploitation and oppression of women, global warming, human rights abuses ever more visible thanks to the Internet, cell phone cameras, uploading pictures to the Internet.

Not only has the Internet changed the nature of communication, but it has enabled new forms of [virtual] community and political formations. Sociologists like Castells, Sassen, and Wellman began to chart the emergence of new forms of networks and organizations in the '90s. Moreover, these networks enable 'virtual public spheres,' where people can not only have access to information but can communicate wide and far. We can suggest that for theorizing Global Justice Movements, given crises, contradiction and adversities and suffering of globalization, that 1) some people, informed by media, become recruited by self or others to form or join networks and organizations. They are often engaged via a computer terminal, where people have access to 'virtual public spheres' where people can freely attempt to create and negotiate understandings, negotiate 'consensual truths,' debate and articulate critiques, propose alternative imaginaries and explore various strategies to realize these goals. As a result, 2) Internetworked Social Movements of various kinds have emerged, with often contentious relations to States. Some provide alternative information, while others initiate various kinds of actions that might contest, resist, and even transform adversities and injustices through pressures on States and/or economic actors to change policies or, in some cases, change governments. These might include lobbying, consumer boycotts, demonstrations, and even direct forms of 'netwar' such as 'hactivism.' As has been noted (Langman, 2005):

> The 'virtual public spheres' of a global civil society not only provide information and communication but act as identity-granting subcultures that foster collective identities. The 'virtual public spheres' of the Internet enable what Kahn and Kellner (2003), call 'post-subcultures,' interpersonal networks of discussion, debate and clarification that, however virtual, nevertheless foster or create spaces for the democratic construction, negotiation, and articulation of new constellations of project identities that are decoupled from national, ethnic, or religious moorings. These 'post-subcultures' allow people the freedom to re-define and construct themselves on the basis of the alternative cultural and/or political forms and experiences.
>
>   Moreover, the global nature of the Internet has fostered a greater awareness of often far-removed injustices and adversities that, in turn, mobilize ameliorative strategies rooted in political or economic practices. Internet 'post-subcultures' have taken up the questions of local and global politics and are attempting to construct globally oriented identities and strategies to act both locally and globally, which are now possible because of nature of the Internet. Social justice movements are organized around articulating collective identities that seek to attain some public good(s).[24] Those who acquire a global justice identity through the Internet are more likely to join Global Justice. Such identity-based networks impel resistance, contestation, and new forms of net-based progressive cyberactivism.[25] These include globally based peace movements, feminisms, gay rights, and environmentalism, as well as AIDS activism. Other AGMs embrace more traditional causes amplified by globalization such as trade unionism, job creation, poverty, inadequate medical services, civil/human rights, genocide, the sex trade, and regional trade agreements (taxes tariffs, migration), landless/homelessness or family violence. (Pp. 57–8)

It is now generally accepted that many "local" problems cannot be solved locally. Acid rain destroys vegetation thousands of miles away. The rapid creation of industrial and service jobs in developing countries has impacted Europe and the US. Much of the tuna in the world now

---

[24] In many cases, membership and participation in a social movement organization serves more to sustain and confirm collective and personal identity than to actually impact policy over what sometimes seem to be intractable adversities. Consider the Israeli-Palestinian conflict. Some of the peace activist groups have spent decades trying to foster reconciliation—so far to no avail.

[25] There have been earlier notions of global justice organization, for example the World Federalists. But these tend to be more formal and less likely to engage in protest mobilizations.

has dangerous levels of mercury, a by product of burning fossil fuels. The pollution of the Pearl River basin impacts every man, woman, and child on the planet. As has been noted, the contradictions of globalization generate negativity that, in turn, might have transformative powers. However, that requires the dedication and devotion of millions of activists devoted to global justice.

Conclusion

While social scientists may quietly debate the nature of social movements, the contemporary world is now dominated by a regime of neoliberal capital that, as such, faces unprecedented contradictions and adversities. Never before has so much wealth been generated in a short time, albeit highly concentrated within the transnational capitalist elites (Sklair 2002). Hundreds of millions of people have moved from abject poverty to moderate levels of comfort, but far more people now face a life of greater poverty, deprivation, and violence. This is especially true after the meltdown of 2008.

Following the fundamental insight of the Hegelian Marxist of the power of negativity, it is clearly evident how globalization in its capitalist phase has intensified the inherent contradictions of capitalism, it growing inequality, it alienation rendering people powerless, dehumanized and socially fragmented, and the contradictions of its promises of freedom, equality and brotherhood. In response to the contradictions and negations of global capital, we have seen the emergence of vast number of Global Justice Movements, Non-Governmental Organizations, International Non-Government Organizations and Social movement organizations. Aided and abetted by the same Internet technologies that make the current moment of globalization possible, there has been a vast and growing proliferation of Global Justice movements. But just as these movements argue that humanity must develop new paradigms of identity and meaning, so too must social scientists rethink the understanding of these new social movements. One of the common themes of the Global Justice movements, most clearly seen as the motto of the World Social Forum, is that another world is possible. Between the growing proliferation of nuclear weapons technology, the growing shortages of resources from oil to land to water, and growing environmental dangers, we might suggest that these movements may not just make the world better, but enable the very survival of humanity.

SMOS, CYBERACTIVISM, AND ENTERTAINMENT AS POLITICS: HOW MOVEON IS EXPANDING PUBLIC DISCOURSE AND POLITICAL STRUGGLE

Victoria Carty

The tremendous impact that information communication technologies (ICTs) have had on social movement organizing, contentious politics, and the electoral political process calls for a re-conceptualization of our definition and understanding of political struggle (Langman 2005; Carty 2004; Earl and Schussman 2003; Castells 2001). The Internet, alternative sources of media, and Netroots organizations have dramatically expanded access to politically relevant information and offer citizens new possibilities for learning, resources, and action (Wellman 2000; Nipp 2004). Some of the most effective grassroots organizing is developing exclusively online, and therefore an examination of electronic social movement organizations (SMOs) and their tactics can help refine our understanding of contemporary social movements.

The website for MoveOn (MoveOn.org), for example, has become the epicenter for campaigns across a variety of progressive issues and electoral politics, and is undoubtedly one of the most successful advocacy operations in the digital era. Its e-activism, in combination with offline engagement in protest and electoral politics demonstrates how conflict between entrenched centers of corporate domination and political parties can be undermined and subverted by marginal groups and an insurgent citizenry. As a grassroots virtual community MoveOn has excited large constituencies by employing experimental methods to give its membership ways to make a creative impact on the increasingly centralized political system (Carty and Onyette 2006). Its pioneering approach of conducting politics through the Internet has been replicated by other SMOs and in formal politics (the Obama campaign for example illustrates how Internet organizing and fundraising have fundamentally transformed the landscape of American politics). By encouraging information sharing, dialogue, and debate within the political landscape MoveOn has uncovered a vast number of frustrated citizens eager to revitalize democracy. Many activists consider its revolutionary use of the Internet as a new form of participatory politics in its ability to bypass mainstream and corporate politics and media.

This paper uses a critical theory framework to examine the ways in which MoveOn has used the Internet and alternative media (including forms of entertainment) to fuse contentious politics with institutional means of reform via the electoral process. Critical theory has had two distinct aims: the analysis and critique of existing forms of oppression and the more emancipatory or reconstructive goal to move beyond current conditions. Habermas, for instance, has long contended that corporate media consolidation has served as a corrosive social force by denying citizens a voice in public affairs and inhibiting the political culture by negating access to honest information while enhancing the power of corporate interests (1981). His hope is that a revitalization of "communicative action" in the public sphere, despite the colonization of public opinion will yield new forms of participatory democracy. Yet, his theory stops short of assessing how technological and media advances may bring this to fruition.

I argue that new ICTs and novel repertoires of grassroots mobilization are helping to decolonize public opinion by expanding public discourse. This analysis supports claims among many social movement scholars for the need to reassess some of the basic premises of critical theory to make sense of how new ICTs and the resulting mediated communities, networks, and identities are transforming the social and political world. New technologies also require further development of the concept of the public sphere as new social and political spaces are constantly being created that allow for the flow of information, mobilization potentials, and wired and concrete communities. Thus, I also incorporate aspects of new social movement (NSM) theories that focus on new sources of collective identity, values, tactics, and organization features among activists and SMOs in conjunction with recent theories regarding the Internet's impact on political struggle.

Critical Theory, New Social Movements, and Theories of the Internet

Though there are various strands of NSM theories, there is consensus among scholars that the newness is to distinguish certain forms of collective action from those based on class-based interests and Marxist reductionism (Laclau and Moufe 1985; Mouffe 1992). Overall, claims are that participants (mainly new middle class professionals) in NSMs are raising new issues, are the carriers of new values and operate in new terrains, employ new modes of action, and have new organizational forms (Cohen 1985). There is also general agreement that new actors struggle for control over the process of meaning, the right to realize their own identity, and creativity of relationships (Habermas 1981; Melucci 1980). NSM theorists attempt to explain the mediated nature of the passage from condition to action via ideological, political, and cultural processes.

Tourraine (1985) and Melucci (1985) explicitly argue that the field of social conflict has shifted from the political sphere to civil society and the cultural realm because it is in these areas where new collective identities and forms of solidarity are being established. For Tourraine culture is the fundamental object of historical contestation and he makes a marked distinction between the social and the political (1988). Like Habermas, Tourraine and Melucci reject the instrumental or strategic forms of action to achieve broad political goals. Melucci holds that participants in NSMs do not necessarily seek material gain, but attempt to challenge the diffuse notions of politics and of society themselves. Actors are now more concerned with retaining or re-creating endangered lifestyles and culture than with changes in the economic or public policy realm. As Tourraine argues, there is reflexivity in some mobilizations that address the issue of the social construction of reality itself (1996).

Laclau and Mouffe (1985) explain social moments in terms of the availability of democratic discourse. They assert the primacy of political articulation and the broadening of politics because multiple points of antagonism have emerged thus leading to a proliferation of political spaces in new areas of social life. Similarly, Offe (1985) suggests that the emergence of NSMs must be understood as a reaction against the deepening and what he perceives to be the irreversibility of the forms of domination in late capitalist societies. He argues that NSMs challenge the boundaries of institutional politics by dismantling the traditional dichotomies between private and public life, institutional and non-institutional action, and political and civil society. In doing so, actors politicize civil society through practices that belong to an intermediate sphere between private pursuits and institutional state-sanctioned modes of politics. Melucci refers to an "intermediate public space" where social movements make society hear their messages and where these messages enter the process of political articulation (1996). Thus, actors can politicize civil society yet in ways that do not reproduce existing forms of control, regulation and state intervention. The literature on NSMs further suggests that organizational features of contemporary social movements are distinct from traditional forms of organization (for example labor unions or political parties) because they are constituted by loosely articulated networks that permit multiple memberships and part-time participation, there is little if any distinction between leaders and rank-and-file members, members and nonmembers, private and public roles, and means and ends (Melucci 1985; Offe 1985).

One of the strengths of NSM theory is the focus on the cultural dimension of social movements and examination of processes of new collective identities; acknowledging pluralistic forms of activism based on articulations among various, flexible, fragmented, and shifting sources of identity (Castells 2001). Haraway (1991) calls for coalitions based on affinity, contingency and mobile positioning—using what is shared in common at a particular time and setting. Another strength of certain strands of NSM theory is that it is in many ways is an extension of some of basis presuppositions of critical theory in its focus on the decentralized nature of both power and resistance and emphasis on cultural and symbolic expressions that challenge forms of domination.

However, there are certain weaknesses in some of the NSM literature. For example, the often exclusive focus on the cultural aspects of contemporary movements and the assertion that civil society is the only arena for collective action precludes an analysis of the political dimension of social movements (Cohen 1983). Many contemporary social movements are much more than cultural phenomena; they are also struggles for institutional reform. Also, an over-emphasis on identity often ignores questions of strategy and a discussion of how identity develops in the process of interaction. Another weakness is that the specific organizational dimension of social movements (organizational dynamics, leadership, recruitment, tactics, and resources that enable or constrain SMOs) is often overlooked. Two final drawbacks are that much of the NSM literature fails to address continuity between new and old actors in terms of their repertoires, organizational structures, and their relationships with political institutions and political reform, as well as the lack of empirical studies to support or discredit the rather general theoretical templates of NSMs to test how/where/under what conditions they operate (Cohen 1980).

Theories of how Technology, Communication, and ICTs Impact Collective Action

Habermas has written extensively on how political and social life in modern society has been impacted by media and communication technologies (1981; 1989; 1993). His premise is that with the rise of late capitalism, the culture industries, and the power of corporations in public life citizens have become passive consumers of goods, services, political administration, and spectacle and the result is a decline in democracy, individuality and freedom (1989). Public opinion, he argues, is now administered by political, economic, and media elites which mediate public opinion as part of social control. Thus, public opinion shifts from one based at least on the possibility of the outcome of debate, discussion, and reflection (what he refers to as communicative action) to the manufactured opinion of polls or media experts and political consulting agencies. For him the function of the media has thus been transformed from facilitating an exchange of ideas and debate within the public sphere into shaping, constructing, and limiting public discourse to those themes validated and approved by media corporations.

Habermas views NSMs as struggles in defense of the public sphere and to regain forms of communicative action. The public sphere refers to the space that mediates between the private sphere and the sphere of public authority; areas of social life where citizens can freely and face-to-face discuss and debate societal concerns that are important to them, and at times, reach a common judgment. It consists of information distributors such as print media as well as physical social areas such as salons, coffee houses, meeting halls, etc. He argues that this realm has been colonized as relationships are increasingly mediated by money and power, and entrenched political parties and interest groups substitute for participatory democracy (1981). Since information has become a crucial resource in modern society collective action designed to change the ways in which public discourse is structured is essential. He is optimistic about the possibility of the revival of the public sphere—one that transcends geographically boundaries to embrace democracy based on a political community that can collectively define its political will and implement it. This political system, he contends, requires an activist public sphere, where matters of common interest and political issues can be discussed and the force of public opinion can influence the decision-making process. Developing theories of the Internet suggest that new ICTS, enabled by collective and individual actors, may indeed be useful in reconstructing the public sphere.

The debate regarding the pros and cons of new ICTs and media is a longstanding one and will remain one into the foreseeable future. Some argue that the Internet may be the most persuasive and effective form of communication technology in diffusing social ideas and actions in history (Castells 2001). Poster (1995) points out that the recent technological advances have "enabled a system of multiple producers, distributors and consumers to use decentralized and newly accessible media technologies in everyday practices... this electronically mediated communication can challenge systems of domination" (28, 57). Similarly, Kidd (2003) espouses that ICTs offer a mode of communication that is fundamentally resistant to state regulation, reducing a state's capacity for repression by hindering its ability to control the flow of information and political communication.

Other utopian-oriented versions claim that the Internet can enhance political mobilization and increase awareness of important social issues outside the control of the dominant media corporations (Langman 2005; Kellner 2004). Bimber (2003) argues that the Internet is democratizing processes of collective action and political organizing by flattening bureaucratic structures and making boundaries more porous. This in turn facilitates collaborative decision-making, coalition-formation among organizations, lowers the obstacles to grass-roots mobilization and organization, and speeds the flow of politics. Another trend he attributes to new communication and information flows is what he calls "accelerated pluralism," a pluralism that contributes to the on-going fragmentation of the present system of interest-based group politics and a shift toward a more fluid, issue-based group politics. Furthermore, new forms of organizational flexibility and efficiency among online groups provided by ICTs thus increases their ability to influence policy processes by subverting the 'professional' campaign model and giving rise to a new type of civic engagement at the grassroots level.

ICT-based virtual communities, like actors in many contemporary movements, therefore are made up of social relations that are decentralized, diverse, heterogeneous, fluid, open, informal, and in many ways self-governing. Many scholars credit the Net for allowing for the development of community in spite of physical distance as it is not bounded by political borders or identities. Also, online links tend to be organized through non-hierarchical channels of individuals who may be geographically and/or socially diverse, but who share common interests, concerns, goals, tactics and strategies (Hampton 2003). Kahn and Kellner (2003) refer to virtual public spheres that coalesce in cyberspace as "post-subcultures," encompassing interpersonal networks of discussion, debate and clarification that create spaces for the democratic construction, negotiation, and articulation of new constellations of project identities. Wellman (2000) describes the organizational, personal, and cultural diversity of cyberactivism as "networked individualism"—the ease of establishing personal links that enable people to join more diverse and numerous online political communities than they would ordinarily join in the material world. Also, recent research shows how digital network configurations can facilitate permanent campaigns and the growth of broad networks despite relatively weak social identity and ideology ties, and that organizers can then mobilize these groups and individuals to participate in political events and protest in face-to-face contexts, which in turn strengthens advocacy networks (Bennett 2003; Van Aelst and Walgrave 2003).

A more critical analysis of electronic mediated information systems, however, reveals a number of limitations. Some claim that virtual social relations in cyberspace are not a substitute for more traditional forms of community, protest, and collective identity due to a lack of interpersonal ties that provide the basis for the consistency of collective identities and ability to mobilize new members (Pickerill 2003). Underlying this concern is an ongoing discussion about whether new forms of media and technology are weakening or strengthening standard forms of political and social engagement (see for example Bimber 2003; Putnam 2000; Kraut et al. 1998). Additionally, many discussion groups and listservs discourage challenges to the information and conclusions drawn by members because they tend to be composed of like-minded people who are often predisposed to issues that draw Internet users to various sites (Jordan 2001; Diani 2000). Other critiques of the Internet note the elite domination over cyberspace and control over listservs by list owners or gatekeepers, and problems regarding access to technology, or the digital divide (Dimaggio et al. 2004).

Despite the pros and cons of new technology and communication systems, there is ample evidence that the Internet has resulted in a significant shift in communication capacity and potential for political organizing. The proliferation of mass-media and ICT communications have dramatically changed the way information is sent, received and accessed, and this has at least compromised the ability of the media, cultural, and political institutions to ensure hegemony. These may serve as a form of resistance and be an important step toward revitalizing Habermas' concept of communicative action in the public sphere, and MoveOn has capitalized on these trends as much as any grassroots entity, and indeed has been one of the central forces driving them. Thus, an analysis of the innovative resources and strategies that

MoveOn utilizes can enhance the explanatory potential of critical social theory and NSM theory by urging us to rethink how different forms of political participation, activism, recruitment, and network-building among groups and individuals are shaped and sustained electronically, and how this in turn impacts the nature of politics and participatory democracy. An empirical analysis of MoveOn also strengthens theories of contemporary social movements by illustrating how it has combined political goals with more culturally-oriented efforts, and examining how repertoires, tactics, decisions, and resources have enabled the SMO.

MoveOn and its Role in Fuelling Contemporary Political Struggles

MoveOn can be viewed as an entity that fosters Habermas' concept of communicative action in the public sphere (yet also a virtual one) because it serves as a central means of communicating grievances, debate and consensus making, sharing and expanding communication, increasing the interconnectedness and consciousness of groups and individuals, and ultimately enhancing participatory democracy. It successfully leverages the Internet to organize people not only online, but more critically in face-to-face forms of both contentious and institutional politics and thereby represents a symbiotic relationship between cyberspace and local space. It does so quickly and cheaply and in ways that were not possible in the past. The SMO was in fact born in cyberspace in the late 1990s and currently has over 3.3 million members (MoveOn.org). It was founded when Eli Pariser and Wes Boyd joined efforts to stop the impeachment trial of President Clinton and later to prevent the U.S. invasion of Iraq. Its running slogan, "Democracy in Action," is indicative of its quintessential grassroots mobilizing efforts.

Pariser explains, "In a sense part of MoveOn's attraction is that it aims for normal people, not just activists, and it engages them successfully... we try to appeal to the highest common denominator, "ordinary, patriotic, mainstream Americans" (Leland 2003). This enables it to build coalitions across diverse constituencies and avoid the discriminating aspects of other mobilizations that reject the people they are countering and thus allows for broad and inclusive communicative discourses. It therefore has credibility which increases its ability to support a genuine kind of populism. Like the formation of many contemporary social movements as theorized by NSM theorists the SMO has no single, identifiable sectional interest or social constituency to represent. What unites members is support for progressive issues and a different type of politics, and the Internet is an essential tool that allows them to stay politically connected. Pariser states, "You would say that MoveOn has a postmodern organizing model. It's opt-in, it's decentralized, and you do it from your home. MoveOn makes it easy for people to participate or not with each solicitation—an approach that embraces the permission-based culture of the Internet, and consumer culture itself" (Jacobs 2005). This is very much is synch with the style of organizing that NSM theorists are addressing and demonstrates how public opinion can become decolonized through new media and computer capabilities.

Though MoveOn does not keep demographic data, anecdotal data shows that most members are middle-class professionals (Boyd 2003). Thus, one of MoveOn's strengths lies in providing an outlet for busy people who may not have the time or energy to be part of more formal, chapter-based organizations and attend regular meetings. Its strategy is to activate people on a few different issues at a time, often for short durations as legislative battles change, and this model allows MoveOn to play an important role as a campaign aggregator. This means it invites people in on a particular issue and then introduces them to additional issues, thus avoiding what Pariser calls "the single-issue balkanization of the progressive movement" (Markels 2003). Therefore, it is different than merely a traditional "protest" group and this has helped to sustain the organization over the past ten years. Also, the multiple issues that the SMO advocates for support Harraways' and other NSM theorists' encouragement of fluid, flexible, and shifting coalitions based on affinity and mobile positioning by focusing on shared beliefs and values at a particular time and place. The organizational nature further illustrates how flexibly articulated networks that permit part-time participation, little distinction between leaders and members, and the merging of private and public roles are a demarcation of SMOs that foster contemporary forms of contentious politics.

In terms of recruitment and tactics, MoveOn's success is clearly different from traditional movements and highlights the importance of these flexible and contingent forms of (wired) collective identity, the blurring of the public and private spheres, and the possibility for expanded forms of communicative action. MoveOn is often the first step for members into political action, and what brings them to take that step is typically an email message sent from one of the organizers or forwarded from a family member, friend, or colleague. Pariser explains:

Every member comes to us with the personal endorsement of someone
they trust. It is word-of-mouth organizing in electronic form. It has made
mixing the personal and political more socially acceptable. Casually passing on a high-content message to a social acquaintance feels completely
natural in a way handing someone a leaflet at a cocktail party never would.
The 'tell-a-friend' phenomenon is key to how organizing happens on the
Net. A small gesture to a friend can contribute to a massive multiplier
effect. It is a grassroots answer to the corporate consolidation of the
media, which has enabled an overwhelmingly conservative punditry to
give White House spin real political momentum, and the semblance of
truth, simply through intensity and repetition (Body 2003).

This statement illustrates how activists in contemporary movements are
questioning the construction of social reality. Also, MoveOn's ability to
draw recruits from variant constituencies over the Internet, and many
first-time participants in political mobilization, supports the claims
of scholars regarding the need to re-conceptualize social mobilization
Additionally it lends weight to Bimber's notion of how the Internet can
represent accelerated pluralism in that the issues MoveOn advocates
for are vast, as well as to the suggestions of Wellman and Hampton
whose research indicates that the Internet allows for new types of
social relations and enhances activism given the ease of participation. Pariser has systematically attempted to establish the SMO as an
interest aggregator and despite the relatively weak collective identity
or ideological ties among its members MoveOn's attempts at online
organizing have facilitated long-term campaigns and developed broad
networks of groups and individuals (this will be discussed in-depth in
the next section).

One of the most powerful mobilizing tactics that MoveOn utilizes
and that facilitates online participatory democracy is the two-way communication with its members in order to generate ideas and strategies
to mobilize around different issues. The Action Forum (a cross between
a blog, a discussion board, and an online rating mechanism), is perhaps one of the best examples. It allows ideas to be rated so that the
organization knows what people feel most passionately about, and asks
members to fill out a progress report to gauge how satisfied they are
with the work MoveOn is doing. Organizing director Justin Ruben states
that, "MoveOn's ideological sensibility is not a product of the staff's
outlook but of the views of its members...we believe strongly in the
wisdom of crowds, giving people the ability to make choices together.
They'll make good choices" (Jacobs 2005). This is highly indicative
of Habermas' concept of rational communicative action, and it also

illustrates the significance of ICTs' ability to diffuse ideas and organize actions while enabling multiple producers, distributors, and consumers of information as theorized by Castelles and Poster. Furthermore, this type of coordinating mechanism parallels Bimber's research on what he claims to be the democratizing process of collective and political action in that the boundaries of online groups are porous and decision-making collaborative, ultimately resulting in more self-governing types of organization.

From the onset MoveOn has sought to empower citizens by combining net activism with meaningful political engagement. In addition to raising money (its political action committee is now one of the leading sources of financial support for Democratic candidates outside of the Democratic Party's committees), MoveOn's website distributes email action alerts that inform its members of important current events and provides petitions and contact information of members' elected officials so that members can respond to those events (Potter 2002). MoveOn also strongly encourages members to be active in their communities and participate in forms of mobilization that will impact the offline world such as physical attendance at rallies and fundraising events, writing letters to newspaper editors and sending written correspondences to political leaders, making phone calls to elected officials, writing postcards to voters, distributing flyers, holding press conferences, donating money for print and television advertising, and organizing events in their communities (one of the most popular being house parties).

These efforts substantiate the claims of Nip, Bennett, and Van Aelst and Walgrave that online organizing and networking often leads to political activism in "real" communities. The continual feedback loop also provides solidarity that activists typically experience on the streets at rallies and protests. For example, emails update members on the progress of the various campaigns as they evolve, often including personal comments and/or photos from members participating in offline activities so that what is happening on the streets ends up back on the Internet. Thus, despite the corporate-dominated media and cultural institutions that attempt to ignore or block dissent and alternative viewpoints, opposition often finds its way into other powerful mediums that have massive audiences and in which information has the potential to spread like wildfire. They also tend to find their way into mainstream media through grassroots fundraising for TV ads and also, inadvertently, due to the criticisms by the owners of the media themselves as will be noted in the following section.

MoveOn Campaigns and Mobilizing Strategies

MoveOn's main focus has been on ending the Iraq war although it is also involved in a host of other progressive issues (see its website for an overview). It has been consistently cognizant of the need to combine e-activism and mobilization with protest and political engagement in the material world. Prior to the U.S. invasion of Iraq, MoveOn worked with Stop the War Coalition, an umbrella organization for the peace movement, to organize a global day of protest to be held on February 15, 2003 to contest the impending war. This resulted in the largest coordinated political protest ever with as many as thirty million people from more than one hundred countries taking to the streets (Kock and Sauerman 2003). Later that month it hosted the online headquarters for the Virtual March on Washington, which was an act of online civil disobedience to protest the imminent invasion of Iraq. This was sponsored by the WinWithoutWar Coalition which is another online umbrella organization for the peace movement. On February 26th over 200,000 individuals signed up and made more than 400,000 phone calls and sent 100,000 faxes to every senate office in the United States with the message: DON'T ATTACK IRAQ! (MoveOn.org). Every member of the U.S. Senate also received a stream of emails that clogged up virtual mailboxes in Washington D.C. The virtual march reinforces Wellman's, Poster's, Kidd's, and Bimber's assessments that advanced communication technologies have resulted in a significant shift in the mechanics of contentious politics and protest, and that the Internet facilitates the interconnections of groups due to the permeable boundaries of organizations that operate online.

Another tactic MoveOn has used repeatedly to organize around certain issues, which combines online planning with community-based organizing in the physical sphere, are candlelight vigils. The March 16th candlelight vigils that involved over one million people in more than 6,000 gatherings in 130 countries were organized in six days by MoveOn over the Internet. Its use of the online resource, Meetup, which is a tool that allows people who are interested in a particular issue to organize meetings by voting on a time and place to meet in their local area, made the event possible. This is another good example of expanding the boundaries of communicative action in both the virtual and public sphere.

Michael Mann (2000) describes such approaches to social issues as "interstitial locations." These consist of the "nooks and crannies in and around the dominant institutions" (57). He argues that groups that are marginal and blocked by the prevailing institutions can link together and cooperate in ways that transcend these institutions. Such movements create "subversive invisible connections across state boundaries and the established channels between them...these interstitial networks translate human goals into organizational means" (13). MoveOn's use of the Internet for electronic political activism, in conjunction with grassroots community-based mobilization illustrates the effectiveness of such interstitial locations as well as Kidd's and Bimber's emphasis on the strengthening of pluralistic politics promoted by grassroots entities being able to work outside of state-regulated and corporate-dominated media. These interstitial locations can further be applied to MoveOn's fundraising tactics, which were also essential to its participation in the anti-war effort and later in the electoral process. In less than one week members raised $37,000 over the Internet to run an advertisement in *The New York Times* calling for a rethinking of the immanent invasion of Iraq (*New York Times* 2002). Although MoveOn and its grassroots allies did not stop the invasion, its involvement in the anti-war movement helped to shift the debate, put the antiwar sentiment on the political map, and brought the organization into the public eye. The SMO further made the case for how powerful the Internet can be in mobilizing social protest and a recruitment opportunity for otherwise disenchanted citizens.

After the invasion of Iraq began MoveOn organized a transnational email drive to enlist signatures for a citizens' declaration that appealed to the international law via the United Nations. Over one million signatures were collected in less than five days and were delivered to the United Nations Security Council and to the petitioners' respective congressional representatives. In the run-up to the Senate vote on the Iraq resolution in October of 2003 MoveOn volunteers met face to face with every U.S. senator with "Let the Inspections Work" petitions (Utne 2003). This again highlights MoveOn's tactics of combining net activism and organization with community-based involvement, and therefore bypasses some of the caveats of online engagement as expressed in some of the literature—that it will replace activism in the material world and serve as an obstacle to social relations.

MoveOn also started to more aggressively engage in political campaigns on behalf of progressive anti-war candidates once the invasion began, urging its supporters to donate money to House and Senate members who had opposed the Iraq resolution. From its inception, key to MoveOn's successful fundraising has been its ability to accumulate small campaign contributions from tens of thousands of rank-and-file citizens. This allows MoveOn to broaden the public sphere and represent the public interest and thus alter the balance of power in politics. Boyd refers to this as "radical decentralization," relying on group efforts to encourage citizens with no affiliation to any political group to donate small sums of money, and most of whom have never contributed money to politicians before (Burress 2003). Yet again this is indicative of Bimber's concept of accelerated pluralism whereby individuals organize around issue-related agendas and outside of elite control, and of critical theory more generally that calls attention to increasing participation in politics via ICTs as ways of self-empowerment and resistance to institutional, structural, and micro-level forms of domination and oppression. In addition, it highlights the potential for the resurgence of Habermas' concept of communicative action.

MoveOn's formal and informal relationship to the Democratic Party has evolved and vacillated over the past several years, and raises important questions regarding the relationship between SMOs (formally organized components of social movements explicitly oriented toward movement goals) and political parties (whose job is to win elections). The Iraq war was a particular point of contention between the two. This climaxed when MoveOn ran an ad in the *New York Times* accusing General Petraeus of "cooking the books for the White House" in assessing the situation in Iraq and labeled him "General Betray Us" (Bai 2007). In response the Senate, including many democrats that MoveOn helped to get into office, passed a resolution denouncing the ad and the organization.

On the other hand, progressive-oriented groups which operate exclusively outside of the Beltway see MoveOn as co-opted by the Democratic Party. For example MoveOn's backing of Nancy Pelosi's (speaker of the House) support for a phased troop withdrawal plan from Iraq rather than pushing for immediate withdrawal led to a fracture between the organization and much of the peace movement, which viewed this as a comprise in order to receive favor with the newly accessible Congressional leadership (Manjoo 2007). Furthermore, certain coalitions within the movement viewed MoveOn's position as one of unprincipled politics that subordinated ending the war to getting Democrats elected to office.

What is resoundingly certain, however, is that MoveOn had a significant impact on the 2004 and 2006 electoral process by supporting democratic candidates. During the 2004 election MoveOn and ACT (America Coming Together) aggressively engaged in electoral politics as they undertook the "Leave No Voter Behind" campaign, an attempt to get democratic supporters to vote at higher rates by communicating with all of them. To correct for the much acknowledged detachment of the Democratic Party from its local membership base and over-reliance on paid consultants and professionals for outreach (and as Habermas would argue the consolidation of public opinion), MoveOn began emphatically connecting with local communities across the country. Together with ACT it used a bottom-up, person-to-person model that involved millions of ordinary citizens and precinct partners (Reilly 2004). The emphasis on face-to-face voter mobilization through social networks increased turnout by seven percentage points (Middleton and Green 2007). This strategy was a clear rejection of the pollster-driven operations and reliance on big donors in previous campaigns. By challenging the lack of leadership and creativity within the Democratic Party MoveOn was able to influence the party to adapt their practices toward more grassroots efforts in exchange for the organization's support. In this way marginal groups were able to collectively impose their will as hoped for but not yet theorized as to how, by Habermas.

The organization continued with its grassroots mobilization during the 2006 election process. In an effort to regroup and rethink its strategies MoveOn invited members to organize and/or attend house parties to debrief the electoral process and to discuss new ideas and strategies. Its email informed members that the best solutions would come not from experts and political consultants but from MoveOn members thinking together. This face-to-face communication and brainstorming was supplemented by web-based organizing and mobilization. All house parties were linked by a network conference call online so attendees could view the event and participate in the discussion. What emerged was the Mandate for Change/Operation Democracy, or "people-powered" campaign (MoveOn.org). In synch with its flexibility and mixing of social events with political engagement to debate issues in the public sphere MoveOn suggested that members kick off the campaign by meeting wherever they felt comfortable—a library, bar, union hall, community center or someone's home.

The Operation Democracy field program asked volunteers to call progressive voters, house local organizers, staff support lines, recruit friends, and host or attend house parties. MoveOn trained volunteers on the ground to organize rapid responses to events and to hold news conferences, editorial board meetings, and rallies to target vulnerable Republican incumbents. Prior to the election MoveOn members held over 6,000 actions in these districts and organized 7,500 house parties (MoveOn.org). The social space of the house parties and other meeting places, and the encouragement of face-to-face dialogue to find the best suggestions/solutions as to how to proceed (with the assistance of ICTs), represents a decolonization of public opinion based on micro-level forms of collective empowerment through grassroots mobilization and fluid collective identities. However, challenging certain positions of NSM theory, these actions also demonstrate the continuity with traditional social movements in that there is an *instrumental* and *strategic* component—the goal being to affect institutional change in formal politics.

As another component of their strategy MoveOn members donated enough money to establish the Call for Change program that used web-based tools and a call-reporting system to reach voters (Doster 2007). The system once again bypassed professional pollsters, allowing ordinary people to connect with one another, and referred to as "cell phone parties for change." The web-based "liquid phone bank" allowed MoveOn members to call from wherever they lived into wherever they were needed within a day or two. Middleton and Green (2007) found that the phone bank was the most effective volunteer calling program ever studied, and that it increased voter turnout by almost 4%. These mobilizing tactics employed by MoveOn are clear examples of how web-based ties and social relations often spill over into the material world, and adds credence to Nipp's and Bennett's research that also finds community-based activism closely related to, or initiated by online activism and organizing. They are also examples of novel forms of communicative action and the bridging of the political and civil spheres of society.

During the 2006 campaign MoveOn's anti-war stance played a significant role in the Democrats' success in taking over the House and Senate. They forced their agenda of making the Iraq war the main Democratic message by pushing the issue relentlessly. Leading up to the election most Democrats were fearful of alienating voters and the party establishment if they were to criticize the war effort. MoveOn filled this void by raising awareness among the public by organizing vigils, rallies, and other forms of direct action in addition to funding advertising campaigns (Holland 2006). It also worked to affect institutional politics by commissioning a poll of sixty potential swing House districts to give Democratic challengers confidence that if they offered direct criticism of the war and a timetable to withdraw troops it would help them win (Berman 2007). This emboldened other candidates and constituents to speak out against the escalation as well, and again demonstrates how collective actors can implement their collective will into formal politics.

To pursue the issue even more aggressively MoveOn launched a project in conjunction with VoteVets.org, an organization that engages in advocacy on behalf of veterans from the Afghanistan and Iraq wars. The project relied on "global witnessing" from soldiers returning from war (many of the vigils also used this tactic). This consists of personal accounts from individuals directly subject to injustices that challengers are forging resistance to. It helps humanize conflict and gives credence to activists on the basis of individuals' first hand experience. VoteVets and MoveOn also produced a number of advertisements during the 2006 cycle denouncing the war escalation. Highlighting how ICTs are expanding the contours of public discourse, mobilization, and participatory democracy MoveOn members were asked to preview and vote on which videos they thought were the most compelling, and the most popular ad was shown on CNN for a week (Lou 2007).

Also during the mid-term election forms of grassroots creativity and identifying issues that deeply disturbed mainstream Americans allowed MoveOn to push second-tier races into first-tier contests. One example is the "Red-Handed" advertisements that criticized Republican incumbents for being caught "red-handed" in accepting money from defense contractors in Iraq while voting to protect them from punishment for war profiteering and defrauding the government, in taking money from oil companies and then failing to push them to pursue clean, cheap energy sources and voting against bills that would have penalized them for price gouging, and in taking money from the pharmaceutical industry while voting to keep drug prices high for seniors. Of the nine long shot races MoveOn targeted with these advertisements Democrats won five (MoveOn.org). The *New York Times* listed the "Red-Handed" advertisement against Representative Thelma Drake, which exposed her receiving money from corporate sponsors, as one of the seven most effective advertisements during the election (Drenttel 2007). Thus, grassroots forms of organization, despite corporate-dominated and controlled media, can gain access to airwaves, even if limited, by raising money in small amounts to subvert traditional ways of doing politics.

Operation Democracy found other creative ways to use the red-handed metaphor to confront representatives, activating cultural-based repertoires that included humor and serious political critique. Displaying giant foam red hands and signs, MoveOn members followed their representatives to town hall meetings, appearances, and fundraisers questioning their allegiance to special interests. The teams also connected with voters by writing letters to the editor and calling into local radio talk shows. In Virginia Beach, members attended every "Coffee with Thelma" event that Representative Drake held to ask questions about her allegiance to special interests. In Louisville, KY members rallied at a gas station to tell voters about Representative Ann Northup's ties to big oil with flyers describing war profiteering. Members in Fayetteville, NC attended a defense contractor tradeshow that Representative Robin Hayes sponsored. The red-handed campaign represents what MoveOn does best—framing issues in a way that resonates with voters and taps into their frustration while using humorous and innovative techniques. During this campaign alone local media wrote over 2,000 stories about MoveOn's actions (MoveOn.org). This illustrates MoveOn's ability to subvert conditions of corporate control to their advantage and its use of symbolic and cultural forms of protest that are indicative of NSMs.

Contentious Politics, Entertainment, and Electoral Mobilization

As MoveOn illustrates, contemporary social movements and SMOs are certainly employing new methods of action through novel organizational forms and new spaces that render themselves to the process of political articulation in new areas of social life. Melucci refers to these as intermediate public spaces, areas in which new forms of solidarity and collective identities emerge through ideological, political and cultural processes. We are also witnessing the merging of private and public life, political and civil society, politics and culture, institutional and non-institutional types of action, and the politicization of the public sphere in intermediate public spaces as theorized by NSM scholars. MoveOn has played a leading role in many of these transformations and one of the best examples is its efforts in the contentious and electoral mobilization of Hollywood. Over the past several years it has employed alternative forms of media, ICTs, and celebrities for political purposes to broaden public discourse and decolonize public opinion. Boyd explains, "We believe in big cultural messages; we believe that politics should be something that is part of mass culture" (Brownstein 2004).

One of the group's first interactions with Hollywood came when filmmaker and co-founder of Artists United to Win Without War, Robert Greenwald, organized celebrities in opposition to the impending war in Iraq as part of the Virtual March on Washington. Artists United had also run a full-page anti-war advertisement in the *New York Times* that was signed by over 100 actors and musicians (*New York Times* 2003). MoveOn has given substantial financial support to a number of Greenwald's films and documentaries to allow for more independent and critical voices outside of mainstream and corporate-dominated media. Its website offered his "Uncovered: The Next War on Iraq" DVD as a premium to members who pledged $30.00 or more, and over 8,000 individuals made pledges within the first three hours. Over 2,600 members hosted screenings in their homes and at community venues, and the movie was ultimately distributed in theaters across the country (Kern 2004). A few years later MoveOn provided free copies of Greenwald's "Iraq for Sale" and "The Ground Truth" documentaries for members to show at house parties. After viewing the films attendees made phone calls and wrote letters to voters. MoveOn also helped Greenwald finance "Outfoxed: Rupert Murdoch's War on Journalism." It promoted this with house parties and took out a full-page ad in the *New York Times* declaring, "The Communists had Pravda. Republicans have Fox" (Deans 2004).

There are other ways that MoveOn has subverted corporate ideology and tools to utilize what Mann describes as interstitial locations. For example, various directors and film producers helped MoveOn construct homemade advertisements once sufficient funds were raised by its members. The "Real People" ads, for instance, were created by documentary film maker Errol Morris and featured ordinary members of the Republican Party explaining why they were crossing party lines to vote for John Kerry (Deans 2004). This was the first time both the content and the funding for an ad campaign came from the grassroots membership of an organization. The "Bush in 30 Seconds" ads challenged the Bush administration's policies and were shown during his State of the Union Address. Moby, a Grammy-nominated musician helped to design them. Drawing on his experience of inviting fans to submit their own videos or remixes for his songs he designed a competition for members to submit ads and recruited a panel of celebrity judges that culminated in an awards show in New York City to raise funds for other anti-Bush television ads (Stevenson 2004). Similar to the "Real People" series, and representative of Habermas' hope for the liberation of public opinion, no agencies, focus-groups, or test screenings were involved.

When CBS refused to air the "Bush in 30 Seconds" ad during the 2004 Super Bowl activists jammed the network's switchboards for a week and condemnations of CBS appeared in the *New York Times* Op-ed page accusing it of limiting the debate to advertisements that were not critical of the political status quo (during the game CBS had run advertisements by the White House in favor of the president's controversial drug proposal) (Karr 2004). The ad did air on CNN during the Halftime show, and because of the free publicity surrounding the censorship issue, as well as Fox News' bashing of CNN for showing the ad, the SMO achieved massive amounts of air and print converge with little money spent. In fact the media coverage that the Right gives to MoveOn's tactics, its website, and political campaigns often far outweighs advertising fees and the money raised in political contributions (Drenttel 2007).

MoveOn had fought against censorship previously when theaters across the Unites States were being pressured by right wing groups to bar "Fahrenheit 9/11," Michael Moore's controversial film. It asked members to pledge to see the film on opening night with other members in order to send a message to theater owners that the public supports Moore's message of peace (MoveOn.org). It furthermore invited viewers of the movie to meet afterwards in house parties to share their analysis of the film and to plan political action to defeat Bush in the upcoming election. Bridging the offline and online worlds and combining entertainment with serious political discussion, there were over 4,600 parties across the United States and at each, on a laptop computer, Moore spoke to members about his movie and his hope that they would each bring at least five nonvoters to the polls for the upcoming November election.

Live forms of entertainment by celebrities were also included in MoveOn's tactics. During the 10-week "Don't Get Mad Get Even!" events preceding the 2004 election MoveOn and ACT held rallies and rock concerts that incorporated celebrity appearances by artists, authors and actors. As part of the Rock the Vote Tour (which promoted volunteer turn out) they jointly held a concert in New York City right before the Republican National Convention that featured rock stars such as Bruce Springsteen, Dave Mathews Band, Pearl Jam, REM, the Dixie Chicks, Jackson Browne, and John Mellencamp. Some MoveOn members threw house parties to watch the concert, at which members wrote letters to swing state voters. Additionally, "Don't Get Mad, Get Even!" television advertisements featured celebrities/activists such as Matt Damon, Rob Reiner, Woody Harrelson, and Al Franken (Karr 2004). The Call for Change initiative also included celebrities such as Stephen King who encouraged members to attend phone parties the weekend before Halloween as part of the get-out-the-vote campaign. A letter emailed to MoveOn members stated, "If I know anything, I know scary. And giving this president and this out-of-control Congress two more years to screw up our future is downright terrifying. Thankfully, this national nightmare is one we can end with-literally-a wake up call" (MoveOn.org).

MoveOn has used other creative tactics that combine mass/popular culture and symbolic forms of resistance to corporate/elite hegemony. In addition to running television advertisements and petitioning Congress to fire Tom Delay, who was accused of legal and ethical breaches of conduct, it held a contest asking members to pick and vote for a slogan for a poster advocating his dismissal that could be downloaded and hung. In its attack on Karl Rove, MoveOn's website provided T-shirts for sale that read, "Karl Rove ruined my country and all I got was this lousy T-shirt." Proceeds from the donation went to a fund to elect a progressive presidential candidate in 2008. MoveOn also provided free bumper stickers that read, "Defend America, Fire the Republicans." Boyd describes the tactics this way: "Think of it as a grassroots advertising campaign, a way to 'brand' the movement to take our country back" (Drenttel 2007). Branding dissent through succinct framing of issues, grabbing media attention through creative forms of activism, and building collective identity through many of these tactics have contributed to MoveOn's popularity. Its success at harnessing popular entertainment to get alternative voices heard, whether in the form of rock concerts, fundraisers, Bush-bashing ads, publicity stunts, or supporting alternative forms of media, and doing this jointly with representatives of the artistic community, is an unprecedented grassroots effort due to MoveOn's use of developing ICTs. MoveOn has mastered the use of the Internet to mobilize, protest, and impact the electoral process, as well as the use of symbolic and cultural expression to affect public policy in order to more accurately reflect the will of its members.

However, at times attempts to grab media attention by pushing the envelope have backfired. For example, MoveOn's "Bush in 30 Seconds" online contest that asked members to submit anti-Bush TV ads drew sharp criticism from certain circles because among the submissions were two ads juxtaposing footage of George Bush and Adolf Hitler (Renuka 2003). Under pressure from many critics MoveOn pulled the advisements off its website and apologized. Another incident occurred in September of 2007 when MoveOn published (the now infamous) full-page ad in the *New York Times* accusing General David Petraeus of "cooking the books for the White House" and labeling him "General Betray Us" (*The Economist* 2007). Later that month the Senate passed an amendment condemning the organization and both Republicans and Democrats (several of which MoveOn supported and fundraised for) publicly criticized MoveOn.

Conclusion

An analysis of MoveOn provides some important insights that can contribute to critical theory, NSM theory, and evolving theories of the Internet by demonstrating how new ICTs allow for new modes of communication, forms of collective identity and solidarity, and grassroots mobilization to resist forms of domination and particularly the colonization of the public sphere and public opinion. The virtual SMO has successfully used media and developing computer-aided technologies to increase socio-political awareness, influence public opinion, mobilize citizens and network with other SMOs, and elect progressive candidates. It demonstrates how new possibilities for information sharing and dialogue, in addition to new opportunities for organizing and mobilizing provided by the Internet, can translate into interest and participation in political offline and online events. It has used tactical innovation to tap into submerged networks that have become a vehicle for the emergence and articulation of Internet-mediated forms of civic engagement based on collaborative decision-making. By combining a flexible entrepreneurial style with a strong ethic of listening to its members it has built a responsive and populist virtual community and is consequently revitalizing grassroots community-based mobilization.

The secondary impact of Web-based mobilization that MoveOn illustrates, such as using online organizing and mobilizing to impact voter turnout, forms of protest politics on the streets, and house parties whereby members can discuss and debate issues meaningful to them and their communities, challenges the assumption that online political participation and activism have replaced face-to-face contacts. This research suggests that the often perceived zero-sum game between new and old activism is a false dichotomy because, as MoveOn depicts, online and offline activism often reinforce each other.

This case study further advances social theory by illustrating the need to re-conceptualize participatory democracy, the public sphere, and public discourse in light of new technologies and forms of media that allow for new forms of collective identity, networks, and communicative action. It also challenges some of the tenets of NSM theory because MoveOn has proven successful by combining old and new tactics, virtual and material forms of organizing, and working both inside and outside of the formal political structure. It has used cultural and symbolic forms of protest but with the underpinnings of instrumental and strategic action for policy reform. Contrary to some strands of NSM theory, the findings of this analysis highlight that contemporary movements are not based merely on cultural phenomena and/or lifestyle issues but are often struggles for institutional and political reform to affect public policy, and gains are achieved through tactical and instrumental organizing and goals. More empirical studies of contemporary social movements, as facilitated by SMOs and their use of new ICTs, will be useful in further addressing the ways in which the Internet is altering the contours of communicative action, public opinion, the public sphere, and forms of collective identity and networks than engage in mobilizing strategies to create new spaces for self- and collective-empowerment.

EXTENDING THEORIES OF NGOS:
COMMITTED HIV/AIDS ACTIVISTS AND
NEOLIBERAL REFORMS IN UKRAINE

Arseniy Gutnik

Introduction[1]

Over the past few decades, many Western scholars, philanthropists and policymakers have considered non-governmental organizations (NGOs) as one of the main vehicles for carrying out projects aimed at global poverty reduction and civil society development.[2] In this paper, I draw on a pilot case study of Western-funded HIV/AIDS NGOs in Ukraine—a country where I had lived during childhood—to examine a number of the claims that have been made about these organizations and highlight areas for additional research. Thus, my objective is to provoke further critical thinking about the politics of non-governmental organizations and civil society, particularly in the post-Soviet environment, rather than to test hypothesis in a comprehensive fashion.

A number of critical scholars have argued that foreign aid to NGOs and other civil society development initiatives have had unintended, sometimes even detrimental effects across the world. While I generally agree with these conclusions, I argue that scholarship could benefit from more direct investigation of the assumptions underlying civil society development through NGOs that take into account broader socio-political conditions of nation-states such as neoliberal reforms. Moreover, scholars studying NGOs have largely focused on the organizational level of analysis, identifying important external relations between NGOs and other stakeholders, but generally only in passing

[1] I would like to thank the following people for assistance during various stages of the research and writing process: all of the Ukrainian interviewees, their program officers and other staff members, Howard Aldrich, Michele Rivkin-Fish, Kenneth (Andy) Andrews, my parents, Inna Khvorostova, and participants of the UNC Sociology Culture and Politics Workshop in the fall of 2007.
[2] Richter (2002) defined civil society as "an overlapping network of autonomous voluntary associations—formal and informal, political and nonpolitical—that creates a space for public action between the individual and the state (p. 55)."

examining internal relations and the meaning of work. I suggest that looking at the individual level is an important step for investigating nuanced distinctions among workers, their motivations, daily experiences and activities, which may modify some of our conclusions about NGOs. Lastly, I propose that scholars could attain greater analytical depth from theorizing that compares and contrasts NGOs' and states' various attributes and functions.

I begin by focusing on Ukrainian socio-economic transformations that followed the collapse of the Soviet Union. In particular, I highlight the roles of Western governments and institutions, such as the Washington-based International Monetary Fund (IMF) and World Bank, elite private consultants, as well as local Ukrainian reformers. These actors embraced a neoliberal skepticism, prevalent in liberal-market regimes, about the centralized power of the state and a positive view of personal choice within market competition. I specify how this transformation affected the provision of social services and diminished the social safety net, instead putting more weight on individual efforts and the capacity of non-governmental organizations to meet citizens' many personal needs and defend their civil, political, and socio-economic rights.

I subsequently summarize some of the main problems attributed to Western-funded NGOs, using the case of women's, particularly feminist, post-Soviet organizations, because they have received the bulk of scholarly attention over the past 15 years. Critiques in the literature highlight that NGOs and their staffs have remained largely disconnected from local constituencies, often engaging in self-serving activities rather than social change, which hinders NGOs' reach and sustainability. However, using data from my own pilot study of Ukrainian HIV/AIDS NGOs, I suggest that: 1) looking inside organizations reveals differences among workers and indicates a contingent of highly committed, innovative, activists with genuine desire for social change; and yet 2) among the most committed activists, individualistic notions inherent in neoliberal reforms and Western civil society models are influencing their activities in complex, sometimes subtle, but significant ways that lead them to take on personal responsibility for systemic problems.

Lastly, I propose that limited corruption and bureaucracy (efficiency), cited as reasons for funding NGOs, rather than providing assistance to democratizing states, may be less objective and more ideologically-grounded claims than previously assumed. Moreover, unpacking how NGOs' service, advocacy, and other functions may be interrelated in complementary and contradictory ways could bring to focus a nuanced set of relationships with their constituencies and the state.

Ukrainian Neoliberal Reforms: Western and Local Actors

Western Players

Following Soviet collapse, Western governments such as the US, and international institutions, like the World Bank, IMF, the European Union (EU) and others, were interested in Ukraine's relatively large population (about 50 million people) and strategic position between Russia and Europe, for national security and other reasons (Pishchikova 2007). After Ukraine's independence in 1991, major Western players, poorly versed in local legal and cultural traditions, called for rapid and sweeping changes while sidelining gradual approaches, just as they did in other former Soviet republics (Trofimenko 2003). With support from sympathetic local political elites, the country embarked on a transition to liberal democratic politics and a market economy (Bandera 2003, Trofimenko 2003).

Outside investment in Ukraine was considerable, but followed sponsors' specific agendas. For instance, between 1992 and 2003, Ukraine received almost 3 billion dollars of U.S. assistance, much of it through USAID, which accounted for one quarter of all US aid to the 12 former Soviet nations. This money was used for economic restructuring, democratization and reforms in the health and social sectors, but not humanitarian aid and economic growth (Pishchikova 2007).

The structure of policy planning initiatives also reflected strong Western bias. The foreword to the edited volume entitled *Ukraine: Accelerating the Transition to Market*, which contained the proceedings of a summer 1996 IMF/World Bank seminar, held in Washington DC, stated that by embracing Western-recommended reforms Ukraine had achieved a degree of credibility in the eyes of the international community.[3] A look at the affiliations of the 80 seminar participants (about 68 men and 12 women) revealed that 53 (66 percent) were either from the IMF or the World Bank. Meanwhile, eight attendees (10 percent) were from Ukraine, but none of them made any presentations.

IMF/World Bank staff labeled some Ukrainian interests counterproductive. During one session, Koch-Weser (1997), a World Bank representative, stated that lobbying from public workers (whose

---

[3] The seminar was a series of presentations by IMF/World Bank staff, followed by a "general discussion." The focus was on IMF/WB policies and programs that would take effect in 1997 (Kavalsky and Odling Smee 1997).

positions were being eliminated), coal miners (i.e. a large part of the energy sector),[4] farming interests, and pressure from elements in the parliament, were slowing down reforms. The rhetoric often had real implications. In Russia, for instance, the IMF essentially blocked the passage of a popular budget of the Russian parliament, in August of 1993. The deficit established in the budget was greater than the IMF wanted and they threatened to pull a promised loan tranche. "In other words, the IMF and its closest US associates saw the actions of the Russian parliament as an obstacle to their priorities and policies that had to be circumvented (Reddaway and Glinski 2001, p. 294)."

Local Reformers

Ukrainian reformers adopted major Western recommendations. After Soviet collapse, state institutions were touted as corrupt, overly bureaucratic and inefficient; moreover, the economy was unstable throughout the 1990s. Many local politicians and middle class professionals, leery of Soviet economic and social controls, considered the reform perspective the necessary, legitimate, solution (Reddaway and Glinski 2001, Zhurzhenko 2001). Some of the most prominent supporters included President Kuchma (1994–2004), former minister of the economy Roman Shpek and current president Victor Yushchenko.[5] Since taking office, President Kuchma pledged to undertake radical reforms to transition Ukraine to a market economy. For instance, in the late 1990s, the National Academy of Science, as well as government ministries, including Ministry of the

---

[4] 500,000 Ukrainian miners, who "earned their living in the official public sector (Mykhnenko 2003, p. 104)," working in one of the world's most dangerous mining conditions, with an average life expectancy of 38 years, struck in 1989. This was followed by much contestation over the following decade, including 1996 protests involving over 600,000 miners, who demanded $122 million in back wages, and another 140,000 miners picketing regional governments and blocking roads and railroad tracks (Mykhnenko 2003).

[5] Victor Yushchenko: current President of Ukraine, former Prime Minister and National Bank Chairman.

Roman Shpek: current Permanent Representative to the European Union, former chairman of the National Agency of Ukraine for Reconstruction and Development, Deputy Prime Minister for Economic Affairs, 1995–6, and Minister of Economy 1993–5 (Aslund and deMenil 2000, Wikipedia 2007).

Economy, sponsored a conference aimed at speeding up the market transition (Bandera 2003).[6]

Social Safety Net Reforms

Social reforms that conformed to neoliberal logic began right after Ukrainian independence. Bandera (2003), for example, wrote that "quite significantly, the government [now] pursues the attainment of public objectives like social security and equity in the context of the market system rather than through the plan-command process (p. 70)." A 1994 World Bank study, "which turned almost into a bible for all those who favour a radical pension reform (Adam 1999, p. 133)," advocated reduction of state-run pensions. The World Bank was critical of monopolistic government management and investment of funds, and emphasized a fully funded, privately run management system, along with a personal or occupational component (Adam 1999). In 1998, the Parliament passed insurance plans for pensions, unemployment, temporary loss of ability to work, childbirth, funeral-related obligations, and occupational disease (Yatsenko 2005).

Ukrainian reforms were similar to those in Russia, where massive efforts on the part of the Yeltsin administration to decrease the budget deficit, with continued pressure from the IMF, resulted in "the government's [default] on domestic obligations, including those due to pensioners and to the work force in the public sector (Reddaway and Glinski 2001, p. 250)." Meanwhile, President Kuchma, "in response to [international monetary agency loan contract] pressures, in July 1998...ordered the halving of government contributions to the state-run Chernobyl Fund. Soon after, the government issued a press release stating [that] Ukraine's budget deficit had dropped from 3.3 to 2.5 percent of [GDP] (Petryna 2002, p. 114)."[7]

---

[6] Despite a large degree of agreement with Western counterparts, or acquiescence to their demands, some local reformers indicated their dependent position and desire for greater Western development of certain local institutions. For example, Shpek (2000) highlighted that Ukraine relied substantially on IMF and World Bank loans, but should instead have access to EU and US trade markets. He also stated that Western nations should provide educational opportunities to young Ukrainians abroad and also invest in the domestic Ukrainian educational system (particularly economics education), to prevent brain-drain of academics.

[7] On the other hand, Goralska (2000) stated that the president had abolished the 12 percent Chernobyl tax in 1998.

People like World Bank representative Koch-Weser (1997), advocated targeted social protections to only help the "truly needy," while reducing others' benefits. Koch-Weser (1997) argued that while it may have been best for the government to allow "inflation to erode pension and other benefits across the board and to compress the benefit structure (p. 7)," to undergo price liberalization during the first five years of reforms, the option of further benefit compression had been exhausted. It was not clear, however, from his comments about the new targeted benefits, who and under what conditions constituted the truly needy, which is one of the problems with this approach.

Neoliberalism: Decentralizing the State, Promoting the Market

Local reformers and their Western counterparts promoted another aspect of the neoliberal agenda, notably working to decrease the size and centralization of the state and increase market competition (Pishchikova 2007). This perspective reflected skepticism about the state, particularly prevalent in the US, although the EU also promoted a policy that rein-forced free trade, the private sector and state retrenchment (Edwards 2004, Hurt 2006). Scholars critical of state retrenchment, however, have called for further investigation of the role state institutions should play in society. Kuzio (2003, following Przeworski), for example, wrote that neoliberal views

> underestimate the role of state institutions in organizing both the public and private life of groups and individuals. If democracy is to be sustained, the state must guarantee territorial integrity and physical security, it must maintain the conditions necessary for an effective exercise of citizenship, it must mobilize public savings, co-ordinate resource allocation, and correct income distribution. And if state institutions are to be capable of performing these tasks, they must be reorganized, rather than simply reduced (Kuzio 2003, p. 25).

Reforms, however, proceeded under assumptions that the state was ineffi-cient, corrupt and overly bureaucratic and therefore should relinquish sig-nificant control to non-state institutions (Bandera 2003, Reimann 2005). Furthermore, according to this view, the state potentially hindered enter-prise development and bred a kind of "culture of dependency;" (Walsh et al. 1997). Neoliberal policies directly impacted the government. Ban-dera (2003) noted that "compared with the preceding Soviet centralized command system, by now, the scope of the [Ukrainian] government has been reduced considerably so that it does not overwhelm the market mechanism (p. 70)."

Decentralizing Social Services, the Contracting Shift and the Role of NGOs

State and social reforms meant the advent of new institutional arrangements for dealing with service delivery as well as other social needs. Services provided through the state were now the responsibility of local authorities and therefore Ukraine was transferring state social assets to local municipalities (Shpek 2000) and private service providers. In the West, such reforms occurred earlier. Walsh et al. (1997, following Flynn 1990), for example, described the logic of the 1980s transformation of the public sector in the UK. These reforms were based on several neoliberal arguments. First, market mechanisms should be applied universally. Second, competition should exist among service providers and should be sharpened by allowing consumers to decline state services. Third, individual choice should trump collective interest. Fourth, state provisions should be minimized. The arguments were based on the presumption of post-WWII failure of the Keynesian welfare state to deliver economic and social stability, and were particularly prevalent in Anglo-Saxon countries.

Walsh et al. (1997), stated that the trend of service contracting, linked to changes in the public sector and adoption of market-based organizational approaches, was global in scope and in some cases resulted in regulatory and normative pressures to conform. Underscoring the wide-reaching influence of neoliberal Western institutions, the authors argued that "[a]n example of [ideological] imposition in the international context includes the relationship between developing countries and the World Bank (Walsh et al. 1997, p. 182)." Westerners, furthermore, advocated for non-governmental organizations, promoted within the context of citizen capacity for self-determination and democratization. Reimann (2005) noted that neoliberal advocates saw NGOs as a better, market-based alternative to corrupt, failing states in developing and democratizing nations, which would bring about grassroots mobilization and civil society.

Hanlon (2000), moreover, argued that donors preferred to fund NGOs and technical assistance contractors because they did not need to negotiate detailed programs with NGOs, as they did with governments. Pishchikova (2007, following Carothers and Ottaway 2000), meanwhile, proposed that the attractiveness of civil society assistance in the form of support for small civic groups was its low cost, compared, for instance, to broad industry or banking restructuring, or engineering projects.

The role of Western sponsorship and NGO initiatives in post-Soviet Ukraine are readily apparent in recent times. In December 2006, on World AIDS Day, President Yushchenko issued a statement calling for collaborative efforts between the government, international donors, NGOs and individuals for curbing the Ukrainian HIV/AIDS crisis (one of the largest in Europe):

> To appreciate the consequences of the epidemic, it is vital to institute medical, social and educational reforms, and to build cooperation between the government and the people, international organizations and NGOs, which should join their efforts to combat the epidemic.
>
> The responsibility of all individuals for their behavior and [their] relatives becomes particularly important.
>
> We must launch a massive educational campaign to forewarn teenagers of the dangers of trying drugs. The easiest and the cheapest way to minimize the risk of getting HIV is to adhere to the everlasting values of family fidelity and respect.
>
> I urge each citizen, ministers, NGOs, business people, medical workers, educators and religious leaders to make a consistent and daily contribution to the cause of fighting the epidemic of HIV/AIDS in Ukraine. We must be tolerant, support the people affected by this evil and never create obstacles in their way.
>
> I would like to give my support to the HIV-positive people: the creation of the National Network of People Living with HIV is an example of courage and hope. Your firm determination to fight the disease and your active cooperation with state institutions and NGOs become a powerful factor in combating the epidemic and help save each individual living with HIV.[8]

The president did not specify how much of a role each of the named parties would or should play, but it was clear that the Ukrainian state was only partly responsible for crisis resolution.[9] Moreover, he tied

---

[8] Source: President Yushchenko's World AIDS Day Address (2006).

[9] In May 2006, the BBC reported that $30 million towards fighting HIV/AIDS came from the Ukrainian government, over $90 million from the Global Fund for HIV/AIDS and tuberculosis (a Geneva-based NGO), and the World Bank loaned $60 million. The loan was then suspended temporarily due to allegations of government fund mismanagement. UNAIDS stated that in "late 2006, the World Bank lifted its suspension of its loan for HIV and tuberculosis, providing an additional US $24 million for national AIDS activities." UNAIDS also reported that in 2007 the government *raised* its domestic funding to $20 million, which contradicts the BBC report but underscores that government contributions were much less than those from international sources; meanwhile, a

to vital reforms the necessity of disparate actors—citizens, ministers, NGOs, business people, medical workers, educators and religious leaders—to take personal responsibility for the crisis.

Throughout the rest of the paper, I focus on NGOs' prominent new role in Ukraine, drawing first on available scholarship and then on my own pilot case study of Ukrainian HIV/AIDS organizations. The NGOs project has not been without its critics, who have cited numerous ways in which these organizations do not live up to promised social change. In the next section, I provide more detailed information about these criticisms. In the subsequent section, I point out that a more nuanced look at variation within NGOs reveals that the prevalent critiques may not apply evenly across NGOs and their staff. Neoliberal reforms, nonetheless, may still be having an impact through a complex causal pathway—consistent with the individualistic notions espoused by the Ukrainian president—leading committed activists to take on personal responsibility for systematic problems.

Critiques of post-Soviet NGOs

Here I summarize recent literature and critiques of NGOs, drawing primarily on examples from post-Soviet women's organizations, because they have received the bulk of scholarly attention over the past 15 years and because the critiques have overlapped considerably across post-Soviet states. Some analogous ideological, organizational and institutional issues have also been documented across a variety of organizations, for example among environmental NGOs in Russia (Powell 2002).

NGOs act as intermediaries between the global (Western) civil society development community and local audiences to promote "social, economic, and political change in developing countries (Brown and Kalegaonkar 2002)." Salamon and Anheier (1997) argued that a common definition is necessary to talk about organizations that have a variety of labels in each nation, across the world and among authors. For instance, the labels "nongovernmental," "nonprofit" "philanthropic," and "civil society organizations [CSOs]" just to name a few, have been

---

new Global Fund grant was approved for up to US $151 million (Finansuvannya Likiv Vid SNIDu 2006, UNAIDS Ukraine: Country Situation Analysis 2007).

applied to similar types of organizations. I adopt three of Salamon and Anheier's (1997) criteria essentially verbatim and a modified fourth criterion, which apply to all organizations henceforth, regardless of the label, unless specified otherwise. First, the organization must have some structural permanence, such as regular meetings, rules and officers; it should not be purely ad hoc and informal. Second, the organization should be private, or not under the majority control of government officials or government apparatus. Third, organizations should not be profit-distributing, meaning that all profits go into sustaining the organizations' activities and the necessary personnel. Fourth, the organizations should be self-governing, having internal procedures that may be substantially influenced, but are not entirely controlled by outside entities.

Western donors sponsoring women's organizations sought independent groups to develop civil society (Hemment 2004). The funding, consequently, was not distributed equally, which led to several problems. Richter (2002) argued that "feminist organizations receive a disproportionate share of Western assistance among women's organizations, and they are more dependent than other women's organizations on such assistance for their survival (p. 54)."[10] He added that Russian feminists were also more likely to look to the West for sponsorship. Hrycak (2006) argued that "[m]any local observers claim that these former 'nationalists' were not 'real feminists,' but rather that they were attracted by the lure of foreign grants and foreign salaries. While most local organizations have no funding, elite NGOs...attract considerable grants and pay their staff sizeable incomes (p. 88)." In Bulgaria, in 2000, for example, international organizations paid their highly skilled workers $900 per month, when the average monthly salary was $200 (Ghodsee 2004).

Kotovskaya (2004) pointed out that the most active participants of the feminist movement were rather elite "representatives of the scientific and artistic intelligentsia; for many of them participation in the movement became an important aspect of self-realization...they all came from educated ['developed'] families, personally engaged in scientific or artistic activities and were on average 43–55 years old (pp. 170, 171)."

---

[10] While little data exists on the numbers and kinds of women's organizations in former Soviet states, some scholarly estimates from the late 1990s indicate that approximately two to four thousand women's organizations were active in Russia (Richter 2002). Feminist organizations made up a minority of these groups.

Chernova (2005) cited among Russian academics (and other researchers) interested in gender studies, a sort of "academic hunger" stemming from a paucity of academic publications based on Russian research, and a lack of professional contacts with Western colleagues, as primary reasons for seeking such connections in the early-mid 1990s. Most had acquired training on gender issues abroad from Western foundations and non-profits (Hrycak 2006). Ghodsee (2004), moreover, quoted an UNDP National Development Report which concluded that "the NGO sector [in Bulgaria] is growing not only because of the availability of a *solvent and low-risk market* represented by donors, but also because of the growing unemployment among intellectuals (p. 739, emphasis original)."

Feminist activists had difficulty finding local connections, due to ideological rifts.[11] They were critical of local women and "traditional" women's organizations that adhered to maternalistic principles, were reluctant to politicize relations between men and women and thus potentially threaten the sanctity of the household. Local women, on the other hand, said that they did not perceive discrimination, or felt that Soviet-era "equality" had not benefited them and were reluctant to join groups advocating for women's rights. NGO feminists saw these arguments as denying women a "choice" (Hrycak 2006, Richter 2002). Gisela Bock's (1989) comment aptly summarizes the problems that funded NGOs encountered in promoting their Western feminist visions: "[t]he difference between women's and men's history does not imply that the history of women is identical for all women...Awareness of the otherness, the difference, the inequality between female and male history has [to be] complemented by an awareness and historical study of the otherness, the *differences and inequalities among women themselves* (Bock 1989, p. 8)." Ghodsee (2004) argued that we could consider Western approaches to foster women's activism a kind of "feminism-by-design." This logic paralleled the flood of Western consultants and foundations promoting the "capitalism-by-design" paradigm that subverted the contextual idiosyncrasies of the post-Soviet space. NGOs were seen as disconnected from and unaccountable to local audiences.

---

[11] I employ the term "Western feminism" synonymously with a kind of "NGO feminism," which generally encompassed three aspects in the literature: (importantly) the use of the word "feminism" (along with other English words, like gender), a focus on women's individual rights and capacity, and a focus on women's substandard social position with respect to men.

NGO Accountability

Accountability, according to Ebrahim (2005), involves reciprocal commitments in a relationship between two or more actors, although the more powerful actor can make claims on the actions of the dependent actor. Scholars have argued that funded NGOs did not have strong incentives to remain accountable to local constituencies because donors served as the main source of support. Donors' quantitative accountability standards, moreover, worked against accountability to local constituencies, because they did not evaluate the qualitative impacts of the projects. Ebrahim (2005) noted that accountability standards established by donors often demand short-term, technical, results, such as the number of people served, pamphlets distributed, and so on, which could distort important qualities, such as the actual impacts of these actions. Stirrat (2000) argued that accountability standards are highly rationalistic and quantitative because "to count is to know—and to control (p. 36)," in modern neoliberal parlance. Scholars like Henderson (2003) have also confirmed that donors working in Russia must meet stringent demands and time-consuming accountability standards of home offices, while attempting to have real impact on the ground, although "evaluations often focus on whether the grantee met the requirements of the project, not on the impact of the work funded (Henderson 2003, p. 88)."

Professionalism and Top-Down NGO Management

Scholars have also discussed how NGOs distribute tasks among staff and carry out projects, in particular highlighting the role of top-down management and professionalism. Western influence was apparent here as well. US donors encouraged bureaucratic professionalism, or structured rule-following, among Ukrainian women's NGOs (Hrycak 2006). Similarly, in the 1990s donors began to professionalize and institute management practices among Russian environmental organizations (and elsewhere) (Powell 2002). Donor funding guidelines assigned directors and upper management in post-Soviet NGOs with the task of implementing donor-specified projects, rather than making their own reflections and assessments (Hemment 2004, Henderson 2003). Elsewhere, Mebrahtu (2003) noted that the British organization ActionAid, active in Ethiopia, which sought to empower local field staff and people, generally failed to do so; instead, local staff had to adhere to donor guidelines. The more flexible, bottom-up approach, which allowed for local input and members' ideas, was generally rare (Lewis 2007).

Thus far, NGOs appear largely ineffective at accomplishing their objectives. Scholars have generally theorized NGO effectiveness as engaging local stakeholders and building up grassroots support for the promised civil society. Instead, what they found fell short of these expectations. Internally, top-down management restricted organizational capacity for local input and reflection, instead emphasizing donor goals. Externally, ideological differences, professional background, lack of accountability, and a restrictive funding structure, led to the formation of boundaries between NGOs and local stakeholders.

Unpacking NGOs: Volunteering and Committed Staff.
A Partial Rejoinder to the Critics

In a partial rejoinder to scholars' critiques, I attempt to show that some NGO activists creatively pushed against their structural constraints to produce local impact. The way staff members understood the meaning of their work and what motivated them varied within organizations. Significantly, the Ukrainian HIV/AIDS NGOs I examined employed a cadre of highly committed activists who closely identified with their constituencies and actively worked to make their work locally relevant, even engaging in unpaid voluntary labor. These activists' efforts, furthermore, engaged people across top-down internal hierarchies and thus potentially expanded a view of what NGOs "do." This more nuanced perspective suggests that a contingent of activists, and possibly NGOs, defies some of the prevalent criticisms. As I show later, however, even among the most committed workers notions of individualism and support for a decentralized safety net arose subtly as the outcome of a complex meaning-making process embedded in broader neoliberal social reforms and relationships with Western donors. In order to illustrate these dynamics, I draw on the literature and employ my interviews with a small sample of HIV/AIDS NGO staff members. But first, I describe my research, Ukrainian NGO demographics and the HIV/AIDS epidemic.

HIV/AIDS NGOs: Sample and Methods

I carried out a pilot study with a small sample of staff members from Western-funded Ukrainian NGOs working on HIV/AIDS issues, who attended an extended training session and "experience exchange" in the United States, in 2007, facilitated by one of their sponsors. I contacted the US organization that was hosting the Ukrainian staff and was allowed to observe workshops during the last several days of their stay. I participated in two workshops during which I took notes on the Ukrainian visitors' presentations, reactions and conversations and handed out a closed-ended survey. I subsequently conducted semi-structured, in-depth, interviews with three staff members, in their hotel. Two additional interviews occurred over the phone, after the visitors had returned to Ukraine. The survey mostly overlapped thematically with the interviews, but provided a brief summary of some responses, as well as numerical, demographic, data that I did not solicit in the interviews (see Appendix).

I surveyed and interviewed the following people: Evgenia, 21, administrator of educational programs in a church-based NGO; Efim, late 20's–early 30's, program coordinator; Isaac, 29, NGO director/head; and Grigory, 32, social worker. I only surveyed Irina, 27, head of a planning council of NGOs, though we had a brief conversation after one of the workshops. I only interviewed Vera, 30's–early 40's, program coordinator. I utilized some information from statements made during workshops by Vera, Irina, as well as Arkady (approximately late 20s, assistant to an NGO coordinating council chairperson). Additional information about the staff is in the Appendix. All names have been changed.

I also used information from follow-up emails with some of the delegation members I met and from personal statements of several regional NGO representatives listed on the website of the All-Ukrainian Network of People Living with HIV/AIDS (PLWH).[12] Additionally, I analyzed a transcript of a round-table discussion between Ukrainian scholars and assorted local NGO staff, about HIV/AIDS representations in the mass media, which took place in February 2005 at the Ukrainian Media Reform Center.[13]

---

[12] Source: All-Ukraine Network of People Living with HIV/AIDS (2007).
[13] Source: Koli Mi Zalyakuemo Chitachiv VIL-infektsieyu (2005).

NGO Demographics in Ukraine

In 2005, there were about 28,000 registered CSOs in Ukraine, but only about 4–5 thousand were active (Palyvoda and Kikot 2006).[14] In a recent study of active civil society organizations (CSOs) of all kinds across Ukraine (N = 583), Palyvoda and Kikot (2006) found that "[45 percent of all] respondents…represented new organizations that registered after 1999; 30 percent of organizations were registered from 1996 to 1999; 13 percent of CSOs started their activities between 1992 and 1995, and four percent were registered before 1991 (Palyvoda and Kikot 2006, p. 22)." Thus, most organizations were quite new. Five percent of all organizations had 71–100 members, seven percent had 51–70 members, 16 percent had 1–10 members, 20 percent had 31–50 members, 25 percent had over 100 members, and 27 percent had 11–30 members. In 2005, 55 percent of all CSOs indicated that they received funding from international grants. On average, these grants constituted 38 percent of the budget for organizations that received them.[15] Participation in HIV/AIDS organizations was found to be equal among men and women.

HIV/AIDS in Ukraine

Ukraine is considered to have one of the worst HIV/AIDS epidemics in Europe. "As of the end of 2005…377,600 [adult] people were estimated to be…living with HIV-infection in Ukraine, or 1.4 percent adult prevalence (UNAIDS 2006)." HIV/AIDS prevalence varies along gender lines and over time, largely because injecting drug users (IDUs, the most risk-prone group) are generally young men, although transmission patterns have shifted recently. USAID (2003) (using 2002 data from the Ukrainian AIDS Center) indicated that in 1997, 87 percent of registered HIV cases in Ukraine were among IDUs, 11 percent were from heterosexual transmission, two percent from perinatal and three percent unknown sources. By 2001, the mode of transmission shifted

---

[14] The CSO must have been legally registered; have had at least two years of experience implementing activities; successfully implemented at least two programs or projects; and been known in the region.

[15] In my survey, four out of five respondents stated that 75–100 percent of the NGO's budget comes from foreign donors, while one respondent indicated 51–75 percent, which shows that either HIV/AIDS organizations tend to receive more foreign funding, or that this was specific to my sample (see Appendix, Q. 23).

to 57 percent among IDUs, 27 percent via heterosexual transmission, 13 percent perinatal and three percent unknown. In 2001, 62 percent of HIV cases in Ukraine were among men and 38 percent among women, while AIDS cases were 76 percent among men and 24 percent among women. In 2005, the estimated HIV infection averages among adults (15–49), were 205,660 for males (54.1 percent), 171,940 for females (45.2 percent), and 2,850 for children 14 and under (0.75 percent). The three highest-risk groups included injecting drug users, with an estimated range of 11–66 percent HIV prevalence, followed by their partners with 8–31 percent HIV prevalence, and female sex workers with 8–31 percent prevalence (UNAIDS 2006).

Discrimination, Rights Abuses, and Public Portrayals

The grim numbers do not clearly show the human side of the epidemic. Infected people also experience discrimination, rights abuses and stigmatization. The Media Reform Center discussion indicated that media portrayals were overwhelmingly negative. They focused on medical statistics rather than preventative information, available services and positive experiences of people who take anti-retroviral drugs and continue to lead fulfilling lives. The Center discussants, as well as my seminar notes and interviews indicated that for years, particularly in the 1990s, but into the 2000s, HIV/AIDS was billed as a death sentence. One NGO worker mentioned that it was also necessary to dispel myths about HIV/AIDS transmission.

Instances when HIV+ individuals were identified in media reports (sometimes by one's clothes, a golden tooth, a ring, etc.), as one lawyer explained, bore consequences such as dismissal from work or school, or refusal to give children vaccine shots. In other cases, some pregnant HIV+ women were segregated in separate facilities, or denied some medical services. Employers sometimes illegally demanded one's medical history. The lawyer described one of his cases when a woman, who was HIV+, along with her infant, was prepared to change jobs rather than disclose her positive status. Disclosure in medical or other facilities sometimes occurred, particularly in small communities. Drug users, moreover, faced potential prosecution, while men who have sex with men faced discrimination. Vera and Grigory also indicated that HIV/AIDS self-help groups had to maintain strict confidentiality and secrecy, because there was danger from groups like skinheads.

HIV/AIDS NGOs: Project-Based Services

Infected people thus need psychological, socio-medical services and protection, and numerous organizations have moved to combat the HIV/AIDS epidemic and related social issues. Grigory, Issac, Efim and Vera indicated that in addition to informational and educational outreach efforts, their NGOs engaged in direct service provision. Services covered a wide range, from psychological assistance, to childcare, home aide services, restoring and filling out legal documents and paperwork, legal defense, supplying food packages, providing crucial anti-retroviral therapy (ART), and personal interventions. Evgenia's organization, which is a church-based foundation that assists other organizations in securing grants, also led preventative informational workshops (primarily for church members).

HIV/AIDS NGO Staff: Unaccountable, Self-Serving Elites and Intellectuals?

Providing services is a demanding and often difficult task. Despite the strain, I suggest that a number of shared characteristics and other circumstances lead to significant commitment among some HIV/AIDS NGO staff to their clients. Staff members are, on average, similar to their clients in age and gender, and, more importantly, share, or have shared, many of the same experiences. Additionally, they have generally joined and remained in their organizations for more "altruistic" reasons than academic curiosity, self-interest, or economic gain, as critics have argued. Staff members in lower positions, in fact, are not highly paid and may endure considerable hardships.

The nature of HIV/AIDS NGO services, moreover, necessitates direct contact between NGO staff and clients, sometimes including difficult interventions. This contact opens up a space for moral accountability, which is generally associated with the "little people—those in subordinate positions. It concerns the informal means by which leaders are forced to be responsive to their followers or patrons to their clients (Hilhorst 2003, p. 127)." Hilhorst (2003) cited an example of moral accountability in action when Philippine locals, instead of accessing a nearby office or sending mail requests, traveled to the central office of an NGO (an "arduous trip") to demand the release of additional funds for an ongoing project in which they were implicated. "The social pressure they thus put on [the office worker] to respond to their needs was so strong that [she] felt she had no choice but to give the money, even though this was against the coordination agreement she had with [her partner organization]. As she said: 'What could I do, they were just standing in the office with their shopping list.' (Hilhorst 2003, p. 138)."

Just like the Philippine locals' presence had a direct effect on the NGO worker, I found numerous situations that likely exhibited a high degree of moral sway over HIV/AIDS staff. Efim and Vera, for instance, mentioned cases when they personally made home visits to convince drug using parents and religious families to allow necessary medical attention for their HIV+ infants and children. Other services, like counseling sessions, distribution of food and medicine also provided opportunities for direct engagement with clients. Isaac, meanwhile, stated the following, as one of the reasons of why he liked his work: "I interacted with clients, I provided them with tangible help, I saw how [my assistance] helped people." Similarly, Grigory described a poignant case, when he and his colleagues saved a client's life:

> **Grigory:** Well...just recently...a young man basically was...could not even walk. [The man's mother contacted the NGO.] Basically, in very bad condition. His only relatives were his mother, a pensioner, and...his children. The children were school age. Three children. And he was alone...basically...He was the sole provider...And he was bedridden...He had meningitis, tuberculosis-induced meningitis; he would not recognize his mother, or anyone else. And we put him back up on his feet. I mean, due to...Well, let's say, my own efforts. I personally traveled...to see him...Called the ambulance. Well, the ambulance...The mother had called the ambulance before, but no one wanted to take him in...We...I...persisted until they took him into the hospital. Quickly found medication there, quickly examined him, did everything [necessary]. And did all this just in time, because later the doctor told us 'guys, thank you so much!' The doctor herself! Even the doctor...not just his mother, who...The mother later came...almost in a stupor [and said]: 'Boys, girls, I will be grateful...all my life...that you put my son back up on his feet.'[16] And then we assigned him [anti-retroviral] therapy...Everything is in order, everything is good [now].

Thus, although Hilhorst (2003) and I focused on situations that occurred in very different cultural contexts and the clients had different objectives,

---

[16] Terms of endearment sometimes used by older people when talking to those who are younger.

I suggest that the moral imperative to remain responsive to clients in light of such direct interactions, is hard to deny.

Client and Staff Similarities

Furthermore, it is important to highlight similarities between some staff members and their clients, which reinforce moral accountability and also contribute to worker commitment. On average, HIV/AIDS clients and staff were close in age and gender. Both were generally in their 20s and 30s (Appendix, Q. 9 and 10)[17] and (in my sample) women made up a slight majority (Appendix, Q. 8 and 11). More importantly, NGO workers had personally experienced, or continued to experience, many of the hardships that their clients faced, and were thus motivated to help them. Hemment (2007) observed a similar trend in her research on a Tver' women's crisis center in mid-late 1990s Russia. Before founding the center, Oktiabrina, the director, had to relocate with her family closer to her in-laws for support, after she and her husband had worked unpaid for six months at an institute in Siberia. They had sold their two-room apartment and deposited the money in a local bank before moving to Tver'. The bank suddenly collapsed a few weeks later and they lost all their savings. Oktiabrina struggled to find work and endured substantial economic hardship, living with her husband and daughter in a "shabby one-room apartment that they rented on the edge of town (Hemment 2007, p. 105)." Her experiences guided her ambitions to engage in practical projects to help local women, like herself (Hemment 2007).

Personal experiences and struggle were also motivating factors among HIV/AIDS NGO staff. Vera, who is openly HIV+, clearly underscored these issues when explaining why she and other colleagues had orga- nized a self-help group in the late 1990s (which they later turned into an NGO):

> **Vera:** We...I worked in an organization, responding to confidential calls about HIV/AIDS prevention and...illnesses transmitted through sexual contact and drug use. And when...people called, I had a lot of difficulty... consulting these people. I mean, when they indicated that they were

---

[17] In Russia, which has HIV infection rates slightly lower but close to those of Ukraine, injecting drug users studied in Moscow hospitals (N = 298) and on the street (N = 126), in the late 1990s, were, respectively, on average 20, 21 years old, 70, 77 percent male and studying (56 percent) or working (58 percent) (Reilley et al. 2004).

HIV+, because I am HIV+ myself. And we decided to create a self-help group. We placed advertisements... People began calling our confidential line... This was 1999. And from this self-help group... Basically, when we had helped ourselves... emotionally... we felt that it was necessary to help other people like ourselves. We started organizing trips to the hospital facility of the regional AIDS center, where the bed-ridden patients were located; I mean, very sick people. We helped them. I mean, there was a certain... sort of this [informational] campaign, if you remember, there were posters [that stated]: 'AIDS—Plague of the 20th Century' and 'You will die alone on a hospital pillow' and so on and so forth. In essence, an HIV+ diagnosis was equal to a death sentence. And a quickly approaching one. In reality, people did not see a possibility to lead a normal life with a positive status—to live, raise children, work, study. So, in reality, the most important thing... initially, the idea is... to revitalize in people the belief that they can live fully.

Vera's account highlights issues echoed in other interviews. Several NGOs began as self-help groups, but then expanded their activity. Isaac's brother, who is HIV+, had founded a self-help group, along with three HIV+ women, which later became the NGO that Isaac now directs. Grigory's NGO grew out of a self-help group as well (though he joined later, when it was already registered), as did Efim's NGO, which split off from Isaac's organization several years ago.

Much like Vera, Grigory, who is HIV+ along with his wife, stated that he found it very important to share with clients his story, his initial experience as a client, and to explain that an HIV+ status was not a death sentence. Both Grigory and Vera, moreover, had been hospitalized for tuberculosis, often associated with HIV infection, and consequently had first-hand experience with this illnesses and its treatment. Other staff members also drew on their own experiences when assisting clients. Efim, for example, mentioned that counselors in his organization, who help injecting drug users take replacement medication in order to quit, were themselves former drug users. Moving beyond my interviews, a look at the regional representatives of the Ukrainian People Living with HIV/AIDS (PLWHA) Network, revealed that many workers were HIV+.[18] Often, engagement with the Network was deeply personal. As

---

[18] An examination of 31 online profiles of the PLWHA Network representatives from across the country, revealed that out of 22 individuals who provided statements, approximately 8 mentioned issues like "... when I found out about my HIV+ status...," "...help for people like me...," "...I live to work and work to live...," etc. which I

one regional branch director stated in his online profile: "...I live to work and work to live..."

I also found evidence that NGO staff members were not elites working for personal gain and fulfillment of intellectual curiosity, despite the fact that the majority of respondents had higher education (with some exceptions, see Appendix, Q. 4, 5, 6). Interviewees mentioned several reasons for initially engaging in HIV/AIDS work, but primary among these were the following: they joined as self-help group participants or clients out of necessity for psychological and medical support (Vera, Grigory); on a voluntary basis because friends and/or family who were in self-help groups asked for help (Efim and Isaac helped with computer applications); on a voluntary basis because of affinity for people in the group (Irina); as a volunteer because of personal (religious) convictions and interests (Evgenia, a medical student, who works in a church-based NGO). They stayed because they found the work interesting and fulfilling and when funding became available, it became possible to devote more time to the NGO.

Pay for work in NGOs, however, was not lavish for many staff members, particularly when taking into account the strains of the work. For example, Isaac said that he made about \$300 per month as the director of his organization.[19] He and Efim nonetheless cited a "temporary burnout effect" that they encountered several times per year, when they felt like abandoning everything and changing jobs. Vera also described considerable strain and low pay among lower positioned workers:

> **Vera:** Well, we had a girl who left [the NGO]; her mother was [HIV] positive, so she began working with us. Now she attends [college] and works in a store...It was just very difficult for her. I mean, the work is difficult—she worked in non-medical care—this means that clients die; it is psychologically very difficult work. And I know that in other countries this is very highly paid work. But in our country it's...well, the maximum pay for a social worker is 750 hryvnas, that's 150 dollars [per month], and that's in [the capital] Kiev.

---

understood as indicative of their HIV+ status. At least three other PLWHA representatives mentioned that their friends or relatives were HIV+.

[19] In early 2007, the approximate average monthly salaries were as follows (by age): 18–28 years: \$120; 29–49 years: \$200; 60+ years: \$100 (N = 2118 across 132 locations) (Srednii Dohod Zhitelya Ukrainy 2007).

Hemment (2007) similarly mentioned in her account of the Tver' crisis center that social workers' salaries were very low. Grigory (a social worker) stated that "you can't make big money as a social worker." This account consequently suggests that scholars should take another look at compensation in foreign-funded organizations; in particular, because of pay and quality of work discrepancies *within* NGOs.

Furthermore, I did not interpret social status, satisfaction from obtaining grants, creative work and self-realization, which came up in most interviews, necessarily as liabilities for NGO effectiveness (i.e. striving for local impact). These may be self-serving objectives in some cases. But my research suggests that such factors, in fact, made work more satisfying and meaningful for NGO employees, and thus buttressed their commitment to alleviating what they perceived as significant problems. Additionally, one of the best indicators of commitment was staff members' engagement in unpaid voluntary work.

Improvisation and Voluntary Work

Improvisation and voluntary work—phenomena that have received sparse attention in the literature (Hilhorst 2003)—came out prominently in my research. Similarly to Oktiabrina's outreach efforts, based out of the Tver' women's crisis center (Hemment 2007), Grigory, Isaac and Efim indicated that they and other staff members engaged in or contributed to unpaid voluntary activities. These activities involved upper management and lower staff members, but were initiated at various levels, for example by social workers, thereby to some extent circumventing hierarchical top-down management structures.

The voluntary activities were part of how ideologically-driven activists attempted to make their work more meaningful, thus seeking out and creating opportunities for action. Hilhorst (2003) maintained that "[i]t is by reshuffling and combining the different 'pulls' and 'pushes', in other words, by improvising, that NGO actors attribute meaning to the organization and arrive at a certain coherence in their everyday practices (p. 218)." Hemment (2007), for example, argued that at times Tver' crisis center members—just like staff at other such centers—used the organization to discuss and plan "ingenious solutions" for self-education, material problems, and socializing, rather than domestic violence. The women adopted the crisis center model, because it was viable with the donors at the time. Simultaneously, however, they wanted to make sure that it would allow them to facilitate their own ideas and hoped that through contact with clients they could assess the need for counseling versus material needs. Oktiabrina, one of the center founders, and her coworkers, moreover, engaged in awareness-raising talks on domestic and sexual violence, when the temporary absence of a phone line prevented the center from running a crisis hotline (Hemment 2007).

Voluntary work in HIV/AIDS NGOs occurred outside funded projects, when some staff members thought that they were not able to engage in certain activities that they considered important. Grigory, for example, stated that he was "very concerned with [preventative measures in educational establishments],"[20] but "no matter how much [he] looked... for donors, organizations, that could give some sum of money for leading these... activities in [his] city... unfortunately there [was] nothing." Consequently, he and some of his colleagues engaged in additional educational work voluntarily.

Grigory's management, although supportive of the idea, was initially hesitant to release staff for this work, which sometimes took hours or days away from workers' functional duties. They eventually agreed, once the issues were negotiated and planned out. Furthermore, not everyone within his organization wanted to work voluntarily because informational meetings in schools "take up a lot of time, there is a lot of resources [needed] and basically, this... is done on a voluntary [unpaid] basis... only through our initiative." "In essence," he added, "we do not shy away from this [work]; we always gladly do it. It would just be preferable for us to do this... on a greater scale."

Grigory proposed to collaborate with a center that had government funding for centralized preventative work among youth because he and his colleagues had "newer technology and more... interesting information and... also training programs, like small workshops, for youth... interactive [workshops]." The center rejected collaboration however, so Grigory and his colleagues continued this work on their own, but "on a smaller scale." One government agency, nonetheless, asked Grigory

---

[20] In 2002, Saenko et al. (2004) interviewed 50 HIV/AIDS experts—law enforcement workers, doctors, city and local administrators, NGO activists, social workers, social educators—in three regional Ukrainian centers, Dnepropetrovsk (central), Donetsk (eastern) and Kherson (southern). 59 percent stated that HIV/AIDS informational talks in schools, community, technical colleges and universities occurred regularly, 33 percent said that they occurred from time to time, eight percent stated that they did not occur. 31 percent of the experts also said that at the city level preventative work with youth was mostly or completely sufficient, 25 percent found it difficult to evaluate, while 44 percent said that it was mostly/completely insufficient.

and some of his colleagues, as HIV/AIDS specialists, to conduct some of their preventative work; so they designed an official plan with the agency.[21] Grigory complained, however, that "again... [the agency staff] receive a salary for this, right? We do not receive anything... for this work for our own [people]."

Similar initiatives took place in Efim and Isaac's NGOs. Isaac wrote "[t]his is truly voluntary work, because it is not written into the project descriptions," and Efim confirmed that donors did not take it into consideration (*ne uchityvaetsya*). Isaac, moreover, was directly involved in planning these activities and even sent me a list of objectives that he developed for a three-session workshop. His staff scheduled and arranged activities with local educational establishments and he had no problem releasing them for these purposes. Like Grigory, Efim added that staff members were released when they were invited to schools as HIV/AIDS specialists (mostly by government agencies that deal with youth and families).

Isaac and Efim revealed another interesting effort to implement ideas that they considered important. At one point I asked them whether they knew of open-ended funding competitions, which I had read were generally rare (Sundstrom 2006). Both had applied for and did not receive such grants in the past, which, indeed, they considered rare and did not know anyone who had obtained them. Isaac wrote a proposal to support a voluntary association of youth organizations created under the regional governor's office. He explained that "[s]tudents gather after class and analyze Ukrainian legislation that pertains to youth... which laws are being upheld and which are not. They make their recommendations to the governor so that he can take action accordingly." Isaac's NGO was part of this association, because "HIV/AIDS is a problem that mostly affects youth." He stated that he wanted to support the group in order to help create leaders who would be more educated on issues and would take them to upper-level authorities. But the problem was that "sooner or later initiative can disappear," because

> it is a lot of work... let's say they work for a year and there are no results, nothing. Just initiative [without material incentives]. Then problems begin. This is all youth... students. They finish their university, go to work, and they have absolutely no time for the social sphere anymore.

---

[21] 63 percent of experts rated cooperation between government agencies and NGOs, on HIV/AIDS informational/educational initiatives with children and youth, as sufficient in the cities (Saenko et al. 2004).

Efim and his colleagues, meanwhile, wrote a proposal for assistance to street children, which they considered important because they were not aware of any such projects in the city or regionally.[22] Efim stated that "[t]here were no [donor-specified] grant competitions [for street children]. I mean, some say that there were competitions for that, but…we have not seen them." Although it is unclear why these projects were not funded, we can see how both men assessed the local situation and substantiated their claims. Isaac's proposal, in particular, was a textbook example of what most social scientists would argue strengthens civil society—a project to build up a cadre of critically engaged youth who analyze the nation's legislation. His proposal, in fact, was not even directly for his organizations' project activities. Both men, who are in upper management positions, attempted to make the best of their structural constraints to fund initiates that they perceived as locally significant.

Not every staff member, however, was as committed as the people I interviewed. A few scholars have also documented variation among NGO workers. Hilhorst (2003), for example, described a three-way staff division within a Philippine NGO that she researched. The first division consisted of highly involved and committed upper management, who were former movement activists. The second division consisted of ideologically committed newer staff. The third division, however, consisted of staff hired for various project purposes and had little or no affiliation with the political movement. They had little loyalty and could easily move on to other job opportunities. It is logical that internal stratification existed across a variety of NGOs. Vera, for instance, stated that some people in her NGO only complete their assigned tasks and "do not think at all how to develop this [project] direction, or how to strengthen it, or what to do so that it becomes stable, regardless of whether there will be donor funds." She can hold workers responsible for their work quality, as long as long as she provides them with a stable salary. "But such people," she added, "do not need anything, except to carry out this work and to receive their stable salary."

Moreover, Vera's comments suggest that perhaps top-down management operates primarily on workers who do not take initiative.[23]

---

[22] 84 percent of experts rated preventative work with street children in the cities mostly or completely insufficient (Saenko et al. 2004).

[23] Alternatively, some of them perhaps forego initiative because of top-down management.

Meanwhile, others, like Grigory, try to influence their NGO's direction and activities despite the organizational hierarchy; in fact, circumventing it by initiating activities and then engaging upper management in the planning.

To sum up, discussion of internal divisions is largely lacking from prevalent accounts of NGOs and they do not show us internal variation that constitutes these organizations. Yet, scholars could benefit from attention to internal stratification because these divisions help to conceptualize and unpack various organizational activities. In fact, through this lens we can see that prevalent NGO critiques in the literature may not apply evenly across workers and possibly NGOs.

Thus, it is important to note that commitment varies among staff members; yet, committed activists may hold positions across the organizational hierarchy. They are distinct in their motivation and efforts to implement ideas that they consider locally relevant.[24] To the extent that activists in lower positions initiate (voluntary) projects and engage upper-level staff, they may mitigate top-down structures. Some upper-level workers, however, also strive to support local initiatives, but within their own spheres of activity. In this case, Efim and Isaac were assisting with administrative and planning tasks (as opposed to direct outreach), as well as attempting to find and secure funding for local initiatives that they considered important. It is also noteworthy that voluntary activities occurred in collaboration with state agencies, either initiated by activists, or the agencies, and, as Grigory noted, were intended to broaden the scale of the outreach efforts.

Making Sense of NGOs

Despite somewhat optimistic findings regarding activists' commitment, I suggest that faced with considerable strain, uncertainty, and new individualistic values, NGO activists took refuge in ideas of personal efficacy and responsibility. The turn to personal responsibility for a fragmented liberalized system came out of an effort to make sense of post-Soviet uncertainty and was manifest in the activists' equivocal perceptions of donors, the state and their own roles. My respondents simultaneously

---

[24] Some discrepancies between clients and NGO workers certainly exist. For example, Grigory mentioned that he considered some clients' requests for money, in lieu of food assistance packages, "mercantilistic."

criticized and sought collaboration with and support from the state, foreign donors (and other local actors, like businesses, the public, etc). They praised donors for providing funding and information. On the other hand, they explicitly lamented the instability and insufficiency of funding and implicitly its competitiveness. Similarly, they listed a litany of grievances against the state ranging from unwieldy bureaucracy, to prejudice against NGOs and HIV/AIDS, to corruption, and other problems. Yet, they voluntarily collaborated with state agencies and extended hopes for state support. Moreover, they hoped for some future stability with state funding or the "third sector" (nonprofit/civil society) and the new NGOs based "social entrepreneurship" models introduced by donors.[25] The following (rearranged) excerpts from Efim and Isaac's interview are exemplary of some of the activists' ambiguity and struggles to make sense of their precarious environment:

> **Efim** [explaining the dependence on foreign funding]: That's the horror of it all. Why are we here [on a donor-sponsored trip in the U.S.]? I mean, the terrible thing in our country is that the government, aside from making speeches, does not help us with anything. And what they tell us, that they are doing something, is all fairy tales. Well, corruption? Yes, I'll admit it, there is corruption everywhere...[On the other hand] if the government does not offer support—then it will be an...enemy (laughs). Yes, an enemy. And what will happen? Well, the third sector, if it survives, will be strong...[But] if we have self-service without government [help], then what will happen in the future?...All these donors [lists several] are planning on leaving [Ukraine]...And now everyone understands that and everyone works with the state, somehow trying to do something there (laughs)...
>
> **Isaac**: Solution to the current situation? Well, I have thought about this a lot and...well, two solutions: of course, financing from the government...at least. And secondly...creation of a social enterprise [an idea Evgenia also championed]. Right now...my central office is working

---

[25] Phillips (2005) argued that in Ukraine, the "logics of the social enterprise and similar programs reinforce [the] burden [of social responsibilities formerly managed by the state] through their implicit dismissal of citizens' claims on state assistance and support, and the stress they place on 'self-sufficiency' and 'independence from donors.'" The prospects for many enterprises to generate necessary operational capital, feed the hungry and employ people with disabilities are limited. NGOs that adopted the social enterprise model sometimes did this out of necessity, when other funding options were foreclosed or severely limited. The ventures were fraught with difficulties and contradictions, ranging from ethical and practical concerns that needy members would have to work to keep the NGO afloat, to cumbersome, mercurial business laws, public skepticism about businesses and NGOs, corruption, and the viability of business success.

on this; [they] already started to implement it. So that...there would be a business which would produce revenue and it would support [NGO] programs...

Efim: Yes...So we have only two solutions.

Isaac: Only two (laughs). And both from the realm of the impossible.

Efim: Everyone begins with [foreign] donors...Some options exist...to receive start-up grants for social enterprises. Small ones...Ten thousand...dollars...They give them for...some small laundromats, small (work)shops...

Isaac: Well, that's just laughable. That's not an amount with which you can start something.

Efim: Well, at least [something]...So, two solutions...

These exchanges indicate that commitment-driven activists, who were unable to overcome the elusive gaps in the social support system, felt personally responsible to both capture and create opportunities from numerous sources thus trying to make sense of, systematize, and channel social resources that had become particularly unsystematic in the post-Soviet period. Consequently, admirable but piecemeal outreach efforts occurred primarily due to the activists' individual sense of responsibility for providing services that were retracted and decentralized during neoliberal reforms.[26] Thus, Grigory and his colleagues, as well as activists at other NGOs, sought out and engaged in voluntary work with state agencies that agreed to collaborate with them (and sometimes even extended invitations). Similarly, Isaac and Efim sought funding and provided administrative support for what they considered important local issues on a case by case basis and through rarely available (and attainable) flexible funding. Rivkin-Fish (2005) made a similar argument, stating that in the reformed Russian healthcare system "personal and privatizing strategies repeatedly produced less than actors hoped: doctors' efforts to resist the 'collective irresponsibility' structured into the health care system through individual, heroic efforts of taking 'personal responsibility' for their work were unable to overcome the range of obstacles stemming from poverty, political disenfranchisement and the fragmented nature of the system itself (pp. 212–213)."

---

[26] Underscoring the idea of decentralization inherent among NGOs, Saenko et al. (2004) argued that inadequate coordination among various international donors' projects leads to duplicate HIV/AIDS studies with similar focus and methodology, rather than investigation of new topics.

While proponents of privatizing service delivery may hail a strong sense of personal responsibility within this system, the interviews suggest that it shifted the momentous burden of helping the disadvantaged to the shoulders of select organizations and activists. Vera, for instance, maintained a constant self-critique to do more, work harder, and push the limits to sustain and create projects at the expense of personal and family time. She described her workday as follows:

> at nine in the morning I leave [home] and at nine at night I return. And I have no strength left for my family (laughs), nor for sex, nor for my [daughter]. I just bark [at them]: 'why are the dishes not washed?' or 'why is something else not done?' Well. Of course...(pause) It's like that.

Her work brought her great satisfaction when she succeeded and disappointment when she did not or could not. Efim, Isaac, and others also mentioned feeling burned out, long hours under grant deadlines, and time away from family, as stated above.

At the same time, social reforms and Western civil society models, have introduced what Neuman (2005) dubbed the shadow (private) welfare state in the U.S. This model includes shifting "the basis for claiming benefits from being a universal and public citizenship right to being a private, contingent patron-client reward" and reducing "pressure to expand and improve public benefit levels by offering private sector alternatives (p. 538)." Thus, fewer resources are devoted to human needs and services, while the trend is toward negotiating subcontracting and division of labor with the private sector, which does not provide equitable coverage (Shaw 2000).

On the other hand, what is a viable alternative? As Kuzio (2003) had argued above, the state should not be reduced, but reorganized to better suit its citizens. In light of this comparison, I critically evaluate two claims that Westerners had made in favor of NGOs, as opposed to the state: NGOs' relative credibility (lack of corruption) and limited bureaucracy (efficiency and effectiveness). First, despite the prevalence of significant state corruption, which I have noted above, corruption among NGOs is also a potential problem that has received little scholarly, or donor attention (who, of course, would be reluctant to publicize it) (Gibelman and Gelman 2004, Hemment 2007, Reimann 2005, Shelley 2005). In my research, several interviewees indicated the existence of this problem. Evgenia, for example, explained that "it is not a secret that...many...[non-governmental] organizations are created—well, it's like that everywhere—they are created for the purpose of money laundering..."

Secondly, lack of bureaucracy in NGOs may be somewhat of a misnomer, which neglects the complexity of running these organizations. Uvin (2000) proposed that even when NGOs are not directly involved in active politics or want to change state behavior, they are nonetheless engaged with the state and political processes. In part, this is due to the registration, taxation and legal requirements, as well as public funding issues, joint projects and personal connections with state officials. My research supports Uvin's claims: an NGO does not simply receive a grant and begin providing services and advocating on behalf of its constituencies. Establishing and maintaining a funded organization, in addition to Uvin's claims, also involves dealing with the sponsors' bureaucracy and oversight, including frequent audits, reports and other guidelines. Moreover, NGOs have infrastructural needs and must deal with authorities at different levels, in order to obtain office space, water, heat, electricity, phone and internet lines (not always easy in the post-Soviet environment). Some organizations, which are located in networks, or are part of federated structures, have to coordinate activities with other NGOs and comply with regulations of and obligations to their central offices or governing boards (Hemment 2006, Henderson 2003, my interviews). We can begin to think of these problems in comparison with the centralized bureaucracy of the state if we imagine some of NGOs' difficulties that stem from dealing with various actors as decentralized bureaucratic hurdles. In other words, we can think of NGOs dealing with a kind of "diffuse bureaucracy" outside of these organizations, which nonetheless "resides" between their goals and the ability to carry them out. The nature of these piecemeal interactions, however, as opposed to the more visible state bureaucracy, potentially obscures a succinct comparative focus between the two. Preliminary findings consequently suggest that donors' claims about NGOs' credibility and lack of bureaucracy warrant further research.

In order to assess the respective roles of states and NGOs, scholars should also begin to unpack their varying functions. Non-governmental organizations not only provide services but also engage in advocacy and policy debates and initiatives. For instance, Vera stated that

> we developed a methodological manual, in partnership with the regional institute for teacher development…called 'Interactive technologies for HIV prevention and formation of tolerant attitudes toward HIV positive people.' It was issued a certificate of authorship and now we are going to move it to the ministerial level, so that we can implement this program at the national level, through the ministry. I think that it is unique—before, there was no such methodological manual in Ukraine.

Thus, some NGOs may provide spaces for critical thought separate from the state; scholars should consequently consider how service and other functions may be interrelated in complementary and contradictory ways.

Conclusion

My aim has been to use a pilot study of Ukrainian HIV/AIDS NGOs to suggest directions for further theorizing about these organizations. First, I explained that scholars should examine the broader environments within which NGOs operate. In the Ukrainian case, neoliberal reforms of the early 1990s shifted many social responsibilities to non-state actors and reduced the social safety net. Meanwhile, Western-funded HIV/AIDS NGOs began to respond to these changes by providing services to and advocating on behalf of thousands of people affected by the burgeoning HIV/AIDS epidemic.

I then proposed that investigating NGOs at the individual level can yield important insights and proceeded to outline how Ukrainian activists, embedded in a reforming nation and complex relationships with local constituencies, foreign donors and the state, sought to make sense of their work. I began to unpack internal NGO dynamics and found variation among workers based on ideological commitment and engagement in voluntary work. Internal variation also revealed that when considering only some of the most committed activists, many of the prevalent NGO critiques in the literature seemed less appropriate. Despite this finding, I suggested that decentralization and ideological underpinnings of Western neoliberal and civil society models led committed activists to adopt personal responsibility for shortcomings of the system.

Finally, I indicated that when considered critically, NGOs may exhibit some of the corruption and bureaucratic problems that are cited as shortcomings of the state. Yet, these organizations have varying functions, such as service provision and advocacy, which could operate in different ways and should be further examined. Ultimately, the issues raised here are intended to provoke questions that scholars could ask in more extensive research about social and political implications of NGOs and civil society at varying levels of analysis.

Appendix

Staff Members' Selected Survey and Interview Responses
About Personal Background, HIV/AIDS NGOs and Clientele (N = 6)

Notes	Q#	Item	Survey#					Interview response only	Mean	Median	Mode	Sum
			1	2	3	4	5					
From donor description (supplied by staff)		Position in HIV/AIDS NGO	Head of coordination board of NGOs	Administrator of educational programs	Program coordinator	Head of organization	Social worker	Program coordinator				
My determination		Sex (1 = female; 2 = male)	1	1	2	2	2	1	1.5	1.5		
	2	Assigned Name	Irina	Evgenia	Efim	Isaac	Grigory	Vera				
Age for Efim and Vera my determination	4	Age (years)	27	21	Late 20s–early 30s	29	32	Mid 30s–early 40s	About 29.5	About 29.5		
	5	Education	Higher	Higher in progress	Night school in progress	Higher	Incomplete higher	Higher			Higher	
	6	Place of education	State university	Medical university	State universities	State institute					State university	
	7	Current workplace										
	a	Only one HIV/AIDS NGO (1 = yes)	1	1	1	1	1	1	1	1	1	
	b	Number of years at NGO (in years)	2	2	5	4	2.5	About 6–7	About 3.7	About 3.1	2	

Survey and Interview Responses (*cont.*)

Notes	Q#	Item	Survey#					Interview response only			
			1	2	3	4	5	Mean	Median	Mode	Sum
	c	Work in other place(s) (number)	0	0	0	0	0	0	0	0	0
	8	Number of people working for NGO									
	a	total	12	7	25	15	14	14.6	14	14	73
	b	men	5	3	12	3	8	6.2	5	5	31
	c	women	7	4	13	12	6	8.4	7	7	42
	9	Age of NGO coworkers (1-8; greatest to smallest category)									
8 = no one (smallest category)	a	under 18	8	8	8	8	8	8	8	8	8
	b	18–25	1	2	3	1	2	1.8	2	1	1
	c	26–35	2	1	1	2	1	1.4	1	1	1
	d	36–45	8	3	2	3	3	3.8	3	3	3
	e	46–55	8	8	4	8	8	7.2	8	8	8
	f	56–65	8	8	8	4	8	7.2	8	8	8
	g	over 65	8	8	8	8	8	8	8	8	8

Survey and Interview Responses (*cont.*)

Notes	Q#	Item	Survey#					Interview response only			
			1	2	3	4	5	Mean	Median	Mode	Sum
10 = no one (smallest category)	10	Age of Clients (1–10: greatest-smallest category)									
		a 0–5	10	10	3	2	4	5.8	4	10	
		b 6–10	10	7	7	4	5	6.6	7	7	
		c 11–17	2	6	6	10	5	5.8	6	6	
		d 18–25	1	2	5	3	3	2.8	3	3	
		e 26–35	3	1	2	1	1	1.6	1	4	
		f 36–45	4	3	1	5	2	3	3	3	
		g 46–55	5	4	4	10	6	5.8	5	4	
		h 56–65	6	5	7	10	7	7	7	7	
		i over 65	7	10	10	10	10	9.4	10	10	
	11	Percent men & women among NGO clients									
		a % women	55	50	55	70	60	58	55	55	
		b % men	45	50	45	30	40	42	45	45	
	23	Percent of budget from sponsors									
		a 0–25%									0
		b 26–50%									0
		c 51–75%	1								1
		d 76–100%		1	1	1	1				4

PART TWO

CHANGING FORMS OF PROTEST

STABILITY AND CHANGE IN THE CONTOURS OF ALLIANCES AMONG MOVEMENTS IN THE SOCIAL FORUM PROCESS[1]

Christopher Chase-Dunn and Matheu Kaneshiro

This chapter examines changes in the organizational space of the transnational social movements that are involved in the World Social Forum (WSF) process. In this study we seek to understand the structure of connections among progressive transnational movements and how those connections may be evolving over time. For this purpose we analyze results obtained from surveys of participants in the WSF in 2005 in Porto Alegre, the WSF in 2007 in Nairobi and the U.S. Social Forum (USSF) that was held in Atlanta in 2007.

We examine the contours of the social movement connections found among WSF participants, and how these may be changing over time. The tricky problem is that our findings probably reflect other things as well as changes in the structure of the network of popular movements in the global public sphere. Undoubtedly the locations of the meetings, the nature of the groups that sponsored the meetings, and the somewhat different purposes of the meetings, also influence the network structures that emerged at each meeting. We shall try to sort out these different elements affecting the structure of alliances.

There is a large scholarly literature on networks, coalitions and alliances among social movements (e.g. Carroll and Ratner 1996; Krinsky and Reese 2006; Obach 2004; Reese, Petit, and Meyer 2008; Rose 2000; Van Dyke 2003). Our study is theoretically motivated by this literature as well as by world-systems analyses of world revolutions (Arrighi, Hopkins and Wallerstein 1989; Boswell and Chase-Dunn 2000) and Antonio Gramsci's analysis of ideological hegemony, counter-hegemonic movements and the formation of historical blocks [see also Carroll and Ratner (1996) and Carroll (2006a, 2006b)].

---

[1] An earlier version was presented at the *Critical Sociology* Conference on "POWER AND RESISTANCE: CRITICAL REFLECTIONS, POSSIBLE FUTURES" The Boston Park Plaza Hotel & Towers, Boston, Massachusetts, USA, August 3, 2008.

Social movement organizations may be integrated both informally and formally. Informally, they are connected by the voluntary choices of individual persons to be active participants in multiple movements. Such linkages enable learning and influence to pass among movement organizations, even when there may be limited official interaction or leadership coordination. In the descriptive analysis below, we assess the extent and pattern of informal linkage by surveying attendees at the WSF. At the formal level, organizations may provide legitimacy and support to one another, and strategically collaborate in joint action. The extent of formal cooperation among movements within "the movement of movements" both causes and reflects the informal connections.

The extent and pattern of linkages among the memberships and among the organizational leaderships of social movement organizations may be highly consequential. Some forms of connection [e.g. "small world" networks, (Watts 2003)] allow the rapid spread of information and influence; other forms of connection (e.g. division into "factions" by region, gender, or issue area) may inhibit communication and make coordinated action more difficult. The ways in which social movements are linked may facilitate or obstruct efforts to organize cross-movement collective action. Network analysis can reveal whether or not the structure of alliances contains separate subsets with only weak ties, or the extent to which the network is organized around one or several central movements that mediate ties among the other movements.

The World Social Forum Surveys

We used previous studies of the global justice movements by Starr (2000), Fisher and Ponniah (2003) and Petit (2004) to construct a list of social movements that we believed would be represented at the January 2005 World Social Forum in Porto Alegre, Brazil. The eighteen movements that we studied in 2005 are listed in Table 1 below. At the WSF in Nairobi, Kenya we used most of these same movements, but we separated human rights from anti-racism and we added nine additional movements (development, landless, immigrant, religious, housing, jobless, open source, and autonomous), and this same larger list was used at the USSF in Atlanta in July of 2007. Most of our results use only the original list of 18, with human rights and anti-racism combined as they were in the 2005 survey.

We asked participants which of these movements they strongly identified with, and with which were they actively involved. Our surveys
also focused on the social characteristics of participants, their political
activism, and their political views (see Reese et al. 2008). The six-page
survey asked participants' opinions on a set of questions designed to
capture the main political divisions within the global justice movement
described in previous research (Byrd 2005; Brecher, Costello, and Smith
2002; Starr 2000; Fisher and Ponniah 2003; Teivainen 2004). In 2005
we collected a total of 639 surveys in three languages: English, Spanish,
and Portuguese.[2]

Although we were unable to survey all linguistic groups, we sought to
ensure that we had a broad sample of WSF participants; we conducted
our survey at a wide variety of venues, including the registration line,
the opening march, Venezuelan President Hugo Chavez's speech (which
drew tens of thousands), various kinds of thematic workshops, solidarity tents at multiple locations, outdoor concerts, and the youth camp.
Our survey of attendees at the World Social Forum in Porto Alegre
is not a perfectly representative sample, though we tried to make it as
representative as possible given the limitations of collecting responses
during the meetings.

Participation in Social Movements at the 2005 World Social Forum

The size distribution of the eighteen movements in terms of number of
participants who say they are **actively involved** is shown in Table 1.

The size distribution of movement selections in Table 1 shows that
the highest percentages of selections were made of human rights/anti-
racism (12%), environmental (11%), alternative media/culture (10%)
and peace (9%). Some activists have refused to participate in the World
Social Forum (or have held counter-events) and some others (those
advocating armed struggle) are excluded by the WSF Charter. These
factors might account for the small numbers of some of the movements
(e.g. anarchists and communists). It is said that anarchists do not fill out

---

[2] Our project web page contains the WSF05, WSF07 and USSF survey instruments.
See http://www.irows.ucr.edu/research/tsmstudy.htm.

Table 1: Total numbers and percentages of movements selected as actively involved at the 2005 WSF

alternative media/culture	133 number of selections	100% % of total selections
anarchist	20	2%
anti-corporate	43	3%
anti-globalization	68	5%
global justice	81	6%
human rights/anti-racism	161	12%
communist	32	2%
environmental	142	11%
fair trade	67	5%
queer rights	37	3%
health/HIV	52	4%
indigenous	48	4%
labor	72	6%
national liberation	38	3%
peace	113	9%
slow food	38	3%
socialist	87	7%
feminist	66	5%
Total Responses	1298	100%
Number of Respondents	560	

questionnaires, but we had very few refusals and 20 of our respondents indicated that they are actively involved anarchists.

We also analyzed the responses to the question about "strong identi-fication" with movements to compare these with the "actively involved" question shown in Table 1. More than twice as many people indicate "identification" as opposed to "active involvement", but the relative percentages are very similar, and the network results (below) on the identification matrix are also very similar to those found for active involvement. The UCINet QAP routine for correlating two network matrices produces a Pearson's r correlation coefficient of .909 between the identification and active involvement matrices.[3]

---

[3] All network calculations employed the UCINET 6.130 software package (Borgatti, Everett & Freeman 2002).

Patterns of Linkage among the Social Movements

We employed two different approaches to analyzing the structure of connections among the movements at the WSF05: bivariate correlations and formal network analysis. First we examined the Spearman's rank-order correlations among the pairs of movements in which respondents said they are actively involved. These correlations tell us how frequently the participants in one movement had similar profiles of participation in other movements. That is, are participants in one particular movement (e.g. anarchism) more likely (positive correlation) or less likely (negative correlation) to participate in another particular movement (e.g. environmentalism). The correlations among movements are based on the patterns of choices of those 418 respondents who said that they were involved in two or more movements.

Of the 153 unique correlations (18*17/2) there are only seven that are negative, and these are small and not statistically significant. That is, there is an overwhelming tendency for solidarity; participation in one movement almost always makes participation in any other more likely—albeit to highly varying degrees. Seventy-eight of the correlations were positive and statistically significant at the .01 level. The correlations are not high. The largest correlation is .488 between the anti-globalization and the anti-corporate movements. The other rather significant positive correlations (above .3) are anti-corporate/alternative globalization; anti-corporate/peace; and queer rights/health-HIV.

We worried that the presence of respondents who had not checked any of the movements might be lowering the correlations and reducing significance levels, and that some of these might be from incomplete questionnaires rather than real responses to the questions. Indeed 24% (135) of the respondents checked none of the movements as ones in which they were actively involved (see Table 2 below). But our fears were allayed by the fact that respondents were far more likely to have checked at least some movements with which they strongly identified. Only 1.3% (8) of the questionnaires had no movements selected as strongly identified. This means that almost all of the 112 respondents who checked no movements as those in which they were actively involved were actually reporting a real situation and our results for the involvement matrix should be accurate.

Network analysis is superior to bivariate correlation analysis because it allows the whole structure of a network to be analyzed including all the direct and indirect links and non-links. This makes it possible to

identify cliques or factions within a network and to examine the centrality or peripherality of network nodes—in this case social movements.

In order to use network analysis we must choose a "cut-off" point
that defines strong versus less strong ties among movement pairs. We
selected a tie strength cut-off of one-half of a standard deviation above
the mean number of movement interconnections to define a "strong"
linkage. Using this cutoff, we display the "strong ties" among the movements in Figure 1.

Even with this rather high cutoff all of the movements are connected
by only one degree of separation, except for the anarchists, communists, queer rights and national liberationists. They are not included in
the network graph because they fall below the dichotomization point
in terms of movement connections using the one-half of a standard
deviation above the mean cut-off. But the matrix of all ties has no
empty cells, so even these movements that are less strongly tied are
not really true isolates.

Figure 1 shows the centrality of Human Rights/Anti-Racism and
Environmental movements in the network of transnational social movements represented at the World Social Forum in 2005. It also indicates
that the Peace, Alternative Media, Anti-Globalization and Global Justice
movements are rather central. These six movements are major "hubs"
or an "inner circle". But the overall structure is multicentric with not
very large differences in network centrality among the most central six.
This pattern is not very hierarchical. No single movement is the most
"inclusive" or a "peak organization" for all of the others.

Comparisons of WSF2005 with WSF2007 and USSF 2007

We have repeated the network analyses above using the results of
our surveys in Nairobi in 2007 and Atlanta in 2007. The purposes of
these comparisons are twofold: to examine the question of stability
and change in the network of transnational social movements participating in the social forum process; and to look for differences that
might be attributable to either the changing structure of global activism, or to the effects that the host country has on the social forum
process (e.g. geographical location, support from the host country's
government, or different organizational influences involved). Brazil
is a semiperipheral country in Latin America. Kenya is a peripheral
country in East Africa. The United States is the reigning hegemon of

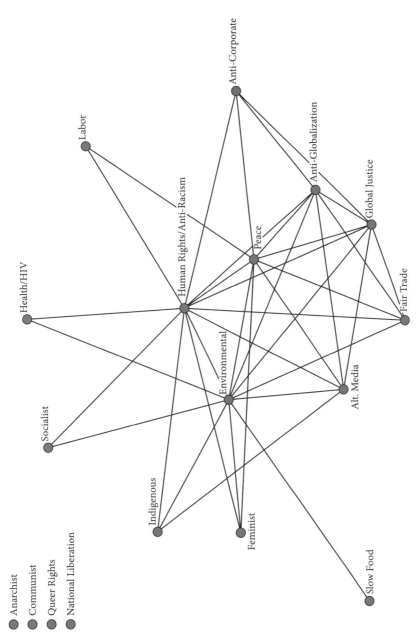

Figure 1: The network of movement linkages at the 2005 WSF in Porto Alegre

the global system. Porto Alegre has been a strong-hold of the Brazilian Workers Party that has been an important source of support for the establishment and continuation of the World Social Forum. The 2005 meeting in Porto Alegre was attended by Brazilian President Lula and Venezuelan President Hugo Chavez.

The World Social Forum was held in 2007 in Nairobi in order to hold an important global-level meeting in Africa, but the Nairobi government was not very sympathetic with the political goals of the social forum process. Rather the government seemed to see the event as an opportunity to increase tourism. The whole tenor of the meeting was affected by this. More conservative groups, especially religious ones, were prominent at the Nairobi meeting. This gathering was also greatly affected by the fact that a large proportion of the attendees were Africans. The United States Social Forum in Atlanta in July of 2007 was explicitly intended by the WSF International Committee to be organized by, and intended for, grass roots movement within the United States. Global and national NGOs and national unions were allowed to participate but they did not play a central role in organizing the meeting. The "internal Third World" and women were important as both organizers and participants in the USSF. These differences, as well as purely geographical factors, probably played a role in shaping the differences that we find in the structure of movement networks across the three meetings.

Table 2 above shows that the percentage of the respondents that did not check any of the eighteen movements to indicate active involvement varied from 22% in Atlanta to 30% in Nairobi. In Porto Alegre it was 24%. Recall that we also asked respondents to check those movements with which they strong identified. Only about 2% checked no movements with which they were strongly identified, so we think that the question about active involvement acted as a high bar that was respected by respondents. From 14% (Nairobi) to 22% (Porto Alegre) indicated that they were actively involved with only one movement, and from 54% (Porto Alegre) to 62% (Atlanta) said they were actively involved in two or more movements. In Nairobi it was 56%. The correlations among movements and the network connections that we are studying are based entirely on the patterns of choices of those respondents who said that they were actively involved in two or more movements. Whereas few respondents indicated that they were actively involved in more than eight movements, more significant numbers indicated involvement in from three to seven movements. Those respondents who are involved in multiple movements may be more likely to be synergists who see

Table 2: Number of movements in which respondents say they are actively involved

# of movements actively involved	WSF2005 # of respondents	percent	WSF2007 # of respondents	percent	USSF2007 # of respondents	percent
0	135	24.1	129	29.9	120	21.6
1	123	21.9	59	13.7	89	16
2	93	16.6	73	16.9	68	12.3
3	69	15.3	52	12.1	55	9.9
4	37	6.6	36	8.4	71	12.8
5	30	5.4	29	6.7	47	8.5
6	23	4.1	16	3.7	24	4.3
7	13	2.3	11	2.6	22	4
8	10	1.8	6	1.4	18	3.2
9	2	0.4	6	1.4	16	2.9
10	2	0.4	5	1.2	10	1.8
11	3	0.5	2	0.5	4	0.7
12	2	0.5	3	0.7	2	0.4
13	0	0	3	0.7	2	0.4
14	2	0.5	0	0	3	0.5
15	0	0	1	0.2	1	0.2
16	0	0	0	0	2	0.4
17	0	0	0	0	1	0.2
Totals (2 or more)	544 (286)		431 (243)		555 (346)	

the connections among different movements and who are more likely to play an active role in facilitating collective action within the larger "movement of movements."

Comparison of the WSF05 and WSF07 network figures shows that the basic multicentric structure of the movement of movements did not change. In both networks there is a set of hub movements that strongly integrate all the other movements. The same cut-off of one-half of a standard deviation above the mean number of connections is used in both Figure 1 and Figure 2 (and also in Figure 3 below), and the same list of movements is used to allow for comparability (see second page of this chapter for an explanation). As was the case for the WSF05 network, the matrix of movement pairs for the WSF07 meeting has no zeros, meaning that all of the 18 movements have at least one participant in all of the other movements. Only a single anarchist (out of forty-three) ties the anarchist movement with the slow food, socialist, and feminist movements. But there are no isolated movements without members who are actively involved in other movements. This was also the case in the WSF05 matrix.

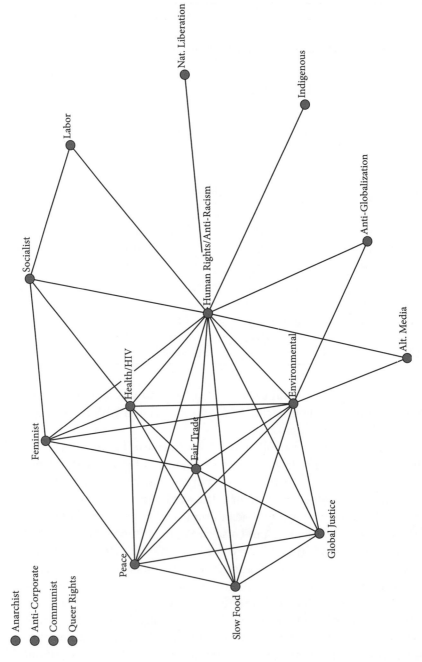

Figure 2: The network of movement linkages at the 2007 WSF in Nairobi

Three of the movements (anarchist, communist and queer rights) that were disconnected by the high bar of connectedness in the WSF05 matrix were also disconnected in WSF07, whereas National Liberation met the test in Nairobi, but not in Porto Alegre, and Anti-corporate failed the test in Nairobi but not in Porto Alegre. One of the same movements appears near the center (Human Rights/Anti-racism), but some that were rather central in 2005 have moved out toward the edge in 2007 (Peace, Global Justice and Alternative Media). The Environmentalists are still toward the center, but not as central as they were in Porto Alegre. Health/HIV is much more central than it was in Brazil, probably reflecting both an increase in global concern and a much greater crisis in Africa. Regarding overall structural differences between the two matrices, the 2007 network is more centered around a single movement (Human Rights/Anti-racism), but there are also more direct connections among some of the movements out on the edge (e.g. feminists and socialists, socialists and labor, slow food and global justice.

Figure 3 shows the network structure of movements obtain from responses by attendees at the United States Social Forum meeting that was held in Atlanta, Georgia in July of 2007. Once again the anarchists and communists do not make the one-half of a standard deviation above the mean number of connections cut-off, but now they are joined by national liberation, socialists and slow food. As with the earlier movement interconnection matrices, there are no empty cells. All the movements are interconnected by at least 2 common participants. Alternative media is rather better connected relative to its position in Nairobi, though not as central and connected as it was at Porto Alegre. The feminists appear rather more central than they were in either Porto Alegre or Nairobi. And Health/HIV is much farther out than it was in Nairobi and somewhat farther out than it was in Porto Alegre. Anti-corporate is closer to the center than it was in Porto Alegre and Nairobi. The USSF network is still multicentric and has the same hubs as in the Porto Alegre network, except that feminism has moved into the center. There are still no separate factions.

These same differences are revealed when we compare the multiplicative coreness scores of the movements across the meetings. Multiplicative coreness indicates the extent to which a node possesses a high density of connections with other nodes. Less coreness is characterized as possessing few interconnections. Nodes with high coreness are often capable of greater coordinated action and a greater mobilization of

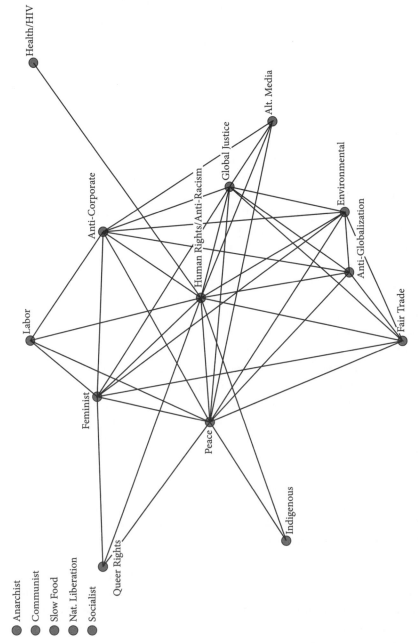

Figure 3: The network of movement linkages at the 2007 USSF in Atlanta

Table 3: Multiplicative Coreness Scores and Ranks of Movements in the
WSF05, WSF07 and USSF07 Networks

| | 2005 | | 2007 | | USSF | |
	Coreness Rank	Multiplicative Coreness Scores	Coreness Rank	Multiplicative Coreness Scores	Coreness Rank	Multiplicative Coreness Scores
Human Rights/						
Anti-Racism	1	0.441	1	0.491	1	0.476
Peace	2	0.364	3	0.309	2	0.363
Environmental	3	0.345	2	0.336	4	0.269
Alternative Media	4	0.300	11	0.194	9	0.228
Global Justice	5	0.272	5	0.272	5	0.267
Anti-Globalization	6	0.251	9	0.198	6	0.252
Fair Trade	7	0.232	6	0.269	8	0.231
Feminist	8	0.202	7	0.249	3	0.290
Socialist	9	0.190	10	0.197	15	0.119
Labor	10	0.199	12	0.169	10	0.210
Anti-Corporate	11	0.177	15	0.107	7	0.251
Indigenous	12	0.174	13	0.159	12	0.163
Health/HIV	13	0.162	4	0.293	14	0.139
Slow Food	14	0.151	8	0.211	13	0.141
National Liberation	15	0.132	14	0.120	17	0.070
Queer Rights	16	0.120	16	0.093	11	0.202
Communist	17	0.098	17	0.083	18	0.060
Anarchist	18	0.070	18	0.027	16	0.093

resources, while nodes with less coreness are not. Table 3 shows the coreness scores and the ranks of the movements.

Both the scores and the ranks tell the story. Seven movements changed their ranks by more than four places: Alternative Media, Feminism, Health/HIV, Anti-Corporate, Socialist, Slow Food and Queer Rights (underlined in Table 3). The other 11 movements were rather stable in terms of their coreness scores and ranks.

It should also be noted that the total number of network connections at the USSF was approximately two times greater than at the WSF05 or the WSF07. The average number of interconnections among movements at both the WSF05 and the WSF06 was sixteen, while at the USSF07 the average number of connections was thirty-one. This is not mainly due to a larger number of respondents. There were 544

Table 4: Pearson's r correlation coefficients of movement interlinks

	WSF05	WSF07	USSF07
WSF05	1	.80	.82
WSF07		1	.71
USSF07			1

respondents in Porto Alegre, 431 in Nairobi and 555 in Atlanta. Rather the level of interconnectedness among movements, that is the number of links produced by people being actively involved in more than one movement, was simply greater at the USSF meeting in Atlanta. Table 2 above shows that a larger percentage of respondents indicated active involvement in a larger number of movements.

While we are interested in detecting and explaining the changes that occurred in the networks, we are also interested in the amount of stability. The progressive wing of the global public sphere, what Boaventura de Sousa Santos (2006) has called the "global left," is an assemblage in formation, but it also exhibits a degree of continuity over time and across space. Our earlier research on the WSF05 movement network examined this issue by comparing the web of social movements derived from the study of WSF05 attendees to a network structure produced by studying the number of joint mentions of movement titles on web pages on the Internet (Chase-Dunn et al. 2007: 11–13). Despite these very different approaches to studying movement interlinks, the results were remarkably consistent.

Another way to estimate the degree of stability across time and space is to use the QAP routine in UCINet to calculate the Pearson's r correlation coefficients between the WSF05, WSF07 and USSF matrices of movement interlinks. Table 4 shows the results. All three of the Pearson's r correlation coefficients were statistically significant. These positive correlations indicate a good degree of stability, though the correlation between Nairobi and the USSF in Atlanta was somewhat smaller than the other two correlations.

Conclusions

Perhaps the biggest finding is that there is a fairly stable network structure of movements across the Social Forum meetings, despite their being held in very different locations and that each of the meetings had differing kinds of support from governments and political organizations. As mentioned above, we even find a similarly structured network when we examine linkages between movements using the contents of web pages. This suggests that there is indeed a global movement of movements that is multicentric, without separate factions, and integrated by a set of central movements that link movements to within one degree of separation from each other. The key role played by the human rights movement in the Social Forum process is important, even though many activists resent the use of human rights discourse by the powers that be to justify the existing structures of global governance. Those who want to democratize global governance should confront this issue head-on by sharply distinguishing between those who genuinely desire to promote economic democracy and civil, economic, and human rights on the one hand, and those who only use human rights discourse to justify neoliberal economic policies.

But we also found interesting differences between the network structures at the three meetings studied. Human rights/anti-racism was more central at the Nairobi meeting than it was at the other two meetings. As can be seen from Figure 3 above, at Nairobi, human rights/anti-racism is the only link between many traditional leftist movements (such as socialism, labor, national liberation, and indigenism) as well as more middle-of-the-road, functionally specific, and newer social movements. In Porto Alegre and Atlanta, on the other hand, older left and labor movements had direct links with the newer or more functionally specific social movements. We have noted above that the Kenyan government was not very sympathetic with the radical political goals of the World Social Forum. It should also be mentioned that Nairobi is a major hub for Northern NGOs operating in Africa. These factors may account for the greater centrality of human rights/anti-racism at the WSF07. The alternative media group was also quite a bit less well linked to other movements at the WSF07 in Nairobi than in the other two meeting locations. We suspect that this may have to do with the greater connections that alternative media activists, who are mainly from Europe and the U.S., have with Latin America than with Africa.

So geography and the nature of local political support have important effects, and we think these are the main explanations for the differences we find in the WSF05, WSF07 and USSF networks of movements. We do not see any strong temporal trends in the development of the movement network. Indeed the WSF05 and USSF07 networks are more strongly correlated with one another than either is with the WSF07 that occurred between them in time (see Table 4 above). This complex entity is a robust multicentric network that has the possibility of engaging in global collective action.

THE GLOBALIZATION MOVEMENT AND WORLD SOCIAL FORUM: FROM PROTEST TO POLITICS

Heather Gautney

Introduction

Changes in the structure of national sovereignty and the emergence of supranational institutions in the last thirty years has been accompanied by a redistribution of power among states, market actors, and civil society. After a half century of intense polarization, the superpowers system gave way to a new arrangement that could accommodate a diversity of cultures, political systems, and people under a unique layer of authority known as Empire. These changes are associated with the increasing dominance of the neoliberal paradigm of globalization, a political-economic system of development, which, by the end of the 1980s, had become so firmly rooted in the common sense, that Francis Fukuyama would resolutely declare its triumph and the "end of history."[1]

Neoliberalism is a political, social, and economic system characterized by the privatization of public services, deregulation of industry, lowering of trade barriers, and reduced public spending on social services. Its underlying ethos reflects a view of human freedom as best realized through free market activity, unregulated competition, and private property rights protected by the neoliberal state. In keeping with this logic, neoliberalism tends to place the burden of market failure on the shoulders of everyday people and prefigure individuals as rational, calculating actors whose value is measured by their ambition, work ethic, and ability to assume responsibility for their life circumstances, rather than look to society for answers. On a global scale, international financial institutions (IFIs) like the World Bank, International Monetary Fund (IMF), and the World Trade Organization (WTO) have attempted, with a great deal of success, to extend the system to the far reaches of the globe, primarily by way of debt, structural adjustment, and "free" trade. Notwithstanding claims to "small government," deregulation

---

[1] See Fukuyama, 1989 or 2006.

and democratic freedom, neoliberalism depends on these regulatory institutions, as well as state power (dictatorial and otherwise), to secure property rights, establish monetary policy in times of crisis, and exploit new markets.

Despite its prevalence, neoliberalism has also given birth to an expansive network of social and political movements—called the Globalization Movement (GM)—that continue to demand increased accountability from IFIs and the governments and corporations that collude with them. The movements were a response to the growing social inequality ushered in by neoliberal reform, but also to the disenfranchisement of local communities from the political and social institutions that shape their lives. According to David Harvey, neoliberalism's success should be understood in part as a failure of the historical left to address people's desires for freedom and prosperity and balance them with the organizational requisites for social justice and change. Neoliberalism has fed desires for autonomy with the promise of private ownership and freedom of consumption, while effectively negating the freedoms associated with cooperative models of political and community life (Harvey, 2005: 61–62; Bourdieu, 1998). The GM attempted to overcome the limitations of previous movements by drawing attention to the devastating effects of neoliberalism by way of open, inclusive protests and movement-building that aimed to prefigure the free, democratic society its constituents sought to create. They also complemented their protest activity with the World Social Forum (WSF), an annual meeting aimed at creating alternative models of economic development and political participation.

This paper looks at the various contributions of the movements and organizations that comprised the GM and WSF and conflicts among them over issues of political organization. Here, political organization is understood as the mechanism through which a movement or class formation articulates its desires for freedom in terms of the broader sets of power relations they seek to contest (Lukacs, 1972: 296; Aronowitz, 2006: 96–97). The paper begins with a discussion of the ideological and historical origins of neoliberalism, and its political economic, and social character, in order to set the stage for an evaluation of the strategies and political alternatives developed by contemporary anti-neoliberal movements. What follows is a discussion of how GM and WSF constituents have conceptualized social change in the 21st century and balance their sometimes disparate ideas regarding freedom and autonomy with the organizational requisites of fighting neoliberal reform and building a democratic, egalitarian society.

Neoliberal Globalization

Neoliberal economic development, also known as "supply side" economics, locates the seeds of economic growth in incentives for production and adjustments to both income and taxes on capital gains. Contrary to Keynesianism's focus on state support, neoliberals argue for a free market, maximal competition, deregulation, and trade liberalization (Brown, 2005: 37–59; Palley, 2005: 20–24). Neoliberalism was the brainchild of Friedrich von Hayek, an Austrian political philosopher associated with the Chicago School of Economics. In 1947, von Hayek formed a study group called the Mont Pelerin Society, which included such notables as Milton Friedman and Ludvig von Mises. Society members called themselves "liberals" to highlight their commitment to personal freedom as well as their antagonism to Keynesianism, which they equated with socialism.

The philosophical basis for liberalism's political economic program can be found in the work of Karl Popper, an early member of the Society. In *The Open Society and Its Enemies*, Popper waged an adamant attack on Marxist historicism, which he identified as a theoretical justification for authoritarianism. For Popper, human history was indeterminate and unknowable, and efforts at prediction or theorizing of historical laws amounted to acts of oppression. An open society was one in which no single person held a monopoly on truth; it enabled debate and the expression of a plurality of views. The rule of law, a democratically elected government, and a vibrant civil society were the stuff of an open society, as was respect for difference and multiculturalism.

In *Objective Knowledge: An Evolutionary Approach*, Popper introduces his concept of "ontological pluralism," which distinguishes three separate, but overlapping worlds: the physical, the mental, and the intelligible (the realm of ideas). For Popper, the world of ideas may be a product of the human mind (the mental world), but once ideas are produced, they can be disembedded from the historical conditions of their production and act autonomously. A second presupposition in Popper is that there are certain objective truths about the physical world that are not directly observable or knowable—they are not locatable in a particular class experience or historical moment. He puts forth an evolutionary view of the world that understands knowledge production as involving processes of trial and error and experimentation. A closed society is one in which the evolution of ideas is thwarted by dogmatism, which he associates with Marxism. An open society, on the other hand, evolves away from dogma and toward "rational criticism" of existing theories by any and all of society's members, such that only the "fittest" ideas survive (Lessnoff, 1980).

Liberalism was the political order that replaced class privilege in the 19th century with modern forms of constitutional democracy rooted in a view of the human selfhood as given, rather than constituted in complex social relations (Brown, 2002: 5–7). It posited the individual as a rational actor, whose humanity was defined and predicated on his or her ability and freedom to choose. *Neo*liberalism has maintained a sharp focus on the individual as such, but it does not consider rational (economic) behavior as given; instead, it manufactures institutions, policies, and crises to facilitate and ensure its function. Moreover, while liberalism once involved the protection of private property by states, the neoliberal state of today is controlled and regulated by the market, which deploys it, when necessary, in the form of monetary policy and deregulation, welfare and housing reform, and even war (Brown, 2002: 5–7). Wendy Brown has aptly termed this force "neoliberal political rationality," which first and foremost involves the submission of politics and all other aspects of social life to the logic of the market—to considerations of efficiency, utility, and profitability. While not all action can be efficient and calculable, neoliberal political rationality evaluates it in these terms, and as such, has become the basis for decision-making at all levels of society (Brown, 2005: 37–59; Munck, 2005: 61).

Alongside issues of state sovereignty and state-centered political power, Brown looks at the ways in which neoliberal states form subjects. Drawing from Foucault's lectures at the Collège de France, she identifies this relationship as a mode of *governmentality*: "techniques of governing that exceed and express state action and orchestrate the subject's conduct toward him- or herself." She points to neoliberalism's tendency to prefigure individuals as rational, calculating actors whose value is measured by their capacity to self-manage and assume responsibility for themselves, to "provide for their own needs and service their own ambitions" (Brown, 2005: 42–44). This model reduces and depoliticizes social life into series of individual pursuits and cost-benefit analyses, rather than toward mutual support, responsibility, and ideas of the good life as collectively defined. Nowhere has this trend shown itself more obviously than in Clinton's welfare reform act of 1996, appropriately named the "Personal Responsibility and Work Opportunity Reconciliation Act of 1996," which radically changed the welfare system designed by Keynes little more than a half a century before. The Act effectively ended welfare as an entitlement and replaced it with "workfare." In the United States, people in need could no longer receive public assistance unless they were working or actively looking for it, nor could they "take advantage" of the system for more than 60 months over the course of their lifetime. As Barbara Ehrenreich has pointed out, welfare reform relied heavily on public perceptions of welfare recipients as "lazy, promiscuous, government-dependent baby machines," encouraged by politicians and members of the media on a massive scale (Ehrenreich, 2004).

Neoliberalism posits human freedom and dignity as bases for democracy, against the threat of fascism, communism, and other kinds of state control, with an understanding of freedom as best realized through free market activity and private property rights. Despite claims to "small government" and its emphasis on democracy, however, Brown and other theorists have demonstrated how it relies heavily on state power and supranational financial institutions like the IMF to protect property rights, set monetary policy in times of crisis, and develop new markets (Brown, 2005: 37–59; Harvey, 2005: 5). In Chile in 1973, for example, the establishment of the Pinochet regime was achieved by way of a violent military coup, covertly facilitated by the U.S. government. Once installed, Pinochet reoriented the economy according to the whims of "the Chicago boys," Chilean economists at the University of Chicago in the 1950s trained in anti-communist strategy in Latin America. The economy was opened to foreign investment, state-owned enterprises sold to private companies, social welfare programs abolished, and property and capital gains taxes cut, against the backdrop of state repression against labor unions and left wing social movements (Colas, 2005: 75–76).

In other parts of the world, such as Thatcher's Britain and Reagan's U.S., neoliberalism relied less on force than on the consent of democratic electorates, facilitated by state actors. Thatcher's impressive dossier of economic reforms and accompanying ideological program, for example, involved dramatic appeals to the virtues of individual freedom and a redefinition of social problems, like unemployment and poverty, as issues of individual responsibility: "Economics are the method, but the object is to change the soul" (Harvey, 2005: 23). Her program of fiscal responsibility involved curbing trade union activity and privatizing public industries. She facilitated foreign investment and competition, which resulted in the transfer of domestic industries, like automobile manufacturing, shipbuilding, and steel, into foreign hands. She also cut deals with foreign and domestic entrepreneurs to sell off state owned industries, including airline, telecommunications, electricity, transportation, and energy services. Her privatization plans involved firing masses of employees to streamline operations and render state assets more attractive to buyers. In addition, much of the country's public housing was sold at low prices, feeding into the middle class dream of owning a home (Harvey, 2005: 61–62; George, 1999).

During this period, Paul Volker became head of the U.S. Federal Reserve. He crusaded against inflation by undoing fiscal policy, which resulted in a surge of unemployment and rise in interest rates that crippled debtor countries. Volker was one of the authors of the Reagan Administration's overhaul to the economy under the mantra of "Reaganomics," which involved fighting inflation by way of fiscal austerity, tax reductions and deregulation. Labor took major hits, including the landmark firing of 11,000 federal air traffic controllers who struck over wages, retirement benefits, and the length of the working week. Low taxation encouraged new investment and the development of new financial markets allowed many companies to move production to right-to-work states in the south or overseas to enjoy low labor costs. Reaganomics was abetted by an ideology that lauded the benefits of flexible work arrangements against the bureaucracy of labor unions, and saw unemployment as a result of low ambition and personal failure. According to Reagan, the economic ills of the 1970s could be cured through entrepreneurial activity, a rollback of government involvement in economic affairs, and tax breaks at the top of the income scale. Wealth would simply "trickle down" to the masses. But it didn't: the Reagan era saw dramatic increases in poverty rates and income inequality, and the Savings and Loan crisis, a by-product of deregulation, cost the U.S. an estimated $160 billion (DiFazio, 2006: 6, 131; Kloby, 2004: 54–86).

During the Reagan and Thatcher years, the World Bank and IMF experienced significant changes as well. The World Bank moved beyond small-scale lending and went into the business of making structural adjustment loans, which required IMF approval that often required strict austerity measures and market liberalization. When a member country needs an IMF loan, they must conform to IMF-determined economic reforms. The content of these reforms conceived at Bretton Woods and into the 1970s reflected a Keynesian approach that emphasized the role of the state in creating jobs and stabilizing markets, but in the 1980s this tendency was replaced by a free market approach to development known as the "Washington Consensus." The "Washington Consensus" referred to the seeming "consensus" among the IMF, World Bank, and

U.S. Treasury over issues related to the economic development and crisis management. More specifically, it signified their agreement to implement neoliberal practices around the world, including privatization of public services and industries on a massive scale, lowering trade barriers for foreign investment and competition, deregulating markets, and imposing extreme fiscal austerity (Palley, 2005: 25).

Despite their successes in implementing neoliberal reform on a massive scale, institutions like the WEF and World Bank continue to be targeted by protest movements around the world. Off the heels of early anti-IMF protests in the 1970s, an expansive complex of social movements emerged in the early 1990s to protest the detrimental effects of neoliberalism on a global scale and demand increased accountability from these and other supranational institutions. In some respects, the movements failed to move beyond protest and build alternative social and political institutions and programs that would garner appeal beyond the usual suspects. In other respects, the cycle of movements effectively disrupted the work of these organizations and exposed their abuses of power, perhaps setting the stage for criticisms of the war in Iraq and the Bush Administration's failed economic policy that have now entered the mainstream. There is no doubt that the movements' critique of neoliberalism is resonating among a nearly depleted American public now forced to "bailout" corrupt lending institutions who wildly benefitted from deregulation and financial speculation, like Enron in the 1990s.

The Globalization Movement and World Social Forum

The Globalization Movement, or GM, has often been called a "movement of movements" to capture the way in which it operated in a decentralized, horizontal. This global network consisted of indigenous peoples, human rights, feminist, and ecology movements; anarchists, socialists and communists; trade unions, and interfaith activists from a variety of backgrounds. The diverse constellation of actors was typically misidentified by neoliberal politicians, corporate leaders, and the press as the "anti-globalization movement," in part to (mis)represent the movements' analyses of neoliberal globalization as a critique of "progress," but also because some of the movements' affiliate groups argued for a strengthening of national sovereignty against the infiltration of supranational financial institutions in countries' domestic affairs. The "anti-globalization" label also reflected some of the movements' concerns over the spread of mass-produced consumer products from the United States that was in part responsible for declines in distinctly national forms of artistic production.

In an effort to combat neoliberals' pejorative use of the "anti-globalist" label, some activists and organizations resorted to the name "Global Justice Movement" to emphasize their orientation toward more egalitarian forms of globalization and social justice. Though popular, especially among NGOs, the title has proven to be less than inadequate for use as an umbrella term since the philosophical and ethical meaning of "justice" varies so significantly among movements' constituents. Inter-faith groups, for example, tend to derive their sense of justice from divine law and posit God as an ultimate authority. Others locate justice in a universal rule of law that they feel has been violated by the privileging of corporate interests and the subsequent uneven distribution of political power away from everyday people. These groups designate "civil society" and public opinion as representatives of justice, but also acknowledge the authority of legal structures and systems of civil and political rights. While these first two groups may welcome the "Global Justice Movement" title, others reject it entirely because they do not acknowledge states, nations, deities, or legal systems as legitimate authorities over social life or guarantors of freedom. Out of respect for these important differences, I use the term "Globalization Movement" or GM throughout this paper to emphasize the movements' common objectives to establish alternative, non-neoliberal forms of globalization that put "people before profits," respect the environment, and enable a freer flow of people, ideas, and cultural forms across legitimate borders.

The origins of the GM can be traced back to the anti-IMF riots of the 1970s in Peru, Liberia, Ghana, Jamaica, and Egypt. The "bread riots" in Egypt, for example, were a result of a drastic increases in the price of bread, a major staple in the Egyptian diet, due to U.S. and IMF-imposed trade policies against food subsidies (Global Exchange, 2001; Katsiaficas, 2001: 29–36; Critchfield, 1992). The Zapatista uprising against North American Free Trade Agreement (NAFTA) on January 1, 1994, the first day the agreement was passed into law, marked a decisive moment in the development of the GM. Against the backdrop of decades, really centuries, of peasant dislocations, the Mexican government repossessed settlement land in the Lacandon Jungle in the name of bioconservation; and, leading up to the signing of NAFTA in 1994, deregulated corn imports and protections on the price of coffee, which tanked the local economy. Shortly after, the Zapatistas—indigenous people of Chiapas—confronted the Mexican government, garnering widespread support among Mexicans as well as the international community (Castells, 1997: 72–81).

According to Naomi Klein, "the strategic victory of the Zapatistas was to insist that what was going on in Chiapas could not be written off as a narrow 'ethnic' or 'local' struggle—that it was universal. They did this by identifying their enemy not only as the Mexican state but as 'neoliberalism'" (Klein, 2002). Their broad, "universal" appeal, ability to rescale indigenous struggle in global terms, and clever use of the Internet not only spurred the *New York Times* to declare it the world's first "postmodern revolutionary movement," but provided a necessary spark for a linking of anti-neoliberal activism across national borders and local communities. For example, the Zapatistas called for a world meeting in 1996 to discuss common issues and tactics among anti-capitalist social movements. The meeting took place in Chiapas and attracted some 6,000 participants from over forty countries. Many of the same groups met again in Spain in 1997, where they drafted a set of organizational objectives for developing an international network of movements. Following the meeting, they coordinated the Global Days of Action, the first of which took place in 1998 during the World Trade Organization (WTO) Ministerial in Geneva, Switzerland. Tens of thousands of protestors participated in more than sixty demonstrations on five continents. Many of these same activists coordinated the Seattle protests in 1999, and subsequent protests in Quebec City and Genoa, which both attracted hundreds of thousands.

In addition to building a large-scale protest network, GM constituent groups met in 2001 in Porto Alegre, Brazil to form a "peoples" counter-summit to the World Economic Forum (WEF) in Davos, a premier meeting of the global elite. The WSF was a reaction to criticisms that the GM was elevating protest to the status of politics and failing to articulate social and political objectives beyond resistance and opposition. While the movement raised public awareness of the adverse effects of corporate globalization, critics on various parts of the political spectrum contended that it still appeared as a loose, incoherent assortment of local and regional struggles that were shortsighted and oftentimes short-lived. In response, the GM forged the WSF to complement its protest activities and counter neoliberalism's "There Is No Alternative" ethic with the positive project of formulating social and political alternatives, epitomized in the slogan "Another World is Possible." In essence, the WSF functioned as a premier meeting of the global left for the purpose of answering the fundamental question: When the Empire falls, what will take its place?

The WSF's organizational form—the "open space"—was derived from the GM's practice of "horizontal," non-hierarchical organizing, which attempted to avoid privileging any one participant group or individual and mitigate existing (and potential) inequalities among them by embracing difference rather than ignoring or suppressing it. The paradigm of the open space was based on organizers' desire to be as inclusive as possible—to create a physical and virtual space for "civil society" groups and movements opposed to neoliberal globalization to socialize, discuss their respective projects, debate alternative economic and political models, and develop decentralized direct action and advocacy networks. The open space process reflected movements' desires to create a free space for the development of alternative modes of globalization, not beholden to special interests, that could prefigure the political communities and social forms that the WSF and its constituents sought to create. Against the WEF and its focus on "economic" development, the WSF was billed as a "social" forum—an independent venue in which sociality would be privileged over private interests. Following this logic, the WSF was founded as a non-party and non-deliberative entity: WSF organizers sought to protect it from cooptation by political party, state, and corporate actors and assumed that the ideological diversity of its participants precluded its potential to operate as a unity and undertake deliberative and action-oriented functions without becoming hierarchical and coercive.

The geographic, political, and cultural diversity of the WSF and its capacity to accommodate difference are often attributed to the open space model and lauded as its greatest achievement. The open space has generated a significant amount of debate, however, over its effectiveness in accomplishing the Forum's anti-neoliberal agenda that reflects fundamental political divisions on the global left over questions of agency, social change, and political organization. While *political organization* often refers specifically to political parties, and *politics*, to the realm of the state, these concepts are treated throughout this paper in their broadest sense, as the ways in which people exercise power over each other in the pursuit of the good life, and the organizational means by which they collectively articulate their desires for freedom in terms of the existing power relations that shape their lives, their generations, and their collective histories.

The concept of *political organization*, and more specifically, the "party," was first theorized by classical Marxists in the early part of the 20th century, who were concerned with how to build a broad-based opposition to capitalism and develop a theory and organizational apparatus to guide the transition from capitalist to classless society. Despite the non-revolutionary character of the 21st century, the problem of how to build a mass movement and more egalitarian social and political structures remains a serious question for contemporary social and political movements, especially in light of debates over state sovereignty and the new power arrangements associated with globalization. In the context of the GM and WSF, activists continue to grapple with a broad range of theoretical and practical issues, but also, an important problematic identified by David Harvey (2005): in light of the left's failure to offer a vision of social justice that has adequately taken into account people's desires for individual freedom, what can contemporary movements do to meet the organizational demands of resistance while protecting the autonomy of their constituents and prefiguring a radically democratic society?

Within the context of the WSF, contests over political organization have taken form among three of the most prominent groups on the contemporary left—social and liberal democratic NGOs, anti-authoritarian (anarchist) social movements, and political parties. While these categories should be understood as "ideal types" in the Weberian sense—as an abstraction from which to draw comparisons and not a reproduction of the concrete reality of the WSF constituency—each group possesses a distinct political history, sets of power resources, and systems of ideas that tell a great deal about the repertoires of today's social movements, and the social and political environments in which they operate. These contests also demonstrate how the WSF as an institution both succeeded and failed in its charge to interconnect such disparate groups, and construct social and political alternatives to neoliberalism.

Non-Governmental Organizations

Non-Governmental Organizations (NGOs) continue to play an important role in the development of the GM and WSF. Many of them participated in the NGO Forums, which were set up alongside large-scale
meetings of the United Nations by NGO lobbyists (Keck and Sikkink,
1998). A London School of Economics (LSE) study suggests that a
significant number of the organizations that participated in the NGO
Forums may have migrated to the WSF. It reported a sharp increase
in the involvement of NGOs and other activists at "civil society" meetings with no corresponding "official summit," i.e., at local, regional and
the world social forum(s). The study also found that in 2005, social
forums—local, regional and global—accounted for 30 percent of all
"global civil society events," whereas parallel summits accounted for
26 percent and UN conferences, 9 percent. Moreover, it reported that
50 percent of respondents took part in a "global civil society event"
without a corresponding "official summit", while 37 percent attended
UN conferences—an increase from 12 percent in the early 1990s. These
data suggest that in 2004–2005, NGO attendance at the social forums
rose and may actually have replaced NGO Forums as the preferred
meeting venue (Pianta et al., 2005).

NGOs have also contributed significant financial and human resources
to the WSF since its inception. The Brazilian Association of Nongovernmental Organizations (ABONG) helped organize the first social
forums, and the WSF International and Organizing committees are
largely comprised of NGOs and international unions (Waterman, 2003).
NGO funders have included: ActionAid; Comité Catholique contre la
Faim et pour le Développement; Christian Aid; Enfants et developpe-
ment "Save the Children;" the Catholic Fund for Overseas Development;
Oxfam GB; Novib; and the Interchurch Organization for Development
Cooperation. Philanthropic non-governmental organizations, such
as the Ford, Rockefeller Brothers, and H. Boll foundations, provided
financial support over the years, except in 2004, when the WSF India
rejected funding from Ford. Ford supported India's Green Revolution
in the 1960s and 1970s, which laid the groundwork for neoliberal agricultural policies, including the privatization of water, seeds, and plants.
The CPI(M), an organizer of the 2004 WSF, contended that Ford and
the Green Revolution veered India away from undergoing communist
revolution (Jordan, 2004). Nonetheless, the Forum had enjoyed Ford
support in years prior.

NGOs that have participated in the WSF operate according to assumptions, functions, and with sets of power resources that are distinct from, and in contention with, other political actors, as well as each other. Debates over the future and function of the WSF, for example, reflect competing views regarding the ways in which problems, like poverty and uneven development, can best be solved by states, NGOs and market actors. These views correspond to differences among NGOs over issues of political organization and democratic practice.

Development and other mainstream NGOs represent a liberal democratic view of freedom and social change and they participate in the WSF with or without actually agreeing to its anti-neoliberal orientation. In some respects, the WSF Charter invites their participation and influence by advocating freedom from political organization and the responsibilities associated with collective decision-making, enabling liberal democratic groups to maintain their focus on issue-based projects at the behest of special interests. Progressive NGOs and social democrats, on the other hand, offer an alternative conception of the WSF that involves the collective regeneration of an independent public sphere aimed rendering market and state actors more accountable to everyday people. They seek to politicize the WSF by arguing for the development of state-run social welfare programs and a strengthening of civil society as a check on multinationals, states, and supranational institutions like the IMF and WTO. Liberals reject such proposals because they assume that the ideological diversity of the WSF constituency precludes its potential to undertake deliberative and action-oriented functions without becoming centralized, hierarchical, and coercive. This version of the "open space" reflects a concept of "openness" as a guarantee of participants' universal (equal) right to access, self-manage and represent themselves in the Forum. It also reflects an understanding of freedom as *freedom from* structure, rather than seeing organization as a way to foster individuals' *freedom to* collectively articulate their desires for change. Social democratic critics, on the other hand, argue that deliberation and other forms of political engagement would not necessarily compromise the "openness" of the space, and that the political fragmentation of the WSF constituency and its overall lack of coordination has stymied its potential to create alternative institutions and directly confront the neoliberal agents it opposes.

The liberal, laissez faire approach to organizing has also, not surprisingly, resulted in logistical difficulties. While most WSF participants point to the "unity through diversity" the WSF promotes and its festival-like atmosphere, others have expressed dissatisfaction at the chaotic, fragmentary nature of the event and the ways in which the open space has actually precluded the forging of inter-movement connections and networks that the WSF claims to facilitate. While no meeting of such a scale could go off without a hitch, without a sound methodology to guide participation and engage participants in the WSF's development, informal (and formal) hierarchies have emerged that helped create a culture of mistrust, especially with the influx of well-funded NGOs and political parties, and oversight committees' failure to make their proceedings more transparent, despite pleas since 2002. Recall Jo Freeman's (1972) famous essay, "The Tyranny of Structurelessness," which elucidates the drawbacks of such structurelessness and the contradictions and difficulties of implementing non-hierarchical, decentralized forms of organization at the practical level. While acknowledging the importance of the New Left's insistence on practicing freedom and democracy at all levels of social life, Freeman criticized laissez-faire organization for its tendency to "mask power." For Freeman, New Left structurelessness did not eliminate power hierarchies within organizations, but allowed for the development of informal elites and hierarchies that were all the worse for not being managed by explicit procedures or operational principles. Moreover, she argued, "structureless" organization was simply not effective in building political organization beyond "consciousness raising" rap groups. While such openness allowed for reflection and discussion in intimate, exploratory settings, it was not effective for goal-oriented projects or large assemblies.

Students for a Democratic Society (SDS) suffered a similar fate when faced with its own expansion and success. At the time of the Port Huron statement in 1962, SDS was firmly rooted in participatory, democratic, and loosely structured organization, but by the late 1960s, it became deeply concerned with questions of political organization in order to satisfy the imperatives of sustaining the movement and ensuring its spread beyond the university into trade unions and other communities. While the New Left maintained its healthy disdain for the authoritarian practices of the Old, its loose organizational structure could not sustain a popular base after the civil rights movement began to dissolve and Nixon abolished the draft (in 1970). Internal conflicts over organization and strategy split SDS along sectarian lines and a portion of its leadership went underground. A veteran of the movement, Stanley Aronowitz has argued that the New Left's lack of a centralized apparatus "lead to bureaucratization and worse, to the inevitable integration of the movement into the liberal mainstream," setting the stage for the movement's devolution into single-issue politics and losing a valuable opportunity to create a broad-based political organization of Left (Aronowitz, 2006).

Social democratic NGOs have been widely criticized in the WSF, albeit to a lesser degree than that of liberals, for their political organizational style and identification as constituents of "civil society." Unlike other groups in the WSF, both liberal and social democratic NGOs posit *civil society* as an antidote to state authority and site democratic freedom, different from Marxists and anarchists who understand civil society as an arm of the neoliberal, capitalist state. During WSF 2002, for example, a large coalition of Brazilian trade unionists widely disseminated an open letter arguing that "the politics of civil society obscure class differences that are critical to understanding the mechanisms underlying global capitalism and how it can be opposed" (Brazilian Trade Unionists, 2002). Other criticisms, from anarchists, autonomous social movements and anti-capitalist political parties contend that social democratic NGOs are beholden to moderate political agendas by warrant of their political relationships. They see the role of institutions like the WSF as informing and influencing states and corporate enterprises, but not as posing fundamental challenges to capitalism as a whole. Moreover, because they occupy leadership positions in WSF committees and have access to mainstream and progressive media, they are empowered to push forth their particular vision of social change without taking into account the political values and contributions of the more radical movements and individuals that politically charged the WSF in its early years.

Anti-Authoritarians

Anarchist-inspired groups in the GM have called themselves various names, including anti-authoritarians, autonomists, and horizontals, but they tend to share a common interest in building a new, participatory culture outside electoral, state, and other forms of conventional politics. Some seek to literally "smash the state," as well as the corporation, school, and other agents of social control, but most are more interested in movement building and challenging what they contend to be *illegitimate* forms of authority. Some of these groups and movements participated in the WSF in the early years to develop networks with other groups, but set up "autonomous spaces" precisely because they did not recognize the authority of WSF organizers.

What distinguishes these groups from others in the WSF (and beyond) is their belief that radical change, and ultimately, freedom and the good life, can be discovered through direct action and the development of cooperative projects and countercultural communities, and not through the realization of a predetermined revolutionary moment or participation in electoral processes, abstracted from the conditions of everyday life. They tend to link their anti-state and anti-capitalist critique of neoliberalism to practical, organizational issues and ethics, against the grain of organizers and large-scale NGOs that wanted the Forum to remain a neutral and apolitical space. They are also critical of progressive NGOs and social democratic groups that have sought to bolster nationally or internationally-sponsored social programs and political influence within legal structures and the electoral sphere. While these groups conceived of the WSF as a renewed public sphere that could function as a check on market actors, anti-authoritarians argued for more systemic change, inspired by the successes of the GM in challenging supranational institutions, like the World Bank, from the streets.

Because of their confrontational approach, anarchists, especially the black bloc, were an ongoing subject of controversy within the GM, especially among activists from liberal democratic NGOs, pacifists, and those associated with political parties and state officials. Some criticized them for escalating police violence and rendering fellow protesters vulnerable to attack, asserting that the black bloc "discredits the movement as a whole and that tactics should be decided democratically, not by small groups acting autonomously" (Epstein, 2001). They were also scrutinized by people outside the movement for the increased police presence they tended to attract during protest events, which, their critics contended, diverted public funds away from much needed social services. Perhaps the most serious criticism was waged after the anti-G8 protests in Genoa when Italian police installed undercover officers and neo-fascists into the demonstration, and, posing as black bloc protesters, vandalized cars and small businesses to foster a poor public image of the GM protesters and exacerbate divisions among them. Many people in the movement scorned the black bloc for its rogue tactics, which, they asserted, made it difficult to differentiate between them and police *provocateurs*, but more importantly, endangered the masses of people who were more interested in civil or social disobedience than in guerilla tactics.

Despite the controversies around the relatively small number of black blockers, many of the "new" anarchists[2] cite Italian Autonomist Marxism of the 1970s as a significant influence and have adopted its concept of autonomy, which understands freedom as a collective and cooperative phenomenon. Autonomia's anti-authoritarian political program involved a rejection of political parties and other centralized political apparatuses and advocated a loosely coordinated network of heterogeneous organizations and movements united by their commitment to the practice of autonomy from the state, political parties, trade unions, and other forms of mediation between them and the interests of capital. For autonomists, autonomy meant preserving the singularity of each person: a *freedom from* the influence of institutional mediations and false unities, and a *freedom to* engage in radical forms of democracy in constructing self-determined communities.

In the context of the WSF, anarchists and autonomists conceived of the open space as a place for the production of a commons, equating "openness" with independence from the interests of states and capital. For them, the open space could facilitate alternative forms of socio-economic relations—"fair" trade agreements, contemporary freedom schools, and other forms of mutual aid—run by self-coordinating communities that decided their own organizational social norms and values. Social democrats in the WSF tended to share anarchists' critique of neoliberal privatization and supranational financial institutions, but they did not reject capitalism entirely. Most of them focused on reforming capitalism toward a Keynesian compromise with capital and the state, rather than building alternative, DIY social and economic formations without state and corporate involvement. They did this in part because the idea of enacting change "from below" rather than change "from the middle" seemed unfeasible to many of them (Grubacic, 2005; Evans, 2005; Wainright, 2004; Jardim, 2004).

Despite the seemingly unrealistic nature of autonomist projects, however, especially in the United States, a surprising number of anarchist bookstores, magazines, recording groups, food cooperatives, concert

---

[2] For an excellent discussion of the "new anarchism," see Graeber, 2002. According to Graeber, "The very notion of direct action, with its rejection of a politics which appeals to governments to modify their behaviour, in favour of physical intervention against state power in a form that itself prefigures an alternative—all of this emerges directly from the libertarian tradition. Anarchism is the heart of the movement, its soul; the source of most of what's new and hopeful about it."

venues, and other social formations continue to flourish in locales around the world. In addition to establishing countercultural venues, anti-authoritarian groups engage in service provision campaigns that are informed by their belief that some things—water, food, and housing—should be understood as commons. The anarchist group, Food Not Bombs (FNB), for instance, was founded on an acknowledgement of food "as a right, not privilege." The first FNB was formed in Cambridge, Massachusetts in 1980 by anti-nuclear activists, but the network has grown to include hundreds of local chapters and has links to various groups like EarthFirst!, the Leonard Peltier Defense Committee, the Anarchist Black Cross, the Industrial Workers of the World (IWW), and several others. FNB chapters do not employ formal leaderships, nor is there a central FNB apparatus. They recover food that would otherwise be thrown out and serve fresh, vegetarian meals to hungry people free of charge. They serve food to anyone—in public places and protests, but also in areas decimated by natural disaster. For example, FNB served food to survivors of California earthquakes, S11 rescue workers, and victims of the Sri Lankan tsunami, as well as New Orleanians abandoned by the local and federal government in the aftermath of Hurricane Katrina (Food Not Bombs, 2008).

The social centers in Italy provide another case and point. Largely influenced by Autonomia, the social center movement began with activists in the 1970s who squatted abandoned buildings in various cities, usually on the outskirts or in industrial areas. The first wave of centers emerged amidst the shift from industrial to flexible forms of production that left vacant large stretches of cityscape in urban centers around the world. In Milan, industrial production gave way to an economy based on the finance, fashion, and service industries, that brought with them high rents and low wages, at least for those lucky enough to still have a job: between 1971 and 1989, 280,000 of the city's workers joined the ranks of the unemployed (Mudu, 2004). By 2004, however, over 250 social centers had been active in Italy over the years, ranging from large complexes like Rivolta in Marghera (outside of Venice) to small spaces in southern Italy, run by two or three people (Ibid.). The first social center, Leoncavallo, was occupied in Milan in 1975, but like many centers, has been closed and reopened over the years due to police pressure.

The common thread among social centers is a desire and effort to take back what neoliberalism has taken away. To that end, they offer an assortment of public services, including housing and documentation services for immigrants and homeless people, condom distribution for prostitutes, day care or housing for homeless children, counseling and other care giving for battered women, and many others. They also provide spaces for a variety of activities: concerts by popular bands, nightlife, art installations, theater, political meetings and conferences, radio and TV broadcasting, and spaces for activist organizing. While corporate music venues tend to charge high admission fees and the spaces themselves are highly regulated, social centers operate outside the coercive realm of corporations and the state, and inhabitants can essentially do as they please (in good faith), without drug crackdowns, age restrictions, and curfews. The low cost of concert admissions enables participation from a broader audience and proceeds are fed back into the centers.

Despite their anti-institutional character, about half of the social centers in Italy have acquired some degree of legal status, but not without controversy. Rivolta, for example, was occupied in 1996. An empty factory in the industrial town of Marghera, it was owned privately and slated to be sold and transformed into a large commercial area. After the space was squatted, the municipality decided, at the urging of sympathetic government officials in the Green and Democratic parties, to designate most of the space for "social use." The other half of the social centers in Italy remain unsanctioned and therefore, subject to enclosure. Legal status tends to be more difficult for those located in areas with higher price tags on real estate (like in Venice proper), and squatters who live and work in those spaces must remain on guard for police infiltration. Moreover, some of them view the sanctioned centers as less authentic in keeping with their antipathy to conventional political entities more generally, but a great many have learned how to use electoral politics to their advantage and use these open political spaces to reclaim their communities and create public venues.

Political Parties

Because of their affiliation with states, and association with coercive forms of power, political parties have been officially excluded from participation in the WSF. The impetus for the ban can be traced to the following factors: First, participants and organizers wanted to ensure that the domestic politics of any one locale did not take over the Forum or supplant its global character. Second, the ban was a response to the failures of left political parties to meet the needs of everyday people, but also because of their historical association with authoritarian and undemocratic regimes. Following the New Left, parties were viewed by constituents of the WSF and GM as sectarian, vanguardist, and generally antagonistic to the radically democratic politics for which they were fighting. Third, WSF participants and founders wanted to create a unique social space for movements and NGOs to build activist networks and bolster their political projects without becoming subsumed in electoral politics or electorally-based definitions of democratic practice.

Despite the ban, political parties played a prominent role in the WSF as key financial and organizational supporters of the process and a significant number of attendees were drawn from their ranks. The Brazilian Partido dos Trabalhadores (PT) or "Worker's Party," for example, hosted the event, and various communist and socialist party members around the world continue to participate regularly. In 2004, when the WSF moved to India, the ban was suspended and political parties played a prominent organizational role, especially members of the Communist Party of India (Marxist) (CPI(M)). Parties have also played a significant part in the development of local and regional social forums. The Austrian Social Forum, for example, attracted roughly 2,000 participants in 2002 and 2003 and was funded by the Green Party and municipal governments; the national German Social Forum was initiated and funded by the Rosa Luxemburg Foundation, the national foundation affiliated with the German Party of Democratic Socialism (PDS); the CPI(M) played a central role in the regional Asian Social Forum that led up to the 2004 WSF in India; and several of the social forums in Italy were funded by Communist and Green parties.

The European Social Forum (ESF) has also been funded by parties each year, but with varying degrees of controversy. The 2003 ESF in Paris, for example, involved French political parties, but only to a limited degree. The 2005 ESF in London, on the other hand, was dominated by the Socialist Workers Party (SWP) and Greater London Authority (GLA), the municipal government headed by Ken Livingston, which drew considerable criticism and protest. These trends date back to the first ESF in Florence in 2002, which was almost entirely sponsored by political parties and government officials. The idea to hold the 2002 ESF in Florence was initiated Claudio Martini, President of the Regional Administration and member of the Democratic Left Party, who attended the first WSF in Porto Alegre. Intimately tied to the local political apparatus in the region, the ESF was funded in part by the Region of Toscane, which also provided translation, housing for 5,000 people, and a fairly elaborate venue. Additional funding was provided by the Partido della Rifondazione Comunista and the SWP in Britain under the front group "Globalize Resistance" (which some activists called "Monopolize Resistance"). In addition to the influence of local parties, the event became a controversial political issue on the national level when Italian President Silvio Berlusconi publicly likened it to the violent, anti-G8 protests in Genoa (Treanor, 2002; Farrer, 2003).

Democratic socialist governments in the South America have also played a major role in the development of the WSF and anti-neoliberal resistance more generally. When Lula was first elected president in 2003, participants in the GM and WSF were wildly enthusiastic about what his administration would do to eradicate poverty and loosen the IMF's grip on Brazil and the rest of Latin America. Lula's party had direct ties to social movements in the country and the party's participatory budget program was lauded as a working case of direct democracy. A few years later, Hugo Chavez and the Fifth Republic Movement (MVR), engaged Venezuela in a "Bolivarian Revolution," joining Evo Morales and the Movimiento al Socialismo (MAS) in nationalizing various industries in their respective countries, including oil and gas, while claiming that "the worst enemy of humanity is U.S. capitalism."[3]

Contests over the involvement of political parties and statesmen in the WSF has been analyzed and debated from essentially three standpoints. First, political parties with limited (if any) electoral involvement (e.g., the SWP in Britain and other European, Indian and Latin American socialist and communist parties) tend to position parties as playing a vital role in the development of a worldwide anti-capitalist movement by providing tight-knit organization, a theoretical basis for understanding class struggle, and leadership to oversee the historical transition from capitalism to socialism. In some cases, they have been able to mobilize large numbers of people for electoral contests or demonstrations and are generally adept at organizing at the grassroots level. They clash, however, with anti-authoritarian groups because of their hierarchical structure, the dark legacy of socialist and communist parties in the Soviet Union and Eastern Europe, and the desire among today's activists to create a new movement culture, free of orthodoxy. Nonetheless, these parties play an important role in the WSF and the global left: the

---

[3] Statement by Bolivian President Evo Morales Ayma on September 24, 2007 during the UN meeting on Climate Change in New York.

SWP, International Socialist Organization (ISO), and International Action Center (IAC) have been extremely active in the global anti-Iraq war movement; the Rosa Luxemburg Foundation funded the German, European, and World Social Forums and supports research on their development (including research for this paper), and many parties were active in supporting local and regional social forums, such as the case in Austria, France, Italy, Greece, and India as well as various countries in Latin America.

Distinct from the first group are state officials and political parties with broad electoral appeal that occupy central roles in state apparatuses (and in the WSF), such as in Brazil and Venezuela, and wield a high degree of political power. Social democrats in the Forum and governmental institutions like the GLA should also be included in this group because of their direct ties to states and electoral parties. Participants in the WSF have been critical of these groups' involvement, but for the most part appear ambivalent. On the one hand, these activists tend to view states as non-representative and corrupt, and even left governments are accused of co-opting movements for political ends. On the other hand, WSF participants recognize the value not only of their support for the social forums, but of the broad variety of progressive policies and programs instituted in their respective countries that run counter to prevailing neoliberal social and economic models of development and political participation. The Brazilian PT, for example, enabled the development of participatory programs, including presiding over municipal budgets, that would otherwise be unthinkable in other countries, and fair trade agreements and redistribution programs in Venezuela and Bolivia are providing models for other countries in the region struggling to cope with the effects of IMF policies on their economies. Along with masses of anti-Bush protesters, these leaders and their parties have effectively lead a charge to disrupt trade agreements like the FTAA in the region, as evinced during Bush's visit to Argentina for the Summit of the Americas in November 2005 (Blanding, 2006).

The third group consists of those who call for a radical rethinking of the concept of the party and political organization itself. These theorists emphasize the importance of movements building their own political and cultural institutions autonomously from state and market actors, but do not dismiss the state and the electoral sphere entirely. Many of them have followed the Latin American shift to the left with great interest and look to Brazil's participatory budget process as a model for the "disarticulation" of states—i.e., the delegation of their control over public goods and services to democratic management by the people of the country—that appears more viable in the 21st century than political programs aimed at seizing or smashing the state (Menser, 2009: 251–271). In Italy, for example, roughly 50 percent of the social centers had entered into agreements with local governments or private land owners by 1998 and many of them are supported by political parties, including the Green Party, Rifondazione Comunista (the Communist Refoundation Party) or PRC, and the Party of Italian Communism (PdC). Otherwise the centers would require constant defense, which would leave little room for the other important activities. Following the Bolivian "water wars," the state began to share management of the water supply with public assemblies in order to prevent another wave of privatization, which had previously rendered water cost-prohibitive for much of the population (Ibid.). These are just two cases among many in which contemporary movements have reappropriated elements of state or corporate enterprise in order to secure a more democratic distribution of land and water resources.

Conclusion

Following the Zapatista call for a worldwide resistance, a regional network in the United States called the Direct Action Network (DAN) emerged to organize against institutions like the WTO and IMF and help build a broader movement against neoliberalism. DAN operated according to two key political organizational principles: First, in contrast to other groups' closed "inner circle" of decision-makers, DAN made use of consensus decision-making processes to prevent any one group from controlling the network and as an experiment in participatory democracy. Second, its structure consisted of autonomous affinity groups that acted as nodes in the larger, organized network or federation, rather than operating as a centralized organization with local affiliates that bore allegiance to a center. It made use of direct democratic procedures based on consensus process as a means to enable a noncoercive climate of egalitarianism and open participation. Each member of the network was encouraged to participate in discussions and decision-making on a relatively equal basis, governed by a cooperative, noncompetitive ethic.

DAN's modus operandi was less about an enforced movement toward some ideal state of affairs or support for a single project or politician than about linking heterogeneous groups with unique histories and producing stable interactions among them. While some of its constituent groups might have been opposed to the anarchist label, DAN abided by anarchist principles: it was non-coercive, non-hierarchical, decentralized and interested in maximizing the autonomy of affinity groups. It joined various movement struggles in major North American cities (most notably linking New York and San Francisco)—and overcame the problems associated with centralized organization by developing an action-oriented network that enabled participation and did not require them to adopt a unified program or party line. DAN demonstrated the effectiveness of loose network organization in staging mass demonstrations against the WTO in Seattle, which succeeded in disrupting the meetings, as well as in Washington, DC in 2000. Soon after it dissolved, new networks sprung up in its place to perform direct actions and civil disobedience against the second Iraq war (Doane et al., 2000).

In its early years, the WSF was particularly successful in bringing together people from a broad variety of social and ideological backgrounds to discover new forms of sociality and enable the same kind of globalization of movements that helped reshape local struggles in terms that moved beyond nationality and local specificity. It reinforced already nascent ideas regarding the global nature of many movements' local struggles and contributed to the appearance that the worldwide movement against neoliberalism had developed an institutional component. While the development of institutional alternatives may have been an overly ambitious charge for such a large and unwieldy event, its function in facilitating the underlying social relations that support radically democratic movements provided many activists with hope that alternatives to neoliberalism were indeed possible and that a significant number of people around the world were committed to waging such an opposition.

In its attempts to safeguard the meeting from the influence of states, corporations, and other potentially coercive entities, Forum organizers created a charter that defined the process as an "open space." But their conception of openness focused less on facilitating the interconnections and contests that enable the construction of new communities and forms of solidarity, than about avoiding structure and conflict at any cost. For many, the WSF came to symbolize a retreat from politics that actually inhibited debate among constituents over substantial political differences and invited participation from groups clearly not committed to opposing neoliberalism or understanding its underlying mechanisms. The WSF's reliance on spontaneity and loose framework, whereby groups and movements were essentially "on their own," only contributed to feelings that it had become "an end in itself" rather than a conduit of transnational activism. Defining openness as structurelessness in such a venue not only disabled democratic participation from its constituency, but it allowed informal hierarchies and power inequalities to flourish.

Anti-authoritarians have attempted to overcome these kinds of limitations by theorizing and developing practices that understand freedom as a capacity for social and political engagement. The GM and groups like the DAN developed participatory, coordinative structures that not only served as organizational bases for large-scale protest activities against the World Bank and IMF, but also enabled ongoing support networks for community-focused projects aimed at reclaiming common spaces. DAN's key insight lay in its ability to connect disparate parts of the fragmented left by focusing on democratic capacity building, including experiments with alternative forms of life based on mutual aid, against the prevailing logic of laissez-faire.

THE TECHNOCRATIZATION OF PROTEST: TRANSNATIONAL ADVOCACY ORGANIZATIONS AND THE WTO[1]

Kristen Hopewell

Introduction

The World Trade Organization (WTO), which is responsible for setting and enforcing the rules of the international trading system, has emerged as a major center of global economic governance and a key driver of neoliberal globalization. The WTO's rules govern not only trade, but also a number of other economic areas such as investment, services and intellectual property, and they have profound implications for a wide range of issues including human rights, poverty, development, the environment, labor and health. Concerns about the neoliberal policies of the WTO and the expansion of its authority have prompted an explosion of social movement activism over the last decade, captured most prominently in the massive street protests surrounding the 1999 Ministerial Meeting in Seattle.

The so-called 'Battle of Seattle' has become an icon of the global justice movement, a movement of protest against the program of neoliberal globalization advanced in large part by and through international economic institutions such as the WTO, International Monetary Fund (IMF) and World Bank. The emergence of this movement has generated considerable excitement in both academic and activist circles. It has been seen as a sign of an emerging transnational social movement or global civil society that could potentially democratize global governance, transform institutions like the WTO and reshape globalization by creating a new 'globalization-from-below', based on values such as democracy, inclusion, participation, justice and equity (Archibugi and Held 1995; Gill 2000; Scholte 2000; Kaldor 2000; Kaldor 2003; Sandbrook 2003; Falk 2003; Anheier 2004; O'Brien 2005; Evans 2005).

[1] This research was supported by the Social Sciences and Humanities Research Council of Canada (SSHRC), the Nonprofit and Public Management Center at the University of Michigan, and the RGK Center for Philanthropy and Community Service at the University of Texas-Austin.

Although there is considerable interest in the global justice movement, there have been surprisingly few empirical studies of how the
global justice movement is actually operating to influence supranational
policy-making, particularly in the case of the WTO. The existing literature on the relationship between the WTO and global civil society has
focused almost exclusively on the former half of the relationship rather
than the latter. Its emphasis has been on the WTO—theorizing what
form the WTO's relationship to civil society should take, examining
the WTO's efforts to engage with civil society and critiquing the measures it has put in place (see, for example, Howse and Nicolaidis 2001;
Scholte 2002; Mortensen 2003; Williams 2005; Wilkinson 2005)—while
paying less attention to what is going on in global civil society itself.
This literature has tended to take the WTO as the object of study and
to treat civil society as a given, leaving it largely unexamined. The result
is that very little is known about the actual dynamics of transnational
advocacy directed at the WTO. Where there has been attention to
transnational advocacy surrounding the WTO, it has focused on the
dramatic street protests at Seattle (Levi and Olson 2000; Gill 2000; Halliday 2000; Kaldor 2000; Smith 2002; Weissman 2003; Murphy 2004;
Murphy and Pfaff 2005), and we know comparatively little about what
has happened in the decade since then and about the contemporary
efforts of the global justice movement at the WTO.

This paper sets out to analyze the current dynamics of transnational
advocacy directed at the WTO, focusing specifically on transnational
advocacy organizations. By *transnational advocacy organizations*, I
refer to groups that transcend the boundaries of the individual nation-
state and work to influence policy at the supra-national level (at the
WTO, for example, these include organizations like Oxfam, Doctors
without Borders, Greenpeace, the Third World Network, and many
others). Transnational advocacy organizations have featured prominently within the global justice movement and in its struggle against
the WTO. Drawing on research involving in-depth interviews with
both transnational advocacy organizations and WTO policy-makers,
I examine the strategies of these organizations and the ways in which
they are engaging with and seeking to influence the WTO. I argue that
an important transformation is taking place in the dynamics of transnational advocacy as these organizations respond to the opportunities and
constraints they face at the WTO. Specifically, transnational advocacy
organizations are coming to rely increasingly on technical knowledge

and expertise as a key source of influence at the WTO. In effect, what is occurring is the 'technocratization' of transnational advocacy, in which these organizations are becoming progressively more technocratic in their approach to the WTO.

While the growing significance of technical expertise and rising prominence of 'experts' in states and international organizations has been extensively charted in the academic literature, I argue that this is driving a parallel process within the realm of transnational advocacy. This growing emphasis on technical sophistication has important implications for the dynamics of political advocacy and contestation in the realm of global economic governance. On the one hand, increased technical expertise and expert knowledge provide an important means for transnational advocacy organizations to gain legitimacy, authority and influence at the WTO. On the other hand, however, the emphasis on technical sophistication may also be reinforcing traditional patterns of exclusion in debates on trade, creating an inner tier of transnational advocacy organizations that are relatively privileged and an outer tier that is further marginalized from the center of power.

Transnational Advocacy Organizations and The WTO

The WTO is an intergovernmental organization, comprised of 153 member states, which was established in 1995 as a successor to the General Agreement on Tariffs and Trade (GATT). It is the central institutional framework for the management of international trade and its functions include: administering and implementing multilateral trade agreements, providing a forum for further trade negotiations, reviewing national trade policies, and administering dispute settlement. The WTO includes a small Geneva-based bureaucratic Secretariat which is charged with facilitating its work and providing technical and administrative assistance.

While its predecessor the GATT was a relatively weak organization, with limited power over its membership and primarily concerned with reducing tariffs, the establishment of the WTO initiated a major transformation in the world trading system (O'Brien and Williams 2004; Williams 2005; Mortensen 2006). This move involved both a deepening of the GATT and a dramatic expansion of the scope of trade rules into new areas including services, agriculture, textiles and apparel, intellectual property, investment, sanitary and phytosanitary measures, and technical barriers to trade. It also marked a significant shift in the trading regime away from simply reducing tariffs towards the development of rules with the potential to significantly impact domestic policies, institutional practices and regulations. This included a move towards policy harmonization, in areas such as subsidies, investment and services. In addition, the establishment of the WTO put in place a trade policy review mechanism and, perhaps most significantly, instituted a binding dispute settlement mechanism.

Since its inception, concerns about the neoliberal policies of the WTO and the growing scope of its power have generated considerable protest and resistance, under the broad label of the global justice movement. This diverse movement has raised questions about the effects of trade liberalization on areas such as human rights, inequality, the environment, labor standards and health and its potential conflicts with efforts to combat global poverty and foster economic and social development. It has also criticized the policy-making process at the WTO for being exclusionary, undemocratic, and lacking in transparency and accountability. Transnational advocacy organizations have played a prominent role within the global justice movement and in activism against the neoliberal policies of the WTO.

Many scholars have argued that the WTO suffers from a severe democratic deficit that calls its legitimacy into question (Mortensen 2003; Scholte 2002; Howse 2003b; Howse and Nicolaidis 2001; Kapoor 2004). The WTO has traditionally operated based on what Keohane and Nye (2001) call a "club model" of international cooperation, characterized by elite decision-making and hostility to direct stakeholder involvement of any kind. The WTO maintains a strongly entrenched "culture of secrecy" (Scholte 2004: 157) and it is exceptional among international organizations in the degree to which it has been closed to stakeholder participation in its activities (Howse 2003a). The closed and secretive nature of decision-making, combined with its growing authority, has prompted calls for greater democratic contestability and inclusion within the WTO. One of the key ways it is thought that the WTO can become more democratic is by improving and expanding its engagement with civil society (Esty 1998; Charnovitz 2000; Mortensen 2003; Kapoor 2004; Howse 2003a; Howse 2003b; Scholte 2004; Nanz and Steffek 2004).

Formally, consultation and cooperation with civil society are written into the very founding text of the WTO: the agreement establishing the WTO states that the organization should make "appropriate arrangements for consultation and cooperation with non-governmental organizations [NGOs]." While initially this stipulation was ignored, over time and in response to considerable pressure, the WTO has slowly put in place measures to facilitate greater access for civil society groups (Williams 2005). These initiatives were significantly ramped-up following the Seattle protests (Moore 2003; Wilkinson 2005). The WTO Secretariat now has several channels of contact with civil society organizations and the public: it allows accredited NGOs to attend Ministerial conferences (though in a highly restricted manner), provides briefings and receives representations from NGOs, organizes symposia and workshops with NGOs representatives, distributes position papers submitted by NGOs to WTO delegations, hosts online discussion forums and live 'chats' with the Director General, and disseminates information to the public through its website. Following a recent decision by the WTO appellate body, dispute settlement panels now also have the authority to accept, at their discretion, *amicus curiae* briefs submitted by civil society organizations.

It is important, however, not to overestimate the extent of interaction between the WTO and civil society. While the WTO has taken some steps towards greater openness, it still remains relatively closed to civil society engagement. The WTO remains the only major international organization without any formal mechanism for consulting with civil society organizations (Williams 2005). Moreover, the WTO uses the term 'non-governmental organization' to encompass essentially all non-state actors, such that the majority of the so-called 'NGOs' that it interacts with are in fact business and industry associations. The WTO also restricts access to NGOs that are able to attain official accreditation. The majority of the WTO's contact with civil society is limited to a small number of large, well-resourced NGOs, primarily based in the Global North and with offices in Geneva. Finally, it has been argued that the WTO has a bias towards associating with organizations that are more friendly to its policies and agenda (Wilkinson 2005).

The Rule of Technocrats

The growing importance of technical expertise and the rise of technocratic elites in government in recent decades has been extensively charted in the academic literature. A considerable body of research has shown the important role of technocrats—whether in states (Bruce 1985; Cheng and White 1990; Rigby 1991; Freeman 2002; Babb 2004; Teichman 2004; Chorev 2007) or international organizations like the WTO, IMF, and World Bank (Howse 2002; Teichman 2004; Xu 2005; Momani 2005)—in the wave of free-market reforms that occurred across the world over the last several decades. For technocrats, legitimacy derives from rationality, impartial objectivity, the appeal to scientific knowledge, and adherence to standards of a community of experts (Centeno 1993; Babb 2004). Their emphasis is on rational, 'objective' decision-making, with a belief in the superiority of professional and technical methodologies and paradigms (such as those of economics). Technocrats see themselves as 'beyond ideology', when in fact they subscribe to the ideology of rationalism, scientism and expertise.

The technocratic paradigm gives rise to faith in the rule of 'experts', as a supposedly "benign authority" (Freeman 2002), whose expertise places them in a superior position to identify the higher good of the whole and the policies needed to achieve it. This claim to the superiority of technocratic decision-making is accompanied by a dismissal of 'politics' as inefficient and possibly corruptive and a profound resistance or scepticism towards democratic forms of decision-making. In the interests of the common good, it is believed that certain issues should be removed from the political arena so that policies are not 'perverted' by political considerations and the undue influence of particular interests (Centeno 1993).

Much of the scholarly interest in the rise of technocracy in the state has come from concerns about its undemocratic implications. The technocratic paradigm works to transform political decisions into technical ones, depoliticizing issues by casting them as technical problems for managers and planners, rather than public, political matters (Ferguson 1990; Fraser 1992; Cooke 2004). This makes the state unresponsive to popular demands and can be used to deny populations a voice and a role in their own governance. As Centeno observes (1993: 318), "the mystique of expert knowledge can serve as a powerful obstacle to those who may wish to challenge the system... Those who wish to challenge the policies of such experts must engage them using the same professional discourse." Technocratic control can result in the exclusion of those not fluent in the expert languages and ultimately restrict policy debates to an exchange between technocrats.

Furthermore, technocratic claims to be pursuing a higher good are deeply questionable. At the very least, the nature and content of the 'common good' is an inherently political and contested question. Moreover, the very concept of a common good is itself problematic. As Nancy Fraser (1992: 131) argues, "when social arrangements operate to the systemic profit of some groups of people and to the systemic detriment of others, there are prima facie reasons for thinking that the postulation of a common good shared by exploiters and exploited may well be a mystification." In such circumstances, any claim to represent the common good must be regarded with suspicion. Technocratic claims to be pursuing the general, public good can serve to mask the specific interests behind them (Centeno 1993; Porter 1995; Babb 2004).

While the existing literature on technocratization has focused on states and international governance institutions, I argue that a parallel process is occurring within the realm of transnational advocacy. Driven by a process of coercive isomorphism (DiMaggio and Powell 1983), whereby organizations conform to the standards of powerful external actors, transnational advocacy organizations seeking to influence the highly technocratic WTO are increasingly coming to adopt its technocratic tendencies. Seeking to increase their chances of being heard at the WTO, transnational advocacy organizations find themselves in a position in which they must work to translate their positions and critiques into the language that is intelligible to trade policy-makers and into a form that will be taken seriously. In response to these constraints and in an effort to adapt to them, transnational advocacy organizations are increasingly coming to engage with the WTO on its own technocratic terms and in its own discourse.

Study Design and Methodology

The field of advocacy activities directed at the WTO is complex and multilayered: it encompasses both national and transnational organizations, efforts targeted at individual member states as well as the WTO as a whole, and (comparatively) well-resourced and institutionalized non-governmental organizations in addition to more informal popular movements. The analysis presented here focuses on transnational advocacy organizations with offices and staff in Geneva seeking to influence the WTO. Transnational advocacy organizations have been prominent actors in the global justice movement and the organizations in this core are, by and large, the most powerful, most visible, and most influential working on the WTO. These are the organizations, for example, that the media will typically go to when seeking a 'counter' perspective to balance out a news story on the WTO (Velthuis 2006), or even that the WTO itself will turn to when seeking a civil society 'representative' for a panel or event that it is organizing. This small group has by far the most extensive and sustained interaction with the WTO, and they are the WTO's principal contacts with civil society.

The study draws upon in-depth, semi-structured interviews (n = 13) with representatives of these transnational advocacy organizations and WTO trade policy-makers in Geneva. Interview respondents were selected to reflect the considerable breadth and diversity of transnational advocacy organizations working on the WTO (which include development, environment, labor, gender, health, agriculture and religious organizations). Policy-makers interviewed included both WTO Secretariat staff and member state delegates. Interviews varied in length from 45 minutes to two hours. This interview data has also been supplemented by the analysis of a wide range of written materials and documents, including WTO documents and materials pertaining to its relationship with civil society, as well as the materials produced by transnational advocacy organizations in their campaigns (including press releases, policy and position papers, websites and member communications.

Changing Dynamics of Transnational Advocacy at the WTO

Advocacy organizations face considerable challenges in seeking to influence the WTO, an elite-based and deeply technocratic institution. WTO delegates and officials, as Howse (2002: 98) observes, tend to understand trade in narrowly economic terms, divorced from political questions and normative disputes. At the core of the WTO's trade liberalization project is a fervent belief in the benefits of self-regulating markets. For WTO policy-makers, free trade is more efficient and produces higher aggregate incomes and thus is inherently in the interest of the common good. From this perspective, trade barriers and protectionism are seen as the result of government policy being captured by narrow special interest groups who profit from the rents they generate at the expense of the greater public good.[2] This view, not surprisingly, produces considerable suspicion of, and even hostility towards, democratic processes. Within the WTO, this has led to a privileging of the knowledge and authority of 'experts', and a resistance to what is seen as 'political' interference in trade policy-making. The result is a highly secretive culture of decision-making, including a major lack of transparency and great resistance to the public dissemination of information.

From the perspective of many WTO policy-makers, efforts by transnational advocacy organizations to influence the trading system are viewed with great suspicion. These actors—particularly if they voice any criticism of the WTO's trade liberalization agenda or challenge its fundamental assumptions—tend to be viewed as opportunistic 'special interest groups' who are either naïve, irrational or opportunistic. The general attitudes of WTO policy-makers towards social movement activism are evident in the comments of Secretariat officials:

> at the beginning the level of misunderstanding [amongst NGOs] was just about, well, sky-high. It was really almost 100%…there was kind of a visceral reaction against [the WTO]. And we had things like the Seattle schemozels and so forth—demonstrations of one kind or another, from people who basically believed it was a kind of a- well, believed it was all kinds of monstrous things.

> it wasn't our job [the WTO Secretariat's] to kind of jump into the debate and say 'no, we don't cause AIDS, um [laughs], and no, we're not the cause of most of the ills of the world, and no, we're not killing Indian farmers, and this is not our business, etc.'…If they're critical of it [the WTO], well that's their right, but at least they should know, what to criticize [laughs] and be correct in their assumptions when they're criticizing.

WTO policy-makers simply cannot make sense of many of the arguments being made by actors in the global justice movement, or their methods. In the first excerpt, we see an idea that civil society protest was a "visceral" reaction (rather, presumably, than one based on rea-

---

[2] An alternate perspective argues that trade liberalization does not always lead to higher aggregate incomes, and in fact some countries (often among the poorest and most vulnerable) are made worse-off from WTO trade agreements. Moreover, even trade economists acknowledge that trade liberalization always results in both winners and losers within a country—some groups are made better off and others made worse off—meaning that claims to a common good are inherently sucpect.

son), based on a lack of understanding of the WTO and the issues involved. In the second excerpt, the official laughs at the criticisms of the WTO that he attributes to civil society actors. Mike Moore, the former Director-General of the WTO, reveals similar sentiments in his autobiographical account of his tenure as head of the organization (Moore 2003). He describes transnational advocacy organizations in general as "uncharitable" "extremists" who "will always be unhappy" (134), suggests they are secretly funded by protectionists and interested primarily in "publicity stunts to raise funds and enlist new members" (199–200), and characterizes their criticism of the WTO as "disinformation" (107) and "cruel self-serving lies orchestrated by selfish observers and self-appointed critics who need to maintain the rage of their supporters to raise funds to stay in business and on the front pages" (134). These statements are indicative of the considerable level of resistance that transnational advocacy organizations face in seeking to deal with policy-makers.

This reality is not lost on transnational advocacy organizations, who are keenly aware of the dismissive, derisive, and even hostile attitudes of trade policy-makers towards civil society actors. Respondents from these organizations see themselves as battling the tendency of WTO policy-makers to view advocacy organizations as "crazy" "trouble-makers". They fear that policy-makers will see them as "ignorant" and "stupid" with "no idea what they're talking about" and as unable to "understand the technical details and political realities of these talks". They struggle against the fact that policy-makers often do not "take them seriously". One respondent, for example, an independent consultant and technical expert who had done a study for a transnational advocacy organization, expressed concern that this connection might damage his professional reputation in the eyes of the policy community. Within this context, representatives of transnational advocacy organizations believe they are highly "stigmatized" and "carrying a lot of baggage" in representing their organizations and attempting to engage with the WTO.

Faced with the negative attitudes of trade policy-makers towards civil society protest, transnational advocacy organizations find themselves in an extremely difficult position in trying to influence the WTO. This has created pressure for organizations to differentiate themselves from the negative image that policy-makers hold of advocacy organizations, in order to have any chance of getting the ear of those policy-makers. This effort at differentiation is evident in the following statement from a representative of a transnational advocacy organization:

I can't speak for the NGO community, though, because I'm like a special animal, in that I'm never protesting, I'm wearing a suit when I go, I'm quite reasonable and nice, you know. There are some other NGOs who are maybe perceived as more troublemakers, or that kind of thing…there's differences in NGOs.

The respondent actively works to distance herself and her organization from "other NGOs" and their tactics, in order to gain legitimacy. The way in which she seeks to define herself is striking, particularly in relation to the previous statements of policy-makers: the WTO officials decry protests ("the Seattle schemozels" and "demonstrations of one kind or another")—this respondent indicates that she never protests, wears a suit, and is not like those organizations that are "troublemakers"; the officials decry the "level of misunderstanding" amongst their civil society critics and laugh at the unreasonableness of their concerns—she stresses that she is "reasonable" and "nice". There is clearly an interplay between the attitudes and standards set by policy-makers and how these transnational advocacy organizations are working to define themselves.

Transnational advocacy organizations are forced to wage a constant struggle for credibility and legitimacy—as they put it, "to be taken seriously"—in the eyes of trade policy-makers. The issue of 'seriousness' shows up repeatedly in the responses of advocacy organization representatives. They stress how essential to their success it is that they be "taken seriously…and that you are considered a serious partner, serious discussant." 'Seriousness' is a major value in the expert-based community of trade bureaucrats and policy-makers and seen as an indicator of one's legitimacy to contribute to trade policy discussions. For transnational advocacy organizations operating in the highly technocratic environment of the WTO, a key measures of 'seriousness' is expertise—technical knowledge, research and policy capacity. Respondents stressed the importance of attention to "good policy research and sound analysis" when dealing with policy-makers in Geneva. It is essential, they indicated, to be "armed with facts and data, and logical arguments that make sense and are well-substantiated", "well-prepared, well-researched", "fully briefed", and to "know your stuff" and show "sophistication" in your analysis.

Advocacy organization representatives consistently reported that their technical expertise and capacity have increased significantly in recent years. In the context of the WTO, this means sophisticated knowledge of trade law, economics and the workings of the WTO; the capacity to engage with complicated WTO rules, legal texts, and negotiating documents and to do legal and economic analyses of them; and the ability to formulate one's intervention in the highly technical language of trade bureaucrats, usually in the form of concrete policy proposals relevant to the current policy issues and debates within negotiations or dispute settlement. In the words of one respondent:

> initially when we were starting to work on this we weren't as knowledgeable about the technical details as we would like to be... But when countries started looking to us and others started looking to us for technical capacity, we had the name, people thought to look to us, and we had managed to create the capacity as well. I think increasingly over the last four years we've come to be an organization that's seen as capable of doing that kind of analysis and technical support.

The growing technical capacity and expertise of this core group of transnational advocacy organizations in Geneva is noted approvingly by trade policy-makers. According to one Secretariat official:

> we look at the kind of debates that are out there from non-state actors, so whether they're real informed debates or they're not. We've seen a great improvement from the Seattle time when it was just outcry against globalization and the WTO was just depicted as one of the, you know, agents of- and people didn't really understand what it's all about... they didn't really understand the benefits of the system... So from that point of view, in terms of the Geneva-based crew [of NGOs], I think we've improved a lot.

This was echoed by a second official:

> I think they have [improved] quite a lot... Because if NGOs have a more informed debate and undertake research that is sound, I mean, the more they are going to be able to help members as well, because... the more informed they are, the more sense that their discussion and papers and proposals etcetera make, they have a greater chance of succeeding in the future. I think it's definitely an improvement... I think the dialogue is really important and to keep it going and make sure it's informed, it's professional, and it's substantive. I mean, otherwise, what's the point then? And they have become a lot more sophisticated in terms of their understanding of the WTO and their views on the system as a whole. I think it's certainly improved.

This finding is consistent with another recent study that also noted an increase in research, expertise and policy capacity amongst civil society organizations engaged in advocacy on trade issues (Mably 2006).

Moving towards greater research capacity and technical expertise is considered essential for transnational advocacy organizations to gain credibility and to prove "that the issues [they] are trying to deal with are real ones". As one respondent explained, if a representative from an advocacy organization is:

> not fully briefed and they rely a lot on the rhetoric and the more broad arguments…that's received less well by policy-makers, because they're like 'don't waste my time [Organization X]', you know. And people love when that happens—the negotiators—because the next time you hear about them talking about us, or the meeting they had with us, including me or other people, they'll be like, 'oh god, [Organization X] was in here the other day, ha-ha-ha, telling me this, this, and this, they're so full of crap'.

Similarly, in speaking of trade policy-makers' negative attitudes towards NGOs, one respondent said:

> And that's changing. That's changed over the last year and a half, maybe two years. And I think it's changed as NGOs have gotten a little more sophisticated in their analysis and done a better job of toning down the rhetoric and replacing it with research.

Interestingly, many respondents made this distinction and comparison between "rhetoric" and "research". As here, they often appeared to be indicating a certain amount of pride in their ability to engage in "sophisticated" research and analysis, rather than just "rhetoric".

Part of demonstrating "expertise" is speaking the language of trade policy. Transnational advocacy organizations indicate that they feel they have to adopt this language, because otherwise they "look stupid" and they "look like they don't know what they're talking about". As one respondent stated:

> That's part of what I've been talking about with playing on the technical level, making proposals. This has been a real challenge for us because if you look back at the trade language, the language in our report when we launched [our trade campaign], I mean I looked at the agriculture recommendations the other day and…I was like, what, god, I've come so far in five years, it's unreal. And we've had to make that shift.

These organizations are not considered credible unless they speak the technical language of trade, and without this they cannot get trade policy-makers to engage with them.

> when you tell [national] affiliates 'well, lobby your government on trade' and they knock on the door and they say 'well, we do not like what you are negotiating because it will be bad for our employment and our working condition and our jobs' then the government- you know, they all

> look at them and say 'yeah, well, maybe you should talk to the Ministry of Labor…we understand but…' So you won't get a real engagement if you don't talk the language.

Adopting the specialized language of trade bureaucrats and gaining technical expertise provides an important means for transnational advocacy organizations to gain credibility and engage with policy-makers at the WTO.

Furthermore, in addition to being a source of legitimacy, technical expertise has itself emerged as an important source of influence for many transnational advocacy organizations. In a highly technocratic setting like the WTO, expertise is a form of power. Policy-makers at times lack specific information or expertise (this is particularly acute in the case of developing countries at the WTO, many of which are severely under-resourced, but can also apply to developed countries), which creates a demand that can be filled by transnational advocacy organizations. In these circumstances, their expertise can provide an important channel of influence.

It is well-known, for example, that Oxfam, a major development NGO and one of the most influential transnational advocacy organizations working on the WTO, uses the trade-policy expertise it has developed to work closely with and advise a number of developing countries at the WTO. Similarly, a transnational environmental advocacy organization has "been advising Switzerland and part of the EU on what to do about the negotiations on multilateral environmental agreements. That's directly related to the negotiations and thinking about proposals that could be put forth, etc…. very specific." The idea is that transnational advocacy organizations can *offer* something to delegates—they can offer something that delegates want, something of use to them. But there are very set parameters around this:

> Delegates know who they want to hear from. The type of people [they are interested in speaking to] are normally quite specialized—either technically or legally—they're not advocacy officers or public relations people, they are a lawyer or technical expert who happens to be working for a particular NGO. Delegates are not looking for positions or statements. They're looking for technical or legal inputs.

Transnational advocacy organizations are more likely to increase their access to policy-makers by de-emphasizing advocacy and instead emphasizing their specialist research, policy, and technical capacity.

One of the key tactics transnational advocacy organizations employ in an effort to use their expertise as a source of influence is to hold events such expert workshops, forums, and dialogues that draw the participation of trade-policy makers. Attendance from trade policy-makers at these events "is quite good actually. It depends, but they know which are the good experts and they take advantage of the fact that they're there." As one respondent explained:

> I think the value added is that you bring a lot of new ideas to the table. Usually we receive we've found a very high degree of interest [for the events we organize]—both among developed as well as developing countries. And also what we try to do is bring new thinking on the table, so we try to bring new experts, new research. So they're always keen to hear all about it.

For many transnational advocacy organizations in Geneva, this is a key means by which they attempt to draw the attention of policy-makers to the issues and perspective they are advocating. There is strong pressure for advocacy organizations to make their work "policy-relevant"; that is, relevant to the existing and current debates taking place within the WTO. By being "useful" to trade policy-makers, they gain access and the potential for influence.

Pressures on transnational advocacy organizations are compounded by the very closed environment of the WTO, where there are no formal channels for the participation of civil society and trade deliberations are highly secretive. In this context, developing and maintaining relationships with trade policy-makers becomes extremely important for these organizations. These personal relationships with WTO delegates and officials are critical for transnational advocacy organizations: they are generally the sole source of up-to-date information on the current state of the negotiations, a vital source of technical information, and provide direct access to policy-makers and therefore an important channel of influence. As one respondent stated:

> Yeah, it's all relationships. Everything is relationships. And that's why you have to be careful what you say, who you attribute what you say to, how you present yourself, all that stuff. It's very personal relationship based here, very diplomacy-oriented. Everything here is relationship-building.

However, while transnational advocacy organizations are heavily reliant on the personal relationships they cultivate with trade policy-makers, those policy-makers can be defensive and highly sensitive to critique.

What often happens unfortunately is delegates just get hit by this stuff—
you know, you're a bad delegate, you're a nasty trade negotiator, because
blah-blah-blah. So they're obviously defensive about it.

When we're critical of the WTO, that is felt as criticism of the hard work
of these smart people who work there. They're very easily offended. And
the rich country negotiators too. Like we did an analysis of the US ag
[agriculture] proposal...and they were so aghast that we said it was smoke
and mirrors and nothing was really on the table and that kind of stuff,
that they even felt that they should call us up and be like '[name], why
did you say that? We need a meeting. We're going to have a meeting'.

This creates a paradoxical 'Catch-22' situation for transnational advocacy organizations: critique is a vital part of their advocacy work on
trade policy, and yet to engage in critique threatens the relationships
they must cultivate with policy-makers in order to carry out their
advocacy work.

It is clear that transnational advocacy organizations are fighting an
up-hill battle in their effort to influence trade-policy deliberations at
the WTO. They are operating in an environment in which their target
is a highly technocratic group of bureaucrats, who view trade policy
in technical, legal and economistic terms and are generally hostile or
dismissive of advocacy organizations. Due to the absence of formal
channels between the WTO and civil society, they are also greatly
dependent on cultivating personal relationships with policy-makers.
Within this context, the ability to demonstrate sophisticated technical
expertise and marshal arguments in the complex professional language
of the WTO provides transnational advocacy organizations with a key
source of credibility and legitimacy, as well as a source of access and
influence.

In the words of one respondent, for an organization to have a chance
of being successful in influencing the WTO, they need to "transition
into a more serious inside-player role". However not all actors within
the global justice movement are equally well-equipped (or willing)
to adapt to the technocratic standards of the WTO and assume this
"insider" role. The existence of "insiders" means there must also be
"outsiders". As another respondent stated, advocacy organizations that
want to function effectively in Geneva have:

really got to invest. Which means you've got to open an office here,
you've got to pay these horrendous salaries and everything because living here is so expensive and you've really got to...get up to speed on
the technicalities—you know, you've got to be able to talk to delegates

at their level. And that's good for some NGOs and civil society groups and not good for others. You know, it depends what you want to do as an NGO...I can see that if you're not in Geneva and you're not able to make that investment, it must seem like a brick wall—very difficult to get your point of view across. And one of the reasons it's difficult to get your point of view across is that, if you're not here, your point of view may very often- it may be well-informed from where you are, but it may be badly informed from where the delegates are...you don't actually have an idea of what's useful here.

Groups who want to influence the WTO face serious constraints: they must formulate their interventions in the highly technical language of trade law and economics and in a way that is relevant to the current debates amongst policy-makers and "useful" to them. Those actors that want to influence the WTO but who cannot or will not adapt to the technocratic standards of policy-makers in Geneva face a "brick wall".

The privileging of technical expertise effectively creates two-tiers of transnational advocacy organizations—those with the ability to "play on a technical level" and "to talk to delegates at their level", and those without. While the former are primarily drawn from the core group of technically-savvy, Geneva-based organizations, the latter are much more likely to be organizations that are based in the Global South, those with fewer organizational, technical and financial resources, and often those that are more radical. The core group of technically-savvy, Geneva-based transnational advocacy organizations form an elite within the global justice movement: they enjoy greater access to policy-makers, greater legitimacy and greater credibility. The result is that this inner-circle of transnational advocacy organizations are drawn closer to the center of power, while an outer-circle of organizations and more informal social movements, that either lack this technical capacity or refuse to engage along these lines, are further distanced and excluded from the center of power and decision-making.

Throughout the responses of the transnational advocacy organiza-tion representatives, we see evidence that they are implicitly adopting the WTO's standards of judgment—in the distinction frequently made between "research" and "rhetoric", for example, in which sophisticated research is seen as valuable and prestigious, juxtaposed against "mere rhetoric" which is derided; in the way they emphasize the value of 'seriousness'; and in the importance they place on technical expertise. These actors are taking for granted and failing to problematize the WTO's standards of legitimacy: if someone lacks the ability to articulate their position in the professional language of trade bureaucrats and to back it with their specialized techniques of research and analysis, then that position is judged less valid. These are signs that transnational advocacy organizations are accepting and assimilating the technocratic paradigm of the WTO. Their own power is enhanced considerably by their ability to work successfully within this paradigm, enabling them to increase their access, authority and influence. But this paradigm is at the heart of the WTO's exclusionary and undemocratic tendencies. In accepting rather than challenging the privileging of expert knowledge at the WTO and staking their own claim to authority on their growing expertise, transnational advocacy organizations legitimate and further entrench a system that excludes those not fluent in the expert languages and techniques.

Conclusion

Transnational advocacy directed at the multilateral trading system is a relatively new phenomenon, occurring for the most part only since the mid-1990s and gathering momentum around the time of the Seattle Ministerial in 1999. The evidence collected in this study suggests that how transnational advocacy organizations *do* advocacy directed at the WTO—that is, their strategies and how they formulate their critique—and how they relate to the WTO has not been static during this time. Rather, it has been changing in important ways as these organizations respond to the constraints they face in targeting a highly technocratic institution like WTO. Transnational advocacy organizations are becoming progressively more technocratic in their approach to the WTO, increasingly relying on sophisticated technical expertise and expert knowledge as a key source of legitimacy, authority and influence. The more these organizations can speak in the language of the WTO and marshal its techniques of justification, the better the reception they receive from policy-makers and the closer they are able to get to the center of power.

However, while the growing emphasis on expertise and technical sophistication amongst transnational advocacy organizations is increasing their access and influence at the WTO, it also serves to reinforce traditional patterns of exclusion in debates on trade. There has been considerable excitement in the literature about the prospects for the global justice movement to democratize global governance institutions like the WTO, challenging their practices of elite-based decision-making, marginalization and exclusion. But there is a real danger that in attempting to adapt to the constraints they face at the WTO, transnational advocacy organizations may in fact be reinforcing some of its un democratic tendencies. Those organizations that are able to successfully conform to the WTO's standards of technocratic expertise increase their access, authority and influence with policy-makers, but in the process they implicitly provide support and legitimation for the dominant paradigm of technocratic control that restricts participation in debates on trade to those in possession of expert knowledge. Rather than challenging the notion that the WTO is the proper domain of experts and that expertise is a legitimate criteria for participation in trade policy debates, they become complicit in a system that marginalizes and excludes those actors who cannot articulate their concerns and critique in the technically sophisticated language of the WTO. Going forward then, a major objective for transnational advocacy organizations seeking to contest the WTO's neoliberal agenda and democratize its trade policy-making processes should be to find ways to engage with the WTO that challenge rather than reinforce its existing patterns of exclusion.

The study presented here has focused on transnational advocacy organizations operating in Geneva. These are the core actors engaged in advocacy directed at the WTO—by far the most active, the most visible, and the most influential, with the greatest contact with the WTO. The results of this research point to an important transformation occurring amongst these organizations and suggest the need for further study in this area. Additional research involving the more peripheral actors seeking to influence the WTO—such as the more marginalized, non-Geneva-based transnational advocacy organizations, as well as national-level organizations and more informal popular movements—would be of great value in furthering our understanding of the changing dynamics of advocacy and contestation within the realm of trade policy. Such research could shed light on the relationship between these different actors engaged in advocacy directed at the WTO (particularly between the core and periphery of advocacy organizations), how the latter are being affected by the changes occurring amongst the Geneva-based organizations, whether they too feel similar pressures to formulate their concerns and critique in the technical methods and language of the WTO, and how they are responding.

PART THREE

POWER AND RESISTANCE IN LATIN AMERICA

EMERGING EMANCIPATORY PROCESSES IN LATIN AMERICA

Ximena de la Barra and R. A. Dello Buono

Latin America of the early 21st century is struggling in a world that craves its natural resources and remains forever perched to capture the fruits of its working people. The majority of Latin Americans have had to endure either overt US interventionism or military dictatorship, or both, at some point during the latter half of the 20th century. The wave of military dictatorships and authoritarian civilian governments that swept the region was supported by the World Bank and International Monetary Fund (IMF), whose main shareholder is the United States. So-called cooperation agencies such as the United States Agency for International Development (USAID) and the National Endowment for Democracy (NED) have continuously operated as agencies of imperial interventionism, actively working to counter the struggles being waged by popular sectors.

In seeking to enhance the US position within the new global alignment emerging from the Cold War, the neoliberal Washington Consensus sought to consolidate access to cheap natural resources and raw materials from the region. Over its lifespan, it showed increasing emphasis on energy and in capitalizing upon its domination over information and technology. The initial installation of the "Consensus" was enabled by the repressive power of military dictatorships. The dictatorships focused their fury upon the most advanced focal points of the region's popular forces. Once Latin American countries were forced into debt, however, these dictatorships were no longer essential to Washington for imposing its policies.

The return to civilian rule towards the end of the century yielded low intensity democracies, propped up in part by faulty electoral mechanisms that helped pave the way for neoliberal civilian regimes to complete and deepen the installation of neoliberal policies. A complex and thoroughly corrupt partnership of elites, both in and outside of the region, worked in collusion to expand the scope of anti-democratic practices in support of transnational interests and the plunder of regional resources.

Continued pressure by International Financial Institutions (IFIs) and international cooperation agencies resulted in the imposition of fundamental policy changes that further usurped national sovereignty. These mechanisms ensured that instead of addressing pressing development needs, "development policy" could effectively continue to line the pockets of the North. The continued willingness of southern elites to stay in this game can only be explained by complicity and self-interest. Since the original prescription contained in the Washington Consensus proved incapable of securing total domination, the response was to impose even more orthodox neoliberal formulas in order to eradicate the "accumulated statist distortions of the past."

An unending mantra of free trade to encourage growth helped support the cause of expropriating national states from essential decision-making, placing them in the hands of non-democratic, supranational financial institutions, transnational enterprises and arbitration tribunals outside the reach of national accountability. Politics became overpowered by economics and old-style politicians by technocrats at the service of foreign capital interests. National sovereignty over the main economic, social and environmental issues was systematically dismantled. The process continued to evolve into a larger, regional strategy to implant neoliberal principles at the constitutional level so as to prevent any return to national sovereignty, keeping all key economic policies perpetually in the hands of international financial institutions.

In summary, the civil successor regimes that brought "democracy" back in force presided over a "premeditated immiseration." Many of the economic activities that previously spawned traditional labor organizations and had provided the social bases for reformist political parties remained crippled. Sharp rises in poverty, malnutrition, diminished basic services, environmental contamination and increased social disparities fueled migration and turned Latin America into the undisputed champion of social inequality among all world regions. The decline in legitimacy of the liberal democratic state and its neoliberal policies reached far and wide, extending to the decline of the region's political parties, including even many of those claiming to espouse a progressive or leftist platform.

At the turn of the century, however, neoliberalism as a monolithic model of development in Latin America had begun to fall into a deep crisis. Fueled by a combination of powerful structural forces, including a decline of US hegemony, impressive social movement mobilizations and significant electoral shifts to the left, crises of governability appeared in one country after another. An eroding public faith and a drastic decline of support for representative democracy, particularly in its traditional presidential form, began to set in. Taken together, these developments marked the beginning of the end of neoliberal ideological hegemony.

New alternatives to the fading "Washington Consensus" have emerged in Latin America, falling mainly into two distinct camps. On one side, there are elite-led attempts to formulate a "kinder, gentler" neoliberal model under the argument that there is no other practical alternative. In the other camp are societies that have experienced far-reaching, popular upsurges that have more decisively rejected neoliberal programs. In these cases, various kinds of mass actions have taken place, deposing elected political leaders who have betrayed the public trust, defending popular governments against reactionary power grabs and coup attempts, and holding popular referendums designed to further empower popular leaders.

Social Movements Push the Envelope

The architects of the Washington Consensus underestimated the capacity of Latin Americans to regroup and reorganize their struggle for national and regional sovereignty, just as they overestimated the ability of neoliberalism to maintain its legitimacy. New forms of popular opposition eventually emerged and various parties of the left and the centre-left have managed to capitalize upon this upsurge.

Especially strong in the early phase of re-awakening were movements demanding "No to the utility price hikes!," "No to privatization!," "No to Deforestation," "No to NAFTA!,"[1] "No to the IMF!," "No to FTAA,"[2] and similar protests. These campaigns involved various "____-less" movements, such as the homeless, jobless, landless, those lacking full citizenship, and others who were receiving the brunt of neoliberalism's assault on the social safety net. At the same time, the struggles of "nation-less" indigenous peoples have energetically joined in these protests, emphasizing the predatory practices of global capital in protecting their ancestral rights and natural environment.

---

[1] North American Free Trade Agreement.
[2] Free Trade Area of the Americas.

Over the course of time, these social movements tended towards consolidation into regional networks of inter-sectoral umbrella groups opposed to the neoliberal model. These broad movements gradually favored the formation of "Yes to...!" movements, yielding new forms of popular participation including demands for constitutional assemblies, the (re-)nationalization of natural resources, people's referendums, clamors for direct participation in public budgets, and a broad insistence upon playing a role in decision-making on larger regional issues such as the presence of foreign military bases and the commercialization of natural resources.

The movement that catapulted Hugo Chávez to power and the dramatic political changes that ensued perhaps best illustrate the powerful transformative potential of social mobilization once it is linked to a revolutionary state committed to fundamental social change. The scene proved to be ripe there for the emergence of new forms of participatory democracy and an alternative emancipatory development agenda centered on the recovery of sovereignty at all levels. The struggle in Venezuela and elsewhere continues to seek a successful articulation of inter-sectorial social movements and political parties capable of challenging, capturing and sustaining popular and democratic state authorities.

In various countries, the creation of electoral party coalitions has proved able to win national elections. The existence of progressive regimes in the region has on the one hand helped strengthen the expansion of alternative social movements, much to the chagrin of their reactionary neighbors, while on the other hand, has usually invited the response of US interventionism. Where reactionary regimes have remained in place, progressive social movements have suffered their share of setbacks at the hands of the state apparatus bent on an expansive criminalization of social protest. The popular challenge to neoliberalism has also been stymied by the cumulative effect of a relentless ideological barrage spearheaded by the region's elite and transnational controlled mass media.

In spite of the setbacks, an overall hopeful trend has begun to emerge in the region, suggesting that the end of neoliberalism may well be in sight. In its most developed form, the dynamic emancipatory process in place in Cuba, Venezuela and Bolivia is being sustained by mass mobilization and other favorable elements, not the least of which includes mutual support of each other via increased solidarity and new forms of intra-regional cooperation.

While re-nationalization was put on the national agenda in Venezuela and Bolivia, the brakes were slammed on privatization in other countries and demands for greater social spending have placed the social debt on the national policy making table for greater scrutiny. Brazil, Uruguay, Ecuador, and Nicaragua have all experienced electoral shifts towards the left, although the emancipatory agenda is either still incipient or remains subordinated by continued elite domination. More recently, there are elements in place in Paraguay, El Salvador, and Guatemala that seem to indicate that the trend is likely to continue.

In some cases, it is true that centrist and center-left elected governments have yielded little structural change and provided scant dividends for the popular sectors. Despite the widespread presence of dedicated activists in parties such as the Brazilian Workers Party (PT), Uruguayan Broad Front (FA), the Socialist Party of Chile (PS), and the progressive Peronist faction in power in Argentina, their electoral coalitions have proven to be incapable of putting forward a transformative agenda in their respective countries. Further progress in these Southern Cone countries can only take place through a heightened mass mobilization of popular forces and a dramatic change in the priorities displayed by parties who speak in name of the popular classes.

Where emerging emancipatory processes have taken better hold, they have tended to be shaped by successive approximation processes, sometimes even on parallel tracks, depending upon the existing conditions at each time. They can be seen as unfolding in several of the traditional arenas of Latin American domination such as the political, financial, social, ideological and military fronts.

Transformative Legal Structures

The stark limitations of existing representative democracies are starting to be strongly contested in Latin America as emerging emancipatory projects seek to transform the legal order in the interests of the popular sectors. In such cases, the idea has been to reformulate the rules of the game in favor of a transitional order in which continual, fundamental change can be protected from derailment by oppositional forces wedded to the status quo. The supra-constitutionality of constitutional assemblies has emerged as a crucial issue in the region for enabling far reaching change. In its absence, the existing legal order generally works to preclude any meaningful constitutional change.

Of equal importance is the way constitutional delegates are elected in ensuring that they can legitimately represent the interests of the broader society. Elections for constituent assemblies where everybody, by definition, is a potential candidate have definitively proven to be more democratic than traditional parliamentary elections. Their participatory character generally favors a constitutional outcome that displays greater inclusiveness and popular incorporation into decision-making.

Other democratic formulas for legal reform have also been proliferating in the region. The use of national referendums of various types has marked a significant step towards direct representation because everybody has an equal say on what is being decided upon. Revocation referendums add another layer of democratic participation since leaders who fail to listen to their bases or who renege on their commitments can be legally ousted at virtually any level of government. Communal and municipal assemblies in countries like Venezuela and Bolivia open up the possibility of permanent decentralized referendums on issues that need to be resolved at that level, or that need to be passed up to confederations of communal assemblies, or even higher up to the ministerial or other appropriate levels.

There are, of course, strategic issues of national concern that need to be made at a centralized level. The articulation among all levels of the state is an issue of great importance. Each level of the state should be able to count on support from higher levels and inputs from lower levels and each should report back to its constituent bases. This is how instances of participatory democracy in some parts of the region, long confined to the municipal level, can best be expanded and turned into a more direct, grassroots democracy.

In the current constitutional processes in Venezuela, Bolivia and Ecuador, there has been an effective combination of popular and charismatic leaders as heads of government and strong pressure from popular bases with a demonstrated ability to unite, organize and mobilize around their agenda. President Morales is fond of repeating a phrase that was originally coined by Zapatista National Liberation Army (EZLN) sub-Commandant Marcos in Chiapas: "There is the need to govern by obeying" (the people). A feature shared in common by the three national processes mentioned above is the inclusion of new forms of direct participative democracy. They are trying to move towards greater popular control over natural resources and seek to use the economy as an indispensable tool to bring about change and fend off sabotage from reactionary opposition forces.

The challenge is to shape a legal structure that will favor continual transformations that can benefit the popular sectors while simultaneously opening the space necessary for mass participation in the governing process. The relative potential for success of these efforts, the speed of the process of change and the revolutionary depth of such changes will certainly vary depending upon the specific political context and prevailing social circumstances.

Challenging the Financial Clamp

Latin America faces an integrated set of challenges to its emerging agenda for transformation. Financial debt first opened the door to harmful conditionalities and the disempowerment of state capacities via public policy impositions from abroad. This resulted in deflated public budgets and a desperate competition for financial resources among developing countries. As the trend deepened, it led to a vastly excessive shift towards export-led economies. This, in turn, increased exposure to unfair trade processes, encouraged the loss of national resources and led to inevitable increases of poverty, hunger and declining essential indicators of human development.

What became increasingly and painfully clear in this process was that the Bretton Woods Institutions were never meant to be development institutions. On the contrary, they remained locked in their post-World War II mindset and singularly concerned with maintaining the stability of global capital. With these priorities in mind, they have sought ways to systematically disempower developing countries in order to maintain the global North's access to essential financial, human and environmental resources. In reality, their greater cause is to sustain the lifestyles of elites in the industrialized world, something that has also paid handsome dividends to rich elites within developing countries.

Perverse measures have been implemented such as ending state control over monetary policy through privatization of central banks and in some cases the elimination of national currencies altogether. International financial institutions pressured states to place significant financial savings in foreign reserve accounts based in the North. This worked to ensure future debt payments and other resource outflows while contributing to the health of wealthy economies. Meanwhile, highly publicized North to South financial flows have become practically negligible. These mainly come in the form of foreign direct investments and migration remittances, making it the region with the highest level of registered remittances at over US$40 billion yearly. The World Bank estimates that this figure is probably at least 50 percent greater once unregistered remittances are taken into consideration (World Bank 2007). For some countries, remittances constitute one of the principal mechanisms for positive financial transfers while for recipient families they constitute almost 50 percent of their family budgets (ECLAC 2006).

Making matters even worse, the traditional outflows of capital have become intensified by a new generation of mechanisms designed to siphon off financial resources. Among them are the so-called "vulture funds," the new generation of free trade agreements, the exporting of national reserve funds, and a massive speculation with oil and food commodity futures that have together compounded the pre-existing pain of the poor and most vulnerable sectors. But thanks to pressure by social movements, progressive governments have begun to challenge the financial clamp and curtail the financial drain. Whether defaulting on debt, establishing budget caps to debt repayments, advance liquidation of debt payments or declaring portions of existing debt illegitimate or "odious," countries are beginning to climb out of debt-related policy conditionalities imposed by IFIs and their juridical entities.

One government that has adamantly defended the idea of independence from the World Bank is the Correa Administration in Ecuador. Correa's government declared the World Bank representative *persona non grata* and ousted him from the country due to an accumulated record of corrupt practices. Bolivia, Ecuador and Nicaragua have asserted that they will no longer recognize the International Center for Settlement of Investment Disputes (ICSID) authority, claiming that it is incapable of being an impartial arbitrator. Venezuela has announced it will step out of both the World Bank and the IMF. The IMF's clients and its main source of income have begun to dwindle and its only clients may soon be only the very poorest or weakest countries that are unable to escape.

This notwithstanding, the full potential of emancipation can only be realized through a more concerted break with imperialism. Progressive governments and social movements alike are quite aware of this and have begun to take action. Concerted efforts have been made to torpedo free trade agreements with the United States and Europe. The outflow of financial resources from the region is being curtailed via the recovery of national sovereignty over natural resources, the recovery of public control over central banks, and the development of instrumental monetary policies. Financial reserves are also being kept at home or in the region, rather than placing them in low interest US Treasury bonds that run the risk of further devaluation via a sinking dollar. These funds are now being better used for supporting other countries in the region in their national development and quest for financial sovereignty.

In the mid-1980s, Alan García during his first presidency in Peru defiantly announced that he would limit debt-repayment to 10 percent of his country's export earnings. His administration was promptly punished by the IMF, denied any further loans and eventually forced to cave in. Similar developments have followed over the years. The *Caracazo* of 1989, consisting of anti-IMF riots in Venezuela, marked an important historical turning point in popular reaction to this state of affairs.

Argentina which briefly shined as a neoliberal showcase by strictly following IMF policy impositions began its descent into a pervasive crisis that similarly proved pivotal in the debt-challenging process. By the end of 2001, under the pressure of the Argentine people who protested day in and day out against rising unemployment and the collapse of the peso, a popular insurrection managed to send the De La Rúa government packing. The depletion of its foreign reserves forced Argentina to suspend payment of private debt and the debt with the Paris Club, thereby proving that such a move was possible.

In May 2003, Néstor Kirchner was sworn in as Argentina's president and appeared ready to stand up to the IMF by refusing to implement some of its most unreasonable and harmful policies. Sensing the power associated with the massive Argentine debt, President Kirchner stipulated his own terms of repayment. Argentina would offer only around 25 cents for each dollar of its defaulted debt still owed to private holders. After much complaint, lobbying and threats of various kinds, a large majority of Argentina's creditors eventually accepted new bonds worth roughly 35 cents on the dollar (Glennie 2007).

Argentina had broken the rules of the global finance game in a spectacular way, much the way that Peru had done almost two decades earlier. The initial consensus amongst the global economic gurus was that Argentina would suffer severe long-term consequences, such as a long drawn-out depression and isolation from international markets. But the result proved to be to the contrary. A very respectable, post-default recovery has restored economic growth that has continued since then, surpassing even the most optimistic predictions.

For its part, Ecuador remains being one of the countries in the region with the highest percentage of its national budget dedicated to servicing foreign debt, hovering around 30 percent by the end of 2007. Correa's successful bid for the presidency allowed him to attempt a unilateral restructuring of Ecuador's debt-service payments by reducing the concentration of payments over upcoming years. Correa has emphasized that Ecuador will not default on all of its external debt. At the same time, however, it will not pay "illegitimate" debts and Correa set up a national commission charged to make all relevant determinations.

In a historical development, Correa initiated the auditing of public debt in order to identify the illegitimate portions of multilateral and bilateral foreign debt, insisting that Ecuador will suspend payment on any debt which is determined to be so. The same applies to public domestic debt for which cancellation measures were implemented prior. There are many legal arguments that favor Ecuador in support of its unilateral decision to stop servicing and even canceling illegitimate debts (Tussaint and Millet, 2007).

Both Ecuador's Rafael Correa and Venezuela's Hugo Chavez have become one of the most adamant defenders of reclaiming central banks in the region and placing them under public control. President Chavez has also sought to exercise public control over foreign investments and exchange rates so as to disarm the financial destabilization schemes of the Venezuelan oligarchy. Needless to say, he has been furiously denounced as interventionist, even in a context when central banks in the United States and the European Union are increasingly intervening in an unprecedented way, especially in subsidizing private banks with public money in the attempt to slow a worsening global financial crisis.

Whereas most other countries have invested their surplus funds in US Treasury Bonds, a coerced way of bailing out the highly indebted United States, President Chávez has proposed to eliminate the macroeconomic stabilization fund imposed earlier by the IMF and replace it with a reasonable amount of reserves under the control of the Central Bank. All remaining funds should be placed in a national development investment fund. These proposals were postponed, however, by his failure by a slim margin to gain voter approval of a 2007 constitutional reform.

The growing popular struggle throughout the region has therefore produced a whole new array of initiatives that seek to challenge existing dependency relations and begin the arduous task of regaining sovereignty. Fully aware of the risks involved in challenging global capital, these new national trends have come accompanied by a greater willingness to link up with alternative forms of regional cooperation and integration. The financial clamps have begun to crumble and with them goes the legitimacy of neoliberal policies.

Nationalization of Non-Renewable Natural Resources

The flawed path to development and democracy pursued throughout the region relied upon growth at any cost. It brought with it an illusory hope (or purposeful misrepresentation) that the cascading benefits reaped by elites would eventually trickle down to the rest of the population. In this context, the natural environment became incapable of sustaining the kind of systematic ecological exploitation being unleashed by transnational corporations. Painfully now aware of this, the region's progressive governments have begun to take countermeasures.

In Ecuador, the Correa administration decided to begin calculating the specific costs represented by the ecological debt of the North during audits of its financial debt in order to deduct them as illegitimate. Bolivia's President Evo Morales has on numerous occasions identified capitalism as the main cause for the grave environmental state of the planet and has made an impassioned call to show greater respect for *Pachamama*, the Mother Earth. He has offered up to the world the possibility of capitalizing upon the valuable ancestral knowledge present in Bolivian indigenous communities, for building a future of hope for humanity based upon harmony with nature.

Prompted by high international market prices for oil and minerals, and tired of seeing their natural resources drained to make foreign companies rich, Bolivia, Ecuador and also Venezuela have sought to renegotiate their agreements with foreign corporations, raising the percentage of royalties and seeking the establishment of joint ventures with the state as a major shareholder. Most large companies, especially the European companies, have accepted the new terms, seeing that they can still make large profits. At the same time, the producer countries have experienced increased and in some cases unprecedented growth in their economies which has enabled the growth of the public budget.

The mechanism of nationalization of natural resources so that their exploitation can benefit its legitimate owners, as well as support other countries in need, has one of the highest emancipatory weights in keeping financial resources at home. In addition to making good financial sense, it is also a matter of dignity as well as national and regional sovereignty. In Venezuela, for example, hydrocarbons had historically been used to make foreign companies and the local oligarchy rich while little benefit arrived to the majority of Venezuelans. After less than a decade since Hugo Chávez was first elected president, contract renegotiations with extracting companies have allowed the state to increase its control over oil revenues. This has helped propel Venezuela forward in providing the resources necessary to carry out a far reaching social transformation.

These oil revenues have also allowed Venezuela to position itself strongly in the global geopolitical scene, including within OPEC,[3] and to establish a well-funded development engine for the region as a whole. This has included the creation of several bi-national oil companies in partnership with PDVSA, the Venezuela State Oil Company. President Chavez claims there are enough energy reserves to outlive this century and is supplying oil and technology to the Caribbean and South America through mechanisms such as PetroCaribe, PetroSur, PetroAndina and long-term energy security treaties. In most of these cases, oil supplied by Venezuela is paid for either in cash or products under a framework of long-term credit. These kinds of special barter arrangements with Cuba, for example, have provided Venezuela with badly needed teachers and medical staff. These arrangements made possible by Venezuelan oil revenues have being extended to many other countries in what amounts to an unprecedented South—South cooperation effort.

A country like Bolivia is in a much weaker position with regard to its options for recovering badly needed resources. Whereas Venezuela has a strong starting point in PDVSA, Bolivia's State Company YPFB was all but dismantled by prior governments that transferred strategic state companies into the hands of transnational corporations. Bolivia's revolutionary MAS[4] government has relatively little choice but to work in partnership with foreign corporations both on account of scarce investment capital and a weak technological and managerial infrastructure. Renegotiations with existing partners, prompted after various discoveries of irregularities in the past, have been successful in dramatically increasing the state portion of oil and gas revenues (from 18 to 50 percent) without having to go further into debt. The state has also become the sole exporter of natural gas (Tabera 2007). With

---

[3] Organization of Petroleum Exporting Countries.
[4] Movement Towards Socialism.

the enactment of recent legislation, foreign companies have stopped owning the resources and have been turned into service providers for the state.

As the latest player in the regional nationalization trend, Ecuador has also enacted new measures. Ecuador's Constitution establishes public ownership of natural resources and so nationalization is not a legal issue per se. In an unprecedented move, President Correa issued a decree whereby 99 percent of the extraordinary revenues emanating from the significantly higher oil prices of recent years have remained in state hands, up from 50 percent which had been past practice.

Resource availability in the region provides the clearest example of the need for a more genuine integration between developing nations towards the aim of achieving energy sovereignty. Horacio Barrancos neatly summed up the principle of complementarity in these simple words:

> Argentina, Chile and Brazil need gas. Bolivia has gas but does not have the resources to exploit, process and commercialize it. Venezuela has the necessary resources, the experience, the managerial capabilities, and it also has gas linked to its oil production, therefore it is looking for markets for its gas. Brazil and Argentina also have resources and they are willing to channel them towards Bolivia in order to guarantee their supply (Barrancos 2007).

In a revolutionary gesture, President Correa has submitted a proposal to the United Nations General Assembly, following previous discussions with local indigenous communities, in order to contribute to the reduction of carbon emissions and the preservation of biodiversity. He has offered to forgo exploitation of oil fields located in a high biodiversity area known as Yasuní Park, preempting the emission of about 111 million tons of carbon. This would result in an annual cost of US$720 million in lost exports for which he has requested international compensation (Correa 2007).

On a more unfortunate note, Biofuels have come to cloud the horizons of regional unity with Brazil taking the lead in a strategy that can only benefit the North, jeopardize regional food security and harm the environment. By jumping to the call to massively produce more biofuels, Brazil opted to strengthen its privileged status among the handful of the world's most powerful countries.

Neutralizing the Military Trap

The use of military force has always been a powerful tool employed by the United States to expand its global power, to guarantee access to strategic natural resources, to repress or intimidate and dissuade resistance, to confront the formation of alternative hegemonic blocks, to enforce the "rules of the game" in favor of global capital, and to enhance its strategic positioning. An important element in this logic of hegemony in US-Latin American relations was first established by President Monroe in 1823. The Monroe Doctrine was a unilateral pronouncement of foreign policy principles designed exclusively in the interests of the US with no consultation whatsoever with the peoples of Latin America. Fundamentally extra-territorial in nature, it had no legal foundation at the time of its unilateral declaration.

During the Cold War era, Washington invoked the Monroe Doctrine to refer to "Soviet expansionism" in the hemisphere in order to justify armed interventions in Guatemala and Cuba in the 1950s and in the Dominican Republic in the mid-1960s. During the 1980s, the Monroe Doctrine was specifically invoked in the advanced Cold War phase of interventionism in Central America. The militarization of the Caribbean Basin was intensively pursued along with a comprehensive deployment of intelligence forces and military aid.

There are of course many subtle ways to support these same objectives, disguised under the cover of humanitarian action, mutual friendship missions, cooperation in illegal drug control, joint participation in peace missions, and anti-terrorism policies. In the haste to trample over the sovereignty of countries, democracy is usually the first casualty and creativity abounds in the attempt of imperial power to utilize supranational and extraterritorial legislation. Military force, nonetheless, forms the central support column for all the rest and is never far from view when popular resistance builds momentum for emancipation.

During the 1990s, the Cold War abruptly evaporated following the collapse of the Soviet Union. This led to the emergence of the "opening of markets" and the "War on Drugs" as the twin pillars of US policies towards the region. The way was now paved for moving on from Central America towards initiating a new wave of interventionism in South America under the cover of "Plan Colombia," soon making Colombia one of the largest recipients of US military assistance in the world. The rapidly expanding "Andean Regional Initiative" as it became called by the Bush (Jr.) Administration, sought to go far beyond the internal crisis of Colombia. It militarized the entire Andean region with a design for controlling various scenarios that could erupt out of the intensifying social conflicts resulting from neoliberal crises. In the process, the Andean operations created a whole series of threats for the region, including ecological devastation via fumigation and biological warfare being waged against illicit crops and large scale displacement that has intensified along with the war.

US strategic interests, particularly regarding petroleum, represents the ultimate significance of these military programs. By 2007, Mexico and Venezuela were respectively the third and fourth largest suppliers of crude oil to the United States, with Ecuador in ninth place and Colombia in twelfth (EIA 2008). In this sense, it should come as little surprise that the "successes" of extending Plan Colombia throughout the Andean region prompted the outgoing Bush (Jr) Administration to propose a "Plan Mexico" for 2008, seeking to weave immigration into its package of justifications for military interventionism.

Throughout the dark history of its interventionism in Latin America, Washington has cultivated close ties with the military establishments throughout the region. Most notable is the School of the Americas (SOA), later re-named The Western Hemisphere Institute for Security Cooperation (WHINSEC). For decades, this controversial US military training facility formed a core element of the "national security doctrine" which instructed Latin American military personnel in the tactics of repression. These methods later became legendary during the dirty wars of South America and in the civil war years of Central America. Latin American military and law-enforcement personnel studied at the SOA along with civilians as they together learned how to effectively wage counterinsurgency campaigns and suppress democratic institutions. Not surprisingly, the school has a long list of notorious graduates that later served as heads of state or high ranking officials in dictatorships and authoritarian governments, some of whom still continue to surface in news reports regarding both current and past human rights cases.

The kind of training provided by the SOA proved instrumental throughout the remainder of the 20th century for extinguishing waves of emancipatory upsurges. The military establishments across the region were trained to see their role as guardians in the face of subversion and the "vulnerabilities" of liberal democracy. The national security doctrine called on military forces to aggressively act and neutralize any attempt to challenge the status quo. Indeed, governments in Latin America were for decades under almost continual threat from their own military and

Latin American elites have repeatedly shown little hesitation to call on the military to preserve their privileges.

The most terrifying era of criminal activity perpetuated by Latin American military establishments took place in a concerted fashion during the 1975–1983 period and was known as Operation Condor. Condor's core members were the military regimes of Argentina, Chile, Uruguay, Paraguay, Bolivia and Brazil, although other countries such as Ecuador and Peru also collaborated. There is now substantial evidence to show that the entire operation counted on organizational, intelligence, financial and technological assistance from the United States and was coordinated, according to US Central Intelligence Agency (CIA) declassified documents, by the Southern Command of the US Army from bases located in the Panama Canal Zone. This highly secret operation involved mass murder of an entire generation of Latin American activists (McSherry 2005).

Unfortunately, much of this repressive infrastructure managed to survive the transition to civilian governments. Indeed, the very transition to civil democracy was in most cases carried out under the close supervision of the dictatorial military establishment, providing a means by which military figures could aspire to continue on as major political actors. The persistence of impunity and the continuing violence of paramilitary activity in various countries, always in close alliance with national armed forces, serve as stark reminders of the contradiction between democratic rule and the prevailing military order.

Another key military issue is the growing number of US military bases positioned in Latin America. In addition to its remaining bases in Puerto Rico, Honduras and Guantanamo, the US military has sought to establish "cooperative security locations" by creating ten year leases for base facilities in other Latin American sites (Isacson, Olson and Haugaard 2007), as well as smaller, less permanent "forward operating sites" in various countries that involve stopover landing arrangements and the use of facilities. Of particular concern, is the potential establishment of new US military bases in Paraguay and Peru. In the former, the US seeks access to the strategic Triple Border area which the Pentagon alleges is a terrorist hub for the Western hemisphere. It also happens to be an area containing the largest non-contaminated reserve of water in the world, the entry point to Amazonia that is a huge natural resources reserve, and is also in proximity to the Bolivian gas reserves of Tarija. In the latter case of Peru, it is generally thought that the establishment of a base was part of the package negotiated between Lima and Washington for concluding a Free Trade Agreement (FTA) in 2007.

In a similar manner, Washington earlier sought to impose the "American Servicemembers Protection Act of 2002" on Latin American countries so as to obtain special advance immunity for US military personnel from possible prosecution by the International Criminal Court. However, in view of refusal from several countries, ignoring the threats of military aid suspension, flexibility had to be introduced to allow continuation of military assistance—and with it, continuation of intervention—to *refusenik* states when deemed in the national security interest.

In virtually every case where a popular government has come to power in Latin America, ties with the US military have been questioned, diminished or eliminated depending on the degree of radicalism involved. The government of Hugo Chávez in Venezuela has been cutting military ties from Washington, while openly increasing the strength of its military forces as a mechanism to dissuade aggressions. This has even included high profile purchases of military aircraft from Russia.

But despite the widespread support that President Chavez enjoys in the armed forces, himself of military origin, he nevertheless fell victim to a short-lived military coup in 2002. The coup was led by the top military leadership that opted to disown the constitution and throw their support to national elites. Rescued by a mass rebellion of the popular sectors and the vast majority of middle and lower level military leaders who remained loyal to the constitution, he was able to remain in power and subsequently clean up the armed forces. Chávez has since involved the armed forces in running strategic services and in accelerating badly needed social programs. Venezuela has thus become a case in Latin America in which a democratic revolutionary process is being actively supported by the military.

Ecuador is similarly developing an agenda for a national defense policy that establishes priorities based on human security and is assigning special importance to the protection of people, natural resources and the effective control of its national territory. The Correa government has backed calls by the social movements to terminate the lease on the US military base at Manta as a question of national sovereignty and intends to keep Ecuador out of the counterinsurgency activities surrounding Plan Colombia. Indeed, the regional criticisms of Plan

Colombia demonstrate the elements of a hemispheric opposition to US interventionism.

In 2007, Leftist political parties from all over the region signed a statement on Hemispheric Security at the Sao Paulo Forum, calling for a regional security framework that supports their own social, economic and political models. The overall aim, they argued, should be to transform Latin America into a zone of peace dedicated to economic development, social inclusion and democratization. The Venezuelan government has in particular proposed on various occasions that the region should contemplate "Bolivarian" strategies for military cooperation and the possibility of a collective military apparatus.

Latin American states effectively exhibited significant signs of independence when they refused to recognize the short-lived Carmona regime in Venezuela during the attempted coup against Chávez. They also did so when they rejected the so-called "military FTAA" in 2004, when US Secretary of Defense Donald Rumsfeld proposed a new security doctrine at the VI Hemispheric Conference of Defense Ministers (Dietrich 2005). They likewise turned back a Colombian proposal for the creation of a multinational military force to intervene in that country and legitimate ongoing government counterinsurgency efforts being funded by Washington. Colombia also failed in its request that the Organization of American States (OAS) be delegated with the task of listing terrorist and insurgent groups (and individuals) in the region for the purpose of preventing them from obtaining visas and traveling between countries. And perhaps most dramatically, the region roundly condemned Colombia's 2008 armed incursion into Ecuadorian territory and assassination of a high ranking FARC[5] guerrilla commander engaged in negotiations for a humanitarian agreement on the exchange of prisoners.

Disappointed in the poor performance of its client states, Washington announced in 2008 that it was revamping the US IV Fleet for assignment to combat terrorism and drug trafficking in the region. But this has had the unintended consequence of alienating center-left governments like Brazil that wish to avoid the kind of regional destabilization that actions from the IV Fleet may bring. As a result, a more autonomous approach to regional security matters seems to be gaining currency in the face of the US Southern Command's attempt to impose its strategic

---

[5] Colombian Revolutionary Armed Forces.

vision. But if indeed the Monroe Doctrine is once more falling out of favor with regional military forces, it is too soon to tell whether the shifting political orientation of the region can lead to genuine forms of counter-hegemonic military cooperation.

Challenging Neoliberal Ideology

An important component of neoliberal domination worldwide is its accumulated ideological hegemony. Leaving virtually no institutional sphere untouched, consolidated neoliberal thought became embedded in Latin America's ideological structures in what became widely known as *pensamiento único* or "one-dimensional thought." The result was a virtual reconstruction of common sense in the service of domination where critical thinking became absorbed into the larger neoliberal logic.

The institutions of mass media and education have been particularly powerful vehicles in this regard. Together, they manufacture and reaffirm the "common sense" of what eventually became summed up in the pervasive notion that "There Is No Alternative." This catch-phrase popularly abbreviated as "TINA" was the oratorical creation of former British Prime Minister Margaret Thatcher who preached that "There is no alternative" to neoliberal globalization. The TINA syndrome later became reproduced over and over again throughout Latin America, enshrined in the "recommendations" of IFIs and regurgitated in the speeches of neoliberal leaders like Fujimori, Menem and many others. In the context of a unipolar world order, the rise of one-dimensional thinking favored a reactionary restoration of conservative, pro-capitalist and pro-imperialist ideas throughout the region.

In recent decades, economic liberalization promoted the privatization and commodification of educational services. This actively transformed the educational process into an act of consumption, something which is economically very significant since educational services normally represent a significant part of every public budget. Privatization also tended to increase the costs of education, thereby deepening an already high level of social exclusion. At the same time, this more "perfect" commodification of education seeped deeply into education's constituent elements, including its curricula, thus favoring the installation of a culture of private enterprise within educational institutions.

The transnationalization of education under neoliberal capitalism compromised the democratic character of the education system by placing important mechanisms of social regulation outside of the reach of the state and public accountability. Meanwhile, the expansion of the private sector in education further intensified the financial pressures upon the public system, accelerating its contraction and auguring for its eventual elimination altogether.

When education loses its special status and becomes treated identically to any other good or service, its regulation falls under the purview of commercial trade agreements which prohibit giving special treatment to local educational agents, insisting instead on "national treatment" of foreign investors. Once this process is consolidated, the educational sector becomes subject to the principle of compensation for any re-nationalization, thus making it effectively "excluded" from any future civil society initiatives that demand the return of its regulation to the public domain.

The justification for this negative trend was sought in the rationalization of education as a training system for "human capital," one designed to competitively service a globally dominated market. But in the process, this effectively transformed teachers into tools of domination instead of agents for teaching the kinds of skills needed for integral, critical thinking. As Paulo Freire (1967) once framed the dilemma: "The choice is between an education for domestication and an education for freedom. Education for the human object or education for the human subject."

Control over mass media has likewise played an important role in maintaining the ideological hegemony of neoliberalism in Latin America. Like many other economic activities, the region's media have become increasingly concentrated into what Aram Aharonian (2007) calls "media *latifundios*." This accumulation of mass media power has occurred in the context of monopoly private sector control over radio, television, and telecommunications service providers. Alongside of a regional media pioneered by the diversifying activities of entrenched traditional oligarchies, a parallel trend has resulted from an accelerated transnational penetration of the industry under neoliberalism. This "CNN-ization" of the region has tended to further homogenize the media products being consumed while it has also imprinted an imperial, pro-US perspective on the flow of news and information.

The power of Latin American mass media "*latifundios*" has traditionally shared a comfortable correspondence with entrenched economic elites. In addition, there is a clearly established pattern of media *lati-fundios* inciting opposition in those countries where populist-reformist and revolutionary governments have come to power. Media power was utilized as a key instrument to promote the counterrevolutionary cause and derail a popular, emancipatory agenda in Chile in the 1970s and Nicaragua in the 1980s. More recently, it can be seen in Venezuela, Bolivia and Ecuador. Elsewhere, mass media serve as the guardians of the dynasty so that continued elite rule can remain unchallenged.

The mass diffusion of neoliberal "common sense" was destined, however, to run up against the objective consequences of neoliberal policies. Just as the economic and political structures of neoliberalism tended towards crisis, so too did the ideological structures that grew up around them. It was this tendency towards ideological crisis that opened opportunities for new and alternative ways of thinking among the region's progressive and revolutionary forces.

Even though the technologically-intensive character of mass media has favored their increasing concentration and transnationalization, it has also opened up new possibilities for popular forces to combat neoliberal ideological hegemony. New radio broadcast technologies for transmission over the internet have significantly expanded the reach of community and alternative media projects. Universities and non-profit, regional research institutions and networks such as Latin American Social Sciences Council (CLACSO) have placed these technologies at the service of training and higher education throughout Latin America.

The recent explosion of blogs and other websites have created dynamic new virtual spaces for anti-hegemonic entities that are vital for discussion and dissemination of information. These spaces accompany the day to day communications of people who are socially network-ing with an agenda for social transformation and this is particularly important in the construction of transnational social movements. One particularly impressive example is *www.rebelion.org*, a radical website in Spanish that is produced in Spain and updated on a daily basis with editorials, analytical essays and other materials submitted from progres-sive intellectuals, social movements and leftist political parties. Among other objectives, they aim to "give news a different treatment so as to reveal the capitalist economic and political interests which the powerful hide in order to maintain their privileges and current status."

Perhaps the most ambitious and well-known example of alternative media in Latin America is the *TeleSUR* project. Financed as a joint ven-ture between Venezuela, Brazil, Argentina and Uruguay, *TeleSUR* has evolved into a region-wide network of independent news and cultural programming, with broadcasting over cable networks, public television systems and its own website where news and internet broadcasting is available worldwide.

Aram Aharonian, its founder and Director, explains that:

> The development of *TeleSUR* is without doubt a political and strategic project. It represents an attempt to recover and promote the construction of hemispheric audiovisual media by broadcasting a real view of the social and cultural diversity of Latin America and the Caribbean. The mission of this alternative media project is to begin to dismantle the Latin American media *latifundios* and to help consolidate emerging processes of political change as an instrument in the battle of ideas against the hegemonic processes of globalization.
>
> ...TeleSUR is a channel to build new bridges for creating a space for integration, escaping from the stereotypes that have kept us in the bounds of others' sight, and with our own language and a visual identity that can allow us to see ourselves from a different perspective: ours (2007).

Predictably, Washington responded aggressively to *TeleSUR* and wasted little time in the US House of Representatives before approving an amendment to the Foreign Appropriations Act. The amendment called for expansion of Voice of America (VOA) propaganda broadcasts to Venezuela so as to counter the "anti-Americanism" being promoted by "Venezuela's *TeleSUR*." The measure was later approved by the Senate to become law for FY2007 (US Office of Management and Budget, 2006).

Engaging the ideological struggle against neoliberal, one-dimensional thought unquestionably forms an important part of social transformation and emancipation. There is a continuing necessity to comprehend the ongoing ideological struggle and to contribute to it. An essential task is to identify and nurture new articulations between anti-neoliberal ideological forces with the aim of consolidating the emerging alternatives that are forming throughout the region. There are many spaces where waging this kind of struggle can take place and the educational sector is clearly a pivotal institution in this regard. It is critically necessary as part of this struggle to defend public education as part of any empowerment strategy for the popular sectors.

Integration for Liberation

The concept of a *"Patria Grande"* or a unified Latin America has deep roots in the region's popular consciousness, tracing back to political visionaries who struggled to liberate the continent from the oppression of Spanish colonialism. Latin American unity did not "automatically" emerge from a common cultural or linguistic heritage but instead out of a history of common struggle against hegemonic powers.

Inspired by this historical vision, the struggle of social movements for a more genuine framework of Latin American integration marks a significant historical turning point. Integration has ceased being solely an issue for governments largely subordinated to foreign capital and imperial designs. Instead, it has become transformed into an element of emancipatory struggle for the peoples of the region.

In the 1960's, calls for integration largely represented a strategy to increase intra-regional trade and to rationalize and extend the bases of the region's incipient industrialization. The first generation agreements established the pattern of reducing regional integration to little more than shared policies of commerce and common tariff arrangements. By the early 1990s, regional agreements like the Andean Community of Nations (CAN) began to assimilate the neoliberal shift of focus "outward" towards market-driven, export oriented growth.

The establishment of the South American Common Market (MERCOSUR) in 1991 formed the paradigmatic case of the second generation of integration agreements. As pre-established by prior, bilateral trade agreements between Brazil and Argentina, the principal beneficiaries of MERCOSUR were set to be the homegrown corporations of those two larger member countries that would benefit from lower costs and a significant increase of sub-regional exchange. The increasing scale of production and expanded markets for member countries effectively amounted to a survival strategy under the twin pressures of cheapening global imports and a declining consumer purchasing power that resulted in reduced national demand.

Gone by that time were the import substitution strategies of the earlier era, leaving the imperfect free trade zone created by the pact devoid of any plan for eventual consolidation into a common market. This relegated the agreement to be a "neoliberal MERCOSUR" that sought to better position the combined export sectors of the two major partners in the global economy. The central argument of the consolidated neoliberal model was that trade would be the motor force for economic growth that can guarantee development.

Although this "trickle-down" argument was largely assimilated by mainstream theorists throughout the region, the fact was that social development was largely deferred and social disparities further increased. The popular sectors that never benefited from this model eventually began to turn against it. The exclusively commercial focus of these initiatives coincided with the deepening consolidation of neoliberal policies and resulted in a profound and well-founded disinterest in regional "integration" on the part of the popular sectors. Elite-driven integration initiatives accorded virtually no role whatsoever for the civil societies of its member countries.

Meanwhile, the integration "alternative" being proposed by Washington, i.e., the FTAA, more closely resembled an "annexation" of Latin America. It promised to reinforce and strengthen an already established asymmetrical order. Ironically, it was the popular *rejection* of hegemonic integration projects such as the FTAA that initially characterized the rekindling of popular interest around the issue of regional integration. The fact that popular movements were successful in detaining the FTAA further consolidated that interest.

By helping to facilitate the transfer of the region's resources to the global market, FTAs operate to the benefit of large transnational corporations. Additionally, FTAs include disadvantageous agreements regarding services, financial and investment flows, public sector procurement and intellectual property. They are heavily implicated in damaging practices to the natural environment and enhanced exploitation of local cheap labor that places the countries on the weaker end at risk and most especially the vulnerable social sectors within those countries. Since Latin America displays the worst distribution of income in the world, it clearly cannot tolerate an integration scheme that further exacerbates these disparities.

By contrast, the Bolivarian perspective holds that no country can achieve its liberation if it remains isolated from its Latin American neighbors. The Bolivarian goal is a *systemic* competitiveness of an entire collection of countries which more closely approximates Bolivar's ideal of the *Patria Grande*.[6] The resulting imperative for achieving regional integration is based upon developing complementary activities, rooted

---

[6] Larger Homeland of United Latin American States.

in solidarity among constituent countries. This differs strongly from the search for competitiveness of one country relative to others as the reigning neoliberal model advocates.

Currently, the rules of the game of regional integration have evolved between three *relatively* autonomous and interrelated dynamics. Firstly, there is Washington's hegemonic project that works to protect the interests of North American-based transnational capital. With practically no difference, the European Union is pursuing a similar track. In a second and parallel process, most Latin American states that are driven by private elite interests continue to push forward with the conventional regional trade frameworks such as CARICOM,[7] MERCOSUR and the CAN. Various state members in these regional pacts have also signed FTAs with the United States (or are in the process of doing so). Others cooperate closely with Washington in strategic areas that work against the region as in the case of Brazil cooperating with the United States in the production of ethanol. The third process began to take shape in 2004 and revolves around the ALBA[8] Agreement proposed by Hugo Chávez. Its adherents openly oppose the neoliberal model and refuse to sign any new asymmetrical agreements with the United States.

The ALBA initiative first surfaced at the time that Venezuela developed its rejection of the FTAA and its introduction constituted a watershed for Latin America. In the guiding principles of ALBA, trade and investment are viewed not as ends in themselves but rather as tools to enable sustainable and fair development. Special treatment is accorded to smaller countries in order to obtain economic complementarity and promote cooperation among member countries. It contains a strong social justice orientation as it sets out to directly engage and reverse existing asymmetries by way of explicit compensatory arrangements. In this sense, ALBA represents a complete rupture with classical, economistic visions of integration and development cooperation. It instead seeks to create a strategic, historical and political alliance that can join capabilities and strengths of its members in order to liberate its peoples and build the *Patria Grande* dreamed of by Miranda, Bolivar, Martí and Sandino.

ALBA seemed to gather momentum by 2008, convening regular summits, including an expanding group of members and observers,

---

[7] Caribbean Community.
[8] Bolivarian Alternative for the Americas.

and seeking to incorporate a role of social movements from through-out the region. From the onset of its formation, it has pioneered the development of "solidarity-led" mechanisms of cooperation, offering generous financing for medical procedures and financial concessions to the poorest nations in the region. More recent developments such as the ALBA Bank suggest that the pact will continue to grow and spawn creative new initiatives from member countries.

When Bolivian President Evo Morales led his country into the ALBA agreement in 2006, he augmented the principles underlying the pact by proposing a series of "Peoples' Trade Agreements" (PTAs). The PTAs were designed to create an alternative to the FTAs that are primarily designed to benefit large corporations. The PTAs are a new type of treaty based in the complementarities that exist between cooperation partners that go well beyond strictly commercial aspects.

Meanwhile, the need for closer cooperation in the field of energy and financial credits is creating a strong impulse for developing innova-tive regional institutions. ALBA has provided a framework for various initiatives in this regard, including the creation of *PetroCaribe*,[9] *Banco del ALBA*[10] and *Bonos del Sur*.[11] Similarly, the *Banco del Sur*[12] reflects this logic on an even greater regional scale, although it has also demon-strated how the geopolitical aspirations of some member states such as Brazil pose limits to the magnitude of the initiative. In all such cases, a forceful "push" from the region's social movements can help ensure that member states live up to their rhetoric and deliver on their promises to reduce poverty and avoid neoliberal prescriptions.

Conclusion

As collectively argued by a large group of the region's social move-ments in the 2006 Declaration of Caracas, it is possible to visualize the construction of a more genuine system of Latin American integration with an emancipatory and transformational character. Such a system presupposes a popular struggle guided by certain basic principles such as the recovery of national sovereignty, the struggle against existing

---

[9] Caribbean Petroleum Alliance.
[10] ALBA Bank.
[11] Bonds of the South.
[12] Bank of the South.

forms of social exclusion, and the expansion of democracy through consolidation of more participatory social forms of decision making and public administration. It is essential that the governments throughout the region move towards a recovery of badly damaged public sectors and their public goods.

With a distinctive Latin American identity at the forefront, the time has arrived for recasting a more endogenous, region-centered strategy for development. The point of departure is the social welfare of its peoples and in this sense, breaking the ties of dependency constitutes a strategic goal. The struggle for genuine regional integration is likely to depend on the level of political mobilization achieved by the region's organized popular forces and their capacity to form proactive proposals amidst the current crisis of neoliberal democracies. The success of this mobilization requires that the social struggle create spaces that are permeable to integration within every social movement, political party, academic and non governmental (NGO) institutions where a popular agenda is being established. This in turn implies the necessity to deepen and institutionalize a permanent dialogue among these key social actors.

The current crisis of Latin American regional integration is in reality a reflection of the crisis of hegemonic integration and the elite-driven initiatives formed by privileged sectors seeking to defend their insertion in the global economy. Popular mobilizations in the region are demonstrating that the only way to create a better world is by strengthening democracy through confronting the existing challenges with a transformative social agenda. In this sense, the struggle for a more genuine regional integration is not a utopian project but rather a strategic one.

The possibility of an "anti-imperialist consensus," one that can replace a discredited Washington Consensus with something more than a reconstituted alliance of local elites, is today no longer just a dream of leftist academics. On the contrary, it forms part of the organized demands of newly mobilizing social sectors that are gaining traction in the region. As global civil society continues to mature and grow more conscious of the adverse impact of the neoliberal debacle, interest is rapidly growing in diverse forms of popular resistance and emerging new bonds of solidarity. The rich experience contained in recent Latin American developments offers important and stimulating insights to peoples throughout the world who believe that another, more just and democratic world is possible.

MIGRATION AND ASYMMETRICAL INTEGRATION IN LATIN AMERICA

Victor M. Figueroa Sepúlveda

There is no question that the phenomenon of international migration of labor defies easy explanation. It is fair to say that dependency theories did not set out to tackle this issue. Some partial and isolated contributions, such as those by Paul Singer, have been duly recognized (José L. Hernández 2008) while more radical sociologists from the region, such as the founders of the marxist school of marginality, mainly Aníbal Quijano (1977) and José Nun (2001) seem to have found no reason to engage in the discussion of the problem. In this case, international labor mobility was not seen as representing any serious theoretical challenge as it was basically solved in the international production of a relative surplus population. The assumption that underlies this is that Marx's general theory of capital satisfies most requirements concerning contemporary explanations of the realities of imperialism. General propositions are supposed to directly serve as a base to tacke actual phenomena. In fact, marginality, i.e., the existence of a surplus population beyond that of the reserve army of labor, was represented as a characteristic phenomenon of capitalism in general. But this falls far short of a fully adequate and useful explanation of migration under today's conditions.

The organization of capital changes as development proceeds and the manifestation of its inherent tendencies becomes modified accordingly. At first glance, it would seem obvious that the emergence of imperialism led to a new manifestation in the form of the tendency to create a surplus population at the international level. This can clearly be seen through migratory movements. Since the 1950s, labor migration experienced a unilateral shift that flowed from the region outward to developed countries. The real process that unfolded suggests to us that Marx's law regarding population does not operate in the same way in both developed and underdeveloped countries. Indeed, this is the case, but still the operation of this law is determined by the social relations of production and therefore the capital relation itself should account for the difference in its manifestation form. The solution to related problems such as wage differentials are also to be found using these same assumptions as a point of departure.

In this essay, I will attempt to outline some mediating propositions that should allow us to reconcile general theory with unfolding historical processes as we build an overall theoretical explanation of migration. I will start off with a brief presentation of Marx's theory of relative surplus population, calling attention to what we see as its shortcomings and suggesting a solution designed to overcome them. Next, I will present some pertinent theses regarding underdeveloped societies and on these grounds propose the outlines of a solution to some of the most serious problems posed by contemporary migration.

A Necessary Amendment to Marx's Theory of Relative Surplus Population

Marx upholds that capital accumulation produces "in direct ratio of its own energy and extent" a relatively redundant population of laborers, a population of greater number than that which suffices for the "average needs of the valorization of capital, and therefore a surplus population" (Marx 1975, Vol. I: 184). This overpopulation is "an industrial reserve army at the disposal of capital" and creates (contains) "for the changing needs of the valorization of capital, a mass of human material always ready for exploitation" regardless of the limits of population (Marx 1975, Vol. I: 786).

The relative character of this surplus population comes from the fact that it serves capital whenever new industries are created or existing ones expand. Thus, the expression "excessive for the average needs of the valorization of capital" must be understood as referring to a surplus-population in relation to capital in motion. The *relative* overpopulation referred to by Marx is the essential human material for future capital, i.e., for the capital that will be realized upon the further expansion of existing industrial branches or creation of new industries. That is how the definition of surplus population as a given "condition of the existence of the capitalist mode of production" makes sense. In short, relative overpopulation is a working population that exceeds the present needs of capital but is entirely necessary for a pending, cyclical expansion of capital. This is precisely why it grows in magnitude during periods of stagnation and shrinks during periods of expansion.

So, the basic idea of a relative overpopulation, equivalent to the industrial reserve army, appears at first perfectly coherent and seems to present no problem. However, when defining the various forms it can assume, various theoretical difficulties begin to surface. For his part, Marx developed the concept by describing typical situations of his era. In so doing, he identified three forms.

The *floating* form refers to workers that are sometimes repelled from employment and later absorbed again by industrial production. Meanwhile, the *latent* form refers to workers expelled from production by the introduction of capital in agriculture since their expulsion is not capable of being re-absorbed as workers in the countryside. That is why their certain destiny is emigration to the cities.

Stagnant overpopulation, the third form, is less clearly identified. According to Marx, this form "is a part of the active army of labor, but its occupation is absolutely irregular." But here, a question arises. As a part of the active working population, involved directly in the valorization of capital, why does this form constitute a part of relative overpopulation? Marx maintains that the main source of the stagnant population is domestic industry, and he adds: "It recruits incessantly its labor amongst the supernumeraries of modern industry and of the agriculture, especially from the decaying branches of industry" (Marx 1975, Vol. I: 801). If its source of labor-power is the supernumeraries created by the accumulation of capital, then it could be the case that the shift of workers just represents changes in their position as members of the relative overpopulation. But this may not be the case because domestic industry, according to Marx, is a "capitalist sphere of exploitation erected in the backyard of large industry" (Marx 1975, Vol. I: 567). It is an extension or "the outside department of the factory, of manufacturing and of large industry" (Marx 1975, Volume I: 562) and it is directly an object of capitalist exploitation. That is why those workers should be considered as members, not of the relative overpopulation, but of the active labor army. Of course, we only refer here to the case where industry provides the means and the materials of production while the workers contribute just their labor-power and receives wages.

In *Capital* a fourth group is brought into discussion: "The lowest sediment of the relative surplus-population dwells in the sphere of *pauperism*" (Marx 1975, Vol. I: 802). This group includes three components: a) indigents able to work; b) orphans and pauper children; and c) the demoralized, ragged and those unable to work. Marx's discourse at this point is somehow confusing. Although Marx seemed more interested in the position of these sectors *vis-à-vis* accumulation and employment, especially with regard to the two first types, the point is that we are not dealing here with categories of the relative surplus population, but rather with living conditions in the midst of the latter. Pauperism can exist within any category of the relative surplus-population, and, as a matter of fact, beyond this category as well.

The case of the third portion of pauperism is somewhat distinct because it becomes linked to the inability to work. While they are a product of accumulation, they do not meet any need of accumulation, either at present or in the future. For this reason, the sector cannot be properly considered as a "condition of existence of the capitalist mode of production." Marx defines them as a burden for capital, one which enters into the *faux frais* (incidental expenses) of capitalist production (Marx 1975, Vol. I: 803) amounting to a deviation of resources that could otherwise be useful to valorization. In fact, they are elements of an *absolute* surplus-population, a kind of advance group of the *consolidated surplus-population* that capitalism is bound to create in its higher stages of development.

In effect, that which Marx calls the consolidated surplus-population (Marx 1975, Vol. I: 803) is one of the elements of a process of disarticulation in the capitalist social relation of production and of its contradiction with the development of the productive forces (Figueroa 1989; 2003). The repulsion of workers tends to be greater than their attraction. At a certain point, the falling number of active workers can no longer be compensated for by an increase in the rate of exploitation in the attempt to prevent the fall of the rate of profit. The introduction of new means of production does nothing but lead to further deterioration of the situation. (Marx 1975, Vol. I: 317–318). It is a frontal collision of the forces of production with existing social relations.

Certainly, no human being is absolutely redundant. This proposition only refers to the position of a sector of proletarians in relation to the needs of capital valorization, in other words, in relation to their significance for capital, and it graphically points out the scarce attention that capital pays to human needs.

These elements, already visible in the social map of capitalism during the time of Marx, have developed progressively with the advance of accumulation. In effect, the general tendency of the capitalist mode of production culminates in the creation of a consolidated surplus-population. As Marx put it: "The increase of the means of production and the productivity of labor which is faster than the increase of the productive population, expresses itself in capitalism in the inverse form, that is, the working population always increases more rapidly than that required by the valorization of capital" (Marx 1975, Vol. I: 804). Thus, the tendency is for relative surplus population to gradually transform itself into absolute surplus population. Once more, mounting quantitative changes come to eventually produce qualitatively different realities.

The forms of existence of an absolute surplus population must tend to multiply and grow beyond the sphere of those who lack the means to survive, such as criminals, vagabonds, etc., and eventually come to include parallel forms of labor organizations and different ways of earning income, stimulated by need and social imagination. Their existence or non-existence at the present time, as a result of the described logic, can be and must be an object of discussion. However, there is no doubt that this situation has *not* been a permanent characteristic of imperialism in developed countries. In underdeveloped countries, on the contrary, their presence is visible, but their adequate explanation must still confront some theoretical difficulties.

We cannot move on without sorting out the uneasiness that the concept of relative surplus-population continues to provoke. If it refers to a reserve army of labor that is essential in order that accumulation can proceed and is therefore a condition of the capitalist mode of production, why should it be called "surplus" population, even if "relative"? It does not seem coherent to do so since these workers are not leftovers who are unwanted or unneeded. On the contrary, they are a necessary population for capitalism and not precisely in a relative sense.

We think that Marx's limited options in this connection are determined by both his aims and his method. He studied capitalism as a closed system where everything appears organized around the capital-wage labor relation and where this social relation is the ultimate determination of all. The production of surplus-value and the exploitation of labor figures as the fundamental driving force of production. This relation is constantly moving and does not stop at contradictions save its own. This rigorous method allowed Marx to construct the most extraordinary representation of capitalism as a mode of production. At the same time, it also leads to proposals that are unsustainable when the point is to analyze societies on the basis of their own concrete historical processes. This is the case, for example, when he suggests that a laborer who works with his own means of production, like the craftsman or the peasant, could be seen as a capitalist and as a wage-worker at the same time. If he appropriates his own surplus labor, then he should be taken as a capitalist, while as a proprietor of his necessary labor, he is to be considered a wage-worker. The fundamental assumption is that separation, and not the unity of direct producers and the means of production, is the normal relation.

In addition, Marx thought that the tendency of the craftsman and the peasant was to become either a capitalist or a wage-worker. So, "in considering the essential relations of capitalist production, it can therefore be assumed that the entire world of commodities, all spheres of material production—the production of material wealth—are (formally or really) subordinated to the capitalist mode of production for this is what is happening more and more completely..." (Marx 1969, Vol. I: 409). In this context, it is only logical to call "surplus-population" the sector of society that does not own means of production and that is unemployed.

Elsewhere, Marx explains his point of view as follows: The owner of labor power, "can live as a worker only in so far as he exchanges his labor capacity for that part of capital which forms the labor fund [...] In different modes of social production, there are different laws of the increase of population and of overpopulation; the latter identical with pauperism. These different laws can simply be reduced to the different modes of relating to the conditions of production [...] The dissolution of these relations with regard to the single individual, or part of the population, places them outside the reproductive conditions of this specific basis, and hence posits them as overpopulation, and not only lacking in means but incapable of appropriating the necessaries through labor, hence as paupers" (Marx 1977, Vol. II: 604). It is also here where it can be seen that other forms of labor organization were seen as irrelevant for the sort of analysis that Marx was carrying out. Those who are not actively participating in production dwell outside the capital relation and relate to it as surplus-population. Once Marx introduces his theory of the industrial reserve army as presented in Capital, it can no longer be said that the surplus population, or at least a part of it, is "outside the reproductive conditions of this specific basis," in this case, the basis of capitalism. On the contrary, it is a condition for it. In short, the approach according to which all unemployed is "surplus" population should have been abandoned.

In the real process of capitalist society, the working population not only obtains their means of subsistence through wage-labor or by charity but also does so through non-capitalist forms of work organization. These forms can evolve either in or out of contact with the processes of capital self-expansion.

With a view to sort out all of these difficulties, we will refer to the *necessary working population* as the sector integrated by the workers directly involved in capitalist production and by the reserve army of labor. We will limit the concept of the latter to its floating and latent forms. We will call *surplus-population* all of the rest and we will distinguish: i) *relative surplus population*, to refer to the workers that from outside the capital relation engage themselves in activities that keep some sort of relationship with the accumulation process, and also those that are exploited by a capital operating outside and against the normal circuit of capital production, and ii) *absolute surplus population* in referring to those whose non-capitalist activities in no way assist the process of capital accumulation.

Population Deficits and Surpluses

Returning to the issue of migration, there is a relevant historical fact that does not seem to be properly addressed in Marxist analyses of labor mobility. The accumulation process in developed countries has for a long time been predicated on labor immigration. In other words, these countries have required legions of workers from abroad in addition to their own domestically available labor force. Besides the migratory movements that constantly take place within developed and underdeveloped countries in conjunction with their changing needs of growth, it is necessary to add the migratory flows between the global South and the global North. In the case of Latin America, this flow has since the 1950s become consolidated as a practically unilateral, South to North movement.

The UN's International Labor Organization (ILO) estimates that in 1998, the portion of migrant workers from "developing countries" reached 4.2% of the entire labor force of the OECD countries, thus reaching 57.8% of the total immigrant force. Moreover, this flow of workers to the industrialized countries has drastically increased over recent decades. The United States is the main recipient country with 81% of new migrants, followed by Canada and Australia at 11% while

France, Germany, Italy and the United Kingdom are the destinations of the rest (ILO 2004). This point is significant in a theoretical sense because it calls into question the existence of a marginal pole in the developed countries, just as it indicates *the existence of difficulties in the operation of the law of the industrial army of reserve labor in those countries.* This constitutes an internal consistency challenge for the theory of accumulation.

According to the Marxist general theory of capital accumulation, production in countries with a lower organic composition of capital, i.e., underdeveloped countries in this case, show a relatively greater capacity to attract labor-power. Their rate of unemployment should be lower than that of developed countries. In practice, however, the opposite is the case. As we have just seen, the developed countries are in fact unable to provide by themselves the required labor-power for their expansion while underdeveloped countries produce an overflowing surplus-population. The theoretical explanation must therefore reconcile these historical realities in a logical manner.

The explanation of Latin America's ability to create a surplus population alongside the industrial reserve army rests upon the confluence of two factors related to the social organization of production, namely, its capitalist character on the one hand and the frustration of the development of the division of labor that separates *general labor* (scientific labor) and *immediate* (operation) labor, on the other. The absence of this social division of labor in relation to global industrial processes is what defines the nature of underdeveloped economies. The underdevelopment of an area is above all an underdevelopment of the capital relation.

The mission of general, scientific labor is to process the development of productive forces. This labor was largely monopolized, however, by the industrialized countries. It was in this manner that they came to control not only the advancement of science but its productive applications in particular and thus the creation of new goods and production processes at each stage of capitalist development. Put another way, those countries managed to gain control over immediate labor with respect to the mass production of processes and goods. That is why they are able to decide the course followed by the process of industrialization and the limited patterns of industrial diversification in the underdeveloped countries.

The absence of the social division of scientific and immediate labor in connection to most industrial activity in underdeveloped countries forces them to satisfy their need of new processes and goods by means of international trade. This is so because, also for them, the adequate method of accumulation turned out to be the production of relative surplus-value. It is precisely the different organization of the capital relation after the emergence of large industry that gave way to the existence of both categories of countries and the imperialist relation between them (Figueroa 1989).

In the course of exchange with underdeveloped countries, more developed nations offer both products of general and immediate labor, while they receive products of immediate labor and also products of general labor, but the latter in such small measure that this flow of products of general labor towards advanced countries can essentially be ignored. The resulting relationship between both categories of countries is a *structurally unequal exchange* involving products of general *and* immediate labor on one side against products of immediate labor on the other. Every time the underdeveloped countries buy new processes and goods for their own processes of accumulation, they consequently *transfer investment*. In general, this proposal is valid for any category of countries. But in dealing with technologically advanced products whose production is controlled by the developed countries, we can observe a purchase that is not compensated for by a corresponding sale, i.e. a sale of the same type of good. The most general manifestation of this unequal exchange is the inherent tendency of the trade balance towards *deficit* in underdeveloped countries, with its corollary of *indebtedness* and periodic *recessions* originated by the need to reduce imports (Figueroa 1986).

The trade balance of underdeveloped countries tends to obfuscate this reality, especially during periods of prosperity when prices and volume of exported natural resources are high. This is something that occurred during the first eight years of the 21st Century for Latin America's exports of oil, mineral, and most agricultural products. On the other hand, looking back over a two decade period, we can see that manufactured export goods with a substantial technological content have grown steadily. Mexico, a major exporter in the region, helped pioneer the evolution of this trend. Products of both average and high technological content are concentrated in the *maquiladora* industry (i.e., those enterprises located on Mexican territory that carry out an industrial process or service by which a good sent by a parent company from abroad is transformed, repaired or used to make products for exports) and represented around 22% of the region's exports by

2001. However, this industrialization which produced greater exports has taken place in strict accordance with the archetypical patterns of underdevelopment.

The *maquiladora* industry is predicated on imported means of production, imports which normally account for more than 70% of the value of the eventual product. Beginning from the time that the *maquiladora* expansion was well underway in 1980, the local input contribution reached its highest point in 2001 at 2.7% of the value of the product. In other words, the *maquiladora* industry has not had any significant impact on the promotion of industries for import substitution. The value of exported manufactures is higher, indeed much higher in this case, than internally produced value. This means that the so-called exports of average and high technological content are predominantly sales of products obtained with poorly skilled labor-power in the exporter country.

It can be readily seen that not only the labor of conception and design of processes and products, but also a large part of the immediate labor related to the former is concentrated in the developed countries. It is also evident, although in a rather extreme way, that not only the creation of new industries but also their operation depends on imports of means of production, something that prolongs an internal deficit in the ability to create. The development of industry deepens both the lack of control over production and the incapacity of the underdeveloped countries to make their own economic decisions. As expressed by UNCTAD experts: "The growing importance of international production networks increased the degree of productive complementarity between the developed and developing countries. This means that a major share of production and exports in developing countries becomes dependant on the decisions and performance of foreign firms and countries" (Mayer, Butkevicius & Kadri 2002).

In Table 1, the balance of goods, broken down by categories, illustrates the above-mentioned trend concerning an industrial deficit in the region.

The Latin American balance of goods rests heavily on the exports of primary and industrial goods based on natural resources. As a whole, it shows a favorable balance between 1987 and 1991, based on a restrictive policy of control of imports and a decline in economic growth. For the next ten years, up through 2001, the balance was showing a deficit. From 2002 up through 2006, this situation was reversed thanks to an increase of prices and to a lesser extent by the volume of primary

Table 1: Latin American and Caribbean Commerce (millions of US dollars)

Exports

Products	1987	1992	1997	2002	2004
Primary	46,906	51,457	85,875	93,371	145,064
Industry based on natural resources	20,651	32,099	52,526	52,823	72,913
Industry with technological intensity	23,680	60,140	132,055	182,193	218,452

Imports

Primary	1987	1992	1997	2002	2004
Primary	14,300	19,999	31,115	32,469	43,981
Industry based on natural resources	13,740	25,772	49,386	50,685	62,415
Industry with technological intensity	40,180	100,237	217,245	234,499	279,506

Source: CEPAL (2006c) Statistical Annex.

Table 2: Latin America and the Caribbean—Balance of Industrial Goods (millions of dollars)

	1987	1992	1997	2002	2004
Total of industrialized	−9,589	−33,801	−82,051	−50,168	−50,554
Based on natural resources	6,911	6,297	3,139	2,137	10,498
Of low technology	2,587	−2,632	−10,154	−6,424	−5,896
Of middle technology	−11,671	−25,098	−50,483	−30,877	−31,692
Of high technology	−7,415	−12,368	−24,553	−15,005	−23,466

Source: CEPAL (2006c) Statistical Annex.

exports, especially oil, gas, copper and some agricultural products (sugar, banana and coffee) (CEPAL 2006a). During each year of the 1987–2004 period, there has been an adverse balance of industrial goods especially due to the deficit of average and high technology goods. The evolution of the balance can be seen in Table 2.

It is evident that the region's production of industrial goods is far from satisfying domestic needs. Even worse, the dependency on externally produced goods tends to grow as industrialization advances. In 1987, imports of these goods made up 78.5% of the total and by 2004, that contribution went up to 87.4%. The goods of average and high technology represented 49.2% of the total during the first year, reaching 57% by 2004. Practically the entire variation is due to the increased importance of high technology goods in industrial imports, going from 13.8% to 21.5% during that same period.

It is worth pointing out that international organizations of the "developing" countries from among the economies from the East and Southeast Asia have a high level of participation in manufacturing. Between 1996–2001, they managed to provide 30% of world exports of information and communication technologies, one of the most dynamic sectors of international trade. This regional area sells a little less than the European Union (34%), but more than the United States (17%) and Japan (15%). Meanwhile, the contribution of Latin America barely reached 4%. It seems that the distinction between "developed" countries and "developing" countries has considerably blurred at the level of trade. To situate the Republic of Korea, Taiwan, Philippines, Singapore, Thailand together with Latin America in the same category as "developing" countries indeed only makes more difficult the comprehension of structured processes which different countries are involved in.

It is not that international organizations ignore relevant differences between the mentioned Asian countries and Latin America. For example, ECLAC indicates that: "in contrast with the experiences of certain countries of Asia, the Mexican export sector, despite its supposed success, has not been able to internally create the economic links in the national economy." It further explains that: "To climb the 'technological ladder' is difficult, especially when the chain of local inputs suppliers is not developed and when enterprises located outside the territory provide parts and components as well as more sophisticated services. In these cases, the services of design and engineering, research and development, and commercialization tend to be offered by parent companies, without any real possibilities of technology transfer" (CEPAL 2003: 109).

What is barely noticed is that countries that are climbing the "technological ladder" are indeed advancing in the development of their capitalist division of labor. They are giving rise to the organization of their general labor and are building the conditions that make it possible for them to appropriate and produce the knowledge and skills that are necessary for the process of accumulation. They do not expect that the export sector will be able to create the necessary economic links. On the contrary, they undertook the task of producing technological progress as national projects, which would raise their nations to a new position relative to the imperialist powers. They are countries and zones that are at the threshold of capitalist development and they have already renegotiated their position in the global market. Latin America, in turn, continues to be trapped in the backyard of imperialism. This also suggests that there is no inevitability in the state of affairs that keeps the region underdeveloped, but rather a political will of governments and ruling classes that seems more inclined to adaptation rather than radical transformation.

To sum up preceding arguments, the underdevelopment of the capital relation, i.e., the absence of the division that organizes general or scientific labor, as different from immediate work, *conveys a transfer to the developed countries of the capacity for accumulation in underdeveloped countries to generate employment.*

Simultaneously, the process by which a reserve army of labor is created also takes place due to relative surplus value production. Historically, the penetration of capitalism in Latin America combined the processes of original accumulation (separation between the producer and his means) with the production of relative surplus, as required by the type of industry that arrived in the region from the end of the 19th century. This combination ended up weakening the ability of capitalism to promote the separation of means and producer. In fact, it has been necessary to reorganize in a non-capitalist way for large sections of the surplus-population, as in the case of agrarian reforms; or else, to send millions of workers abroad as with the *bracero* program that was established by mutual accord between Mexico and the USA (1942–1964).

As for the effects of the consolidation of capitalism over the working population, there is no single pattern. In a country like Mexico, for example, the relatively low capacity of accumulation to absorb labor-power, together with the increasing disposal of a "free" labor force promotes a very slow evolution of capitalism in agriculture. Argentina, in contrast, combines a huge availability of lands and a relatively low population that favors labor immigration, extends wage-labor and promotes the introduction of capitalist techniques. In other words, the starting point in different areas will be translated into diverse circumstances of the population that will have a distinct impact over subsequent years. Once capitalism is consolidated inside definite territorial limits and with predominance in all the branches, production nevertheless tends to always create a reserve army, whatever the average composition of capital.

Alongside of this general feature of capitalism, we find in Latin America that there is a steady transfer of investment and jobs that accompanies accumulation. Due to these reasons, underdeveloped capitalist production not only creates a reserve army but also a surplus population, that is, one that *extends itself beyond the average needs of the valorization of capital*, i.e. the needs of capital either working or latent.

The *opposite situation* is to be found in developed capitalism. While in underdevelopment, accumulation consumes more than what it produces, accumulation in developed countries produces more than what it consumes. The shortage of production in one pole is satisfied with the excess of production in the other. Therefore, while in underdeveloped countries accumulation generates an overflowing overpopulation, the developed countries witness an *insufficiency in the creation* of their reserve army of labor. The imperialist organization of production that condemns certain countries to concentrate on immediate labor also distributes in an unequal way the energy with which each pole of the system generates available labor-power.

The History and Nature of the One-Sided Immigrant

We can now begin to see the nature of the migrant worker. The emigrating laborer can be regarded as one for whom accumulation lacks a productive function in their own country, be it in actual or potential production. Governments are not interested to retain him at home but on the contrary, they are inclined to support his relocation on account of the problems that this shift alleviates and of the advantages that it creates. Generally speaking the laborer is a member of the surplus population and his situation is redefined so soon as the migration takes place and his incorporation into productive activity in the developed country that receives him is consummated. It thus becomes clear that his true nature is to be a part of a *reserve army of labor created in one pole of the international system so as to serve in the other*. But this nature is a historical one and the situation of these migrants is an unsettled one since they gained worldwide fame for joining the ranks of poverty and unemployment within developed countries (Levine 2002).

If we take as reference the lot of Latin American migrants to the United States, not including either undocumented laborers or temporary shifts, it was estimated that by 2000, there were almost 14.5 million Latinos now settled (Pellegrino 2003) of which almost 7.8 million came from Mexico. Another 2.7 million were settled in Spain, Canada, the United Kingdom and Japan (CELADE 2002).

The fact that regional emigration to developed countries has grown over recent decades is challenging. The United States as a main destination registered around 820 thousand people during the 1960s. This amount steadily increased, almost doubling the next decade, although the growth of migration rates seemed to decline somewhat in the 1980s and 1990s. This evolution might be interpreted as the response to a *growing insufficiency* of the developed economy to produce its own reserve army of labor which would mean that the theory of accumulation, in its more general formulation, would still have to wait before falling into alignment with reality. But this is not actually the case.

It is a fact that unemployment rates in developed countries have been growing over the long run (Maddison 1996; OECD, 2003). Today, nobody refers any longer to 3% or even 4% as "normal" unemployment rates. In 2005, the rate of unemployment in OECD countries reached 6.6%, including a 5.1% rate for the United States and an 8.6% rate for Europe. In 2002, OECD registered 8.4 million unemployed for the United States and another 13.5 million in the European Union. For the OECD countries as a whole, the number of unemployed reached 36.4 million (OECD 2003). These figures should suffice to demonstrate that developed capitalism can already rely on its own reserve army of labor. However, there is more to the picture.

The participation of part-time labor in total employment has also been increasing steadily, going from 11.6% in 1994 up to 15.4% in 2005 in the OECD countries. It is clear that a sector of part-time workers must be considered partial unemployment, available for work, and therefore construed as a reserve of labor. The OECD itself put it rightly: "There is a potential supply of labor amongst people who are unintentionally employed on a partial basis" (OECD 2003: 105). Those who are able to work but who do not participate in the labor market should also be considered as a potentially employable labor force. At the same time, temporary labor has also grown. "Although temporary work was in general less dynamic than part-time labor, its expansion generates concerns because most temporary workers would prefer permanent jobs" (OECD 2003: 20).

At the same time, the exploitation of workers has become more intense so the proportion of workers that report that "they are working at very high intensity or under very tense limits of time is increasing. Those who work many hours or at an intense pace also report a growing number of stress-related health problems and major difficulties in reconciling work with their family life" (OECD 2003: 20).

The devaluation of jobs, the greater exploitation of labor, the growing perception that employment is more and more uncertain, and all the conditions related to labor precariousness and flexibility would simply not be possible under conditions of scarcity in the labor force. Likewise is the case with the worsening of poverty. In the United States, the population living poverty reached 37 million by 2005, or about 12.6% of the total (US Census Bureau 2007). This figure was 5 million greater than in 2001 and 6 million more than in 2000. It is estimated that 15.6 million now live under extreme poverty (i.e. people receiving an income lower than the half the poverty threshold), representing the highest level since 1975 (US Conference of Catholic Bishops 2006). This course of events is not normal under conditions of a limited supply of labor-power. Developed capitalism *has already overcome* its limitations for the internal creation of its reserve labor force.

There is no doubt that for a long time, the migration of workers made it possible for developed countries to respond to their limited capacity to create a reserve army of labor. But the migratory flow to the global North during the last few decades, especially to the United States in the case of Latin America, can only partly be attributed to that reason. Other causes related to the economic order created by neo-liberal globalization further contributed. First, the processes of economic restructuring in Latin America further weakened the ability of production to create employment. The commercial liberalization forced countries to improve their productivity levels, thus changing the technical and organic composition of local capital, with a view to compete abroad and with imports at the level of the domestic market.

Second, many industries went bankrupt as a result of their inability to carry out their re-structuring. Exports, handled by international capital, did grow at high rates, but the gross domestic product increased far below the levels of the decades of the 1950s, 1960s and 1970s. As a result, Latin America lost further ground in the world market. World production became ever more concentrated in the former developed countries as well as in emergent ones. Estimates by the ILO revealed that the gap between the high and middle income countries grew from eight to fourteen times between 1975 and 2000, and that the gap between the high and low income countries extended from forty-one to sixty-six times in the same period (ILO 2004). Third, state economic activity abruptly went down everywhere thus further expanding unemployment (ILO 2004).

So, it can be see that the great mass of available labor-power ready to emigrate, and ever more motivated to do so as a result of weakening local conditions, began to take off. The international movement of workers was further encouraged by the existence of a *dense net of relationships* that the long tradition of migration had created. In this sense, it can be said that labor migration to the North was further motivated by institutional conditions. Yet, this spatial redistribution of labor that followed the restructuring of world production is not without limit, since the host countries have their own problems as we have already seen. Immigration to the developed countries at present is no longer as welcome as it was in prior decades, although highly qualified and temporary labor still enjoys the support of recipient governments.

During the 1980s, it is true that the US did promote immigration even in a context of high unemployment. The reason for this was that the government was devoted to the task of introducing greater labor flexibility and the de-regulation of labor relations. Immigration was assigned a new functional role of overloading the labor market with the aim of weakening unions and introducing a new regime of labor relations (CELADE 2002). In short, immigration was encouraged so at to assist U.S. political goals.

Remittances and Wage Differentials

From the underdeveloped country's perspective, the advantages of migration are many. Not only are potential conflicts avoided, allowing governments to better handle internal tensions, but considerable economic advantages are also obtained. Migrating laborers in large part carry with them the responsibility to maintain their family being left behind. As the migrants work abroad, they perform this role via cash remittances. The volume of money that workers send to the region from the North has steadily increased over recent decades. For 1990, total remittances were calculated at about US$5.8 billion and by 2005, it had grown to an estimated US$53.5 billion. Although these amounts could be distorted because of methodological problems in measuring their magnitude (CEPAL 2006b), they suggest an impressive dynamic. Remittances represented around 2.6% of the regional GDP in 2005, although it has more recently been found that their rate of growth is slowing (Cortina; de la Garza and Ochoa-Reza 2005).

There is no need to explain the excitement that remittances have created for national and international public organizations and private economic and banking interests. With the rationale of promoting a better impact of remittances on development, these institutions have jockeyed within the framework of their respective interests to obtain the best possible benefit for themselves.

These remittances are destined overwhelmingly to consumption (80–85%) and this indicates the extent to which the reproduction of the region's labor-power is accomplished by means of value created abroad. That is to say, a part of internal production, equivalent to the consumption that takes place on account of foreign remittances which is not satisfied with imports, rests on the value created by migrant workers. It follows that the regional production of wage-goods for internal consumption is bigger than the income generated internally for those purposes. The remittances take the production of wage-goods beyond the limits determined by domestic wages and therefore have a positive impact on local production and employment.

Remittances have other positive effects, such as the strengthening of current accounts and the increase of government income by means of taxes, and even the "reduction of poverty" without any cost for governments and employers. At the same time, they have undesired effects such as the weakening of the competitiveness of export products and the promotion of imports caused by a strengthened local currency. But these disadvantages are just "collateral damage" in the context of the larger process, the export of labor-power that has been assumed as a business by the region governments.

The question of wage differentials between the different categories of countries, something that make remittances possible, demands specific attention in this context. The surplus-population certainly bears upon it and according to the perspective we have been working on, the point must be clarified. According to Marx in Chapter 25 of Capital (Vol. I): "Taking them as a whole, the general movement of wages is exclusively regulated by the expansion and contraction of the industrial reserve army and this again corresponds to the periodic changes of the industrial cycle" (Marx 1975). So, it is not the reserve army of labor that regulates the general movements of wages, but rather accumulation determines the size of this reserve and the negotiating power of the workers. Accumulation produces a labor reserve of a magnitude that varies with the succession of phases in the process of production. In periods of expansion, the surplus-population decreases, the trade union movement is strengthened, competition between workers weakens, and wages tend to rise. The opposite then occurs during the contraction phase. That is to say, the functioning of capital produces *different correlations of power between social classes*, thereby creating different contexts for the negotiation of wage levels.

In the underdeveloped countries, a permanent overflowing of surplus-population can only act as a constant downward pressure on wage levels. Indeed, the surplus-population is one of the main reasons for the value of labor-power being low,[1] since it weakens the position of the active labor force. This thesis is by itself so clear that in fact what must be explained is why the relative value of labor-power in Latin America is not even lower than what it is, or why there are occasionally periods when *wages* register significant increases.

The influence of the surplus-population over the level of wages clearly contains two elements: one objective and the other subjective. The former is defined by the existence of the surplus-population as an element that results from the organization of the relations of production. In this context, surplus-population is a burden for active labor and its effect is negative. The subjective element appears because the

---

[1] This is not to say that the labour-power is paid underneath its value; its value itself is lower than in developed countries (Figueroa 1986).

surplus-population contributes to a highly explosive concentration of discontent and unrest. It has frequently formed part of the region's great social and political movements. Landless laborers, "marginals," and the unemployed in the countryside and in the cities, along with "informal workers" and the like have organized themselves to pursue their own specific demands or have coalesced around wider populist upsurges. Most recently, they have been prominent in the movements that culminated with progressive governments in Venezuela, Bolivia, Ecuador and Nicaragua, and have constituted an important element of significant regional political resistance to neoliberalism. Probably no significant movement that has ended with concessions to the working class has lacked the participation of the surplus-population.

This social movement dynamic has nevertheless exhibited its ups and downs. Dramatic episodes of repression in Latin America have also been as consistent as social discontent. Such repression is the method by which capital restricts concession. It not only obstructs but eventually orients in an opposite direction the improvement of living conditions for the popular sectors. Political struggle is a prominent factor in the determination of wage levels and the surplus-population is an important actor in this conflict. The larger difficulties facing the democratization of Latin American societies are strongly rooted in the active relationship between discontent and repression.

The relatively low value of the region's labor-power has other objective causes which can be mentioned here. The lower skill level of labor-power required by capital with a lower average technical composition is one factor. The so-called "educational deficiencies" as visualized from the developed countries correspond to that situation. In addition, a lower average intensity of labor corresponds to a lower technical composition. As the worker's energy expended in developed countries is greater, the reward that he receives must be larger. A union movement free from the burden of a surplus-population enjoys a more advantageous position to win the necessary compensation.

Conclusion

The emergence of imperialism opened some novel routes to the operation of Marx's law of population, unequally delivering its effects on developed and underdeveloped countries. This neither eliminated the law itself nor prevented its originally anticipated effects from taking place in the long run. A Marxist theory of migration is possible so long as general categories and actual processes become mediated through a logical approximation.

There will be an irresolvable conflict between general theory and historical process if the forces that capital mobilizes to counter those tendencies that restrain its development and their impact on capital organization are ignored. For example, a number of measures such as capital export, colonial control, and the creation of monopolies were aimed to counter the tendency of the rate of profit to fall. These measures led the way to imperialism, i.e., a new phase in the development of capital. Every new phase implies a change in the relation of capital.

In this sense, we can distinguish three major phases: 1) labor's formal subsumption in capital (manufacture); b) real subsumption of immediate labor by capital (large industry—free competition) and c) real subsumption of immediate labor combined with formal subsumption of general labor by monopoly capital (imperialism). As suggested earlier, underdeveloped capitalism did not organize the formal subsumption of general labor. Therefore, the operation of capital at the international level was bound to display a specific logic, one that would differ from the more abstract logic outlined in *Capital*. But this is no more than the logic of a *phase* of the historical process of capital which sooner or later has to end up coming to terms with more abstract postulates.

We have pointed out that the worker who leaves his underdeveloped country for the United States shows himself as a part of a reserve army of labor that was created to serve the interests of this latter country. In principle, he appeared as a member of his own country's surplus population. Yet, this does not mean that he was necessarily unemployed. In most cases, it only means that he lacked a job under capitalist conditions. As shown here, the surplus population is forced to do something in order to acquire the means of economic survival. This seems to support the theory that wage differentials and not precarious jobs and unemployment are the real cause of migration. In the same way that neo-classical theories pay no attention to structural causes, they also do not seem to worry about the fact that migration has done nothing to equalize wages.

The international articulation of the labor market through migration is starting to become depleted. The development of productive forces is allowing advanced countries to not only create their own reserve army of labor but also their own surplus population. The attraction of migrant labor power is increasingly limited to skilled segments of workers and temporary workers. This attraction should continue to weaken as well. In accordance with this trend, Latin America's surplus population will also grow. This is its fate under capitalism. While the trend could be moderated by the reorientation of productions towards a more inward-oriented strategy of economic growth, a path which the present world crisis makes ever more likely, it does not offer any possibility of its elimination.

WHAT IS THE POTENTIAL OF LATIN AMERICA'S "THIRD LEFT"?

Marie Kennedy, Fernando Leiva and Chris Tilly

September 11, 1973 symbolically marked an important turning point for the left in Latin America. On that day the armed forces of Chile, with the collusion of the U.S. government, overthrew the constitutionally elected social democratic government of Salvador Allende. This coup d'état was far from unprecedented (the memory of coups in Guatemala in 1954, Brazil in 1964, the Dominican Republic in 1965, and Peru in 1968 was still fresh at the time), and did not signify an end to all left advances in Latin America (popular movements unseated dictators in Nicaragua in 1979 and Haiti in 1986). But the toppling of a broadly popular government in a nation with a long, continuous history of constitutional democracy marked a new aggressiveness of conservative regional elites. They preferred to combine laissez faire economics with state terror to restructure Latin American society, signaling a reversal of the region-wide left upsurge initiated by the 1959 victory of the Cuban revolution. Over the next two decades most of Latin America fell under the sway of authoritarian governments, and left parties, programs, and movements were severely repressed, battered and marginalized. The economic, political and cultural structures that underpinned the left's support were to be radically restructured by neoliberal policies.

Almost three decades later, October 28, 2002 represented another kind of turning point for Latin America's left. That day brought the election of former factory worker and Workers' Party leader Lula da Silva to the presidency of Brazil, Latin America's largest country. Lula's election seemed to be the clearest example of the political realignment that was unfolding throughout the region during the first decade of the 21st Century. Left governments of various stripes would be elected in half a dozen other countries, with close defeats in a number of others. Latin American populations were, and are, mounting "the struggle for post-neoliberalism," as Brazilian sociologist Emir Sader puts it (Hernández 2007). Lula's victory certainly did not define a sharp boundary—new stirrings of revolt dated back at least to the 1994 Zapatista uprising—but it signified a decisive shift in momentum.

Though it is indisputable that the left has gained ground in Latin America, the left movements and governments in ascendance across the region are a heterogeneous lot. Michelle Bachelet's moderate center-left social democratic government in Chile has little in common with the anarcho-communalist Zapatista movement. There is considerable value, then, in distinguishing among left currents in what Cuban nationalist José Martí called Nuestra América (Our America), and assessing their varied prospects.

In this paper, we argue that a particularly important component of Latin America's current radical resurgence is what we call the "third left."[1] The easiest way to identify the third left may be to contrast it with the "old" left approaches that have dominated the region for the last five decades. One such approach was the armed guerilla movements, inspired by the Cuban revolution, but now largely extinct (with Colombia as the chief, now waning, exception). The other was the mass populist movements linked by patronage or party discipline to left or center-left electoral parties. While the guerrilleros have declined, left political parties much like the traditional ones, far from disappearing, have surged in the last several years across much of Latin America.

Both of these lefts have helped make progressive changes in Latin America—challenging inequality, attacking illiteracy, improving services to the poor, redistributing land, and mobilizing ordinary people to defend their rights. But neither has had a strong tradition of bottom-up organizing. The military model at the core of the guerilla insurgencies and the model of charismatic leadership at the core of electoral leftism are centralized, top-down models—structures that can represent the interests of poor majorities, but usually without directly involving them in the decisions that affect their lives.

The third left takes a different direction. According to Sader,

> The old strategies of reforms promoted by Latin America's lefts have been left behind. The same is true of guerilla warfare. By moving from social to

---

[1] We thank participants in the annual meetings of the Latin American Studies Association (Montréal, 2007), Society for the Advancement of Socioeconomics (San José, Costa Rica 2008) and *Critical Sociology* (Boston, 2008) for useful input into this paper. Parts of this discussion have appeared in Kennedy and Tilly 2006 and 2008. Where we do not provide references for quotations or descriptions of movements, they come from interviews conducted by Kennedy and Tilly or syntheses of previous publications by us (these publications are all cited at one point or another). Quotations in English from references in Spanish were translated by the authors.

political struggle, resistance struggles against neoliberalism have forged a new strategy for the left of the continent (Hernández 2007).

In previous work (Kennedy and Tilly 2006a, 2008), we have contrasted the third left with the other two in terms of promotion of bottom-up decision-making and the pursuit of autonomy from the state rather than of state power. Uruguayan analyst Raúl Zibechi (2008), in his own analysis of new directions in the Latin American left, likewise pointed to these two characteristics. He went on to suggest two others that accurately describe the same set of movements, and we are now adopting one part of Zibechi's expanded framework as definitional, the second as descriptive. A third definitional feature, then, is that these movements all stake claims on territory, whether it be a community or simply an empty building. Finally, and more descriptively, these movements are primarily grounded in identities other than those of Latin America's traditional social movement actors—employed workers, peasants, and students. Third left movements have especially erupted among newly active groups: indigenous people (Mattiace 2005), slum dwellers (Álvarez-Rivadulla 2008), laid-off workers (Lavaca 2007).

Others have also emphasized elements of this three-plus-part definition in describing what is new about Latin America's left movements. For example, NACLA (2005) focused on autonomy, Vanden (2008) on participation while Stahler-Sholk, Vanden, and Kuecker (2008) highlighted both autonomy and participation. José Luis Coraggio captured the same sense in describing Latin America's search for how to name a variety of social practices and experiences that involve the construction of noncapitalist economic forms and seek to institutionalize the values of "…a solidarity which is not easy to produce, because it presupposes a complex praxis involving politico-ideological, technological, organizational, juridical, communicational and emotional aspects, as well as a constant struggle to preserve, expand, and consolidate it" (Coraggio 2008).

As we explore below, the boundaries of this third left are debatable. We would definitely include Brazil's Landless Workers' Movement (MST) (Kennedy and Tilly 2002; Stedile and Fernandes 1999; Vanden 2005; Welch 2006; Wright and Wolford 2003), Argentina's autonomista current of workplace and community organizations (Collin in this volume; Kennedy and Tilly 2005a,b,c; Lavaca 2007; Sitrin 2006), Mexico's Zapatista movement (Cerullo in this volume, Harvey 2005, Kennedy and Tilly 2006b, Stahler-Sholk 2005, 2008), and the Federation of Neighborhood Councils (FEJUVE) in the indigenous metropolis of El Alto, Bolivia (near La Paz), a grassroots community organization at the center of the strikes and protests that brought down two governments and carried Evo Morales to power (Achtenberg in this volume; Vanden 2008). But beyond these high profile examples, this political current includes varied other groups in just about every country in Latin America. Zibechi (2008) enumerated such groups in Bolivia, Colombia, and Ecuador. We have written about the rise of self-defined autonomous indigenous communities across Mexico from Tlalnepantla, Morelos to Zirahuén, Michoacan (Kennedy and Tilly 2004), and Mexico's Popular Assembly of the Peoples of Oaxaca (APPO), which controlled parts of Oaxaca's capital city for months in 2006, and these fit the mold as well (Davies 2007). So do Brazil's quilombos, i.e., Afro-Brazilian rural communities that are descended from runaway slaves and fighting for communal control over their land (Kogan 2007). These characteristics are also shared by a wide range of environmental movements led by residents and users of the land, water, plant, and animal resources under threat (for example, Árias 2008; Bacon 2007; Kuecker 2008; Witte 2006; 2007).

In this paper, we seek to do five things. First, we examine the strengths and limitations of our definition of a third left. Second, we elaborate how the four defining elements play out in the actual movements in question. Third, we distinguish among three main political directions adopted by adherents to the third left. Fourth and fifth, we summarize the key achievements of Latin America's third left and then consider at greater length some of the challenges facing this new brand of politics. We close with very brief conclusions.

Strengths and Limitations of Our Definition

We would argue that our definition has two chief strengths. The first is that it corresponds empirically to an important subset of Latin American social movements struggling to displace state power by popular power with varying degrees of local, regional, and national success. The second is that the definition has a certain coherence, and coheres as well with the spread of neoliberal policies that has diminished the national state's capacity for, and commitment to, income redistribution, provision of social service and infrastructure, and support of national industries and agriculture. By battering traditional industries and agriculture, neoliberalism erodes the economic base for traditional proletarian and peasant identities, driving social groups toward both older identities (indigenous people) and newer ones (landless people, the unemployed), producing "new articulations of culture with class" across diverse social sectors (Albro 2005: 433–34). In the face of the shrunken redistributive capacity of the neoliberal state, and the restructuring of the state and political systems to render the market and the new regime of accumulation immune to popular demands, a shift toward autonomy makes sense. Control of territory and widespread participation make autonomy, rather than dependence on state provision of jobs and subsidies, more viable. Autonomy also neutralizes the fragmentation, cooptation and commodification embedded in the social policies of a new type that the restructured and recalibrated state seeks to deploy in the region. Participation itself helps construct robust new identities.

But like any ideal type, the concept of the third left frays somewhat upon closer examination. Concrete historical processes are messy and all categorizations used to try to interpret them have limitations. In this regard, the differentiation of the Latin American left into a military, electoral and autonomist left, is useful as an expository device as long as we acknowledge that these boundaries are not fixed in stone. The past five or six decades have given us many examples of processes that ultimately transgress and violate such clear demarcations. In Latin America, various armed organizations became electoral parties—for example, El Salvador's FMLN (Farabundo Martí National Liberation Front), URNG (Guatemalan National Revolutionary Unity), Nicaragua's FSLN (Sandinista National Liberation Front.), Colombia's Patriotic Union, etc. We have also witneseed how electoral political parties have decided to take up arms and shift their strategic and/or tactical initiative towards armed struggle—the origins of the FARC (Armed Revolutionary Forces of Colombia), the Communist Party of El Salvador, the Communist Party of Chile in the 1980s, etc. It can further be seen that some social movements expand and develop into armed organizations, while elsewhere, armed struggle and armed organizations become social movements—for example, the genesis and current practice of Mexico's EZLN (the Zapatista Army of National Liberation).

If we are clear that the boundaries are not always solid but porous, it nonetheless behooves us to determine whether the array of social practices encompassed in our definitions, effectively distinguish a third left in Latin America. Beyond the particular forms of struggle in a particular historical moment, what needs to be determined can be summed up in the following two questions: Is there a distinct strategic or epistemological stance that is unique to Latin America's third left? Do the conceptions and practices of what is tentatively grouped as third left, represent a historical rupture from the past and a new synthesis of the present? As becomes clear below where we discuss particular cases (and even more so in the more detailed papers by Achtenberg, Cerullo and Collin in this volume), this rich set of social practices originated as ways to ensure livelihood and give voice to those excluded. At what point can we say that they have taken the leap into a strategy for societal transformation? What signals that these social practices have jumped from being a conjunctural response into enacting an epistemological break and a self-aware political project for the self-transformation and self-liberation in the Latin American context? Although we contend that the evidence suggests that such a jump has occurred, we concede that more careful study of these and other movements is required to fully make the case.

Moreover, the kind of practices that are gouped under the umbrella of the third left—horizontality, direct democracy, territorially-grounded multi-sector alliances—are not new in the history of Latin America's social movements. Zibechi (2008) identifies movements fitting this profile beginning in the early 1970s, including the CRIC (Regional Indigenous Council of Cauca in Colombia, 1971), Ecuarunari (Ecuador, 1972), Bolivia's Tiahuanaco Manifesto (1973), and the Indigenous Congress of Mexico (1974). We can add that these traits, in various combinations, have been present in a number of other mobilizations of previous decades—the Cordones Industriales and Comandos Comunales in Chile during the 1972–1973 period and the Asamblea Popular and other examples of dual power already experienced in Bolivia (Zavaleta Mercado 1979), or under conditions of military dictatorship (Leiva and Petras 1986). In other words, there is a rich tradition of constructing "popular power" that has been practiced by social movements, grass-roots activists and militants at different historical junctures, during pre-revolutionary as well as counter-revolutionary periods.

There is little question that the scale of such strategies has expanded. Nonetheless, can we say that a qualitative tipping point has been reached given the scope and amplitude reached by such practices over recent years? The question remains whether autonomy, horizontality, transparency, self-transformation through praxis and direct democracy, all constitute characteristics of sophisticated social movements or whether they have become the founding principles for a qualitatively new historical project and its corresponding strategy and tactics. Noting these concerns, we move to an elaboration of how the three elements of the definition along with the added descriptive element of new identities appear to play out in practice.

The Four Elements in Practice

Autonomy and territorial control

The two older lefts emphasized making demands on the state with the goal of taking it over. But in the context of states with shrunken capacities, this approach falls short. The third left instead pursues autonomy—still making demands on the state, but with much more focus on organizing people to do things for themselves. This includes economic, political, and cultural autonomy.

Economic autonomy is closely linked to control of territory. MST settlements in Brazil cultivate previously unused agricultural lands they have occupied. In Argentina workers take over and run bankrupt enterprises. Mexico's Zapatistas carry out subsistence agriculture as well as producing fair trade coffee and indigenous crafts for sale. The Bolivian FEJUVE neighborhood councils pool community resources to purchase land and install infrastructure as well as regulate the buying and selling of land and homes. Indigenous activists in Zirahuén, Mexico seek to safeguard their lake, the treasure of their community and a basis for sustainable tourism as well as farming, from developers who seek to build a golf course and resort. In step with these economic strategies, many of these movements seek to develop independent technical and investment resources. For example, the MST has built a network of technical experts who can provide advice and has even established its own seed bank. In all of these instances, the idea is to link scattered productive projects into a broader "social economy" prioritizing human needs rather than profits.

In many cases, environmental sustainability is part of the package. Some MST settlements provide successful models of organic and agro-ecological production. In 2005, the MST worked in cooperation with La Via Campesina[2] to establish the Latin American School of Agro-

---

[2] *La Via Campesina* is a peasant producers' organization that brings together movements involved in the struggle for land from all over the world.

ecology. By 2008, the school graduated its first class of 100 technicians from peasant organizations throughout Latin America.

Political autonomy means independence from the state and political parties. The degree of independence varies. As Lula wound up his successful 2002 run for the presidency, MST organizer Jonas da Silva in 2002 told us: "We are critical of Lula, but we're campaigning for him. What matters is not the election, but democratizing the media and breaking up the large land-holdings." When Lula won, the MST challenged him with an accelerated program of land occupations. For the most part, MST leaders eschewed positions in the left government and the MST is sharply critical of Lula for his retreat from a broader progressive program (Stedile 2008).

Similarly, in Bolivia and Argentina, third left organizations have generally supported Evo Morales and Néstor Kirchner and now Cristina Fernández de Kirchner, but continue to make independent criticisms and demands. In contrast, the Zapatistas declined to support center-left populist Andrés Manuel López Obrador in the 2006 Mexican presidential elections, arguing that his program simply put a kinder face on a brutal system. The MST demands government funding to buy agricultural inputs and create community infrastructure; FEJUVE likewise presses the government for financial assistance for community development—including joining the successful struggle to establish a public university in El Alto. On the other hand, the Zapatistas refuse all government aid, instead "taxing" the government and NGOs for projects they carry out on Zapatista turf. They have, however led the long and (so far) unsuccessful struggle for legislation guaranteeing stronger rights for Mexican indigenous people to control their land, resources, and lives.

Some organizations walk a fine line. For example, Argentina's Unemployed Workers' Movement (MTD) of La Matanza seeks government funds for projects but refuses the patronage-linked welfare checks that have "destroyed many organizations," this according to one activist we interviewed by the name of Soledad (who prefers to be identified only by her first name). All of these organizations combine building broad alliances with maintaining independent politics, including the right to criticize any party as well as the state itself.

To help build cultural autonomy, Latin America's third left places enormous emphasis on education. Both the MST and the Zapatistas take over the schools in their communities, train their own teachers, and implement their own curriculum. Autonomista workplace and community organizations in Argentina typically require members to take classes in principles of cooperativism, and quite a few of the worker-run businesses host adult education classes and community cultural centers. Activists from Haiti to Chile use low-powered, local FM radio stations to promote discussions about social justice and give voice to the voiceless.

Bottom-up decision-making

In addition to autonomy, the other axis of Latin America's third left is horizontalidad, a word that translates rather poorly as "horizontality"—in contrast with the top-down verticalismo (or verticality) that continues to characterize much left activity in Latin America (and elsewhere). This means "having everybody decide," says Argentine social psychologist/activist Maiqui Pixton, who works with the cooperative housing movement in Buenos Aires. The specifics vary. The Zapatistas use village-wide meetings to decide local issues, rotate regional leaders, and use intensive consultation to reach movement-wide decisions. The MST uses a more traditional set of pyramidal elected councils (with some less traditional aspects, such as mandating an equal number of women and men representatives at every level). Indeed, some have criticized the MST for being excessively hierarchical (Rubin 2006). Argentina's worker-run companies typically combine frequent workplace-wide assemblies with an elected management council that has executive powers. Housing cooperatives in Argentina bring together coop members and skilled professionals (architects, psychologists, and others) in participatory design and planning. But in every case, these organizations are committed to broad participation, bottom-up decision-making and transparent governance. This is participatory planning in practice, with plenty of imperfections but a genuine effort to shift power downward, and a goal of empowering people to move beyond the immediate project to tackle other issues in their lives. Again, education is a key ingredient as activists seek to give people the tools to participate meaningfully, break down dependencies and transform themselves into active decision-makers.

Broad participation can provide an opening for the formerly excluded, but it can also simply obscure domination of decision-making by informal elites. Both tendencies are present in third left organizations (See Kennedy and Tilly 2005a; Rubin 2006). But evolving gender dynamics in these movements suggest that they are indeed giving voice to subordinate groups. While women in the MST or the Zapatista movement certainly do not occupy a position equal to that of men, these movements' efforts to promote women's participation and equality have unleashed discussion of gender relations and created far more egalitarian relations than in the surrounding rural societies (Kampwirth 2002). A conversation we and other colleagues have had with the Junta de Buen Gobierno (Good Government Council—the Zapatistas' name for their town councils) at the autonomous community of Magdalena La Paz in the Chiapas highlands illustrates the advances and continuing challenges. The Junta proudly pointed out that they consisted of seven women and six men, despite a prevailing culture in which women walk several steps behind their husbands, carry heavy burdens as their husbands walk empty-handed, and often suffer domestic abuse. When it was pointed out that all six men were there but only two of the women, they explained, "The other women are married," and therefore unable to attend the meeting due to their domestic duties. Asked if it was new for women to be involved in government, they replied, "No, they were involved until the Spanish came." Whether accurate or not, their vision of self-governing pre-Hispanic indigenous communities includes equal political participation by women.

Horizontalidad is an ongoing experiment. As Soledad of MTD in La Matanza recounted, "When a small group of us was dreaming about a community center, we had a lot of prejudices. We doubted that the community would accept the values and principles that we had agreed on. But we were wrong—the community was able to contribute." She laughed, "When we formed the 'educational community' to govern our day care center, we feared that the parents wouldn't speak up. The other day, one of the mothers said, 'Now, you can't get us to shut up, can you?'"

Autonomy and horizontalidad complement each other. Fewer strings leading to the economic and political centers of power means more room for input from people at the base. On the flip side, autonomy is a hard road, and mass participation increases the chance of success. "None of us alone is as good as all of us together," declared Soledad, quoting a movement slogan.

New identities

An exciting characteristic of many of the movements that we would define as third left is their mobilization of identities distinct from those of traditional left actors, such as students and trade unionists. In Argentina, workers laid off from closed businesses are building organizations at just the point when trade union struggles ended. Similarly, homeless Argentines are now organizing themselves into housing cooperatives where tenant union struggles have left off. Other movements to seize and cooperatively run businesses and housing have arisen in many other Latin American countries. In Brazil, the MST and competing landless movements have provided avenues for encouraging landless rural workers to organize themselves outside the purview of existing peasant organizations. In Mexico, first peoples from the Zapatistas to Zirahuén are mobilizing and building institutions around their indigenous identities, not just plugging into already existing movements. In so doing, they are joining similar movements on the South American continent from Colombia to Chile, and above all in Bolivia. As Zibechi (2008) notes in speaking of these new organizations: "...they started to stir the deep waters of social sectors that up until that moment had not made their voices heard independently. Instead, they had joined large conglomerates in which their voices were barely audible." This plethora of new identities greatly extends the reach of left movements at a time when neoliberal reforms have undermined the material base for traditional labor union and peasant organization, even though they also contain the potential for a fragmentation of struggles.

Three Options Within the Third Left

The Latin American third left's political strategies vary widely, with neither the benefit nor the limitation of a numbered International to provide guidance, with varied class roots, and building on diverse local traditions in a context of decentralization and local autonomy. Reacting to the World Social Forum's slogan that "Another world is possible," the Zapatistas called for "A world within which many worlds will fit."

Within this range of variation, new movements on Latin America's left have taken three political directions. First, some have gravitated toward the more totalizing visions of the guerrilleros and the traditional left parties—seeking to solidify unity in action by subordinating autonomous movements to a single ideology and organization, often with a goal of pushing the state or contending for state power (or consolidating state power after an electoral victory). Venezuela's Bolivarian left has some of this tendency (Chirino 2008; Hawkins and Hansen 2006;

Wilkinson 2008). "Venezuela has a politically mobilized population, but it is a population that has been mobilized by [President Hugo] Chávez himself," remarked left Venezuelan historian Margarita López Maya (Rosen 2007). Kirk Hawkins and David Hansen (2006: 102) concluded that Venezuela's Bolivarian Circles "embodied a charismatic mode of linkage to Chávez," and "often reinforced clientelistic relations between Chávez and the voters." We see such movements as part of the "first left" rather than forming part of the third one.

A second thrust has been withdrawal from national politics as such, deepening autonomy but limiting impact. When we asked a rank-and-file Maya activist of the Zapatista movement as to why the Zapatistas so rarely take part in broader alliances, his answer made it clear that for him the word alianza was a negative one connoting back-scratching politics. But the "purity" of the resulting politics has reduced Zapatismo's impact on Mexican politics in recent years. Similarly, Emir Sader noted the limits of the "Que se vayan todos!" ("All of them [politicians] must go!") slogan of the piqueteros (unemployed "picketers" movement) and other dissidents in Argentina. "Faced with the election [of 1995], their main slogan was 'que se vayan todos,'" he observed. "Well, 'they' did not leave, and the movements ran the risk of getting Menem"—the Peronist president who brought neoliberalism to Argentina, and who was indeed re-elected in 1995 (Hernández 2007).

The third option, which we find the most promising, is to maintain a creative tension between attempts to build national-level power in order to influence or—in increasing numbers of cases—manage the state, and a continuing commitment to autonomy and participation. This describes the tense but productive relationships between the MST and Lula da Silva, or between Argentina's recuperated business movement (in which workers form cooperatives and take over shut down businesses) and former President Nestor Kirchner. Bolivia's vice president, Alvaro García Linera (2007; see also Carlsen 2007; Romer 2008), distanced himself from a centralizing model when he recently declared, "We as a government do not seek to lead the social movements, we seek to be led by them." (However, in the face of the right-wing offensive in process in Bolivia as we write, the space between the left in government and third left movements outside governments has narrowed dramatically.) Conversely, when we commented to Lee Young-soo of the Korean Peasants League, which has a close working relationship with Brazil's MST, that the MST keeps its distance from state power, he smiled and replied, "The MST wants to take part in running the state in Brazil—they just want to take part in building and running a different state."

In actuality, even in instances where third left movements have shifted in one of the first two directions, a productive tension persists. Hugo Chávez's drive for a single, unified socialist party is tempered by the presence of supportive but often critical independent organizations: "The fragmented social movements that predate Chávez have not abandoned their existing structures," reported Venezuela-based journalist Jonah Gindin (2005) While the Zapatistas passed on supporting a candidate in Mexico's 2006 presidential election, they took the occasion to launch the Other Campaign, an attempt (still continuing) to build a broad front (we would even call it an alliance) "from below and to the left" across Mexico (Aguirre Rojas 2007; Kennedy and Tilly 2006b).

Achievements

The strategy of building "popular power" in El Alto, the Lacandón Jungle, Argentina's worker-run factories, and in the rural settlements organized by Brazil's MST, and other third left movements in Latin America have accomplished three achievements of notable proportions.

First, against great odds they have carried out two significant redistributions. They have redistributed productive resources (land, businesses, housing), creating spaces within the harsh landscape of neoliberalism within which people can survive and organize. They have also redistributed skills and knowledge. When the MST develops an elementary school curriculum grounded in region-specific rural life, Zapatistas run schools in their communities' native Maya languages, or Argentinean worker-run factories host adult education classes, they make knowledge available to those who otherwise would not have access to it. At a more sophisticated level, these movements build networks of technical expertise ranging from agroecology to factory management.

Second, third left movements have helped to build new identities and consciousness among formerly atomized, marginalized, or demoralized communities. The effective reconstitution of collective identities and collective action on the part of popular sectors that have experienced the devastating effects of neoliberal-imposed decomposition and de-structuring is itself a remarkable accomplishment. Through the combination of democratic political practice, the influence of proximity and territory, and the activation of historical memory, the

Lacandón jungle, the neighborhoods of El Alto and the shut-down workplaces of Argentina became sites where heterogeneous and fragmented popular sectors have been capable of constructing new social, political and cultural identities. The accompanying consciousness not only challenges the subordination of these subaltern groups, but often challenges inequality and subordination within such groups, as in the case of gender inequality. The new consciousness is most powerful within third left movements, but also has ripple effects throughout the society. Ernesto González, a worker at the Chilavert print shop, one of Argentina's "recuperated," worker-run businesses, commented, "The possibility of recuperation means there is one less argument for the boss. It used to be that bosses could say, 'If you don't make these concessions, I'll close down the plant.' But now workers know they can run the factory for themselves."

Third, these practices have placed on the table the discussion of what constitutes an effective strategy for social change under the current historical circumstances. In this regard, it seems to us that what they offer is not so much Holloway's (2002) new notion of changing the world without taking power, the notion of "praxis as practical negativity" (Dinestein 2005), or the rejection of the state as a tool for radical change, but rather the placement of a very old notion at the center of debate. It is the notion that only genuinely democratic experiences can produce moral self-transformation (self-esteem, sense of control over one's life's options) and the sense of community capable of nurturing the process of conscientización, that is, the expansion of individual self-interest to the point where it can incorporate, feel identified, and co-constitutive of collective interests and society-wide interests (Piñero Harnecker 2007). By carrying out this argument in practice, Latin America's third left movements have become a model for a wide range of other movements the world over (Leyva-Solano 2006; Starr and Adams 2003).

Again, these are significant achievements. In particular, the conformation of new political subjects and the (re-)opening of the discussion of political strategy go beyond what either the armed left or the electoral left in Latin America have been able to accomplish in the wake of neoliberal restructuring. Herein lies the nub of what needs to be further explored to determine if these accomplishments, and their conceptual and practical interconnectedness, provide enough epistemic and historical material to allow us to speak of a distinct third left—or whether perhaps they constitute a necessary but not sufficient condition for a third left in Latin America.

Challenges

The social, political and cultural practices discussed in this paper face numerous challenges in not just surviving, but consolidating and scaling up these experiences. We would like to suggest that these can be organized around four interrelated nodes of issues: (1) the relationship with the state, (2) the relationship between social movement and political representation, (3) the question of the economic surplus, and finally, (4) the overall challenge of the ability of such movements to spread and replicate themselves.

The relationship with the state

The social practices classified as belonging to Latin America's third left defend autonomy from the state both in rhetoric as well as principle. In practice, however, such autonomy has always been shown to be relative.

Historically, left governments have recruited leadership cadre of social movements to fill positions in the state apparatus. Their organizations become vehicles for the deployment of unemployment assistance, housing and other aspects of state social policy at the national and local level ensuring that these policies and resources reach targeted communities. Even short of such outright cooptation and incorporation, rhetoric may diverge from reality.

Uruguayan sociologist Maria José Álvarez-Rivadulla (2008) has pointed out that although Montevideo squatter movements employ a discourse of autonomy from parties and the state, in practice they are involved in constant interaction, negotiation, and cooperation with those same parties and state. In addition, the dynamics of class conflict can force autonomous movements and their leadership to subordinate their demands to the defense of an embattled government that, ultimately, is seen as representing their interests and aspirations. In Venezuela and increasingly in Bolivia, sharpening political polarization has reduced the scope for autonomous organization.

Various authors share our argument on the necessity of maintaining a creative tension between social movements and the state (Rockefeller 2007; Zavaleta Mercado 1979). In this sense, the notion of "dual power" is currently being re-theorized as not being temporary as in 1905 or 1917 Russia, but rather as a permanent condition. While this is indeed an important possibility to explore, it should be clear—as the situation of the Zapatista autonomous communities and the reactionary counter-offensive underway in Bolivia clearly show—that the span of time over which such creative tension can be maintained, that is the duration of a situation of dual power, is not always a decision that can be made unilaterally by popular forces. Imperialism and bourgeois reaction can often dictate the duration and conditions under which dual power situations are maintained.

In sum, the relationship between social movements and the state needs to be explored further in terms of conjunctural and strategic dynamics, examining the complexities that shape such a relationship historically. In this sense, the choices of the Zapatistas, the MST, the Argentine autonomous movements, and of social movements in Bolivia, as well as other like movements, need to be studied to reveal not only the overarching similarity in their posture with the state—the claim of autonomy—but also their differences so as to reveal how such autonomy is negotiated, bartered, surrendered and defended, along with the resulting consequences.

Social movements and political representation

As the case studies discussed clearly show, third left practices fill a void in the mechanisms of societal coordination left by the market and/or by the state. Given the vacuum, social movements fill that space and coordinate actions and multiple decisions through reliance on what they have at their disposal, the deployment of social energies and social cooperation based on trust and networks. Two issues need to be addressed here to be able to adequately gauge the potential and limits of such mechanisms in replacing market and state-based forms.

First, these practices of autonomy, direct democracy, horizontality, accountability and transparent governance, harness and channel the social energy of specific social and territorially-based social groups. Their effectiveness within these socio-spatial scales is unparalleled. How can they be used to represent the interests of broader sectors of society without addressing the issue of political representation and the eminently political nature of the historical project of societal transformation? Can political parties and a political instrument be completely eschewed? These questions place front and center the relationship between third left practices and political parties. Yes, political parties have been deficient and derelict, and have demonstrated a disheartening inability to rise to the historical challenges of the present, but is there something inherently irreplaceable about their role as mechanisms for representing the interests of highly differentiated and spatially distant social groups? Moreover, the nature of the relationship between leaderships emerging from social movements and the political parties has turned out to be many times much less idealistic, innovative and transparent, as the concrete history of Bolivia's MAS (Movement to Socialism) compiled by Marta Harnecker and Federico Fuentes shows (Harnecker and Fuentes 2008). Backroom deals, manipulation, authoritarianism, are not only a trait of political parties, but can also be deeply imprinted in social movement leaders.

Second, the celebration of trust-based cooperation and networks as an alternative, must consider something else. At present, both international development agencies as well as the center-left governments intent on legitimizing and regulating the export-oriented regime of accumulation hewn by their neoliberal predecessors, are deploying policies aimed at capturing social energy. The emphasis of government policies on social capital and constructing a new type of civil society-state alliances, of elite interventions in cultural and socioemotional realm directed and financed by international development agencies such as the IDB, the World Bank and ECLAC, many times end up coopting social practices that initially appear as autonomous (Leiva 2008; Leiva and Smith 2008).

In other words, what are the limits of direct self-representation? What supporting role if any, can or must political parties play in universalizing the values and interests enacted by these movements?

The issue of economic surplus

From the point of view of political economy, these experiences also need to be evaluated from the lens of that classical question: who produces, appropriates and distributes the economic surplus? While the worker-managed enterprise, the rural settlement, the barter clubs or the indigeneous communities practicing the principles of the third left offer concrete answers to this question at the local level, important issues remain as to how these experiences are to be scaled up to the regional, national and global level.

The economies of Latin American countries are dominated not by petty commodity production, but by internationally integrated global production systems and the hegemony of finance capital. Scaling up third left experiences requires forging answers as to how these principles can be applied in an economy dominated by global value chains, the international production system and the global markets that characterize the present economy. Certainly spaces for noncapitalist economic organization exist and these have been creatively seized by social movements. What needs to be discussed is the historical potential for these practices to influence the course of overall local, national and regional economies, the only way in which the livelihoods of broader sectors of the population can be impacted.

Ability to spread and replicate

All of these issues and others cumulate into the ultimate question, namely, the ability of these movements to grow to a critical mass within their countries. Autonomy limits access to resources and political leverage, and participation places exigent demands on constituents; both can limit the attractive power of third left movements. This question arises acutely in today's Argentina where a range of creative movement improvisations developed in the heat of economic crisis appear to be waning as the country's economy recovers (Collin, this volume; Kennedy and Tilly 2005a,b,c). When the Argentine government began offering monthly checks to the unemployed in 2002, most piquetero organizations in Argentina gladly accepted this source of extra income to stem hunger, thus re-connecting themselves in the process with patronage networks. MTD La Matanza refused in the interest of maintaining political autonomy and they consequently paid a steep price. "We went from thousands of people to six," said leader Toty Flores.[3] This concern was echoed by Argentine sociologist Javier Auyero who commented:

---

[3] They had subsequently rebuilt to fifty members when we met with them in 2005.

"One question I keep having about these horizontal movements is their relative failure to involve more people in them and their difficulties in competing against machine politics" (personal email, 2005). The Zapatistas even refuse as a matter of principle to extend their organization outside of their home region of Chiapas. Instead, they urge people throughout Mexico (and the world) to form their own autonomous, regionally based organizations.

The MST, which claims two million members and is "arguably the largest and most powerful social movement in Latin America" (Vanden 2005: 23) would seem to stand at the other extreme in terms of reach. But two million in a country of 160 million, the majority of them poor, still falls short of a decisive force. "We projected a shadow that is much larger than what we really were and we became famous for that," commented MST leader João Pedro Stedile. He added, "In fact, the MST as a force of the organized workers in Brazil is very small; we cannot even organize all the landless of Brazil who number four million" (Stedile 2008: 195).

Conclusion

What we have called Latin America's third left, marked by autonomy, bottom-up participation, territorial claims, and in large part by new social identities, has already accomplished a great deal. While this assemblage of organizations and movements does not dispose of the resources and power of left governments now governing roughly half of the region's people, it has done much to redistribute land and other productive resources. It has forged new collective identities and sparked discussion of strategy for social transformation in ways unparalleled by the traditional left parties or the surviving guerilla movements. Though the precise boundaries of such a third left are far from clear and our cases have revealed much variation within the third left category, there is little question that this set of actors has developed a fresh and important set of strategic innovations.

But the spokespeople of these movements—Subcomandante Marcos, João Pedro Stedile, and many others lesser known like Toty Flores and Soledad—have set rather ambitious goals: not just reclaiming ground from the depredations of neoliberalism, but helping to carry out a broader social transformation "from below and to the left," in the words of the Zapatista Army of National Liberation (EZLN). If the experiences we have labelled as belonging to the third left are to persist and scale up, then the issues associated with the four challenges we have identified—relationship with political parties, the state, control over economic surplus, and ability to spread and replicate—must all be addressed. The answers will determine if indeed a Latin American Third Left is in the process of being born. These answers will also clarify which of the three options we have outlined in our analysis of emerging and innovative experiences will be followed in the future: reproduce the old hierarchical top-down model, withdraw from national politics, or move forward through a creative and fertile tension between the social, political, economic and cultural practices of the exploited and oppressed and the forces of global capitalism. The latter would indeed signify the blazing of a new path to how the region's peoples can become architects of their own future in the 21st century.

RESURRECTED ENTERPRISES AND SOCIAL MOBILIZATION IN ARGENTINA[1]

Laura Collin Harguindeguy[2]

Introduction

Argentina, more than any other country, became immersed in a neoliberal economic model that led to an economic and political crisis, resulting in the removal of four consecutive presidents over a three month period. In response to the implementation of the neoliberal model and the resultant recession and crises, new and different kinds of social reactions and social movements began to emerge. Although this article will touch on a variety of these new social movements, it will particularly focus on the experience and transformation of workers as they took over bankrupt factories and put them back into production.

Once workers control is exerted over enterprises, their organized activities just like other forms of popular mobilization give rise to a new kind of political behavior—bottom-up organization, participatory democracy, autonomy and self-management, that analysts Kennedy and Tilly (in this volume) qualify as *third left*. To understand the context in which workers could take production under their control, I present a brief analysis of the economic and social crisis in Argentina, followed by a description of the varied social reactions over the last decade of the twentieth century, with emphasis on the vast mobilization that forced more than one president to resign. In so doing, I point to novel characteristics of social mobilization that differ from more traditional forms. After a succinct description of the enterprise recuperation process, I argue that the new relations described were a result of social practices more than a consequence of ideology.

Similarly, I show in the following section how these emerging social practices introduced a new discussion inside of the academic left. It

[1] My recognition and thanks to Marie Keneddy and Chris Tilly who helped me in the translation of this paper.
[2] Research professor at the Colegio de Tlaxcala A.C. in Mexico and member of the National System of Researchers.

stimulated the desire not only to understand what was going on, but to recognize their importance and to theorize about these new ways of practicing social agency. It suggested the development of new types of relations between the vanguard and the people, learning "how to accompany", instead of trying to coerce them. I conclude the chapter by reflecting on what may happen with this new left in the context of a retreat of social mobilization.

Neoliberal Policies and Crises in Argentina

If the origins of the crisis can be traced to the Argentine military dictatorship when Martinez de Hoz,[3] a member of the cattle export sector, began to impose the idea of a financial model of development in place of an industrial one, the complete application of the model took place during the two administrations of President Carlos Menem,[4] when:

> Argentina, more than any other developing country, bought into the promises of U.S.—promoted neoliberalism. Tariffs were slashed, state enterprises were privatized, multinational corporations were welcomed, and the peso was pegged to the dollar…(Krugman, 2002: 2).

During Menem's administration, almost all public services were privatized[5] and financial speculation was rampant, resulting in massive deindustrialization and a horrifying loss of jobs. The impact of public services privatization was extensive. It impacted the market such that prices increased dramatically for services such as water, energy, and telephone while those services that could not be easily privatized, such as schools and healthcare, suffered a loss in quality and covered ever fewer people. The increasing costs of public services thrust groups who had never previously been poor into poverty as people were forced to spend almost all of their income on services that the government used to provide. As the peso was pegged to the dollar, contracts that allowed an

---

[3] José Alfredo Martínez de Hoz was an Argentine policy maker and executive, best known as the Minister of Economy under *de facto* President Jorge Rafael Videla between 1976 and 1981, during the military dictatorship that called itself the National Reorganization Process.

[4] Menem was from the *Partido Justicialista*, by their own definition, the "party of pizza and champagne".

[5] The plan included the privatization of 93 governmental enterprises, tax exemption, deregulation of labor and financial markets, and the cooptation of unions (Dinerstein, 2002).

index of tariff increases generated inflation in dollars. Argentina became one of the most expensive countries in the world in which to live and produce. As a result, many owners moved their businesses to other countries, or became importers. Following the establishment of the *plan de convertibilidad*[6] (Argentine convertibility plan), unemployment began to grow, increasing from 6% in 1991 to 18% in 1995. Drastic declines of production coincided with deregulation of the labor market. Since the most power unions were affiliated with the same *Partido Justicialista*, unions became accomplices to Menem's neoliberal policies.

Throughout the nineties, thousands of business collapsed and half of Argentina's industry had stopped working. In a country where 69% of workers are urban, the industrial crash became a national disaster. The new century began with 18% unemployment and between 2000 and 2001; it increased to 25% (SIEMPRO, 2001). Without work, others sectors, mainly the middle class, soon followed the working class and joined the ranks of the newly poor.

New Social Movements

Lacking a response from the traditional unions, an upsurge in working class militancy took place that led to the creation of the *Central de Trabajadores Argentinos* (CTA, Argentine Workers' Union) in 1992 and the *Movimiento de los Trabajadores* (Workers' Movement) in 1994, both of which split off from the *Confederación General de trabajadores* (CGT, Workers General confederation), the traditional corporatist union (Dinerstein, 2002). Other new movements soon appeared in reaction to the neoliberal policies. These movements indicated the emergence of new social subjects, mainly those excluded by the system such as the unemployed, but also those conceptualized as the "new poor" (Bauman, 2003), i.e., people trying to survive in an extremely difficult situation. Some of the more important of these movements emerging in the 1990s are briefly described below:

Central de Trabajadores de Argentina (CTA). The CTA is a workers union federation, the first to enroll workers, both employed and

---

[6] The Argentine Convertibility Plan established a 1 to 1 exchange rate between the U.S. Dollar and the Argentine Peso.

unemployed, by direct and personal affiliation. CTA's principles include political autonomy (which in the Argentine context means from the Peronist (*Justicialista*) Party) and full democracy (CTA, 2008). The CTA was founded as an alternative in the face of what leaders considered the betrayal of existing unions that they viewed as pro-management (Barandel y Godoy, 2007). Members of this new federation include traditional unions, community organizations, and the unemployed movements.

Piqueteros. Organizations of unemployed workers—*movimientos de trabajadores desempleados*- are referred to as *piqueteros* (picketers). The defining tactic used by these organizations was blocking major roads and bridges, brining traffic to a halt to demand work (Rodriguez, 2007).[7] Their demands were not met by jobs, but rather by cash subsidies, first called *Planes Trabajar* (work subsidies) and later, perhaps in recognition that these subsidies had nothing to do with providing work, called *Planes Jefes y Jefas de Familia* (head of household subsidies). In the course of the crisis, left parties were able to insert themselves into worker neighborhoods and take control of the *piqueteros* using the clientelist tactics of the right. A new structural power pyramid emerged where the government at the top issues subsidies; in the middle, the "leaders" direct the organization; and at the bottom, unemployed people decide nothing but are mobilized to block streets and support certain candidates, etc., as a condition for receiving their subsidies (Alvarez, 2007). There were (and are) different types of *piqueteros*, corresponding to the political orientation of the leaders. For example:

1) The *Justicialista Party*, Argentina's populist Peronist party run by *punteros* (middlemen who buy votes), which practices clientelism.
2) The *Partido Comunista Revolucionario* (*PCR*), a Maoist tendency led by Delia Bisutti, who frequently negotiates with governments in power.

---

[7] Carrera and Cotarelo (2002: 100), register from 1993 to 2001 a change in the composition of those who participated in blocking street traffic. Originally (1993–1997) about 35% were working class people with a job, while in 2001, 34% were unemployed, and 33% were owners of small business. The change was related to what was happening in Argentina and how the recession threw enterprises into bankruptcy with subsequent loss of jobs.

3) The *Movimiento de Trabajadores Desocupados de la Matanza* (MTD La Matanza), the only *Piqueteros* group that refused cash subsidies. Instead, MTD-La Matanza insisted on having legitimate and dignified jobs and so they focused on building working class culture and on developing enterprises with a sense of self sufficiency and autonomy (Flores, 2007). With these enterprises, workers began to build a new "us" by making alliances with other like-minded social movements (e.g., *las Madres de Plaza de Mayo* in Argentina, the Landless Workers' Movement in Brazil, the Zapatistas in Mexico), as well as with academics, non-governmental organizations (NGOs), and company owners such as the powerful CGE (General Economic Confederation) (Fitz-Patrik, 2006).

MTD La Matanza represented a diferent voice, in that they considered clintelism to be a cancer that "erodes each of society's living cells" (Flores, 2007:44). Given their refusal to accept governmental subsides, MTD La Matanza challenged traditional left ideas in developing new social enterprises. Flores (2007: 23) points out that there is a prevailing confusion between autonomy and self-management or *autogestión*. In his opinion, any project can be self-managed, but that is not what gives strength to a movement. Instead, he argues that it is the "depth of political autonomy that determines dependence or independence from the government and traditional parties".

Clubes de trueque (barter clubs). Barter clubs used alternative or complementary currency in reciprocal and multilateral interchanges that became a means of subsistence during the crisis. The movement began in 1994 and became divided in 1999 into 2 different movements, the Global Net and the Solidarity Net (Primavera, 2002). The former is more business-oriented, while the latter emphasizes greater consciousness, autonomy and capacity-building. Barter clubs had an exponential growth and at the peak of the crisis involved more than a million people. The solidarity net emphasizes being "prosumers", a concept of Toffler's (1979) that signifies being producers and consumers at the same time.

In addition, a wide range of NGOs worked with vulnerable and unemployed people, utilizing participatory methods, empowering people and building a sense of autonomy while developing production projects, housing, health care, child care, and social organizations. Still other movements included the young people's organization HIJOS,[8] which made *escraches* (denunciatory performances in front of the homes of military officials involved with repression in the military dictatorship of the 1970s) and *puebladas*, whole towns mobilized to demand jobs or to oppose some government project. As Rodriguez (2007) points out, people in the 1990s were strongly politicized in the absence of the organized left. In fact, what happened later demonstrated: "…a lack of power in the existing political class, but also lack of capacity on the part of civil society for building a new political class (Nievas, 2002:90).

Movements Emerging from the Social Mobilization of 2001

When elections finally dismissed the *Justicialista* administration from power, the recession had already begun. After 18 months of recession, Argentina was completely fed up. The president at that time, Fernando de la Rua, proved incapable of understanding what was going on. First, he instituted an austerity plan. When that didn't work, he asked the people to increase their spending. When people tried to take their money from banks, the banks refused to allow withdrawals and instituted the *corralito*,[9] in order to stop a run on the banks. With their bank accounts effectively frozen, Argentines from all walks of life said "no." In an unusual social mobilization, citizens rose up together to throw out the government, sending a multitude of people were in the streets.

The first participants in the mobilization were probably sent by one of the future presidents of Argentina, Eduardo Duhalde. But the gathering rapidly grew into a completely spontaneous or media-driven uprising. Some people were directed to go to the center of Buenos Aires and demonstrate against the president, but others, the majority, went on their own as they heard the news on radio or television. For two days, the capital city Buenos Aires was taken over by the people who chanted, fought the police and destroyed property—mostly property associated with globalization such as transnational banks, AFORE (the

---

[8] *Hijos e Hijas por la Identidad y la Justicia contra el Olvido y el Silencio* (sons and daughters for identity and for justice against forgetting and silence). These are the sons and daughters of those who "disappeared" during the military dictatorship.

[9] Corralito was the name given to the economic measures taken in 2001 in order to stop a bank run, which were in force for one year and almost completely froze bank accounts.

privatized social insurance system), telephones owned by *Telefónica*, a Spanish enterprise, and McDonald's (Bonnet, 2002: 129). After several skirmishes that included 21 deaths, the president resigned but order still could not be restored.

It was a state of permanent mobilization, mostly in Buenos Aires, that was reminiscent of the Paris Commune. A preferred slogan was *que se vayan todos, que no quede uno* (all of them must go, not one should remain). Those that should go, included the president and all politicians as well as judges, police, in short, the entire government power structure. It amounted to a *"coup d'état* of the multitude" that some authors described as an "insurrectional situation" (Sztulwark, 2002: 50), and others as a gap in hegemony (Nievas, 2002). A succession of presidents that, briefly assumed power and then almost immediately resigned, ended when Duhalde took power and called for new elections.

In addition to the traditional stakeholders of social mobilizations (of whom there are suspicions about their independence or spontaneity),[10] there were two other kinds of new stakeholders in the popular *coup d'état*: 1) those movements that emerged in recent years as a response to the effects of neoliberalism, and 2) new actors not previously conceptualized as movements, but that were set into motion on December 17–21, 2001, and which remained mobilized in subsequent years, some of which still existed towards the end of the decade.

At the height of the mass action, neighbors who had never met before came together in the street and went together downtown or wherever the demonstration was going to take place. Street meetings were soon transformed into *Asambleas barriales* (Neighborhood assemblies) that gathered first for discussion during the mobilization and soon developed varied social strategies, such as occupation of outdoor and indoor spaces (public buildings, vacant government buildings or banks) for use as meeting places and for collective cooking and feeding and/or as places for selling and buying, and offering personal services, markets, and social entrepreneurs (Fernandez, 2003). Neighbors decided to take in their own hands what government had abandoned with neoliberal restructuring, building social networks of reciprocal help (De-Angelis, 2003). During the final days of 2001 and all of 2002, people never before

---

[10] As Nievas (2002: 87) argues, "…it is hard to believe that it was a spontaneous movement given the synchronization in the morning when local leaders from the *Partido Justicialista* promoted the mobilization against President de la Rua".

involved in politics were busily attending demonstrations or participating in assemblies to discuss and design projects. It was in that context that a new epidemic grew—an epidemic of enterprise seizures.

Enterprise Recuperation

Between 2002 and 2004, a rash of occupations of factories and other businesses took place. By 2007, 160 enterprises had been seized by their workers and were in operation including large, small, and middle-sized firms of all kinds—from services such as restaurants, hotels, and supermarkets, to a metallurgical business—involving a total of 10 thousand workers (Rebon and Saavedra, 2006). See Table 1.

In a context in which neither market nor government were able to guarantee social reproduction or production, local governments, legislators and judges not only permitted that process but also promoted it with timely expropriation decrees. Workers also counted on the support of union leaders with experience in a similar process during the nineties.[11]

During the final years of the 1990s, a lot of enterprises failed as a result of the recession. Even before that time, quite a number of enterprises failed, but for a different reason. As the Argentine peso was pegged 1-for-1 to the dollar, it was cheaper to produce in other countries, so a great number of Argentine entrepreneurs either became importers or relocated to Brazil, China or elsewhere, leaving their workers without jobs, and making a reality of workers saying, "wealthy owners, poor enterprises." The first wave of failures was a consequence of capitalist rational choice and the volatility of capital investment. The second wave was a consequence of the first one. The unemployment generated by capital movements provoked the recession that for 32 months plunged Argentina into chaos and was only ended by the 2004 devaluation of peso (Collin, 2003).

In the early 1990s, Argentine workers began to occupy factories as part of mass strikes conducted by the unions as a way of pressuring for

---

[11] "The legal form most used by workers has been expropriation as defined by the National Constitution that becomes acquired via the declaration of public use of the factory, making it subject to temporary occupation as sanctioned by the legislatures of various provinces" (Gracia, 2006: 26).

Table 1: Enterprises Run by Workers

Category	Number of businesses
Food	17
Construction	9
Press	4
Electric-mechanical	4
Thermoplastic	1
Graphics	6
Meat	12
Wood	1
Glass	4
Shoes makers	2
Rubber	2
Leather industry	1
Paper	2
Plastics	3
Railroads	1
Shipping	1
Chemical	3
Textile	7
Mechanics	12
Metallurgic	18
Radio	1
Health	8
Communitarian services	1
Restaurants	3
Commerce	5 / 2
Transportation	5
Tourism	2
Total	135

Source: Author's calculation from data from the Self-Managed Work (Trabajo Auto-gestionado) Program (Secretaria de Empleo. Ministerio de Trabajo, 2007)

higher severance pay, since the businesses were still functioning without the owners (Rebon, 2004: 14). Then between 2002 and 2004, workers seized 160 enterprises and held them. If workers in the 1990s wanted more severance pay while searching for a new job, those acting in the new century knew they would be unable to find new jobs. They were essentially dealing with their survival as workers' and became forced to "disobey unemployment" (Rebon, 2004: 10) upon seeing themselves reflected in the mirror of the *piqueteros*.

In this new and completely different situation, most unions were opposed to or at best indifferent to what was going on. Only a few of the unions were with the movement.[12] Instead of the support of their natural allies, the new wave of enterprise occupations counted on the approval and mobilization of neighbors and new social movements mobilized during the popular *coup d' etat* in 2001 Other allies came from the universities, activists and the left, a new and autonomist left (Cieza, 2006).

Occupied, Recuperated, or Resuscitated Enterprises?

The workers took over or occupied enterprises because they were afraid of being jobless. They had no previous consciousness about workers' control or autonomous management. As one worker pointed out: "the owners made a mistake, because, if they had offered us 10 pesos, surely we would have taken them and left."[13] Another worker put it this way: "There was no decision to occupy the factory, instead there was a decision to stay waiting for the owner to bring money"[14] (Lavaca, 2007: 27). They didn't seek to be radical. Indeed, some occupiers saw the use of the term "occupied" as too radical and began to search for other concepts that implied less conflict so to soften the image of their movement. They wished to say: "we're not occupying, we're just staying in our workplace."

According to Rebon (2004), the workers stayed on in 35% of cases by consensus (between owner, judge, and workers) and in 12% of the cases, the owner just disappeared, leaving the workers in place. When the occupations began, Argentina was still in a deep crisis so even judges and politicians, the guarantors of the system, were suddenly in favor of suspending the expulsion of the workers, thereby recognizing labor rights ahead of capital privileges. Legislators and local governments modified laws to allow workers to take control of workplaces. As a Chilavert worker said at the time,[15] "If we continue working, we

---

[12] Only a section of the powerful UOM (Metallurgical Union) and the printers' union, with a progressive heritage from its historical leader Ongaro, were involved in the occupation or recuperation of enterprises.

[13] Matilde Adorno, a textile worker at Brukman Factory.

[14] Celia Martinez, a worker at Brukman Factory.

[15] Candido, a worker at Chilavert Printing Enterprise.

pay taxes, provide services, and jobs...it not only meant fewer subsidies to give, but also more revenue for the government". But in other cases (45%) the relationship was not so easy and involved a struggle with the owner. Those workers rightly stated that they were occupying the workplace; that they were taking it from the owner, and so they adopted the slogan "occupy, resist, and produce!"

From an external point of view, to occupy means usurpation, an illegal act carried out by force, and the one who does it is a criminal. From the Argentine workers' perspective, "occupy" means "take care of." "To occupy" was a concept that reflected the situation at the very beginning when the task was to stop the *vaciamiento* (decapitalization) of factories, to preserve the business, and to take control of the workplace for negotiation purposes. But it soon became transformed into something else. The workers couldn't just remain in place. They needed to restart production and begin to work and from that moment onward they were not just occupying, but now involved in a process of recuperation.[16]

In terms of formal organization, three distinct ways were adopted: cooperative, private, and governmental under workers control. While left parties favored government ownership, there is only one example where this was attempted and that one ultimately failed: the Buenos Aires City government took control of an enterprise and hired the workers as municipal employees, but subsequently closed the enterprise. In contrast, those that adopted the form of a private society reached an agreement with the owners or managers. The vast majority of cases, however, are cooperatives which were easier to register and offered the advantage of having to pay less taxes.

Over time, distinctions in the ways workers saw themselves became a division in the movement. Recuperated businesses formed two different, though similarly named, associations:[17] the MNFERT (National Movement of Factories and Businesses Recuperated by the Workers) and the MNER (National Movement of Recuperated Businesses). The

---

[16] The most descriptive term is *recuperated*, but the one I would prefer is *resurrected*, the most joyful term, because it implies that the businesses died and what workers did was to generate a rebirth.

[17] The difference is that in Spanish, "factory" has a direct relation with the working class (in the strict sense of the proletariat), while enterprise is related to the working class only in a broad sense, so it includes the service sector. The distinction also is related to location. MNFRT is located in the periphery, the factory district, while MNER is located mainly in Buenos Aires with more participation in the service sector.

first proposed that workers hold the business while waiting for the owner to return or a new owner to buy, whereas the second foresaw a new vision in which workers may and can produce without an external management.

"Recuperated" has a significant meaning because it implies that a workplace is a right of the working class, or more than that, that work generates rights, property rights. According to liberal economic philosophy, owners can open or shut up enterprises as they like, move the production from one country to another, and hire or fire at their convenience. The claim of the workplace as a right challenges that liberal point of view. Recognizing the right of recuperation implied a change in workers' worldview. It was not the only change. As Marx put it, "Social practice changes consciousness."

Changes and Practice

Most of the participants in this movement were not radical, did not recognize themselves as political actors, and only participated superficially in their unions. But unions in Argentina were strongly controlled by the Peronist (*Justicialista*) party, locked into a hierarchical structure with top-down decision-making. The unions had long been *oficialista* with the era of struggle having ended long before. If the workers now took a progressive and even radical position, it was because they learned from practice. But what they learned also changed their practice.

Solidarity from and with other social movements: The fact is that the movement did not have the support of the unions (or only minimal support) so what they formed were alliances with sympathetic neighbors, other social movements, and left political parties. In the process, they learned that they were part of a larger mobilization. As their allies got involved with them in the struggle, helping them to confront the police or to build a demonstration, the workers were in return expected to participate in other kinds of mobilizations. They became politicized in this process and part of a larger, diverse, and pluralistic movement—not as a result of a conscious decision, but as a consequence of reciprocity. As Lewis and Klein (2007: 11) argue, "Some of the most powerful workers leaders...had begun as non-political and discovered solidarity along the way." Workers passed from a "defensive strategy to an offensive one" (Fajn, 2004: 22), and from a worker movement to a political fight.

Spatial roots: The enterprises used to be like islands in geographic space where workers would stay for 8 hours and then return home. President Juan Peron used to say, "From house to work, and from work to home." This situation changed with the occupations. Workers began to build relationships with the surrounding neighborhood, turning to the neighbors for help, coffee, or for help in keeping a lookout for the police. In return, some of the recuperated enterprises have opened their doors to the community, opening cultural centers, adult education programs, health clinics and other ways of relating to the community. They transformed their island into an open park. This new kind of spatial relation gave greater importance to territories for political expression (Polleri, 2007).

New ways of working: in the absence of the owner, but also without technical workers, the workers needed to learn how to make decisions for themselves. So they broke with the traditional distinction between manual and intellectual work, and learned to work without supervision, establishing workers' control and autonomy—all without reading Gramsci (e.g., 1985) or Korsch (e.g., 1972).

Democracy: Not all the former workers participated in the recuperation of their enterprises (typically about 50%), but those involved needed to learn how to form new kinds of relations. Without central supervision, they needed to make collective decisions. The enterprise-wide assembly was the place and consensus-building was the way. Democratic discussion covered salaries, production decisions, planning, political discussions, and how to deal with differences: "moving from an individual logic to a collective one" (Fajn, 2004, 130).

Networking: The workers had to deal with unfamiliar situations not just in production but also the acquisition of inputs, and finding out where and how to sell their products. Loans between enterprises become frequent as did various kinds of joint ventures to buy or sell products. They learned how to share capital and contacts with other enterprises. Instead of competitive relations, they learned how to practice solidarity.

Analytical capacity: In addition to the workers' leap across the division between manual and intellectual work, some intellectuals in a spirit of solidarity sought to place their knowledge at the service of the movements.[18] Professors and students not only conducted research

---

[18] In the city of Buenos Aires, groups of intellectual supporters include the Picasso Project and others at the University of Buenos Aires. In the Buenos Aires hinterland,

or helped with social programs, but they also engaged in discussions with workers. As a result, anybody who talks with one of these workers gets the impression that they are speaking with an intellectual full of concepts and theoretical ideas.

Autonomy: With no directions from the boss, no support from unions, or help from the government, the movement confronted the elimination of social programs and assistance. Autonomy was not the final state but the initial starting point since workers were really alone, at first with no institutional help and with only the assistance of a few advisers with experience. So they had to depend on their own resources, a situation that became empowering. Autonomy marked the struggle at the onset and introduced another power, an alternative power (Ouviña, 2007: 190).

These new practices, values, and ideas were shared with some of the other movements within the broader landscape of mobilization: MTD La Matanza, neighborhood assemblies, barter networks, and NGOs supporting autonomy, self-management, participatory democracy and solidarity. Rodgers (2007: 126) adds "identity" construction to the list. A new human being, opposed to liberal values such as individualism, lack of solidarity, and *salvese quien pueda* (each for his/herself), was being formed that, according to Flores (2007: 26), represented a "communitarian culture against an individualistic one".

Can the workers involved in this process be considered part of a leftist movement? If one were to ask them, they would probably answer "no." Consciousness doesn't always reflect practice. Indeed, they seem to act and think as leftists since they deny property rights, hierarchical authority, and obedience to power, while fostering new social practices such as autonomy, self management and solidarity. But they are not just any kind of left. They seem to agree with the autonomist left that began to grow in the world since the student movements in the seventies and after the crash of "real socialism" and the Berlin wall. Kennedy and Tilly propose the existence of three kinds of left in Latin America, namely, the armed guerrilla movements, populist movements linked by patronage electoral parties, both hierarchical, and those engaged in "bottom-up organizing" (Kennedy and Tilly, 2005a). New social movements in Argentina seem to conform to the botton-up models.

---

there were projects based at Quilmes University, and one at San Martin University. In Santa Fe State, Rosario National University, and Litoral National University were involved.

From their daily practices, workers involved with recuperated enterprises learned many of the principles that were previously proposed by left-oriented parties and alternative movements. On the other side, militants from the left had to change their conceptions of what was going on with the social movements. Among the advantages offered by the recuperated enterprises are: control over production, popular support, technical abilities, human capital, sense of belonging, democracy, participation, solidarity, horizontality and cooperation (Magnani, 2003).

The New Left

The intellectuals and activists of left parties that supported the various social movements saw that these new and novel forms of self-organization needed to be analyzed. Some activists from the left began to discuss and confront old notions such as the working class as the natural subject of revolution, instead introducing the notion of popular power. They also pointed to the need to recover other ideas that "actually existing socialism" had forgotten or abandoned, such as autonomy and self-management. One part of the left remained faithful to the old spirit and orthodox "theological" interpretation of the classics. Others, meanwhile, adopted an ultra-autonomist position and rejected all preexistent theory. Still others tried to analyze what was happening in the spirit of recovering and reconstructing socialist and social theory.

Trying to build new or recover old notions such as "popular power" (Stratta, 2007; Rodriguez, 2007) and using people, instead of class, as the formula that articulates subaltern particularities, various authors opened the discussion. The first matter is who is the revolutionary subject? Toty Flores, leader of MTD La Matanza, tried to define the new identity as a different kind of "us," a collective us based in solidarities, cooperative, plural and inclusive, oriented to integration (Krymkiewicz y Aiello, 2007). This definition points out a difference between his movement and others that focus on a class perspective. It reflects their alliance with entrepreneurs (March, 2007), other local or continental movements such as the *Madres*, the Zapatistas of Mexico, the landless workers movement of Brazil (Fitz-Patrik, 2006), and with a huge number of social organizations from North America as pointed out by Bordegaray (2007). The most frequent alliance was between unemployed workers and recuperated enterprises with territorial roots. Understanding these movements as an insurrection, a new social force, a new popular class alliance of workers, employed and unemployed, and the middle class Bonnet (2002), nonetheless, felt that this kind of configuration could not be considered permanent since the middle class often acts as a conservative force. Bonnet was later proved right when in 2008; the middle class allied itself with big agribusiness against progressive government tax policies and the interests of workers.

Popular power appears as the process that permits the places of everyday life (work, residential, recreation) of the subaltern classes, to become cells of an alternative social power (Stratta and Mazzeo, 2007; Fernandez, 2003) from which to build contra-hegemonic power. This implies different kinds of social actors, plural and from different classes and social experiences, instead of the traditional concept of social classes. The construction of power signified the discussion of notions such as "dual power" (Trotsky) or "counter-hegemony" (Gramsci). For Caviasca (2007: 59), dual power means contesting existing institutions through the creation of new ones and as such can be considered to include neighborhood assemblies and recuperated enterprises. In his opinion, postmodern, autonomist versions of socialism propose power-building on the edges, outside the states, building autonomist relations, but most of all a different way of life. Caviasca focuses on the meaning of power, introducing the distinction between "power of, power over, and power to do". He disagrees with those who insist on seizing power, "because neither power nor the state can be treated as a thing that can be used or appropriated by revolution."

Casas (2007: 140) disagrees with Holloway's (2002), formula of "changing the world without taking power" and proposes a new formula: neither taking power, nor renouncing power, but "building a new power! popular power. The heritage of this thought comes from workers' councils, and self-management, and differs from the concept of dual power. Some authors shift the focus and instead of saying "take power" propose the "power of making revolution". While "dual power" implies an exceptional situation during revolutionary crisis, counter-power or popular power implies the construction of new kind of relationship within everyday spaces and the building of autonomy means communitarian appropriation of the conditions of existence and social praxis, fashioning a new way of living (Ouviña, 2007).

With respect to the concept of a future society, it is significant that not all the authors involved in the discussion of the new left refer to socialism or revolution. It seems that some essentially avoid the subject. But when they do refer to revolution, it differs from the preexisting one and becomes defined as "emancipation" (Casas, 2007: 137). Instead of replacing a capitalist government by another government built with the same logic, the project includes building from the bottom-up a political alternative that could go far beyond capital and capitalism. Avoiding a definition, they often utilize the word "alternative". When an author refers to socialism, as Acha (2007: 28) does, he affirms that, "The only version of socialism that fits with popular power is the bottom-up one". If this is not a class mobilization, the question is not only who the new stakeholders are, but how they have built (and can build) a shared consciousness.

Touraine (2006) proposes that identity assumes an important place in new social movements. In Argentina, Dri (2007: 65), a philosopher and theologian of liberation theology, focuses on the social self-construction of new subjects. In this interpretation, assemblies or recuperated enterprises are not yet new social subjects but may be a subject or subjects in construction if they prove able to build shared programs. The new subject does not seem to identify its movement as one for working class socialism, nor as a part of the Peronist party as in the past (Acha, 2007: 17), although some authors recognize that the working class still plays a relevant role.

In relation to strategies, Rodriguez (2007) makes a distinction between social movements and political movements. In his opinion, the social movement is the instrument of grassroots organizations, while the political movement is the instrument of social movements. He also distinguishes between articulation and coordination: articulation refer to the relations between experiences that have the same construction criteria while coordination links experiences with different criteria of construction. While articulation may be strategic, coordination is mainly tactical. Articulation may be useful in the long term while coordination is key in the short term. Adding or building concepts to understand reality, intellectual thought was trying to develop ever more adequate concepts to reflect bottom-up political practices.

Theory and practice

In practice, each type of social reaction or mobilization presents a rainbow of positions, ranging from populist nationalism to the radical left with a center of participants that refuse to consider themselves as involved in politics, and from top-down leaders to horizontal democracy.

In the case of recuperated enterprises, some enterprises are completely democratic, others vertical, some decided on wages according to the complexity or responsibility involved with work while others applied notions of equal distribution, and still others preferred to have compensation awarded on the basis of need (Fitz-Patrik, 2006).

Most of the participants in recuperated enterprises or in neighborhood assemblies do not presume to be doing politics.[19] Many neighborhood assemblies rejected left parties because the parties tried to direct or impose their own point of view or their strategies on the movement. Sztulwark (2002) judges that the participation of left parties in the assemblies and *piquetes* was largely destructive, while Ouviña (2002) considerers that the rejection of left participation does not mean a rejection of left politics but of politicians (Dinerstein, 2002: 45). To understand the contradiction of a left social mobilization that rejects left party participation, it is necessary to recognize that the different preexisting left parties and movements in Latin America were as Kennedy and Tilly (2005a) point out centralized, top-down models.

While some portions of the left try to assume their role as a vanguard and participate in assemblies or recuperated enterprises to *"tirar linea"* (tell them what to do and what to think), other left activists discarded the vanguard position and instead are trying to learn how to accompany them. This kind of activist now works in the enterprises, attends assemblies, and proposes ideas without trying to impose them. These new left activists know that it is not necessary to be recognized as a socialist or a communist, if the social practice is autonomist socialism. They know that some who are recognized as socialists contradict socialist principles in their practice. This new breed of left activist is "re-inventing politics" (De-Angelis, 2003: 160).

In practice, new left ideas coincided with new left practices. The new left activist discuses concepts such as autonomy, self-management and popular power, while the disagreement is over the taking or not of state power, and between the concept of socialism and the building of new ways of life, i.e., an "alternative model".

---

[19] Federico Tonarelli Interview, December 2007, January 2008.

Last but Not Least

While most neighborhood assemblies are no longer active, recuperated enterprises which are workplaces still persist. Is it possible to support labor under distributive equity in a competitive economy? Are recuperated enterprises viable in the long term? Based in his own field work in a recuperated glass metallurgical factory, Klimberg (2005) affirms that worker-owned and run enterprises lead to solid economic growth and competitive conditions that foretell prosperity. He gives several reasons for this prosperity: enterprises managed by workers have less permanent costs,[20] pay fewer taxes,[21] show strong financial discipline as a result of participative management, have no debts or financial cost,[22] and are focused on maintaining workplaces rather than fast accumulation, so they appear to be more careful in their decisions. In Klinberg's opinion, all these conditions shape more solid economic units. He recognizes that part of the success of recuperated enterprises and factories can be explained by national economic recuperation, post-crisis or post-devaluation, and the subsequent importations of a substitutive process. But that is not the only explanation, as recuperated enterprises grew more than the rest of the economy.

Such assertions are contrary to common sense. People generally think that workers are unable to manage a business. In my research, I frequently heard that kind of opinion and pessimism expressed by other workers, left academics and militants, just as Klimberg (2005) heard when he interviewed students from the University of Buenos Aires. Magnani noted the opinions of some former owners:

> They cannot produce without a head, without technicians, they cannot produce for export, not even for the local market...chances are that they can only make cheap products for street selling. A Chilavert worker told me that he was challenged in an even worse way: How can you do it?... you are 'negroes'[23] (Magnani, 2003: 159).

---

[20] The owner's profit, and management and administrative cost.

[21] A cooperative in Argentina is recognized by law as a social organization, pays low taxes and has less regulation.

[22] Either as a refusal of being in debt or as a result of the difficulty of obtaining credit.

[23] Negro in Argentina does not refer to skin color, or a racial definition, but instead refers to a class definition.

Instead of losing clients, most recuperated enterprises increased the number of clients. Why? Part of the answer that Klimberg (2005) gives could also be applied to enterprises under a Toyota or Kalmar productive restructuring: workers feel part of the enterprise and show more engagement, so they are able to finish work more quickly than the competition. But they don't only commit time, but also capital, knowledge, and most important of all, will power. For instance:

> They self-financed by their own sales. After paying their ongoing costs, they divided the remainder 50–50. One half was distributed in equal parts among all members of the cooperative and the other half was converted into working capital (Klimberg, 2005: 13).

In other words, capital and work under these conditions are not different or opposing values, but complementary. If workers contribute capital of their own, there is no surplus value but rather self-investing. Even when they make a solidarity investment by helping other enterprises, it loses the sense of capital that reproduces capital to instead become social and constitutive of solidarity relations. This type of capital can be conceptualized as a new form of accumulation oriented to social group and workplace reproduction instead of capital reproduction and accumulation (Barkin, 2006).

What we are discussing is the relation between recuperated enterprises, social movements, and the emergence of a new left in South America. Pervellini and Tifni (2007) propose that workers' new forms of association may be considered part of the solidarity economy as Razzeto (1988) defines it because they reproduce principles of self-management, coordination, cooperation and participatory democracy, in what he calls factor C: community, cooperation, collaboration, collective. The question is if that would be enough to define a different production logic or a different rationality. Cooperatives in general (and recuperated enterprises are cooperatives) are no longer ago part of the left. While some authors believe that the solidarity economy and cooperatives are the same, and others that cooperatives are part of a solidarity economy, cooperatives in general display solidarity relations only inside their walls as they participate in the larger economy without any larger social commitment.

The importance of self-management, independent thought and self construction as identity references (Allegrone, 2006) for many recuperated enterprises points to the difference between the traditional cooperative movement and recuperated enterprises which adopted a cooperative organization as a useful framework. The MNER, recognizing the necessity of a kind of differentiation, created the FACTA (Federation of Argentine Self-Managed Worker Cooperatives) as a way of saying "we are cooperatives, but a different kind of cooperative" (FACTA, 2007).

Recuperated enterprises emerged without a political identification but turned to the left as a result of mobilization needs, only to remain there. To establish themselves, they required support and they still need support because most are not recognized by law as the owners of the enterprises.[24]

> Each recuperated enterprise realized that their survival depended on the networks they could build. Protection is based on worker conviction but also on the support from neighbors, assemblies, human rights organizations and political parties (Lavaca, 2007: 41).

In the future, some may become like traditional cooperatives, like any other enterprise, while others could be destroyed by incompetence or recovered by private owners. Whether some of the enterprises under workers control remain part of a new left movement depends on the extension of the movement, or its persistence as a social movement. This means joining with other worker-managed enterprises and with other social movements to resist and subvert the profit and private logic.

Argentine overall level of social mobilization has decreased since the country's economy has recovered (Zibechi, 2008). Government-sponsored clientelism has once again grown as the successive Kirchner presidents (Nestor and Cristina) have used public funds to provide stipends to the unemployed and to co-opt some of the social movements that were previously autonomous. Moreover, the renewed social mobilization of wealthy business owners has arisen as a new enemy to face. As Marin (2004: 15) says, referring to the slogan "All of them must go", "Neither did all of them go, nor was revolution made." The bulk of the mobilization that some identified as prerevolutionary shifted to supporting the populist government against new enemies, while some continue fighting to preserve their power over particular spaces. Still, out of this history of struggle, new knowledge, experiences, and concepts will remain as an available repertoire for future movements (Tilly,

---

[24] In most of the cases, the legal authority gave workers the right to produce during some time, from 2 to five years, but not the final eminent domain.

1978–2004). Democracy, autonomy, self-management, as new *habitus* (Bordieu, 1995), or practices will continue in popular consciousness waiting for a new wave of mobilization. If left parties or militants want to be with the movement they must accept this change, and become a new left, or third left.

COMMUNITY ORGANIZING, REBELLION, AND THE PROGRESSIVE STATE: NEIGHBORHOOD COUNCILS IN EL ALTO, BOLIVIA[1]

Emily P. Achtenberg

Introduction

Visitors to La Paz in August 2004 experienced a rare event: a day without car horns, gasoline fumes, and traffic congestion in a major Latin American capital city. A strike by transportation workers protesting an increase in gasoline prices had sparked a series of road blockades, converting major downtown arteries into impromptu soccer fields and pedestrian-friendly boulevards.

Soon the streets were filled with thousands of indigenous demonstrators demanding the nationalization of gas. Women in traditional wide skirts and bowler hats discoursed eloquently on the link between the lack of basic neighborhood services (including cooking gas) and the role of transnational corporations in exploiting Bolivia's natural resources. To a progressive urban planner, even more remarkable was the realization that these groups were marching for nationalization under the banners of their local neighborhood councils—chapters of FEJUVE (the Federation of Neighborhood Councils), a grassroots community organization in the neighboring indigenous city of El Alto.[2]

In fact, during the tumultuous "Gas Wars" of 2003–5, while many groups (including *campesinos*, coca-growers, workers, and students) participated in the broad-based social movements that brought down two neoliberal governments and ultimately elected Evo Morales as Bolivia's first indigenous president, the role played by FEJUVE-El Alto was decisive.

---

[1] An earlier version of this article was published in Progressive Planning, No. 172, Summer 2007.

[2] References to FEJUVE throughout this article are to FEJUVE-El Alto. FEJUVEs also exist in each of Bolivia's nine departments and are loosely affiliated through their federation, CONALJUVE. While all FEJUVEs are involved in community organizing activities, their national political orientations and affiliations vary. FEJUVE-El Alto is the largest and most dominant of the organizations.

It was FEJUVE that forged a national consensus and mobilization around the demand for nationalization of gas. By barricading El Alto's gas storage plant, blockading road access into La Paz, and carrying out massive civic strikes, FEJUVE and its allies created a prolonged state of siege that paralyzed the national economy and government. And El Alto paid the price, providing most of the Gas Wars' 67 victims.

How did a grassroots urban community organization, focused on the delivery of basic neighborhood services, become the major protagonist in a civil insurrection against the neoliberal order? How did FEJUVE move from organizing the community to organizing rebellion? What challenges do FEJUVE and the neighborhood councils now confront in relation to the new MAS (Movement Towards Socialism) government? These issues are of interest to progressive planners and others seeking to understand the relationship between urban neighborhood organizations, popular movements, and new left governments in Latin America and elsewhere.

El Alto and the Neoliberal City

As Bolivia analysts Linda Farthing, Juan Arbona, and Benjamin Kohl have noted (2006), the La Paz/El Alto metropolis is a dramatic expression of the neoliberal globalized city. El Alto, an impoverished township of rural migrants steeped in traditional indigenous customs, sits on the rim of the altiplano overlooking and nearly surrounding La Paz, the colonial capital driven by market forces and the perpetuation of elite privilege.

El Alto itself is largely a product of the Bolivian state's failed agricultural and economic policies over the past 50 years. While the 1952 revolution redistributed land to highland *campesinos*, credit and price supports were channeled primarily into lowland commercial agriculture. Fragmented through inheritance and buffeted by drought, traditional peasant farms could not compete with the cheap food imports introduced by neoliberal structural adjustment policies of the 1980s and '90s. Massive numbers of *campesinos* were expelled from the Altiplano, along with 30,000 miners displaced by the shutdown of government-owned mines (Kohl and Farthing 2006).

Fueled by these migratory forces, El Alto grew from a village of 11,000 in the 1950s to become an independent municipality in 1988.

Today, with close to 1 million residents, it has overtaken La Paz and is the second largest city in Bolivia, after Santa Cruz (Rojas 2008).

This explosive population growth has vastly outstripped El Alto's capacity to provide basic services to its residents and neighborhoods. Land use and urban settlement patterns are basically unregulated, allowing the creation of subdivisions without public services or community facilities (schools, churches, parks). Most neighborhoods have no paved streets, trash pick up, or telephone service; most homes lack indoor plumbing, potable water, and electricity. Seventy-five percent of the population lacks basic health care, and 40% are illiterate (Zibechi 2005).

Unlike other third-world cities with large reserve labor pools, El Alto has not attracted a significant transnational corporate presence. It is dominated by the informal economy, which has increased by 162% since 1985 (Farthing, Arbona, and Kohl 2006).[3] Seventy percent of the economically active population works in the family-run or "semi-business" sector, including sales, food, trade, construction, and artisanry (Zibechi 2005). An estimated 50% of the population participates in the informal street vending economy (Dangl 2007).

Many *alteños* commute daily into La Paz where they build the infrastructure and provide the services that enable the reproduction of global elite lifestyles. Many El Alto businesses, too, are headquartered in La Paz and pay taxes there instead of in El Alto, further depleting El Alto's economic base (Gill 2000).

Significantly, more than 80% of El Alto's residents self-identify as indigenous (Zibechi 2005). While the rural migrant population is predominantly Aymara, former miners are mostly Quechua. The City's ethnically diverse indigenous population also includes many urbanized and urban-born mestizos, and is predominantly youthful. Sixty percent of El Alto residents are under the age of 25 (Zibechi 2005).

---

[3] This exponential growth of the informal sector also reflects the increased participation of women and children in the labor force, as households struggle to make ends meet (Arbona 2007).

Community Organizing

The earliest neighborhood councils in El Alto were established in 1957 to provide basic services for the recently urbanized migrant population, becoming affiliated through FEJUVE in 1979 (Crabtree 2005). Historically, the councils have played a variety of roles in relation to civil society and the state.

- *Self-help.* Through the neighborhood councils, ex-miners and *campesinos* have pooled their resources (including miners' pension funds) and technical skills to buy land, build schools and parks, and install basic utility services. This has enabled residents to basically self-construct their communities and neighborhoods without reliance on the state.
- *Regulation.* A primary function of the neighborhood councils in newly settled peripheral areas is to protect new migrants from predatory land speculators (*loteadores*) and assist them in securing legal title. In established neighborhoods, the councils regulate transactions such as the buying and selling of homes, mediate neighborhood disputes, and administer community justice (with sanctions ranging from community service to forms of corporal punishment). Perhaps due to the vigilance of its neighborhood assemblies (whose tactics include hanging dolls in effigy from lampposts to warn prospective thieves), El Alto reportedly has fewer mob lynchings than Cochabamba or Santa Cruz (Albó 2007).
- *Protest.* The neighborhood councils also have a long tradition of mobilizing residents to demand from government authorities what they cannot build or deliver themselves. In 1998, FEJUVE was a major protagonist in the struggle to found the Public University of El Alto. In 2003, FEJUVE successfully resisted a municipal tax on building and house construction. In 2005, FEJUVE spearheaded a campaign to oust the privatized water company. In this role, FEJUVE mediates between residents and the state outside the traditional political party structure, to make government more accountable.

The neighborhood councils were greatly strengthened in 1994 by the Law of Popular Participation, a neoliberal democratic reform that devolved 20% of the national budget to municipalities and gave local groups an enhanced role in participatory planning and budgeting. The ability to demand and deliver funds for neighborhood projects significantly increased FEJUVE's power and influence. In many respects, El Alto's neighborhood councils have functioned as micro-governments, substituting for the mostly absent state.

Today there are some 570 neighborhood councils in El Alto, organized by geographic zone in each of the city's nine districts and affiliated at the citywide level through FEJUVE (Crabtree 2005). The basic unit at neighborhood level must have at least 200 members (Zibechi 2005). The elected leadership committee meets regularly and calls a general neighborhood assembly monthly or semi-monthly. Elected leaders must reside in the zone for at least two years; may not be a merchant, transportation worker, real estate speculator, or political party leader; and cannot be a traitor or have colluded with dictators (Zibechi 2005). Women reportedly represent 20%–30% of the neighborhood council leadership, a higher percentage than is found in most popular organizations in Bolivia (Kohl and Farthing 2006; Reel 2007).

A parallel set of territorially-based organizational structures exists for small proprietors and workers in El Alto's informal economy, who are highly organized. As anthropologist Sian Lazar (2008) explains, the street merchants' association represents vendors (mostly women) who sell in the same street or market; it regulates access to stalls, monitors upkeep and cleanliness, mediates disputes, and negotiates relations with the municipality. Taxi and bus drivers are organized by route; the union (*sindicato*) regulates departures, allocates profitable vs. unprofitable itineraries, and performs other functions similar to the vendors' association. These types of organizations dominate El Alto's citywide trade union federation (COR-El Alto) and ally with FEJUVE on critical issues.

Both the neighborhood councils and their counterparts in the informal economy are patterned after the traditional socio-political organization of rural indigenous communities (*ayllus* and peasant unions), which draw on territorially-based kinship networks. They also reflect the political traditions and organizational experience of the radical miners, who for decades led Bolivia's militant, class-conscious trade union movement. Fusing these legacies, El Alto's migrants have effectively transplanted, reproduced, and adapted their communities of origin to facilitate survival in a hostile urban setting.

Rebellion

FEJUVE's success in broadening its role from community organizing to rebellion against the neoliberal state is grounded in the collective traditions and experiences that find contemporary expression in El Alto's neighborhood councils. These include a deeply-rooted culture of collective identity, consensual obligation, direct democracy, and autonomy. During the Gas Wars, these traditions provided the infrastructure that allowed social resistance to flourish.

Collective Identity. El Alto residents identify strongly with their neighborhoods, making territorially-based organizations the logical vehicle for collective action. But many Alteños also maintain strong ties with their rural communities of origin—owning land in the *campo* and returning to grow crops, participating in assemblies, even maintaining leadership positions (Albó 2007; Lazar 2006, 2008). Some rural mayors live in El Alto during the week, effectively establishing a second headquarters for their Altiplano municipalities.

For anthropologist Xavier Albó (2007), these dual residency arrangements recall the traditional Andean practice of vertical ecological integration, linking rural and urban zones as a strategy for economic survival. During the Gas Wars, these relationships were instrumental in promoting indigenous solidarity across urban-rural boundaries: when peasant-led blockades caused food shortages and rising prices in El Alto, most Alteños identified with the *campo* despite their immediate economic hardship as consumers (Lazar 2008).

For historians Forrest Hylton and Sinclair Thomson, the Gas Wars in El Alto also represent a historic convergence of indigenous and "national-popular" identities (Hylton and Thomson 2007). Throughout most of Bolivia's history, these dual traditions of resistance have coexisted uneasily and sometimes antagonistically, with indigenous interests generally subordinated to class-conscious trade union and progressive mestizo elements in unstable alliances that have ultimately fractured.[4]

In the contemporary struggle, protests by Aymara peasant migrants and militant ex-miners in their respective El Alto neighborhoods rein-

---

[4] A dramatic example of this instability occurred in the 1960s, when indigenous peasants who had united with insurgent miners to bring about the national Revolution of 1952 formed new alliances with the reactionary military dictatorship to suppress the militant trade union movement.

forced and amplified one another with a common purpose. Both indigenous and mining cultures contributed to an urban resistance grounded in non-liberal forms of collective organization and drawing on traditional tactics (such as the urban siege). Even the symbols of the resistance (slingshots, dynamite, miners' helmets, and *wiphalas*—the checkered flag of indigenous self-determination) fused elements of both cultures. The symbolic moment of convergence occurred at the height of the mobilizations with the entry of truckloads of highland miners into El Alto—waving the *wiphala* to affirm their newly-discovered indigenous identity, and overcoming long-standing ethnic-class and urban-rural divisions (Hylton and Thomson 2007).

Consensual Obligation/Participation. A high degree of member participation in collective organizational activities is expected and achieved in El Alto. During the civil strikes that characterized the Gas Wars, all shops, markets, and businesses closed, transportation stopped, and thousands mobilized for daily marches and demonstrations. This solidarity was produced by a unique blend of social coercion and incentives that dates back to the *ayllu*, where members who fulfill their collective obligations are entitled to greater benefits, services, and protection from the association. Similarly, failure to participate in a neighborhood campaign or *sindicato* activity might result in a fine, a denial of neighborhood services won by the community, or assignment to a less favored market stall or taxi route (Lazar 2006, 2008).

While these "consensual obligations" depart from the liberal democratic tradition, they are generally accepted in El Alto as part of the way the community works. As Lazar observes, Alteños typically do not perceive these participatory requirements as incompatible with the essentially democratic nature of their neighborhood assemblies, because they support the ultimate goals (Lazar 2008). As long as the penalty for non-participation in protest activities does not significantly exceed the day's lost wages and transportation costs, it is considered reasonable.

Direct Democracy/Horizontal Governance. During the Gas Wars, grassroots mobilizations were strengthened by the traditional practice of community assembly where residents meet to exchange information, deliberate in public, and reach decisions by consensus. In many El Alto neighborhoods, assemblies were held regularly at the block level. Community radio facilitated direct communication and the growth of "horizontal" decision-making networks.

Individual neighborhood councils took responsibility for organizing road blockades, communal cooking, and neighborhood defense, utilizing the traditional tactic of shift rotation to allow the protest to continue indefinitely. They negotiated with (or pressured) street vendors and transport drivers to regulate the opening and closing of markets and access roads (Lazar 2006). In many cases, the neighborhood councils simply provided cover for grassroots networks acting independently, drawing on their everyday experiences of collective organization. As Hylton and Thomson (2007: 115) observe:

> In the climactic days of October, heterogeneous popular forces organized themselves, deliberated in open assemblies, and took action in their own sphere without waiting for orders from political party, trade union, or other established leaders.

That the FEJUVE leadership, at the height of the struggle, was forced to follow rather than direct events is fully consistent with the indigenous concept of *mandar obedeciendo* (to lead by obeying). In the communal culture, leadership is not a privilege but a form of community service, always accountable to the base. As one FEJUVE leader explained to Sian Lazar (2008: 235):

> We were no longer an executive, the people didn't take any notice [of us]. The people rose up... They triumphed, not us [the leaders]. We simply obeyed orders.

Autonomy. Through the neighborhood councils, El Alto has developed as a self-constructed city largely independent of the state. In Zibechi's view (2005), the autonomous organization of labor in the informal sector, based on productivity and family ties instead of the hierarchical boss-worker relationship, has reinforced this sense of empowerment: that citizens can self-manage and control their own environment. While neighborhood self-help activities in some contexts may serve to legitimize public sector disinvestment and the privatization of social service costs (Gill 2000), FEJUVE's combination of autonomist and protest politics, which makes continuing demands on the state, has helped to mitigate this risk.

At the height of the Gas Wars in October 2003, the practice of self-organization enabled Alteños to achieve an extraordinary level of institutional autonomy as the state effectively ceded control over resources, territory, commerce, and even police functions to the neighborhood "microgovernments" (and to parallel formations in the Altiplano provincial capitals). It also allowed FEJUVE and other popular organizations to exploit El Alto's strategic geographic location on the rim of the Altiplano, linking La Paz by road with the rest of Bolivia. In a tradition dating back to Tupaj Katari's indigenous rebellion in 1781, and continuing with the militant miners' entry into the capital during the 1952 revolution, El Alto residents used road blockades and massive demonstrations to lay siege to La Paz from above. Since—thanks to globalization—El Alto is now also the site of La Paz's international airport, these tactics applied in the contemporary context effectively cut off La Paz from the rest of the *world*.

The resulting institutional and territorial autonomy achieved by the social movements in 2003 has been likened by some analysts to the "dual power" exercised by revolutionary soviets, providing the basis for creation of an alternative state (Hylton and Thompson 2006). However, consistent with their non-statist orientation, FEJUVE, the neighborhood councils, and other popular organizations did not move to "seize state power" once a vacuum of authority was created. Instead, their collective experience of autonomous grassroots mobilization opened up a broad political space, paving the way for the democratic election of Evo Morales eighteen months later.

The Progressive State: New Challenges

Since the inauguration of the new MAS government—a self-proclaimed "government of the social movements" (Carlsen 2007)—in December 2005, FEJUVE and the neighborhood councils have faced new and substantial challenges in defining their relationship to the progressive state.

The MAS government came to power on a pledge to implement the "October Agenda" put forth by FEJUVE and the social movements: to regain popular sovereignty over natural resources and refound Bolivia as a plurinational state. For more than two and a half years, the government's efforts, though partially successful, have been constrained by the political power of lowland agrobusiness elites, the economy's continued dependence on transnational finance capital, and the weakened capacity of the state after 20 years of neoliberal restructuring.

Thus, while the "nationalization" of hydrocarbons—in reality a combination of buybacks and forced negotiations—has vastly increased state revenues, energy production has been severely curtailed by cutbacks in private investment and the limited capacity of Bolivia's public energy company. Agrarian reform, though targeting only large estates held for non-productive use, has been thwarted by regional agrobusiness interests and limited to the redistribution of publicly-owned land. Most important, the drafting of a new constitution by an elected Constituent Assembly was stymied for more than two years by opposition forces, culminating in "autonomy" votes in the four lowlands departments.[5] Regional agrobusiness elites then mounted an increasingly violent campaign to prevent adoption of the constitution and destabilize the MAS government, despite (or because of) the resounding reaffirmation of Evo Morales' popular mandate by two-thirds of the voters in the August 2008 recall referendum.

In this polarized political environment, FEJUVE and the social movements have struggled with the tensions and contradictions inherent in seeking to maintain an autonomous stance while defending the besieged government. While FEJUVE remains a major protagonist in El Alto (La Razón 2008b), some question whether its independence has been compromised by the cooptation of its leaders into high-level government positions (Spronk 2008) and the alleged delivery of patronage jobs to its members (La Razón 2008a). FEJUVE's former president, appointed Water Minister by Evo Morales, was roundly criticized—and ultimately dismissed—for mismanaging the return of El Alto's privatized water company to public ownership (Spronk 2008).

How to incorporate the forms of collective organization and participatory decision-making that flourished during the Gas Wars into alternative models of political and institutional representation has presented another major challenge. For example, as a member of the government commission set up to design the new La Paz-El Alto public water company, FEJUVE originally proposed a structure with a high degree of popular participation—including an elected delegate assembly to determine water policy. However, under pressure from international funders and the La Paz and El Alto mayors, this participatory model was significantly scaled back (Spronk 2008).

---

[5] In these resource-rich regions, "autonomy" is essentially a demand for departmental control of land and hydrocarbons revenues to benefit local elites. This contrasts sharply with the autonomist politics of grassroots organizations like FEJUVE and the neighborhood councils, which emphasize self-organization and participatory democracy within the context of popular/state sovereignty over natural resources in order to ensure their equitable distribution.

Similarly, a proposal advanced by indigenous and popular organizations to allow collective forms of delegate representation to the Constituent Assembly outside the traditional political parties (based on ethnic, *sindicato*, or neighborhood affiliation) was rejected by MAS, whether for practical or political reasons. This episode attests to the weakened state of the social movements as well as MAS' increasing efforts to consolidate power under party control (Hylton and Thomson 2007). For some critics, even the manner in which FEJUVE and other popular organizations have collaborated with the government to defend the Constituent Assembly against rightist attacks (Los Tiempos 2007) suggests elements of MAS manipulation:

> The government has sought continuously either to demobilize autonomous rural and urban protest…or to strategically mobilize its bases against the *media luna* [lowlands departments]…but within very strict perimeters, predetermined by government elites…FEJUVE-El Alto, one of the most powerful organizations in the 2000–2005 wave of revolt, has sadly lost its independence from the government, and is unable to mobilize its bases effectively to advance the cause of the city's indigenous informal proletarian masses (Webber 2008: 8).

Yet in the fall of 2008, when escalating rightwing violence brought Bolivia to the brink of civil war, popular neighborhood-based resistance to the civil coup in the eastern city of Santa Cruz recalled the autonomist communitarian practices that characterized El Alto in 2003–5, signaling a resurgence of the social movements' independence (Zibechi 2008). In Plan 3000, a sprawling settlement of indigenous migrants (primarily from the western highlands) that has been called the "El Alto of Santa Cruz," entire neighborhoods rose up to defend their public markets against paramilitary attacks, after growing impatient with the government's refusal to take action (Gutiérrez Aguilar 2008). Following a massacre of pro-MAS peasants in the Pando department, a broad coalition of popular organizations responded with a siege of Santa Cruz, followed by an epic 200-mile march to La Paz to demand that Congress convoke a referendum on the new constitution. With FEJUVE and Evo Morales in the lead, 200,000 arrived at the Plaza Murillo equally prepared to besiege the Congress or celebrate the vote, as appropriate (La Razón 2008c; Do Alto 2008).

The compromise constitution negotiated by the political parties in Congress, which is virtually certain to be approved in the January referendum, reflects significant concessions to the opposition (e.g. with respect to agrarian reform, departmental autonomies, and presidential term limits). For some, the outcome (as well as the process by which it was achieved) represents a betrayal of the Constituent Assembly that leaves the power of entrenched agrobusiness elites intact, while relegitimizing the tradition of political party "pacts" at the expense of more democratic forms of decision-making. For others, the achievement of a constitutional framework that reflects the essential core of the social movements' October agenda—a plurinational state with greater indigenous rights and state control over national resources—represents a historic victory (Do Alto 2008). With the rightwing opposition divided and demoralized by the compromise vote, MAS supporters perceive an unprecedented opportunity to consolidate their gains, increase political power, and advance the program for "decolonization" of the state.

Today the relationship between the social movements, the MAS government, and Evo Morales, characterized by "a contradictory mix of verticalism and autonomy" (Fuentes 2008; Stefanoni and Bajo 2008), appears to be more complex than ever. The recently-formed CONAL-CAM (National Coalition for Change), representing the largest indigenous, peasant, and urban social movements—including FEJUVE-El Alto—has joined with the COB (Bolivian Workers Central) to mobilize support for the compromise constitution and is a new force to be reckoned with (Fuentes 2008). Arguably, both the government and the social movements have been strengthened by recent events; but whether the new popular formation will serve to check or reinforce MAS' growing hegemony is still uncertain. Clearly, tensions and challenges in the relationship remain.

Now that Bolivia's political turmoil has subsided, at least for the moment, both the MAS government and the social movements must confront the real—and perhaps more difficult—challenge of how to deliver on their promises. At the end of the day, popular organizations like FEJUVE need to provide concrete benefits (jobs, housing, and services) to retain the allegiance of their constituents. This will require significant public resources which, to date, the government has been unable (or unwilling) to deliver. Whether FEJUVE and other popular organizations can successfully shift from their past confrontational and current defensive postures to a new mode of constructive but critical collaboration with the progressive state, while continuing to affirm their autonomist and participatory traditions, remains to be seen.

Some fruitful areas for collaboration in the economic sphere may be emerging, with particular reference to El Alto. For example, the government has launched a social housing program using public and private sector employee contribution funds to provide direct zero- or low-interest loans to both informal sector and salaried workers (La Razón 2007). Major suppliers are providing building materials (such as cement) at discounted prices. Projects can be targeted to neighborhood groups, *sindicatos*, and indigenous organizations, among others. FEJUVE and allied organizations (such as COR) participated in pilot programs and are now pressing to direct more funds to El Alto's social sector, with increased community participation in planning and control of the housing (El Diario 2008a, 2008b). Red Habitat, an activist housing NGO in El Alto, is seeking to promote greater emphasis on traditional and collective self-help building methods (Achtenberg 2009).

Additionally, the new Ministry of Production and Microenterprise is providing credit and technical support to micro-enterprises, producer associations, and small businesses (Claure 2007). Significant loans have been made to established social enterprises in El Alto that are organized around native resources and traditional participatory practices, including a fiber processing company (COPROCA) owned by a federation of llama herders and a cocoa processing plant (El Ceibo) owned by an organic farmers' cooperative (La Prensa 2007).

As sociologist Kevin Healy has noted (2001, 2004), these highly integrated operations allow the collective producer associations to control and benefit from the full chain of production and commercialization, while providing good manufacturing jobs for El Alto workers. The development model also extends the Andean tradition of "verticality," linking non-contiguous ecological zones to promote self-sufficiency. COR and FEJUVE are demanding an expansion of the program to give El Alto's less established microbusinesses similar access to national and international markets (El Diario 2008b).

According to Vice President Alvaro Garcia Linera, the MAS government seeks to promote a kind of "Andean capitalism" which combines community-based, family-based, and modern industrial economies. The goal is to "transfer a part of the surplus from the nationalized hydrocarbons in order to encourage…forms of self-organization, self-management, and commercial development that are really Andean and Amazonian" (Stefanoni 2005). To the extent that FEJUVE and the neighborhood councils can help to shape the realization of this vision in El Alto, in ways that further their autonomist and participatory traditions, progressive planners and community activists will continue to draw inspiration from this creative grassroots organization.

THE ZAPATISTAS' OTHER POLITICS: THE SUBJECTS OF AUTONOMY

Margaret Cerullo

In a devastating summation of the "progressive decade" in Latin America, signaled by the elections of Lula, Tabaré Vázquez, the Kirchners, and also Evo Morales, Hugo Chávez and Rafael Correa, Raul Zibechi recently concluded that one of its outstanding results has been the demobilization of social movements. (Zibechi, 2008) Aside from the cooptive strategies of left governments in power, he identified the new strategies of the elites (finance capital aligned with Empire) to foment destabilizing internal polarization and force left social movements to ally with the left parties against the Right. Zibechi concludes by raising the key question of the role of the state in processes of fundamental social transformation in this historical (neoliberal) moment in Latin America. Threatened no longer by the artillery and bombs of old style imperial interventions (e.g., Guatemala 1954; Dominican Republic 1965) but rather by what Subcomandante Marcos (1997: 261) calls "financial hyperbombs,"[1] left governments have not been able or willing to risk economic destabilization as a punishment for putting the brakes on multinational speculation and accumulation.

The Zapatistas have witnessed what happens to the Left in power. They have concluded that just as they ceased to believe in the *foco guerrillero*,[2] they can no longer believe that a group or a person (such as López Obrador, the "left" (PRD) candidate for the presidency in 2006) can fundamentally transform the lives of those at the bottom (the poor, small farmers, maquila workers, those who are marginalized for being different or other (the indigenous, sex workers, "other

---

[1] An indigenous farmer interviewed by Neil Harvey (2005: 15) in Tumbalá, describes Plan Puebla Panama, a neoliberal meta 'development' (and counter-insurgency) scheme, as "a cold war...a war of low prices, so that we die off."

[2] The *foco*, an idea of Che's, is that a small group of the "enlightened" would demonstrate the courage to take up arms against the government, provoking the masses to follow their lead, rise up, overthrow the existing government, and install a socialist state. In the Zapatistas' critique, the problem with the *foco* is that it envisions change as a top down process.

loves," women)) through controlling the national state.[3] Thus, rather
than mobilize to support Lopez Obrador's candidacy, they launched
an "Other Campaign," a national listening campaign to connect those
throughout the country engaged in struggles against neoliberalism and
for humanity. Due to what is widely regarded as a fraudulent election in
2006, the Zapatistas confront not a government of the institutional Left
as they had anticipated, but the militarized Right wing government of
Felipe Calderon (2006–present). They have developed their politics in
a specifically Mexican context where transforming the passive political
culture and subjectivity of the entrenched system of *clientelism*[4] has been
a central focus. Beyond Mexico, however, in the broader regional politi-
cal/economic context Zibechi analyzes, the Zapatistas' "other" politics,
centered on integrating politics (as the art and practice of governing
and being governed) into everyday life and identity, (a "de-alienation"
of politics) as the principal barrier to de-politicization, passivity, and
paternalism, acquires special significance.

This paper will address only one aspect of current Zapatista practice
and theory: the construction of new social subjects through the exercise
of autonomy in the Zapatista communities, since it is the aspect that
most directly addresses the context and issues described above. It is
part of a larger project to explore the distinctive Zapatista combination
of the utopian and the strategic, manifest in its history and practice.
That larger project will address as well the explicitly anticapitalist Other
Campaign, launched in 2006 as an alternative to the presidential campaign; the rising of the women, one of the principal internal dynamics
of Zapatismo; the primacy of ethics in the Zapatista vision and practice;

---

[3] According to Subcomandante Marcos (Marcos, 2008), the Zapatistas refer to the
inexorable transformation of the Left in power as the "stomach effect": power either
assimilates you or turns you into shit.

[4] *Clientelism* refers to the long-standing political culture and system of political
control practiced by the PRI (the party that ruled Mexico for 70 years); and, arguably,
continued today outside the PRI. On the one hand, desperately needed material concessions are exchanged for political subordination (which, as Jonathan Fox reminds
us, does not imply submission). *Caciquism* refers to the *caciques* or local, regional, or
national "bosses" who are the funnels between the state and the people, who maintain
unity via threats as well as serving as channels for the distribution of benefits. In the
corporatist version, society is compartmentalized (into peasants, workers, teachers,
etc.) and organized by strong leaders. In the current neoliberal version of *clientelism*,
state programs establish a direct relationship with individuals without the mediation
of corporatist sectors. The usual manipulative balance between concession and repression typically shifts to the latter under threat of significant popular mobilization. (See
Adler, 1994; Fox, 1994)

and the centrality to Zapatismo's political project of parody and poetry in its discourse—making visible other worlds, invisible or devalued within dominant paradigms of thought, while unsettling hierarchies of social, political, economic, and cultural value and sense.

Zapatista Autonomy: Cultures of Resistance and Transformation

In the Summer of 2003, the Zapatistas officially proclaimed five autonomous governments or *caracoles* consisting of more than thirty autonomous municipalities that comprise Zapatista territory.[5] This proclamation resulted from the Zapatistas' recognition that the path of negotiation with the federal government that they had pursued since 1994 had proven deceptive and futile; and that indigenous autonomy had to be exercised rather than demanded from the state.[6] It also represented a recognition by the *comandancia* (general command) of the EZLN that the effective government by an army, even an army of national liberation, was incompatible with the development of democracy in the communities, and that the army had to withdraw and delineate its responsibilities. As Subcomandante Marcos explained:

> ....the EZLN's military structure in some way 'contaminated' a tradition of democracy and self-governance. The EZLN was, in a manner of speaking, one of the 'undemocratic' elements in a relationship of direct community democracy (another anti-democratic element is the Church, but

---

[5] It is perhaps not always recognized that Zapatista territory is an archipelago of communities scattered throughout the state of Chiapas, in the midst of other non-Zapatista communities. Even within small villages, there are frequently two local governments, one Zapatista, the other, the official government, aligned with the state.

[6] The major re-orientation of strategy represented by the proclamation of the *caracoles* and the dedication to the development of internal autonomy was primarily the result of the government's failure to honor the 1996 San Andres Accords on indigenous autonomy and culture. As the Accords moved nowhere for four years after their signing, in 2001 the Zapatistas organized the March of the People of the Color of the Earth from Chiapas to Mexico City, where an indigenous woman addressed the Congress for the first time in history to demand legislation that fulfilled the Accords. When in April 2001, the three major political parties colluded in the introduction of an indigenous rights law that stripped away all the important features of the San Andres accords, principally the right to indigenous autonomy, the Zapatistas broke off all contact with the government, and began to reassess their relationship not only to the PRI but to the PRD (the supposed party of the Left) as well. The proclamation of the *caracoles* after two years of internal consultation and public silence expressed the Zapatistas' recognition that the path of institutional, constitutional reform was definitively closed.

that's a matter for another paper). When the Autonomous Municipalities began operating, self-governance did not move just from the local to the regional, it also emerged (always tendentially) from the 'shadow' of the military structure. (Marcos, 2003b)

Additionally, the declaration of the *juntas de buen gobierno* (good government councils) in each of the five Zapatista hubs as the interface with civil society was a way to track and redistribute resources more equitably within the communities, and to become more vigilant about the paternalism that had often accompanied civil society initiatives.

In "The Thirteenth Stele, Part Two: A Death," Marcos (2003a) describes the pile-up in the Zapatista communities of useless computers, expired medicines, extravagant clothes, and even shoes without their mates, going on to note

> ...a more sophisticated kind of handout which is practiced by some NGOs and international organizations. It consists more or less in their deciding what the communities need and, without even consulting them, imposing not just particular projects but also the timing and form of their execution. Imagine the desperation of a community that needs potable water and instead is given a library or needs a school for children and is given a course in herbiculture.

Finally, as González Casanova (2005) reminds us, the proclamation of the caracoles, the decision to "build up the autonomy of the rebel territories," was a decision for a peaceful alternative to taking up arms again when the government and the political parties betrayed them. It represents a wager that it is possible to construct a "peaceful transition toward a viable world which is less authoritarian, less oppressive, less unjust, and which can continue to struggle for peace with democracy, justice and liberty."

All of these contextual factors contributed to the 2003 declaration. But it is important to emphasize that the official proclamation of autonomy formalized the Zapatista autonomous municipalities declared since 1994. The occupation of land, its reinscription with indigenous identity[7] and

---

[7] Andres Aubry, for example, contrasts the vernacular architecture and planning of the autonomous Zapatista communities with the urbanization projects of the INI (Instituto Nacional Indigenista). The former are built around the geography (material and/or symbolic) of the place, around a hill in one community; along the banks of the river in another; on either side of the formal road in the center of Oventic (sometimes dubbed the "road to modernity.") In the free zones, the principle of organization is meeting needs. By contrast, the state government-funded "urbanization" projects seek

anti-capitalist logic through the development of alternative practices—sustainable and equitable economies, the use of indigenous languages, distinctive practices of justice, participatory self-government—has been one of the basic motives and achievements of Zapatismo since, and indeed before, the uprising in 1994. As Comandanta Kelly explained as she embarked from Chiapas on the stage of the Other Campaign[8] dedicated to the "Defense of Territory":

> For the rural, *campesino*, indigenous communities land and territory are more than work and food: they are also culture, community, history, ancestors, dreams, the future, life and mother. But for two centuries the capitalist system has de-ruralized, expelled *campesinos* and indigenous from their land, changed the face of the earth, dehumanized it. (Quoted in Aubry, 2007b)

Land, territory the material base of both survival and autonomy, has come to be in Aubry's words "embodied Zapatismo" and is therefore the logical target of counter-insurgency, whose goal is to unsettle the "geography of resistance," the land recuperated by the Zapatistas since before the uprising. Specifically, the government of the state of Chiapas awards claims to landless *campesinos* on land that the Zapatistas have reclaimed and occupy, and back up their awards with the threat of (military or paramilitary) force, unmasking the "new face of counterinsurgency." (Aubry, 2007a) I mention this since it is important to understand the highly militarized and constantly threatening context within which the Zapatista autonomy project is being carried out.

The substance and significance of Zapatista autonomy has been intriguing and elusive and the subject of considerable political interest and commentary (Richard Stahler-Sholk, 2007; Pablo González Casanova, 2005; Neil Harvey, 2005; Atilio Borón, 2005; Andres Aubry in

---

to imitate *mestizo* cities, with networks of streets, "central parks" with kiosks, identical city halls and warehouses, used or not. (Aubry, 2003a: 229–30)

[8] The "Other Campaign," the most recent initiative in the Zapatistas' search for an other way of doing politics, was proclaimed to coincide with the presidential campaign of 2006. Unlike the official campaign, the Otra sought to make visible the great national problems the presidential candidates ignore. Its form was a national "listening campaign" in which Subcomandante Marcos and at times various members of the *comandancia*, such as Comandanta Kelly, traveled throughout the country to meet with those "from the left and at the bottom," Mexico's excluded. Its goals were to discover the concrete problems and struggles that exist throughout the country, in this way concretizing neoliberalism as well as the collectivity of those who are struggling against it. The ultimate goal, still pending, is to formulate a national progressive agenda, a program of struggle, created from the bottom up.

Jan Rus, et al., 2003; Gilberto López y Rivas, 2006). Neil Harvey, for example, regards the *caracoles* as the Zapatistas' most significant political achievement, even though autonomy has not gained recognition at the level of the state; while Atilio Borón insists that the Zapatistas bypass what remains the critical locus of power, the state, and substitute "ingenious plays on words" for the task of actually making power holders "rule by obeying" the people. For Richard Stahler-Sholk, the creation of autonomous, community-controlled institutions—schools, clinics, systems of justice and local governance—is a critical part of the struggle against neoliberalism, as they articulate and enact collective priorities independent of the logic of the market; while for Pablo González Casanova, the *caracoles* are an alternative form of social and political organization that draw their strength from internal participatory and direct democracy and a structure of connected and coordinated organizations of resistance. They represent, he argues "an 'anti-systemic' proposal in that the creation of autonomous rebel municipalities strengthens the people's capacity for resistance and for the creation of an alternative system." Neil Harvey identifies autonomy with the struggle to defend access to common property and social solidarity in the face of neoliberalism's advance through destruction of the material bases of collective projects and solidarity, while Andres Aubry and Gilberto López y Rivas both emphasize that autonomy has to be understood as a rejection of "indigenism," the long, paternalist project of the Mexican state to incorporate the indigenous into the nation on the condition that they cease to be indigenous.

Concretely, what does Zapatista autonomy for which so much is claimed (rightly, I believe) consist in? Guided by, or rather, embodying the idea of *mandar obedeciendo* (lead by obeying the people), the Zapatista communities as systems of self-government are characterized by rotation of authorities. Each municipality sends two representatives to the *Junta de Buen Gobierno* (good government council) of the region for terms of 10–15 days; with the principle of recall if the chosen authority does not fulfill his or her charge. While permanent commissions on such areas as education, health and security provide continuity, they take their direction from the *juntas*, one of whose principal functions is the resolution of conflicts between non-Zapatistas and Zapatista supporters living side by side in many communities. The government of local communities is carried out by elected municipal councils and judges who serve longer terms (approximately two years). Critical to this structure, as mentioned above, is the removal of the *comandancia* (general command) of the EZLN (the Zapatista army) from the internal governance of the communities, an explicit goal of the formation of the caracoles. The *juntas* are the mediator between the Zapatistas and civil society, receiving all visitors and all proposals for research or cooperative projects with the communities. They are responsible for resolving disputes in the communities and Zapatista judges are widely respected and appealed to by non-Zapatistas as well.[9] The *juntas de buen gobierno*, along with the municipal governing councils, are, in short, an active participatory democratic school "resistance turned into a school" (Marcos, 2008) that engages thousands of indigenous men and women in the practice of self-government. They are a continual vaccination against *caciquism* and *clientelism* that have effectively eliminated a political class in the Zapatista communities and returned politics to the intimate quotidian practice of the people, effecting what I have called above, a "de-alienation" of politics. Discussions of the practice of autonomy in Zapatista communities tend to be somewhat general, drawn from the communiqués of Subcomandante Marcos rather than from ethnographic work. Stahler Sholk provides two rare glimpses from his field observations of Zapatista communities' interactions with the clientelist state. One is of a community in the *Cañadas* recently returned from a month's refuge in the hills during the government's 1995 offensive that was visited, almost upon arrival back to their community, by a helicopter full of Mexican Congress people offering aid. The community held a long open-air assembly to discuss the offer, while the legislators grew ever more impatient. After careful consideration they returned their decision to reject aid from the government that had just sent the army after them, and demanded instead the withdrawal of troops. In a second community, where a brigade to investigate for malaria arrived without notice, suddenly no one in the village could speak a world of Spanish.

---

[9] Richard Stahler Sholk reports one case of two paramilitaries following a machete fight appealing to Zapatista judges to settle their dispute.

Roots and reasons of autonomy

There is a tendency (at least in the US) to romanticize indigenous communities and practices, and to attribute them to a "culture"—more communal and egalitarian—preserved despite 500 years of Conquest and several hundred years of incorporation into the capitalist world system. In response to the prevalence of this (imperial) common sense, I emphasize following López y Rivas, Andres Aubry, and Neil Harvey that autonomy should be understood as at base a historically resilient political culture of resistance. Its practices of broad democratic participation and the construction of consensus have made a critical contribution to the remarkable internal cohesion of the Zapatistas over the last fifteen years of their public existence, preceded by ten years underground, in which a clandestine indigenous army was organized throughout the state of Chiapas without being exposed. Aubry (emphasizes a longer time frame—the famous "*usos y costumbres*" (traditional practices and customs) should be understood as "nothing more than the current evolving and changing expression of indigenous resistance regulated by successive forms of clandestine organization. Its principal form, autonomy, was lived at the margin of the law, under cover, until after January 1, 1994 it became necessary to bring it out into the open." (Aubry, 2003a: 221) Or, in a more poetic rendition,

> Custom...is the form of struggle adopted by a people to secure a future and a place in society other than that of the inhuman labor of the farm, the desperate search for land and work, the prison cell, the denigration of women, and the governmental obstacles to aspirations for a different political life. It is a daily struggle to prevent macroeconomic, police, or military genocide. (*Ibid.*: 220)

For Aubry (2003a: 229) then, "the declarations of the EZLN do not follow a theory but theorize old practices that represent a 'gradual gathering of forces in silence.'" In another language, we might interpret indigenous *usos y costumbres* as akin to James Scott's famous "hidden transcripts" of resistance (1992), a collective culture elaborated "offstage" out of a reworking of daily indignities and insults, a culture of resistance that preserves blocked intentions, possible futures, other logics. For Aubry, the key difference between the Zapastista negotiations with the government and the old patronizing indigenism is the acknowledgement that the terms of the discussion have fundamentally changed—the future of Mexico depends not on an alteration of the indigenous to conform to the imaginary *mestizo* national standard, but rather "a change of the society that would put them in a new relation to the nation *that owe[s] them its existence.*" [emphasis his]. That is, he proposes that at San Andres the indigenous Zapatistas were nation building, refounding the nation, insisting on their inclusion on their own terms, establishing "the collective right to be different." Insistently not separatist, but inclusive, this represents a indigenous contribution to contemporary democratic theory and practice—tempering equal rights with the right to be different, a right whose ultimate collective expression is autonomy with neither segregation nor secession.

More than self-government...

Gilberto López y Rivas is the analyst who has most emphasized the transformative character of the practice of autonomy in Zapatista communities, and presumably in other contexts as well. Underlining the "planned and programmed" participation of women and young people, the equitable and sustainable reorganization of the economy, the adoption of anticapitalist and antisystemic political identities, as well as the active search for alliances, both national and international, he argues that these practices have brought about a qualitative change in the meaning of autonomy and in the constitution of autonomous subjects. In particular, beyond the practices of self-government but integral to them, Zapatista communities have seen an internal transformation of relations of age and gender, due precisely, I propose to the expansive character of autonomy, conceptualized by the Zapatistas "not as a program or a rigid plan, but a process that unfolds in its own way, from below." It is this expansive, protean character of autonomy that I noted in conversations during two visits to the Highlands, in May 2007 and October 2008. Young Zapatista women have extended the discourse of autonomy to fashion a distinctive position on abortion (a subject of intense political discussion in Mexico after the city of Mexico decriminalized abortion in 2006). This brief example will, I hope, give some flesh to the idea of new autonomous social subjects. It was the Zapatista women who initiated a discussion of abortion in 2007 in the light of the law in Mexico City. "500,000 women annually in Mexico have an abortion," one explained, *"sin pedir permiso del estado"* without asking the state's permission, connecting women's practice of clandestine abortions with the project of autonomy that they have undertaken *sin pedir permiso del estado.* "Abortion is murder, is the taking of life of a human being," another affirmed, "but women have the right." In this discourse Zapatista women rather startlingly claim the right to usurp the classical patriarchal prerogative, the right over the life of their children, as, in their willingness to take up arms to defend justice, equality and dignity, they have already usurped the prerogative of the state, its monopoly on the legitimate use of force.[10] "To not be allowed to have an abortion is how they impede us—by forcing us to have 10, 12 children."

Impede them from what? If one turns to the Revolutionary Law on Women, the basis of the interviews I conducted in Chiapas, the text chosen by the young Zapatista militants to discuss, the Law's principles include the right to participate in the revolutionary struggle, to have *cargos*, positions of authority in their communities, and to participate in the revolutionary armed forces, that is the right to be part of a collective project to transform the world. If the Revolutionary Law is an articulation of their rights, it is the practice of autonomy that has made those rights concrete, and extended their meanings. The young Zapatista women I met in the Highlands have claimed a woman's right to bodily autonomy, reclaiming the territory of their bodies and collectively inscribing them with new possibilities—these are bodies that play basketball, sometimes abandon *traje* (traditional dress of heavy woolen skirts and embroidered blouses) for more comfortable and mobile blue jeans. These are women who will take into their own hands the determination of how many children to have. They have articulated a distinctive Zapatista feminism, expressing a collective gendered challenge that links the multiple powers that they as indigenous Zapatista women contend with—the state or the "*mal gobierno,*" neoliberalism, and the norms of their communities and expectations of their families, particularly husbands and fathers. They have introduced a body politics into Zapatismo which perhaps has made the movement receptive to

---

[10] According to Subcomandante Marcos's most recent history of the EZLN (Marcos 2008), in the years leading up to the uprising, it was indigenous women who began to spread the idea that became an insistent refrain throughout the Highlands and the jungle of Chiapas that, "'ya basta,' something had to be done" to forestall or at least call attention to the death worlds—no child in the Selva Lacandona between 1990 and 1992 survived more than 5 years—that the indigenous inhabited.

both lesbians and gays and to sex workers who have become important adherents of the Other Campaign.

As the above discussions with some new social subjects of autonomy suggests, Zapatista autonomy makes another contribution to the democratic imaginary in its open-ended character, as an ever expanding horizon of subjective and communal transformation. López y Rivas (2008) catches some of the motion in Zapatista collective and individual identities, when he points to the adoption of explicit anti-capitalist and anti-systemic identities since 2003 (by a movement that previously had identified itself primarily as indigenous), and the constant search for national and international alliances, a complex process of identity construction and transformation through shifting (political) identifications.[11] Along with others, I have often wondered about the Zapatistas' ongoing appeal to young people in the US and throughout the world. Perhaps it is their recognition that you can't stay who you are and create something new, their refusal to restrict their lives to a single narrative, to codify their being into a single category, to present one official authentic transcript, to stay fixed, that appeals to young people, themselves in a position of becoming. To create a space where multiple identities are legitimized, and where conflicting narratives coexist is after all the project of the *caracol*, the conch, that symbol of openness to the exterior that nurtures the interior of the communities, the shell used to call people to the assembly where together, in a process that like the Maya conception of time (see Aubry, 2003b) is neither linear nor circular but takes a thousand turns, they reach a mutual understanding and the ability to "walk together, but separated and in agreement," which, as Lynn Stephen reminds us, is crucial to building any social movement. (Stephen, 2002: 162)

---

[11] In May 2007, Zapatista education *promotoras* introduced a discussion on homosexuality. "We don't know any homosexuals, but we are sure there must be some in our communities."

CONTRIBUTOR INFORMATION

Emily Achtenberg is a Boston-based urban planner and affordable housing consultant to community-based non-profit development organizations. She has been researching urban social movements and social housing in Bolivia as an independent scholar. Her recent articles on Bolivia, published in *Progressive Planning: The Magazine of Planners Network* (www.plannersnetwork.org), include: "Social Housing in Bolivia: Challenges and Contradictions" (No. 178, Winter 2009); "Community Organizing and Rebellion: Neighborhood Councils in El Alto, Bolivia" (No. 172, Summer 2007); and "Bolivia: Reclaiming Natural Resources and Popular Sovereignty" (No. 170, Winter 2007).

Christopher Chase-Dunn is Distinguished Professor of Sociology and Director of the Institute for Research on World-Systems at the University of California, Riverside. He is the author of *Rise and Demise: Comparing World-Systems* (with Thomas D. Hall), *The Wintu and Their Neighbors* (with Kelly Mann) and *The Spiral of Capitalism and Socialism* (with Terry Boswell). He is the founder and former editor of the *Journal of World-Systems Research*. Chase-Dunn is currently doing research on global party formation and antisystemic social movements. He also studies the growth/decline phases and upward sweeps of settlements and polities since the Stone Age, and he is working on simulation models of future global state formation.

Ximena de la Barra is a Spanish/Chilean social scientist initially trained as an architect. She was part of the Allende Popular Unity Government and of the first democratically elected Madrid local government, both in a technical capacity and as a community activist. In New York, she previously taught at Columbia University in the fields of urban and social policy planning. She later worked with the United Nations, first at UN Habitat and most recently at UNICEF, serving in high-level positions including head of office in El Salvador, regional advisor for public policy for Latin America and senior global advisor for public policy and urban affairs. Recently retired from UNICEF, she is now an independent consultant and co-author (with R. A. Dello Buono) of

Latin America after the Neoliberal Debacle: Another Region is Possible (Rowman and Littlefield, 2009), and many articles on regional integration in Latin America.

Melanie E. L. Bush is the author of *Breaking the Code of Good Intentions: Everyday Forms of Whiteness* (Rowman and Littlefield Publishers, Inc., 2004), co-author of a forthcoming book entitled *Tensions in the American Dream: The Imperial Nation Confronts the Liberation of Nations* (Temple University Press with Dr. R. D. Bush, St. Johns University) and numerous articles in scholarly journals. She is currently Assistant Professor of Sociology at Adelphi University (Garden City, NY) and has been active for many years in struggles for equality and justice.

Victoria Carty is Assistant Professor of Sociology at Chapman University. She has published several articles on social movements in the United States, Mexico, and Panama across the dimensions of labor and peace issues. One of her main emphasis has been on "globalization from below" and how the Global Justice Movement, as an umbrella social movement, is bringing together previously distinct mobilizing efforts. Her most recent work examines how new information communication technologies such as MySPace, Utube, and Facebook are impacting mobilizing efforts for participants engaged in both contentious and electoral politics, with a specific focus on the role of these technologies in the 2008 presidential campaign.

Margaret Cerullo teaches sociology and feminist studies at Hampshire College. She has had a long-standing interest in the Zapatista movement. Her current research is on queer formations of gender and sexuality in rural Mexico.

Laura Collin, born in Argentina, has lived in Mexico since 1976, where she has been involved as a researcher and activist with indigenous and social movements. She is an active member of the national Solidarity Economy Network. Collin has a PhD in anthropology, is a professor and researcher at El Colegio de Tlaxcala in Mexico, and is a member of SNI (National System of Researchers). She focuses her research on conflict, power and identities and has written 5 books and more than 80 articles and book chapters. Currently, with support from CONACYT (National Council of Science and Technology), she is examining counter cultural social movements.

Richard "Ricardo" A. Dello Buono is a sociologist whose research areas include comparative social problems and Latin American/Caribbean Studies. He has been a visiting professor at various Latin American universities, including the National University of Colombia, a Fulbright Professor at the University of Panama, and invited professor of political science at the Autonomous University of Zacatecas, Mexico. He is the former Vice-President of the Society for the Study of Social Problems (SSSP), and Series Editor of *Critical Global Studies*, Brill (Leiden). Currently, he is associate professor and chair of the sociology department at Manhattan College. He is co-editor (with José Bell Lara) of *Imperialism, Neoliberalism and Social Struggles in Latin America* (Brill, 2007). He is the co-author (with Ximena de la Barra) of *Latin America after the Neoliberal Debacle: Another Region is Possible*, published by Rowman and Littlefield, and many articles on regional integration in Latin America.

David Fasenfest, Associate Professor of Sociology and Urban Affairs, College of Liberal Arts and Sciences, Wayne State University, is an economist and sociologist whose research focuses on regional and urban economic development, labor market analysis and work force development, and income inequality. He received his graduate training at the University of Michigan. His work has appeared in *Economic Development Quarterly, Urban Affairs Review, International Journal of Urban and Regional Review*, and *International Journal of Sociology*. He is the editor of *Community Economic Development: Policy Formation in the U.S. and U.K.* (1993, MacMillan Press) and *Critical Perspectives on Local Development Policy Evaluation* (2004, Wayne State University Press). In addition, he edits the journal *Critical Sociology* published by SAGE.

Víctor M. Figueroa Sepúlveda, a Chilean sociologist, is a distinguished development theorist and Director of the Graduate Studies Program in Political Science at the Universidad Autónoma de Zacatecas en Zacatecas, Mexico. He is the author of *Reinterpretando el subdesarrollo* (Siglo XXI Editores, 1986), *América Latina en la crisis del patrón neoliberal de crecimiento* (Tribunal Superior de Justicia del Estado, 2003) and numerous other studies in the field.

Heather Gautney is an assistant professor of sociology at Fordham University. She is author of *Between Protest and Political Organization: NGOs, Anti-authoritarian Movements, and Political Parties* (forthcoming, Palgrave Macmillan), and co-editor of *Democracy, States and the Struggle for Global Justice* (Routledge, 2009), and *Implicating Empire: Globalization and Resistance in the 21st Century* (Basic Books, 2003). She is also on the editorial board of *Social Text*.

Kristen Hopewell is a Ph.D. Candidate, Department of Sociology, University of Michigan and Visiting Fellow, Graduate Institute of International and Development Studies, University of Geneva, September 2008–June 2009. In her dissertation research, she is examining the rise of developing country powers at the World Trade Organization (WTO). She is the author of "Globalization and Authority: Analyzing the 'Public Information' Discourse of the World Trade Organization," in Rex, L., ed. *Authoring and Authorizing Self, Community and Globalized Society*. Cresskill, NJ: Hampton Press and (with M. Margulis) "The Comedores Populares: Responding to Neoliberalism's Legacy of Poverty and Hunger in Argentina," *Journal for the Critique of Science* 222, special review issue on neoliberalism and Latin America.

Matheu Kaneshiro is an advanced graduate student in sociology at the University of California-Riverside. He studies transnational social movements, global governance, and the social impacts of environmental degradation.

Marie Kennedy is professor emerita of Community Planning at the University of Massachusetts Boston and visiting professor of Urban Planning at the University of California Los Angeles. She combines the roles of activist and scholar, teaching, working in and writing about community development, planning education and participatory action research. Marie has worked extensively with community organizations in the Greater Boston Area, as well as in San Francisco, Brazil, Cuba, Haiti, Mexico, and Nicaragua. She is co-chair of the Steering Committee of Planners Network, co-editor of Progressive Planning, and is a member of the board of directors of Grassroots International, a human rights and international development organization with many partners in Latin America.

Lauren Langman is a professor of sociology at Loyola University of Chicago. He received his Ph.D. at the University of Chicago from the Committee on Human Development and had further training at the Chicago Institute for Psychoanalysis. He has long worked in the tradition of the Frankfurt School of Critical Theory, especially relationships between culture, politics/political movements and the psychosocial. He is current President of Alienation Research and Theory, Research Committee 36, of the International Sociological Association. He served a 5 year term on the editorial board of Sociological Theory, and remains on boards of Current Perspectives in Social Theory and Critical Sociology. Recent publications include a special issue of American Behavioral Politics devoted to the presidency in a television age as well as a number of articles and book chapters on alienation, social movements, Islamic fundamentalism, the body, nationalism and national character. His most recent book is *Trauma Promise and Millennium: The Evolution of Alienation*, Rowman and Littlefield (with Devorah Kalekin). His forthcoming book, *The Carnivalization of America*, Pine Forge Press, looks at the role of the alienation of youth and their embrace of transgressive life styles, identities and moments of popular culture.

Fernando Leiva is Associate Professor of Latin American, Caribbean and US Latino Studies at the University at Albany (SUNY) and has a PhD in Economics (UMass-Amherst). His research focuses on how the economic, political, and social restructuring of the past three decades has transformed how power is exercised and contested in the region. His current work is on the intersection of flexible accumulation, inequality and the production of social cohesion. He is the author of the book *Latin American Neostructuralism: The Contradictions of Post-Neoliberal Development* (University of Minnesota Press, 2008). His other books are *Democracy in Chile: The Legacy of September 11, 1973* (with Silvia Nagy-Zekmi) and *Democracy and Poverty in Chile* (with James Petras).

Deborah Little is an assistant professor of sociology at Adelphi University in New York where she teaches courses in qualitative methods, law and inequality, disability studies, and gender. She began teaching sociology following years of work as a legal aid attorney. Dr. Little has done research on welfare and gender, care theory, and disability studies. Her current research examines leadership and organizing efforts of caregivers and the relationship between care theory and disability theory.

Arseniy Gutnik is a sociologist whose interests include qualitative methods, cultural and political sociology and social movements, with an emphasis on post-Soviet Russia and Ukraine. His future research will focus on the political and cultural contestation of Russian urban space.

Chris Tilly, Professor of Urban Planning and Director of the Institute for Research on Labor and Employment at the University of California Los Angeles, specializes in labor, income distribution, and local economic development, with research focusing on the United States and Mexico. Tilly's books include *Half a Job: Bad and Good Part-Time Jobs in a Changing Labor Market, Glass Ceilings and Bottomless Pits: Women's Work, Women's Poverty, Work Under Capitalism, Stories Employers Tell: Race, Skill, and Hiring in America,* and *The Gloves-Off Economy: Labor Standards at the Bottom of America's Labor Market.*

REFERENCES CITED

Abendroth, Mark. 2008. "Book review of McLaren, Peter and Nathalia Jaramillo. 2007. *Pedagogy and Praxis in the Age of Empire: Towards a new Humanism.* Sense Publishers." *Radical Teacher.* 82: 41–2.

Acha, Omar. 2007. "Poder Popular y Socialismo desde abajo" ["Popular Power and Socialism from Below"], in Omar Acha, et al., *Reflexiones sobre el poder popular [Reflections on Popular Power]*, Buenos Aires: El Colectivo: 17–36.

Acha, Omar. Campione y Aldo Casas. 2007. *Reflexiones sobre poder popular [Reflections on Popular Power].* Buenos Aires: El Colectivo.

Achtenberg, Emily. 2007. "Community Organizing and Rebellion: Neighborhood Councils in El Alto, Bolivia," *Progressive Planning: The Magazine of Planners Network,* 172 (Summer): 40–43.

——. 2009. "Social Housing in Bolivia: Challenges and Contradictions." *Progressive Planning: The Magazine of Planners' Network,* 178 (Winter).

Adam, Jan. *Social Costs of Transformation to a Market Economy in Post-Socialist Countries: The Cases of Poland, Czech Republic and Hungary.* NY: New York: St. Martin's Press, Inc., 1999.

Aguirre Rojas, Carlos Antonio. 2007. "Generando Contrapoder desde Abajo y a la Izquierda" ["Creating Counterpower from Below and the Left"] *Rebelión.* January 17. http://www.rebelion.org/noticia.php?id=44955

Aharonian, Aram. 2007. *Vernos con Nuestros Propios Ojos: Apuntes sobre Comunicación y Democracia [Seeing Ourselves Through Our Own Eyes].* Caracas: Fondo Editorial Question.

Albó, Xavier. 2007. "El Alto: Mobilizing Block By Block," *NACLA Report on the Americas* 40(4) (July/August): 34–38.

Albro, Robert. 2005. "The Indigenous in the Plural in Bolivian Oppositional Politics." *Bulletin of Latin American Research.* 24(4): 433–453.

Allegrone, Veronica. 2006. "La construcción de la identidad colectiva en los procesos de recuperación de fabricas y empresas en argentina. Un estudio de caso" ["Construction of a Collective Identity in the Process of Recovering Factories and Companies in Argentina"], in *e-l@tina. Revista electrónica de estudios latinoamericanos Vol. 4, N 15 abril-junio.*

All-Ukraine Network of People Living with HIV/AIDS (PLWH). 1 Aug. 2007, Ukraine. 11 Apr. 2007 <http://network.org.ua/joomla/index.php?option=com_content&task=view&id=5&Itemid=217□=en>.

Alvarez, Fernando. 2007. "La mirada de Ulises" ["Ulysses' Gaze"], in Toty Flores, ed., *Cuando con otros somos nosotros[When with Others We are Ourselves]*, Buenos Aires: Peña Lillo-Ed Continente: 175–83.

Álvarez-Rivadulla, Maria José. 2008. "How to Study Elusive Collective Action: A Call for Mixed Methods." Unpublished paper, Department of Sociology, University of Pittsburgh.

Amin, Samir. 1997. *Capitalism in an Age of Globalization.* London: Zed Books.

——. 2006. "Towards the fifth international?" Pp. 121–144 in Katarina Sehm-Patomaki and Marko Ulvila (eds.) *Democratic Politics Globally.* Network Institute for Global Democratization (NIGD Working Paper 1/2006), Tampere, Finland.

Anheier, Helmut. 2004. *Civil Society: Measurement, Evaluation, Policy.* Sterling, VA: Earthscan.

Arbona, Juan Manuel. 2005. "Reading the City as (Social) Movement: El Alto, Bolivia—October 2003," *Delaware Review of Latin American Studies*, 6(1) (June 30).

Archibugi, Daniele and David Held, eds. 1995. *Cosmopolitan Democracy: An Agenda for a New World Order*. Cambridge: Polity Press.

Árias, Eliézer. 2008. "Our History Is in Our Land/Nuestra Historia Está en la Tierra." Film. Mérida, Venezuela.

Aronowitz, Stanley. 2006. *Left Turn: Forging a New Political Future*. New York: Paradigm Publishers.

Arrighi, Giovanni, Terence K. Hopkins, and Immanuel Wallerstein. 1989. *Antisystemic Movements*. London: Verso.

Aslund, Anders, and De Menil Georges. *Economic Reforms in Ukraine: The Unfinished Agenda*. Eds. Anders Aslund and De Menil Georges. NY: Armonk: M. E. Sharpe, Inc., 2000.

Astin, Alexander W. 1999. "Promoting Leadership, Service and Democracy: What Higher Education Can Do." In *Colleges and Universities as Citizens*, ed. R. G. Bringle, R. Games, and E. A. Malloy. Boston: Allyn and Bacon.

Astin, Alexander W., Lori J. Vogelgesang, Kimberly Misa, Jodi Anderson, Nida Denson, Uma Jayakumar, Victor Saenz, Erica Yamamura. 2006. "Report to the Atlantic Philanthropies, U.S.A. Understanding the Effects of Service-Learning: A Study of Students and Faculty." The Higher Education Research Institute Graduate School of Education and Information Studies. University of California, Los Angeles (July 31).

Aubry, Andres. 2003a. "Autonomy in the San Andres Accords: Expression and Fulfillment of a New Federal Pact," in Jan Rus, Rosalva Aida Hernandez Castillo and Shannan L. Mattiace, eds., *Mayan Lives Mayan Utopias: The Indigenous Peoples of Chiapas and the Zapatista Rebellion*. Lanham, Md.: Rowman and Littlefield, pp. 219–241

——. 2003b. "Los *caracoles* Zapatistas: tema y variaciones" ["Zapatista Enclaves: Theme and Variations"], *La Jornada*, Suplemento mensual Ojarasca, Nov. 23.

——. 2007a. "Chiapas: la nueva cara de la guerra"["Chiapas: The New Face of War] *La Jornada*, March 27.

——. 2007b. "Tierra, terruño, territorio I & II ["Land, Terrain, Territory I & II"], *La Jornada*, June 1.

Babb, Sarah. 2004. *Managing Mexico: Economists from Nationalism to Neoliberalism*. Princeton: Princeton University Press.

Bacon, David. 2007. "Blood on the Palms: Afro-Colombians Fight New Plantations." *Dollars and Sense*, July/August: 28–34.

Bagdikian, Ben H. 1997. *The Media Monopoly*. Boston: Beacon.

Bai, Matt. 2007. "Profiting from the Pummeling." *New York Times*. September 23.

Bandera, Volodimir N. "Formation of a Market-Oriented Social Economy of Ukraine." *Society in Transition: Social Change in Ukraine in Western Perspective*. Ed. Wsevolod W. Isajiw. Toronto, ON: Canadian Scholars' Press, Inc, 2003. 53–77.

Barandel, Hugo and Roberto Godoy. 2007. A dos voces ["To Two Voices"]. *CTA: Publicación de la Central de Trabajadores de Argentina. Año V*, 47: 9–12.

Barkin, David. 2006. "¿Es posible un modelo alterno de acumulación? Una propuesta para la Nueva Ruralidad" ["Is an Alternate Model of Accumulation Possible?"]. *Revista Polis (on-Line) de la Universidad Bolivariana, Volumen 5, Número 13*.

Barrancos Bellot, Horacio. 2007. "El negocio de los energéticos, sus cifras y las estratégias políticas" ["The Business of Energy Sources, their Figures and Political Strategies"] *Bolpress* Aug. 15.<http://www.bolpress.com/art.php?Cod=2007081516>.

Bartholomew, Amy, and Margit Mayer. 1992. "*Nomads of the Present*: Melucci's Contribution to 'New Social Movement' Theory." *Theory, Culture and Society* 9: 141–159.

Bauman, Zigmund. 2003. *Trabajo, consumismo y nuevos pobres [Work, Consumerism and the Newly Poor]*. Barcelona: Gedisa.

Beck, Ulrich. 2006. "Living in the world risk society." *Economy and Society* 35: 329–345.

Bell, Brenda, John Gaventa and John Peters. (Eds.) 1990. *We Make the Road by Walking: Conversations on Education and Social Change / Myles Horton and Paulo Freire.* Philadelphi: Temple University Press.

Bennett, William. 2003. "Communicating Global Activism." *Information, Communication and Society* 6(2): 143–68.

Berman, Ari. 2007. "Not Your Father's Antiwar Activist." *The Nation*: 32–37.

Bimber, Bruce. 2003. *Information and American Democracy: Technology in the Evolution of Political Power.* Cambridge: Cambridge University Press.

Blanding, Michael. 2006. "The World Social Forum: Protest or Celebration?" *The Nation.* March 6.

Bock, Gisela. "Women's History and Gender History: Aspects of an International Debate." *Gender and History* 1.1 (1989): 7–30.

Bonnet, Alberto. 2002. "Crisis e insurrección en Argentina 2001" ["Crisis and Insurrection in Argentina-2001"]. *Bajo el Volcan*, año 3, 5: 109–136.

Bordegaray, Soledad. 2007. "La conspiración de los Nosotros" ["The Conspiracy of the We's"], in Toty Flores, ed., *Cuando con otros somos nosotros [When with Others We are Ourselves].* Buenos Aires: Peña lillo / Ediciones Continente: 49–76.

Borgatti, S. P., Everett, M. G. and Freeman, L. C. 2002 *UCINET 6 For Windows: Software for Social Network Analysis.* http://www.analytictech.com/

Borón, Atilio. 2005. "Civil Society and Democracy: the Zapatista Experience," *Development*, 48, 2: 29–34.

Boswell, Terry and Christopher Chase-Dunn. 2000. *The Spiral of Capitalism and Socialism: Toward Global Democracy.* Boulder, CO: Lynne Reinner.

Bourdieu, Pierre. 1998. "The Essence of Neoliberalism." *Le Monde Diplomatique.* December.

Bourdieu, Pierre and Loic Wacquant. 1995. *Respuestas por una Antropología Reflexiva [Responses by a Reflexive Anthropology].* México: Editorial Grijalbo.

Boyd, Andrew. 2003. "The Web Rewires the Movement." *Why War.* Available at http://www.whywar.com/news/lead.php21d-3972.html.

Braudel, Fernand 1972. "History and the Social Sciences: The *longue duree*," in Peter Burke (ed.). *Economy and Society in Early Modern Europe.* Harper and Row.

Brazilian Trade Unionists. 2002. "Critique of Porto Alegre: Open Letter to the Trade Unionists and Activists Participating in the World Social Forum 2002 in Porto Alegre, Brazil: Is it Possible to Put a human Face on Globalization and War?" January 2. http://www.ainfos.ca/02/jan/ainfos00502.html.

Brecher, Jeremy, Tim Costello, and Brendan Smith. 2002. *Globalization from Below.* Cambridge: South End.

Brown, David L., and Archana Kalegaonkar. "Support Organizations and the Evolution of the NGO Sector." *Nonprofit and Voluntary Sector Quarterly* 31.2 (2002): 231–258.

Brown, Wendy. 2005. "Neoliberalism and the End of Liberal Democracy." *Edgework: Critical Essays on Knowledge and Politics.* New Jersey: Princeton University Press and Oxford.

Brown, Wendy and Halley, Janet. 2002. *Left Legalism, Left Critique.* Durham: Duke University Press.

Brownstein, Ronald. 2004. "MoveOn Works the Hollywood Spotlight to Amplify its Voice." *The Los Angeles Times*, October 17, p. A13.

Bruce, David. 1985. "Brazilian Technocrats and Economic Development Policy." *Public Administration and Development* (April–June): 169–175.

Buechler, Steven M. 2000. *Social Movements in Advanced Capitalism: The Political Economy and Cultural Construction of Social Activism.* New York: Oxford University Press.

Burawoy, Michael. 2004. "Public Sociologies: Contradictions, Dilemmas, and Possibilities*." *Social Forces* 82: 1603–18.

Burawoy, Michael. 2005. "2004 American Sociological Association Presidential address: For public sociology." *American Sociological Review* 70: 4–28.

Burawoy, Michael, William Gamson, Charlotte Ryan, Stephen Pfohl, Diane Vaughan, Charles Derber, and Juliet Schor. 2004. "Sociologies: A Symposium from Boston College" *Social Problems* (Feb) 51: 103–30.

Burress, Charles. 2003. "Making Their Move." *San Francisco Chronicle*, February 9, p. A23.

Bush, Melanie E. L. 2004. *Breaking the Code of Good Intentions: Everyday Forms of Whiteness.* Lanham, MD: Rowman and Littlefield Publishing, Inc.

——. 2005. "The Movement for an "Academic Bill of Rights: A New Assault on Academic Freedom." *North American Dialogue*: The Newsletter of the Society for the Anthropology of North America. Section of the American Anthropological Association. Alisse Waterston, Ed. Volume 8. Number 1. April. 16–19.

Bush, Roderick D. 2009. *The End of White World Supremacy*. Philadelphia: Temple University Press. Forthcoming.

Butin, Dan W. 2003. "Of What Use Is It? Multiple Conceptualizations of Service Learning Within Education." *Teachers College Record* 105: 1674–92.

Byrd, Scott C. 2005. "The Porto Alegre Consensus: Theorizing the Forum Movement." *Globalizations*. 2(1): 151–163.

Carlsen, Laura. 2007. "An Interview with Álvaro García Linera, Vice President of Bolivia: Bolivia—Coming to Terms with Diversity." Americas Policy Program Special Report, November 16. Washington, DC: Center for International Policy.

Carrera, Nicolas y Maria Cecilia Cotarelo. 2002. "Luchas sociales en la Argentina Actual (1993–2001)" ["Social Struggles in Present Day Argentina (1993–2001)"]. *Bajo el Volcan*, año 3, 5: 95–108.

Carroll, William K. 2006a. "Hegemony and counter-hegemony in a global field of action" Presented at a joint RC02–RC07 session on alternative visions of world society, World Congress of Sociology, Durban, South Africa, July 28.

——. 2006b "Hegemony, counter-hegemony, anti-hegemony" Keynote address to the annual meeting of the Society for Socialist Studies, York University, Toronto, June. Socialist Studies, *Fall, 2006.*

Carroll, William K. and R. S. Ratner 1996 *"Master framing and cross-movement networking in contemporary social movements"* Sociological Quarterly 37,4: 601–625.

Carty, Victoria. 2002. "Technology and Counter-hegemonic Movements." *Social Movement Studies* 1(2): 129–146.

Carty, Victoria and Jake Onyette. 2006. "Protest, Cyberactivsm and New Social Movements: The Reemergence of the Peace Movement Post 9/11." *Social Movement Studies* 5(3): 229–249.

Casas, Aldo. 2007. "Actualidad de la Revolución y poder popular" ["The Timeliness of Revolution and Popular Power], In Acha, et al, *Reflexiones sobre el poder Popular [Reflections on Popular Power]*. Buenos Aires: El colectivo, pp. 129–144.

Castells, Manuel. 1997a. *The Power of Identity: The Information Age: Economy, Society and Culture.* Cambridge, MA: Oxford.

——. 1997b. *The Information Age: Economy, Society and Culture, Volume II: The Power of Identity.* Oxford: Blackwell Publishing.

——. 2001. *The Internet Galaxy: Reflections on the Internet, Business and Society.* Malden, MA: Blackwell Publishers.

Caviasca, Guillermo. 2007. "Poder Popular, Estado y revolución" ["Popular Power, the State and Revolution"]. In Acha et al. *Reflexiones sobre el poder popular [Reflections on Popular Power]*. Buenos Aires: El colectivo: 37–61.

CELADE (Centro Latinoamericano de Demografía). 2002. "La migración internacional y el desarrollo de las Américas" ["International Migration and the Development of the Americas"] NU-CEPAL 15 (July). Santiago de Chile. http://www.eclac.cl

Centeno, Miguel A. 1993. "The New Leviathan: The Dynamics and Limits of Technocracy." *Theory and Society* 22(3): 307–335.

CEPAL (Comisión Económica para América Latina). 2003. *Panorama de la inserción internacional de América Latina y el Caribe 2001-2002) [Panorama of the International Insertion of Latin America and the Caribbean—2001-2002].* March. Santiago de Chile: United Nations-CEPAL. http://www.eclac.org/publicaciones/xml/3/11663/lcg2189e.pdf

——. 2006a. *Estudio Económico de América Latina y el Caribe 2005–2006 ["Economic Study of Latin America and the Caribbean 2005–2006"].* July. Santiago de Chile: United Nations. <*http://www.eclac.org/cgi-bin/getProd.asp?xml=/publicaciones/xml/5/26135/P26135.xml&xsl=/de/tpl/p9f.xsl&base=tpl/top-bottom.xslt* >

——. 2006b. *Migración internacional, derechos humanos y desarrollo [International Migration, Human Rights and Development].* August. Santiago de Chile: United Nations-CEPAL) agosto. <http://www.eclac.cl/publicaciones/xml/8/26608/LCW98-migracion.pdf>

——. 2006c. *Panorama de la inserción internacional de América Latina y el Caribe 2005-2006 [Panorama of the International Insertion of Latin America and the Caribbean—2005-2006].* September. Santiago de Chile: United Nations. <http://www.eclac.cl/publicaciones/xml/9/26619/2006-380-PANINSAL-ESPANOL.pdf>

Charnovitz, Steve. 2000. "Opening the WTO to Non-Governmental Interests." *Fordham International Law Journal* 24: 173–216.

Chase-Dunn, Christopher, Christine Petit, Richard Niemeyer, Robert A. Hanneman and Ellen Reese 2007 *"The contours of solidarity and division among global movements"* International Journal of Peace Studies 12(2): 1–15 (Autumn/Winter)

Cheng, Li and Lynn White. 1990. "Elite Technocrats and Modern Change in Mainland China and Taiwan." *China Quarterly* (March): 1–35.

Chernova, Zhanna. "Genderniye Issledovaniya: Zapadniy I Rossiyskiy Opyt." *Gendernoye Ustroystvo: Social'nye Instituty I Praktiki.* [Gender Studies: Western and Russian Experience] Ed. Zhanna Chernova. St. Petersburg: European University Publishing, 2005. 8–22.

Chirino, Orlando. 2008. "Venezuela's PSUV and Socialism from Below." Interview. *New Politics*, Winter: 15–20.

Chorev, Nitsan. 2007. *Remaking US Trade Policy: From Protectionism to Globalization.* Ithaca: Cornell University.

Cieza, Guillermo. 2006. *Borradores sobre la lucha popular y la organización [Drafts on Organization and the Popular Struggle].* Avellaneda, Argentina: Manuel Suarez Editor.

Claure, Bernarda. 2007. "May Day-Bolivia: New Style Workforce," *Inter Press Service News Agency*, May 3.

Cohen, Jean. 1980. *Crisis and Civil Society: The Limits of Marxian Critical Theory.* Amherst, MA: University of Massachusetts Press.

——. 1983. "Rethinking Social Movements." *Berkeley Journal of Sociology* 28: 97–113.

——. 1985. "Strategy and Identity: New Theoretical Paradigms for Social Movements" *Social Research* 52: 663–716.

Colas, Alejandro. 2005. "Neoliberalism, Globalization and International Relations" in *Neoliberalism: A Critical Reader*, edited by Saad-Filho and Johnston. London: Pluto Press.

Colby, Anne. 2007. "Educating for Democracy." *Carnegie Perspectives.* The Carnegie Foundation for the Advancement of Teaching. Stanford, CA. Accessible online at < http://www.carnegiefoundation.org/perspectives/sub.asp?key=245&subkey=2433>

——. 2008. "The Place of Political Learning in College." *Peer Review*. Spring-Summer: 4–8.

Colby, Anne, Elizabeth Beaumont, Thomas Ehrlich, Josh Corngold. 2007. *Educating for Democracy: Preparing Undergraduates for Responsible Political Engagement*. San Francisco: Jossey Bass.

Colby, Anne, Thomas Ehrlich, Elizabeth Beaumont, and Jason Stephens. 2003. *Educating Citizens: Preparing America's Undergraduates for Lives of Moral and Civic Responsibility*. San Francisco: Jossey-Boss.

Collin-Harguindeguy, Laura. 2003. "Los riesgos de la desindustrialización" ["The Risks of Deindustrialization"]. In Ursula Oswald (comp), *Soberania y Desarrollo Regional. El México que todos queremos [Sovereignty and Regional Development: The Mexico that We All Want]*. México: UNAM / CANACINTRA /El Colegio de Tlaxcala / Gobierno del Estado de Tlaxcala: 337–392.

Collins, Patricia Hill. 1990. *Black Feminist Thought: Knowledge, Consciousness, and the Politics of Empowerment*. New York: Routledge.

Cooke, Bill. 2004. "The Managing of the (Third) World." *Organization* 11(5): 603–29.

Coraggio, José Luis. 2008. "Necesidad y Posibilidades de Otra Economía" ["The Need for and the Possibilities of Another Economy"]. *Rebelión*. March 27. http://www.rebelion.org/noticia.php?id=65155

Correa, Rafael. 2007. *Speech of Ecuador President Rafael Correa to the 62nd Session of the General Assembly of the United Nations*. 26 Sept., New York: United Nations.

Cortina, Jerónimo, De la Garza, Rodolfo and Ochoa-Reza, Enrique. 2005. "Remesas: limites al optimism" ["Remittances: Limits to the Optimism"]. *Foreign Affairs* 5(3) July-September (Spanish edition).

Crabtree, John. 2005. *Patterns of Protest: Politics and Social Movements in Bolivia*. London: Latin America Bureau.

Critchfield, Richard. 1992. "Patient Old Egypt Can't Go on Like This." *International Herald Tribune*. March 3.

CTA. 2008. *Sitio oficial de la CTA [Official Site of the CTA]*. Recuperado el 17 de junio de 2008, de pagina institucional: www.cta.org.ar/institucional

Dale, Chris and Dennis Kalob. 2006. "Embracing Social Activism: Sociology in the Service of Social Justice and Peace." *Humanity and Society* 30: 121–32.

Dangl, Benjamin. 2007. *The Price of Fire: Resource Wars and Social Movements in Bolivia*. Edinburgh, Oakland, West Virginia: AK Press.

Davies, Nancy. 2007. *The People Decide: Oaxaca's Popular Assembly*. Narco News Books.

De-Angelis, Massimo. 2003. "Reflexiones sobre alternativas, espacios comunales y comunidades o como construir un mundo nuevo desde abajo" ["Reflections on Alternatives, Comunity Spaces and Communities, or How to Construct a New World from Below"]. *Bajo el Volcan Año*, 6: 143–167.

Deans, Jason. 2004. "Fox News Documentary Tops Amazon Sales Chart." *Guardian Unlimited News*, July 21. Available at http://www.film.guardian.co.uk/news/story/012589.html.

Deegan, Mary Jo. 1988. *Jane Addams and the Men of the Chicago School, 1892–1918*. New Brunswick, NJ: Transaction Books.

——. 2002. "Back to the Future: Settlement Sociology, 1885–1930." *American Sociologist* 33: 5–20.

della Porta, Donatella. 2005a. "Multiple Belongings, Tolerant Identities, and the Construction of 'Another Politics': Between the European Social Forum and the Local Social Fora," Pp. 175–202 in *Transnational Protest and Global Activism*, edited by Donatella della Porta and Sidney Tarrow. Lanham: Rowman & Littlefield Publishers, Inc.

Diani, Mario. 2000. "Social Movement Networks Virtual and Real." *Information, Communication and Society* 3(3): 386–401.

Dietrich, Heinz. 2005. *La Integración Militar del Bloque Regional de Poder Latino-americano [The Military Integration of the Regional Bloc of Latin American Power.]*. <http://www.rebelion.org/docs/9526.pdf>.

DiFazio, William H. 2006. *Ordinary Poverty: A Little Food and Cold Storage*. Philadelphia, Temple University Press.

DiMaggio, Paul J. and Walter W. Powell. 1983. "The Iron Cage Revisited: Institutional Isomorphism and Collective Rationality in Organizational Fields." *American Sociological Review* 48(2): 147–160.

DiMaggio, Paul, Estzer Hargiattai and Steven Shafer. 2004. "From Unequal Access to Differentiated Use: A Literature Review and Agenda for Research on Digital Inequality." Pp. 355–400 in *Social Inequality*, K. Neckerman (ed). New York: Russell Sage Foundation.

Dinerstein, Ana C. 2002. "¡Que se vayan todos! Crisis, insurrección y la reinvención de lo político en Argentina" ["Out with All of Them! Crisis, Insurrection and the Reinvention of the Political in Argentina"]. *Bajo el Volcan*, 5: 11–46.

——. 2005. "A Call for Emancipatory Reflection. Introduction to the Forum 'On John Holloway's Changing the World Without Taking Power. The Meaning of Revolution Today," *Capital and Class* 85: 13–16.

Do Alto, Herve. 2008. "Bolivia: Compromise Agreement Allows Progress." *Green Left*, October 31. www.greenleft.org.au/2008/773/39855.

Doane, Randall; Menser, Michael; Ausch, Robert; and Gautney, Heather. 2000. The Politics of Assembly: Building an Urban Ecology from A16." *Found Object* #9, Fall.

Doster, Adam. 2007. "Dancing into the Majority." *In These Times*. Available at http://www.inthesetimes.com/article/3201/dancing_into_the_majority.

Drenttel, William. 2007. 'MoveOn's Muddled Symbolism." *The New Republic*, June 28, p. 17.

Dri, Ruben. 2007. "El Poder Popular" ["Popular Power"]. In Acha et al. *Reflexiones sobre el poder popular [Reflections on Popular Power]*. Buenos Aires: El Colectivo: 63–85.

Earl, Jennifer and Alan Schussman. 2003. "The New Site of Activism: Online Organizations, Movement Entrepreneurs the Changing Location of Social Movement Decision Making." *Research in Social Movements and Change* 24: 155–87.

Ebrahim, Alnoor D. "Accountability Myopia: Losing Sight of Organizational Learning." *Nonprofit and Voluntary Sector Quarterly* 33.1 (2005): 56–87.

Eby, John W. 1998. "Why Service Learning is Bad." Vol. 2007: Agape Center for Service and Learning.

ECLAC. 2006. *International Migration, Human Rights and Development in Latin America*, Santiago: United Nations.

——. 2008. *Notes N°56*, Jan., Santiago: United Nations.

Edwards, Michael. 2004. *Civil Society*. Malden, MA: Polity Press.

Ehrenreich, Barbara. 2004. "The New Cosby Kids." *The New York Times*, July 8.

EIA (Energy Information Administration). 2008. *Crude Oil and Total Petroleum Imports Top 15 Countries*, Energy Information Administration. Washington, DE: United States Department of Energy.

EIU (Economic Intelligence Unit). 2007. *2007 Country Forecast: Latin America Regional Overview*. London: EIU.

——. 2008. *Ecuador—The Operating Environment: Political Conditions*. Jan. 16. London: EIU.

El Diario. 2008a. "Conaljuve sera contraparte en construcción de viviendas" ["CONALJUVE Will be a Partner in the Construction of Housing"]. April 3.

——. 2008b. "Trabajadores alteños presentarán pliego petitorio al Gobierno en julio" [Workers of El Alto Will Present their Petition to the Government in July"] June 24.

Ender, Morten G., Lee Martin, David A. Cotter, and Brenda Marsteller Kowalewski. 2000. "Given an Opportunity to Reach out: Heterogeneous Participation in Optional Service-Learning Projects." *Teaching Sociology* 28: 206–19.

Engle, Shaena. 2006. "More College Freshmen Committed to Social and Civic Responsibility, UCLA Survey Reveals: Survey reports significant rise in volunteering and community service work." Press Release: *UCLA News*. Retrieved July 15, 2007 from http://newsroom.ucla.edu/portal/ucla/More-College-Freshmen-Committed-6754 .aspx

Epstein, Barbara. 2001. "Anarchism and the Anti-Globalization Movement." *Monthly Review*, v53n4.

Esty, Daniel C. 1998. "Non-Governmental Organizations at the World Trade Organization: Cooperation, Competition, or Exclusion." *Journal of International Economic Law* 1 (1).

Evans, Peter. 2005. "Counter-Hegemonic Globalization: Transnational Social Movements." *Handbook of Political Sociology: States, Civil Societies and Globalization*, Janoski, Thomas; Alford, Robert R.; Hicks, Alexander M. and Schwartz, Mildred (eds.) New York: Cambridge University Press.

——, and John Braxton. 1997. "The Impact of Service-Learning on College Students." *Michigan Journal of Community Service Learning*, Vol. 4: 5–15

Eyler, Janet and Dwight E. Giles, Jr. 1999. *Where's the Learning in Service-Learning?* San Francisco: Jossey-Bass.

Eyler, Janet, Dwight E. Giles Jr., and John Braxton. 1997. "The Impact of Service-Learning on College Students." *Michigan Journal of Community Service Learning*, Vol. 4: 5–15.

——. 1999. *Where's the Learning in Service-Learning?* San Francisco: Jossey-Bass.

FACTA 2007. "En Facta votamos todos los dias" ["In FACTA, We Vote Everyday"]. *La revista de Facta*, año 1, 3: 3–5. de Federacion Argentina de Cooperativas de Trabajadores Autogestionados.

Fajn, Gabriel. 2004. *Fábricas y empresas recuperadas. Protesta social, autogestion y rupturas de subjetividad [Factories and Recuperated Companies: Social Protest, Self-Management and Ruptures of Subjectivity]*. Buenos Aires: ediciones del Instituto movilizador de fondos cooperativos IMFC.

Falk, Richard. 2003. "Globalization-from-Below: An Innovative Politics of Resistance", in Richard Sandbrook, ed., *Civilizing Globalization: A Survival Guide*. Albany, NY: SUNY Press.

Fanon, Frantz. 1986. *Black Skin, White Masks*. Translated by C. L. Marhham. London: Pluto Press.

Farrer, Linden. 2002 "World Forum Movement: Abandon or Contaminate?" December 9. <www.nadir.org/nadir/initiativ/agp/free/wsf/worldforum.htm>.

Farthing, Linda, Juan Manuel Arbona, and Benjamin Kohl. 2006. "The Cities That Neoliberalism Built," *Harvard International Review*, 28(2).

Feagin, Joe R. 2001. "Social Justice and Sociology: Agendas for the Twenty-First Century." *American Sociological Review* 66: 1–20.

Feagin, Joe R. and Hernan Vera. 2008. *Liberation Sociology* (2nd Ed.). Boulder, CO: Paradigm Publishers.

Ferguson, James. 1990. *The Anti-Politics Machine: 'Development", Depoliticization and Bureaucratic State Power in Lesotho*. Cambridge: Cambridge University Press.

Fernandez, Ana María. 2003. "La lógica situacional de las Asambleas, los juguetes rabiosos de los barrios" ["The Situational Logic of the Assemblies, the Furious Games of the Neighborhoods"]. *Bajo el Volcan Año* 3, 6: 221–240.

Figueroa S., Víctor. 1986. *Reinterpretando el subdesarrollo. Trabajo general, clase y fuerza productiva en América Latina [Reinterpreting Underdevelopment: General Work, Class and the Productive Forces in Latin America]*. Mexico City: Siglo XXI Editores.

——. 1989. *La identidad perdida del socialism [The Lost Identity of Socialism]*. Mexico City: UAM-UAZ.

——. 2003. "La actualidad del imperialismo, la actualidad de la crítica" ["The Continuing Relevance of Imperialism, the Continuing Relevance of Crisis"], in Víctor Figueroa, ed., *América Latina en la crisis del patrón neoliberal de crecimiento [Latin America in the Crisis of the Neoliberal Growth Pattern]*. Zacatecas: Tribunal Superior de Justicia del Estado.

Finansuvannya Likiv Vid SNIDu—Pid Zagrozoyu. [Financing for AIDS Drugs in Peril] 3 May 2006. BBC Ukrainian. Nov. 2007 <http://www.bbc.co.uk/ukrainian/news/story/2006/05/060503_aids_ukraine_it.shtml>.

Fisher, William F. and Thomas Ponniah (eds.). 2003. *Another World is Possible: Popular Alternatives to Globalization at the World Social Forum*. London: Zed Books.

Fitz-Patrik, Mariel. 2007. "Para superar la cultura de la sobrevivencia" ["Overcoming the Culture of Survival"]. In Toty Flores, *Cuando con otros somos nosotros [When with Others We are Ourselves]*. Buenos Aires: Peña Lillo / ediciones Continente, pp. 97–124.

Flores, Toty. 2007. *Cuando Con otros Somos Nosotros: La experiencia Asociativa del MTD La Matanza [When with Others We are Ourselves: The Associative Experience of the MTD La Matanza]*. Buenos Aires: Peña Lilio /Ediciones Continente / ediciones MTD.

Food Not Bombs. 2008. Food Not Bombs Website: http://www.foodnotbombs.net/.

Foster, John Bellamy. 2002. *Ecology Against Capitalism*. New York: Monthly Review Press.

Fox, Jonathan. 1994. "The Difficult Transition from Clientelism to Citizenship: Lessons from Mexico," World Politics 46, 2: 151–184.

Fraser, Nancy. 1992. "Rethinking the Public Sphere: A Contribution to the Critique of Actually Existing Democracy", in Craig Calhoun, ed., *Habermas and the Public Sphere*. Cambridge: MIT: 109–142.

Freeman, Jo. 1972. "The Tyranny of Structurelessness." *Berkeley Journal of Sociology*, v17.

Freeman, John R. 2002. "Competing Commitments: Technocracy and Democracy in the Design of Monetary Institutions." *International Organization* 56(4): 889–910.

Freire, Paulo. 1967. *La Educación como Práctica de la Libertad [Education as the Practice of Freedom]*. Rio de Janeiro: Editorial Paz e Terra.

Fromm, Erich. 1941; 1994. Escape From Freedom. New York: Henry Holt and Company.

Fuentes, Federico. 2008. "Bolivia: The Struggle for Change." *Green Left*, November 29. www.greenleft.org.au/2008/777/40070.

Fukuyama, Francis 1989. "The End of History?" *The National Interest*. http://www.wesjones.com/eoh.htm

——. 2006. *The End of History and the Last Man*. New York: Free Press.

Gans, Herbert J. 1989. "Sociology in America: The Discipline and the Public. American Sociological Association, 1988 Presidential Address." *American Sociological Review* 54: 1–16.

García Linera, Álvaro. 2007. Speech at the Latin American Studies Association, Montreal, September 6.

George, Susan. 1999. "A Short History of Neoliberalism." Paper presented at the Conference on Economic Sovereignty in a Globalizing World, Bangkok. March 24–26.

Ghodsee, Kristen D. "Feminism-by-Design: Emerging Capitalisms, Cultural Feminism, and Women's Nongovernmental Organizations in Postsocialist Eastern Europe." *Signs* 29.3 (2004): 727–753.

Gibelman, Margaret, and Sheldon R. Gelman. "A Loss of Credibility: Patterns of Wrongdoing Among Nongovernmental Organizations." *Voluntas: International Journal of Voluntary and Nonprofit Organizations* 15.4 (2004): 355–381.

Gibson, Cynthia M. 2006. "Citizens at the Center: A New Approach to Civic Engagement," The Case Foundation.

Giddens, Andrew. 1991. *Modernity and Self-Identity: Self and Society in the Late Modern Age*. Stanford: Stanford University Press.

Gill, Leslie. 2000. *Teetering on the Rim: Global Restructuring, Daily Life, and the Armed Retreat of the Bolivian State*. New York: Columbia University Press.

Gill, Steven. 2000. "Toward a Post-Modern Prince? The Battle of Seattle as a Moment in the New Politics of Globalization." *Millennium: Journal of International Studies* 29(1): 131–140.

Gindin, Jonah. 2005. "Chavistas in the Halls of Power, Chavistas on the Street." *NACLA Report on the Americas* 38(5): 27–29.

Glennie, Jonathan. 2007. *Enough is Enough: The Debt Repudiation Option*. London: Christian Aid.

Global Exchange. 2001. "How the International Monetary Fund and the World Bank Undermine Democracy and Erode Human Rights: Five Case Studies." September. <www.globalexchange.org/campaigns/wbimf/imfwbReport2001.html

González Casanova, Pablo. 2005 "The Zapatista 'Caracoles': Networks of Resistance and Autonomy," *Socialism and Democracy* 19, 3: 79–92.

Goodwin, Jeff, James M. Jasper, and Francesca Polletta. 2000. "The Return of the Repressed: The Fall and Rise of Emotions in Social Movement Theory." *Mobilization* 5: 65–84.

——, eds. 2001. *Passionate Politics: Emotions and Social Movements*. Chicago: University of Chicago Press.

Goralska, Helena. "Funding of Social Benefits and the Social Service System in Ukraine." *Economic Reforms in Ukraine: The Unfinished Agenda*. Eds. Anders Aslund and De Menil Georges. NY: Armonk: M. E. Sharpe, Inc., 2000: 232–254.

Gore, Al. 2007. *The Assault on Reason*. New York: Penguin Press.

Gracia, Amalia. 2007. "Invención y difusión de los procesos de recuperación fabril en Argentina" [Invention and Spreading the Word of the Factory Recuperation Processes in Argentina]. Manuscript.

Graeber, David. 2002. "The New Anarchists," *New Left Review*, 13, January–February, http://www.newleftreview.org/A2368.

Gramsci, Aantonio. 1985. *Cuadernos de la Carcel [Prison Notebooks]*. Puebla: ERA.

Grant, Linda, Marybeth C. Stalp, and Kathryn B. Ward. 2002. "Women's Sociological Research and Writing in the AJS in the Pre-World War II Era." *American Sociologist* 70: 69–91.

Gray, Maryann J., Elizabeth H. Ondaatje, and Laura Zakaras. 1999. *Combining Service and Learning in Higher Education: Summary Report*. Santa Monica: RAND.

Grubacic, Andrej. 2005. "The Archaic Burden on the Global Movement." ZNet. February 3. <www.zmag.com>.

Guarasci. Richard. 2001. Developing the Democratic Arts. *About Campus*, Jan./Feb.

Gutiérrez Aguilar, Raquel. 2008. "Winds of Civil War in Bolivia: Understanding a Four-Party Conflict." Americas Policy Program Special Report (Washington DC: Center for International Policy, October 29).

Habermas, Jurgen. 1975. *Legitimation Crisis*. Boston: Beacon Press.

——. 1981. "New Social Movements." *Telos* 49: 33–77.

——. 1989. Structural Transformation of the Public Sphere. Cambridge, Mass: MIT Press.

——. 1993. "Further Reflections on the Public Sphere." Pp. 421–461 in *Habermas and the Public Sphere*, Craig Calhoun (ed). Boston, MA: MIT Press.

Halliday, Fred. 2000. "Getting Real About Seattle." *Millennium: Journal of International Studies* 29(1): 131–140.

Hampton, Keith. 2003. "Grieving for a Lost Network: Collective Activism in a Wired Suburb. *The Information Society* 19(5): 417–28.

Hanlon, Joseph. "An 'Ambitious and Extensive Political Agenda': The Role of NGOs and the AID Industry." *Global Institutions and Local Empowerment.* Ed. Kendall Stiles. New York, NY: St. Martin's Press, 2000: 132–145.

Hanneman, Robert and Mark Riddle 2005. Introduction to Social Network Methods. Riverside, CA: http://faculty.ucr.edu/~hanneman/

Haraway, Donna. 1991. *Simians, Cyborgs and Women.* New York: Routledge.

Hardt, Michael and Tony Negri. 2002. *Imperio [Empire].* Buenos Aires: Paidos.

Harnecker, Marta and Federico Fuentes. 2008. "MAS-IPSP. Instrumento Político que Surge de los Movimientos Sociales" ["MAS-ISPS: The Political Instrument that Emerged from the Social Movements"]. *Rebelión*, May 9. http://www.rebelion.org/docs/67155.pdf

Harvey, David. 2005. *A Brief History of Neoliberalism.* London: Oxford University Press.

Harvey, Neil. 2005. "Inclusion through Autonomy: Zapatistas and Dissent." *NACLA Report on the Americas* 39(2): 12–16.

Hawkins, Kirk A. and David R. Hansen. 2006. "Dependent Civil Society: The Círculos Bolivarianos in Venezuela." *Latin American Research Review* 41(1): 102–132.

Healy, Kevin. 2001. *Llamas, Weavings, and Organic Chocolate: Multicultural Grassroots Development in the Andes and Amazon of Bolivia.* Notre Dame, Indiana: University of Notre Dame.

——. 2004. "Towards an Andean Rural Development Paradigm?" in *NACLA Report on the Americas,* 38(3) (November-December): 28–33.

Hedges, Chris. 2008. "The Lessons of Violence." Truthdig, Jan. 21. Retrieved January 21, 2008 (http://www.truthdig.com/report/item/20080121_the_lessons_of_violence/).

Hemment, Julie. *Empowering Women in Russia: Activism, Aid and NGOs.* Bloomington, IN: Indiana University Press, 2007.

——. "The Riddle of the Third Sector: Civil Society, International Aid and NGOs in Russia." *Anthropological Quarterly* 77.2 (2004): 215–241.

Henderson, Sarah L. *Building Democracy in Contemporary Russia: Western Support for Grassroots Organizations.* Ithaca: Cornell University Press, 2003.

Hepburn, Mary A., Richard G. Niemi, and Chris Chapman. 2000. "Service Learning in College Political Science: Queries and Commentary." *PS: Political Science and Politics,* Vol. 33, No. 3 (Sep.): 617–622.

Hernández, Jose Luis. 2008. "El Posneoliberalismo Será Anticapitalista, No Socialista" ["Post-neoliberalism Will be Anti-capitalist, Not Socialist"]. Interview with Emir Sader. *La Jornada* (Mexico City). October 12, p. 12.

Hernández, José Luis. 2007. *Perspectivas de la migración México-Estados Unidos. Una interpretación desde el subdesarrollo [Perspectives on Mexico-US Migration: An Underdevelopment Interpretation].* Doctoral Thesis in Political Science. Zacatecas, Mexico: Universidad Autónoma de Zacatecas.

Higher Education Research Institute. 2006. "The American Freshman: National Norms for Fall 2005." UCLA, Graduate School of Education & Information Studies. http://www.gseis.ucla.edu/heri/heri.html

——. 2007. "The American Freshman: National Norms for Fall 2006." UCLA, Graduate School of Education & Information Studies.

Hilhorst, Dorothea. *The Real World of NGOs: Discourses, Diversity and Development.* New York, NY: Zed Book Ltd., 2003.

Hochschild, Arlie. 1997. *The Time Bind: When Work Becomes Home and Home Becomes Work.* New York: Metropolitan Books.

Holland, Joshua. 2006. "The Right Wing Sets its Sights on MoveOn." Available at http://www.alternet.org/story/49935.

Hollister, Robert M., Nancy Wilson, Peter Levine. 2008. "Educating Students to Foster Active Citizenship." *Peer Review.* Spring-Summer: 18–21.

Holloway, John. 2002. *Change the World without Taking Power: The Meaning of Revolution Today*. London: Pluto Press.

Howse, Robert. 2002. "From Politics to Technocracy—and Back Again: The Fate of the Multilateral Trading Regime." *The American Journal of International Law* 96: 94.

——. 2003a. "Membership and its Privileges: the WTO, Civil Society and the *Amicus* Brief Controversy." *European Law Journal* 9(4): 496–510.

——. 2003b. "How to Begin to Think About the Democratic Deficit at the WTO", in Stefan Griller, ed., *International Economic Governance and Non-Economic Concerns: New Challenges for the International Legal Order*. New York: Springer.

Howse, Robert and Kalypso Nicolaidis. 2001. "Legitimacy and Global Governance: Why Constitutionalizing the WTO Is a Step Too Far", in Roger B. Porter, Raymond Vernon, Pierre Sauvé, Arvind Subramanian and Americo Beviglia Zampetti, eds., *Efficiency, Equity, and Legitimacy: the Multilateral Trading System at the Millennium*. Harrisonburg, VA: Brookings Institution Press.

Hrycak, Alexandra D. "Foundation Feminisms and the Articulation of Hybrid Feminisms in Post-Socialist Ukraine." *East European Politics and Societies* 20.1 (2006): 69–100.

Hurt, Stephen R. "Civil Society and European Union Development Policy." *New Pathways in International Development: Gender and Civil Society in EU Policy*. Eds. Marjorie Lister and Maurizio Carbone. Burlington, VT: Ashgate Publishing, 2006: 109–122.

Hurtado, Sylvia, Linda J. Sax, Victor Saenz, Casandra E. Harper, Leticia Oseguera, Jennifer Curley, Lina Lopez, De'Sha Wolf, Lucy Arellano. 2007. "Table 19. Change in First-Year Students' Life Goals." *Findings from the 2005 Administration of Your First College Year (YFCY): National Aggregates*. Higher Education Research Institute. University of California, Los Angeles (February 24).

Hylton, Forrest and Sinclair Thomson. 2007. *Revolutionary Horizons: Past and Present in Bolivian Politics*. London and New York: Verso.

IBASE (Brazilian Institute of Social and Economic Analyses) 2005. *An X-Ray of Participation in the 2005 Forum: Elements for a Debate* Rio de Janeiro: IBASE http://www .ibase.org.br/userimages/relatorio_fsm2005_INGLES2.pdf

ILO (International Labor Organization). 2004. International Labour Conference, 92nd Session "Towards a fair deal for migrant workers in the global economy." Geneve: ILO. <http://www.ilo.org/public/english/standards/relm/ilc/ilc92/pdf/rep-vi.pdf>

Isacson, Adam, Joy Olson and Lisa Haugaard. 2007. *Below the Radar US Military Programs with Latin America, 1997–2007*. Washington: LAWGEF/Center for International Policy and WOLA.

Jacobs, David. 2005. "Internet Activism and the Democratic Emergency in the United States." *Ephemera: Theory & Politics in Organization* 5(1): 68–77.

Jacoby, Barbara. 2006. "Bottom line—Making politics matter to students." *About Campus* 11, 4 (Sep/Oct): 30–32.

Jardim, Claudia and Ginden, Jonah. 2004. "Venezuela: Changing the World by Taking Power." *Counterpunch*. July 24–25. <www.counterpunch.org/tariq07242004.html>.

Jordan, Lisa. 2004. "The Ford Foundation and the World Social Forum." OpenDemocracy. January 15. <www.opendemocracy.net>.

Jordan, Tim. 2001. "Measuring the Net: Host Counts Versus Business Plans." *Information, Communication and Society* 4(1): 34–53.

Kahn, Richard and Douglas Kellner 2003. "Internet Communication and Oppositional Politics." Pp. 299–314 in *The Post Subcultures Reader*. Oxford: Berg.

Kaldor, Mary. 2000. "'Civilizing' Globalization? The Implications of the 'Battle in Seattle'." *Millennium: Journal of International Studies* 29(1): 131–140.

——. 2003. *Global Civil Society: An Answer to War*. Malden, MA: Blackwell.

Kampwirth, Karen. 2002. *Women and Guerilla Movements: Nicaragua, El Salvador, Chiapas, Cuba*. University Park, PA: Pennsylvania State University Press.

Kapoor, Ilan. 2006. "Deliberative Democracy and the WTO." *Review of International Political Economy* 11(3): 522–541.

Karr, Timothy. 2004. "CBS Cuts MoveOn, Allows White House Ads During Super Bowl." Available at http://www.meidacannel.org/views/affalert131/html.

Katsiaficas, George. 2001. "Seattle was not the Beginning" in *The Battle of Seattle: the New Challenge to Capitalist Globalization.* E. Yuen, G. Katsiaficas and B. Rose (eds.) New York: Soft Skull Press.

Katz-Fishman, Walda and Jerome S. Scott. 2005. "Comments on Burawoy: A View from the Bottom Up." *Critical Sociology,* Vol. 31, No. 3: 371–74.

Kavalsky, Basil and John Odling-Smee. "Foreword." *Ukraine: Accelerating the Transition to Market.* Eds. Peter K. Cornelius and Patrick Lenain. Washington, D.C.: International Monetary Fund, 1997: iii–iv.

Keck, Margaret E. and Sikkink, Kathryn. 1998. *Activists Between Borders: Advocacy Networks in International Politics.* Ithaca: Cornell University Press.

Kellner, Douglas. 2004. *Globalization, Technopolitics and Revolution.* Pp. 180–194 in *The Future of Revolution: Rethinking Radical Change in the Age of Globalization,* John Foran (ed). New York: Zed Books.

Kenfield, Isabella. 2007. "Taking on Big Cellulose: Brazilian Indigenous Communities Reclaim Their Land." *NACLA Report on the Americas* 40(6): 9–13.

Kennedy, Marie. 2004. "Empowerment through community development". *Progressive Planaing:* 7–14.

Kennedy, Marie and Chris Tilly. 2002. "Dancing to a Different Samba: A Visit to Brazil Reveals Lively Movements Hammering at Inequality." *Dollars and Sense.* September/October: 26–29 & 36–37.

——. 2004. "'We've Been Fighting For the Land Since Time Immemorial': Indigenous Land Struggles in Michoacan, Mexico." *Progressive Planning,* Summer: 21–23.

——. 2005a. "Argentinean Grassroots Movements at the Crossroads: Dilemmas of Horizontalidad." *Z Magazine,* October: 15–20.

——. 2005b. "From Resistance to Production in Argentina: Worker-Controlled Businesses Take the Next Step ." *Dollars and Sense,* November/December: 28–33.

——. 2005c. "Participatory Housing Cooperatives: An Argentinean Experiment." *Progressive Planning,* Summer: 1 & 7–11.

——. 2006a. "Bottom-up Planning: Lessons from Latin America's Third Left." *Progressive Planning,* Summer: 30–32.

——. 2006b. "Chiapas: Counter-campaigns and Autonomous Communities—The Zapatistas' New Fight." *Against the Current,* July/August: 21–25.

——. 2006c. "From Here to Autonomy: Mexico's Zapatistas Combine Local Administration And National Politics." *Progressive Planning,* Spring: 12–17.

——. 2008. "Making Sense of Latin America's 'Third Left'." *New Politics,* Winter: 11–16.

Keohane, Robert O. and Joseph S. Nye. 2001. "The Club Model of Multilateral Cooperation and Problems of Democratic Legitimacy", in Roger B. Porter, Raymond Vernon, Pierre Sauvé, Arvind Subramanian, and Americo Beviglia Zampetti, eds., *Efficiency, Equity, and Legitimacy: the Multilateral Trading System at the Millennium.* Harrisonburg, VA: Brookings Institution Press.

Kern, Montague. 2004. "Web and Mass Media Campaigns by Political Candidates." *School of Communication, Information and Library Studies.* Rutgers: April 19.

Kidd, David. 2003. "Indymedia: a New Communications Commons." Pp. 47–69 in *Cyberactivism: Online Acts in Theory and Practice,* Barbara McCaughney and Michael Ayers (eds). New York: Routledge.

Kiesa, Abby, Alexander P. Orlowski, Peter Levine, Deborah Both, Emily Hoban Kirby, Mark Hugo Lopez, Karlo Barrios Marcelo. "Millenials Talk Politics: A Study of College Student Political Engagement." The Center for Information & Research on Civic Learning and Engagement. College Park, MD.

Kirk, Gwyn and Margo Okazawa-Rey. 2007. *Women's Lives: Multicultural Perspectives.* New York: McGraw Hill.

Klein, Naomi. 2002. "Farewell to the End of History: "Organization and Vision in Anti-Corporate Movements." *A World of Contradictions.* Panich, Leo and Leys, Colin (eds.) New York: Monthly Review Press.

——. 2007. "De Zanon a Irak" [From Zanon to Iraq]. In Lavaca, *Sin Patron. Fabricas y empresas recuperadas por sus trabajadores [No Boss: Factories and Enterprises Recuperated by their Workers].* Buenos Aires, Argentina: Lavaca, pp. 5–11.

Klimberg, Nicolas. 2005. "*Fabricas recuperadas por los trabajadores y su viabilidad economica" [Factories Recuperated by their Workers and their Economic Viability].* Febrero de 2008. www.fabricas recuperadas.org.ar

Kloby, Jerry. 2003 *Inequality, Power, and Development: Issues in Political Sociology.* New York: Humanity Books.

Koch, Connie and Barbara Sauerman. 2003. *The Day the World Said NO to War.* New York: AK Press.

Koch-Weser, Caio. "Introductory Remarks." *Ukraine: Accelerating the Transition to Market.* Eds. Peter K. Cornelius and Patrick Lenain. Washington, D.C.: International Monetary Fund, 1997: 3–6.

Kogan, Karen. 2007. "Can Brazil's *Quilombos* Survive? *In These Times,* September 25. http://www.inthesetimes.com/article/3321/can_brazils_quilombos_survive/

Kohl, Benjamin and Linda Farthing. 2006. *Impasse in Bolivia.* London and New York: Zed Books.

Koli Mi Zalyakuemo Chitachiv VIL-infektsieyu, to Zalyakuemo Timi Lyud'mi, Yaki Hvoriyut'. [When We Scare Readers with HIV-infection, We Are Scaring Them with People Who Are Ill] 17 Feb. 2005. Tsentr Media Reform, Ukraine. Apr. 2007 <http://mediareform.com.ua/old/article.php?articleID=383>.

Korsch, Karl. 1972. *Autogestion [Self-Management].* Cordoba, Argentina: Cuadernos de Pasado y Presente.

Korten, David. 2001. *When Corporations Rule the World.* San Francisco: Berrett-Koehler.

Kotovskaya, M. G. *Gendernye Ocherki: Istoriya, Sovremennost',* [Gender Sketches: History and Modernity] *Facty. Moskva:* Rossiskaya Akademiya Nauk. 2004.

Kovel, Joel. 2002. *The Enemy of Nature: The End of Capitalism or the End of the World?* New York: Zed Books.

Kraut, Robert, Michael Paterson, Sara Kiesler, Vicki Lundmark, Ridas Ukopadtyah, and William Scheller. 1998. "Internet Paradox: A Social Technology that Reduces Social Involvement and Psychological Well-Being?" Carnegie Mellon University. Available at http:///ww.es.cmu.edu.

Krinsky, John and Ellen Reese. 2006. "Forging and Sustaining Labor-Community Coalitions: The Workfare Justice Movement in Three Cities." *Sociological Forum* 21(4): 623–658.

Kruggman, Paul. 2002. "Crying with Argentina". *The New York Times ,* january 1: 2.

Krymkiewicz, Vanesa y Martin Aiello. 2007. "La experiencia del Nosotros" ["The Experience of the We's]. In Toty Flores (Comp), *Cuando con otros somos nosotros[When with Others We are Ourselves].* Buenos Aires: Peña Lillo / Ed Continente: 135–152.

Kuecker, Glen David. 2008. "Fighting for the Forest Revisited: Grassroots Resistance to Mining in Northern Ecuador," in Richard Stahler-Sholk, Harry E. Vanden, and Glen David Kuecker, eds., *Latin American Movements in the Twenty-First Century.* Lanham, MD: Rowman and Littlefield: 97–112.

Kuzio, Taras. "Ukraine's Post-Soviet Transition: A Theoretical and Comparative Perspective." *Society in Transition: Social Change in Ukraine in Western Perspective.* Ed. Isajiw W. Wsevolod. Toronto, ON: Canadian Scholars' Press, Inc, 2003: 21–52.

La Prensa. 2007. "El Gobierno entrega créditos por $US 3.3 millones del BDP" ["The Government Gives Credits for US$3.3 million of the BDP"]. October 21.

La Razón. 2007. "El crédito de vivienda beneficiará a quienes ganan desde Bs 361" ["Housing Credit will Benefit those who earn over 361 *Bolivianos*]. April 4.

———. 2008a. "Los sindicatos del MAS se lotearon el Poder Ejecutivo" ["The MAS Unions Throw in their Lot with the Executive Power"]. March 23.

———. 2008b. "Sectores sociales alteños deciden el destino de la urbe" ["Social Sectors of El Alto Decide the Fate of their City"], September 14.

———. 2008c. "Los alteños llegan hoy a La Paz a cercar el Congreso" [The People of El Alto Arrive Today to La Paz to Converge on the Congress]. October 18.

LaClau, Ernesto, and Chantal Mouffe. 1985. *Hegemony and Socialist Strategy: Towards a Radical Democratic Politics.* New York: Verso.

Langman, Lauren. 1992. "Neon Cages: Shopping for Subjectivity." Lifestyle Shopping: The Subject of Consumption, edited by R. Shields. New York: Routledge: 41–82.

Langman, Lauren. 2000. "Identity, Hegemony and the Reproduction of Domination", in Richard Altschuler, ed., *Marx, Weber and Durkheim.* New York: Gordian Knot Press: 238–290.

———. 2002. "Globalization, Cyberspace and Identity," *Information Technology, Education and Society* 3: 2.

———. 2005. "From Virtual Public Spheres to Global Justice: A Critical Theory of International Social Movements." *Sociological Theory* 23(1): 42–74.

———. 2008. The News of the Death of Nationalism May be Premature. Plenary Address, Annual Meeting, *Global Studies Association,* Pace University, New York.

Lavaca. 2007. *Sin Patrón: Fábricas y Empresas Recuperadas por sus Trabajadores [No Boss: Factories and Enterprises Recuperated by their Workers].* Buenos Aires: Editora Lavaca.

Lazar, Sian. 2006. "El Alto, Ciudad Rebelde: Organisational Bases for Revolt," in *Bulletin of Latin American Research,* 25(2): 183–199.

———. 2008. *El Alto, Rebel City: Self and Citizenship in Andean Bolivia.* Durham and London: Duke University Press.

Leiva, Fernando Ignacio. 2008. *Latin American Neostructuralism: The Contradictions of Post-Neoliberal Development.* Minneapolis and London: The University of Minneapolis Press.

Leiva, Fernando Ignacio and James Petras. 1986. "Chile's Poor in the Struggle for Democracy." *Latin American Perspectives,* Vol. 13, No. 4: 5–25.

Leiva, Fernando Ignacio and Michelle Smith. 2008. "Ethnodevelopment, Globalization and the State: Programa Orígenes and Aymara Communities in Northern Chile." Paper presented at the Globalization Studies Association conference, "The Nation in the Global Era: Nationalism and Globalization in Conflict and Transition," Pace University, New York, June 6–8.

Leland, John. 2003. "A Movement Yes, but No Counterculture." *New York Times,* March 23, p. A14.

Lengermann, Patricia Madoo and Jill Niebrugge-Brantley. 1998. *The Women Founders: Sociology and Social Theory, 1830–1930.* New York: McGraw-Hill.

———. 2002. "Back to the Future: Settlement Sociology, 1885–1930." *American Sociologist* 33: 5–20.

Lessnoff, Michael. 1980. "The Political Philosophy of Karl Popper." *British Journal of Political Science* 10(1) January.

Levi, Margaret and Olson, David. 2000. "The Battles in Seattle." *Politics and Society* 28(3): 309–329.

Levine, Elaine. 2002. "Los trabajadores más pobres del país más rico: los inmigrantes mexicanos en Estados Unidos" [The Poorest Workers of the Richest Country: Mexican Immigrants in the United States], in Leticia Campos Aragón, ed., *La realidad económica actual y las corrientes teóricas de su interpretación: un debate inicial [The Current Economic Reality and the Theoretical Currents of its Interpretation: An Initial Debate].* Mexico City: UNAM.

Lewis, David Levering. 2000. *W. E. B. DuBois: The Fight for Equality and the American Century, 1919–1963*. New York: Henry Holt.

Lewis, David. 2007. *The Management of Non-Governmental Development Organizations*. NY: Routledge.

Lewis, Tammy L. 2004. "Service Learning for Social Change? Lessons from a Liberal Arts College." *Teaching Sociology* 32: 94–108.

Leyva-Solano, Xochitl. 2006. "Zapatista Movement Networks Respond to Globalization." *Latin American Studies Association Forum* 37(1), pp. 37–39.

López y Rivas, Gilberto. 2008. "Por los caminos de la autonomía: algo más que autogobiernos" ["Taking the Paths of Autonomy: Something More than Self-governments"], *La Jornada*, June 27.

Lopez, Mark Hugo and Karlo Barrios Marcelo. 2007. "Volunteering Among Young People." Vol. 2007: The Center for Information & Research on Civic Learning & Engagement. College Park, MD.

Los Tiempos. 2007. "García Linera llama a sectores sociales a defender la Asamblea" ["García Linera Calls upon the Social Sectors to Defend the Constituent Assembly"]. November 8.

Lukacs, Georg. 1972. *History and Class Consciousness*. Boston: MIT Press.

Luo, Michael. 2007. "Antiwar Groups Use New Clout to Influence Democrats on Iraq." *The New York Times*, May 4.

Mably, Paul. 2006. *Evidence Based Advocacy: NGO Research Capacities and Policy Influence in the Field of International Trade*. IDRC Working Paper on Globalization, Growth and Poverty.

Maddison, Angus. 1996. *Problemas del crecimiento económico de las naciones [Problems of Economic Growth of Nations]*. Mexico City: Ariel.

Magnani, Esteban. 2003. *El Cambio Silencioso. Empresas y Fábricas Recuperadas por los Trabajadores en la Argentina [Silent Change: Companies and Factors Recuperated by the Workers of Argentina]*. Buenos Aires: Prometeo Libros.

Majnoo, Farhed. 2007. "MoveOn Moves in with Pelosi." http://www.salon.com/news/feature/2007/03.html.

Mann, Michael. 2000. *The Global Transformations Reader*, David Hert and Andrew McCrew (eds). Cambridge, MA: Polity Press: 136–147.

March, Carlos. 2007. "La democracia de los desaparecidos" ["The Democracy of the Disappeared"]. In Toty Flores, *Cuando con otros somos nosotros [When with Others We are Ourselves]*. Buenos Aires: Peña Lillo / Ediciones continente: 77–96.

Marcos, Subcomandante. 1997. "The Fourth World War Has Begun," *Nepantla: Views from the South.* 2: 3.

——. 2003a. "Chiapas: The Thirteenth Stele—Part II—A Death," tr. Irlandesa, accessed at http://www.zmag.org/znet/viewArticle/10094

——. 2003b. "Chiapas: The Thirteenth Stele—Part V: A History," tr. Irlandesa, accessed at http://www.narconews.com/Issue31/article830.html

——. 2008. "No nos rendimos, no nos vendimos, no claudicamos" ["We Won't Give Up, Won't Sell Out, Won't Back Down"]. Words of Subcomandante Marcos, Zapatista Enclave of La Garrucha, Aug. 2. www.ecoportal.net/content/view/full/80621

Marin, Juan Carlos. 2004. "Hacia la desobediencia debida" ["Towards Due Disobedience"]. In Julian Rebon, *Desobedeciendo al desempleo [Disobeying Unemployment]*. Buenos Aires: Picaso / La Rosa Blindada: 13–22.

Markels, Alex. 2003. "Virtual Peacenik." May 5. Available at http://www.MotherJones.com/news/hellriiser/2003/05/ma_379_01.html.

Marx, Karl. 1966. *La ideologia Alemana [The German Ideology]*. Buenos Aires: Cartago.

——. 1969. *Theories of Surplus Value (Vols. I–III)*. London: Lawrence & Wishart.

——. 1972. *Grundrisse: Elementos fundamentales para la crítica de la economía política. [Grundrisse: Outline of the Critique of Political Economy]*. Mexico City: Siglo XXI

——. 1975; 1977; 1982. *El Capital [Capital—Vols. I–III]*. Mexico City: Siglo XXI.

Mattiace, Shannan. 2005. "Representation and Rights: Recent Scholarship on Social Movements in Latin America." *Latin American Research Review* 40(1): 237–250.

Mayer, Jörg, Butkevicius, Arunas, and Kadri, Ali. 2002. "Dynamic Products in World Exports." *Discussion Papers* 159 (May). Geneve: UNCTAD. <http://www.unctad.org/en/docs/dp_159.en.pdf>.

McAdam, Doug and David A. Snow. 1997. *Social Movements: Readings on Their Emergence, Mobilization, and Dynamics*. Los Angeles: Roxbury Publishing Company.

McChesney, Robert. 2000. *Rich Media, Poor Democracy: Communication Politics in Dubious Times*. New York: The New Press.

McSherry, J. Patrice. 2005. *Predatory State, Operation Condor and Covert War in Latin America*. Boulder, CO: Rowman & Littlefield.

Mebrahtu, Esther. 2003. "Perceptions and Practices of Monitoring and Evaluation: International NGO Experiences in Ethiopia. Laura Roper, Jethro Pettit, and Deborah Eade (eds) *Development and the Learning Organisation*. Oxford, UK: Oxfam: 332–355.

Meikle, Graham. 2002. *Future Active: Media Access and the Internet*. New York: Routledge.

Melucci, Alberto. 1980. "The New Social Movements: A Theoretical Approach." *Social Science Information*, 19(2): 197–226.

——. 1985. "The Symbolic Challenge of Contemporary Movements." *Social Research* 52: 789–816.

——. 1989. *Nomads of the Present: Social Movements and Individual Needsi in Contemporary Society*. Philadelphia: Temple University Press.

——. 1992. "Frontier Land: Collective Action Between Actor and Systems", in Mario Diani and Ron Eyerman, eds., *Studying Collective Action*. London: Sage.

——. 1995 in "The Process of Collective Identity", in Hank Johnston and Bert Klandermans, eds., *Social Movements and Culture*. Minneapolis, MN: University of Minnesota Press: 41–63.

——. 1996. *Challenging Codes*. Cambridge, MA: Cambridge University Press.

Menser, Michael. 2009. "Disarticulate the State! Maximizing Democracy in "New" Autonomous Movements in the Americas" in *Democracy, States, and the Struggle for Global Justice*. New York: Routledge.

Middleton, Joel and Donald Green. 2007. "Do Community-Based Voter Mobilization Campaigns Work Even in Battleground States?" Unpublished paper. Yale University. Available at www.yale.edu/csap/seminars/middleton.pdf.

Mills, C. Wright. 1959. *The Sociological Imagination*. London: Oxford University Press.

Moghadam, Valentine M. 2000. "Transnational Feminist Networks: Collective Action in an Era of Globalization." *International Sociology* 15: 57–85.

Momani, Bessma. 2005. "Recruiting and Diversifying IMF Technocrats." *Global Society* 19(2): 167–187.

Moore, Mike. 2003. *A World Without Walls: Freedom, Development, Free Trade and Global Governance*. Cambridge: Cambridge University Press.

Mortensen, Jens L. 2003. "Recasting the World Trade Organization", in Richard Sandbrook, ed., *Civilizing Globalization: A Survival Guide*. Albany, NY: SUNY Press.

Mouffe, Chantal. 1992. *Dimensions of Radical Democracy: Pluralism, Citizenship, Community*. New York: Verso.

MoveOn.org. Available at http://www.moveon.org, various years.

Mudu, Pierpaolo. 2004. "Resisting and Challenging Neoliberalism: The Development of the Italian Social Centers." *Antipode*. November.

Munck, Ronaldo. 2005. "Neoliberalism and Politics, and the Politics of Neoliberalism" in *Neoliberalism: A Critical Reader*, edited by Saad-Filho and Johnston. London: Pluto Press.

Murphy, G. H. and Pfaff, S. 2005. "Thinking Locally, Acting Globally? What the Seattle WTO Protests Tell Us About the Global Justice Movement," *Political Power and Social Theory* 17: 151–176.

Murphy, Gillian H. 2004. "The Seattle WTO Protests: Building a Global Movement", in Rupert Taylor, ed., *Creating a better world: interpreting global civil society*. Bloomfield, CT: Kumarian Press.

Mykhnenko, Vlad. "State, Society and Protest Under Post-communism: Ukrainian Miners and Their Defeat." *Uncivil Society?: Contentious Politics in Post-communist Europe.* Eds. Petr Kopecky and Cas Mudde. New York, NY: Routledge, 2003. 93–113.

NACLA (North American Conference on Latin America). 2005. "Introduction." *NACLA Report on the Americas* 38(5): 13.

Nagourney, Adam and Megan Thee. 2007. "Young Americans Are Leaning Left, New Poll Finds." *The New York Times*. Nytimes.com. June 27.

Nanz, Patrizia and Steffek, Jens. 2004. "Global Governance, Participation and the Public Sphere." *Government and Opposition* 39(2): 314.

Neuman, W. L. *Power, State and Society: An Introduction to Political Sociology.* New York, NY: McGraw-Hill, 2005.

New York Times. 2002. MoveOn paid advertisement. December 11, p. 12.

———. 2003. Artists United to Win Without War paid advertisement. February 15, p. 9.

Nievas, Fabian. 2002. "La crisis en Argentina" ["The Crisis in Argentina"]. *Bajo el Volcan*, 5: 73–93.

Nipp, Joyce. 2004. "The Queer Sisters and its Electronic Bulletin Board: A Study of the Internet for Social Movement Mobilization." Pp. 233–258 in *Cyberprotest: New Media, Citizens and Social Movements*, Wim Van De Donk, Brian Loader, Paul Nixon and Dieter Ructh (eds). New York: Routledge.

Nun, José. 2001. *Marginalidad y exclusión social [Marginality and Social Exclusion].* Buenos Aires: Fondo de Cultura Económica.

O'Brien, R. and Williams, M. 2004. *Global Political Economy: Evolution and Dynamics.* New York: Palgrave MacMillan.

O'Brien, Robert. 2005. "Global Civil Society and Global Governance", in Alice D. Baa, ed., *Contending Perspectives on Global Governance: Coherence, Contestation and World Order.* New York: Routledge.

O'Connor, John S. 2006. "Civic Engagement in Higher Education." *Change*, Vol. 38, No. 5 (Sept/Oct): 52–58.

Obach, Brian K. 2004 *Labor and the Environmental Movement: The Quest for Common Ground.* Cambridge, MA: MIT Press.

Obreros de la Zona Norte. 2006. *Zanon bajo control obrero y la comuna de Paris [Zanon Under Workers' Control and the Paris Commune].* Buenos Aires: Nuestra Lucha.

OECD. 2003. *Employment Outlook 2003.* Paris: OECD.

Offe, Claus. 1985. "New Social Movements: Changing Boundaries of the Political. *Social Research* 52: 817–68.

Ouviña, Hernan. 2002. "Las Asambleas Barriales. Apuntes a modo de hipotesis de trabajo" ["The Neighborhood Assemblies: Elements of a Working Hypothesis"]. *Bajo el Volcan*, año 3, 5: 59–72.

———. 2007. "Hacia una politica prefigurativa. Algunas hipotesis en torno a la construcción del poder popular" ["Towards a Prefigurative Politics: Some Hypotheses on the Construction of Popular Power"]. In Acha, et al *Reflexiones sobre el poder Popular.* Buenos Aires: El Colectivo: 163–192.

Palley, Thomas I. 2005. "From Keynesianism to Neoliberalism: Shifting Paradigms in Economies." in *Neoliberalism: A Critical Reader*, edited by Saad-Filho and Johnston. London: Pluto Press.

Palyvoda, Lyubov and Oksana Kikot. "Civil Society Organizations in Ukraine: The State and Dynamics 2002–2006." Counterpart Creative Center (2006). Available http://ccc.kiev.ua

Patomäki, Heikki and Teivo Teivainen. 2004. "The World Social Forum: An Open Space or a Movement of Movements?" *Theory, Culture & Society* 21(5): 145–154.

Pellegrino, Adela. 2003. "La migración internacional en América Latina y el Caribe: tendencias y perfiles de los migrantes" ["International Migration in Latin America and the Caribbean: Trends and Profiles of Migrants"]. *Serie Población y Desarrollo* 35 (March). Santiago de Chile: United Nations-CEPAL). http://www.eclac.org/cgi-bin/getProd.asp?xml=/publicaciones/xml/0/12270/P12270.xml&xsl=/celade/tpl/p9f.xsl&base=/tpl/top-bottom.xslt

Perbellini, Melina and Evangelina, Ana Tifni. 2007. "Las empresas recuperadas: una experiencia autogestionaria. El caso de la Cooperativa de trabajo Cristaleria Vitrofín" ["The Recuperated Enterprises: A Self-managing Experience. The Case of the Work Cooperative Cristaleria Vitrofín"]. *Otra economia* Vol I, N° 1: 109–125.

Perucci, Robert, and Earl Wysong. 2002. *The New Class Society*. Langham, MD: Rowman & Littlefield Publishing, Inc.

Petit, Christine. 2004. "Social Movement Networks in Internet Discourse." IROWS working paper #25.

Petryna, Adriana. *Life Exposed: Biological Citizens After Chernobyl*. New Jersey: Princeton: Princeton University Press, 2002.

Phillips, Sarah D. "Will the Market Set Them Free? Women, NGOs, and Social Enterprise in Ukraine." *Human Organization* 64.3 (2005): 251–264.

Pianta, Mario; Silva, Federico; and Zola, Duccio. 2005. "Global Civil Society Events: Parallel Summits, Social Fora, Global Days of Action." Text for the website of Global Civil Society 2004–2005, London School of Economics Centre for the Study of Global Governance and Centre on Civil Society.

Pickerill, Jenny. 2003. *Cyberprotest: Environmental Activism*. New York: Manchester University Press.

Piñero Harnecker, Camila. 2007. Democracia Laboral y Conciencia Colectiva: Un Estudio De Cooperativas en Venezuela ["Labor Democracy and Collective Consciousness: A Study of Cooperatives in Venezuela"]. *Rebelión*, May. http:www.rebelion.org/docs/53984.pdf

Pishchikova, Kateryna. "What Happened After the 'end of History'? Foreign Aid and Civic Organizations in Ukraine." *Civil Societies and Social Movements: Potentials and Problems*. Ed. Derrick Purdue. NY: New York: Routledge, 2007. 35–52.

Polleri, Federico. 2007. "Elogio de la Imprudencia. Sujeto, identidad y poder popular" ["Praising Imprudence: Subject, Identity and Popular Power"]. In Acha, Omar. Campione y Aldo Casas. *Reflexiones sobre el poder popular [Reflections on Popular Power]*. Bueno Aires: El Colectivo: 193–206.

Porter, Theodore. 1995. *Trust in Numbers: The Pursuit of Objectivity in Science and Public Life*. Princeton, NJ: Princeton University Press.

Poster, Michael. 1995. *Second Media Age*. Cambridge, MA: Polity Press.

Potter, Trevor. 2002. "Internet Politics 2000: Over-hyped, then Under-hyped, the Revolution Begins." *Election Law Journal* 1(1): 25–33.

Powell, Leslie. "Western and Russian Environmental NGOs: A Greener Russia?" *The Power and Limits of NGOs*. Eds. Sarah E. Mendelson and John K. Glenn. NY: Columbia University Press, 2002: 126–151.

President Yushchenko's World AIDS Day Address. 1 Dec. 2006. President Of Ukraine. Official Website. Nov. 2007 <http://ww8.president.gov.ua/en/news/data/11_12351.html>.

Primavera, Heloisa. 2002. *Moneda Social: ¿Gattopardismo o Ruptura de Paradigma? [Social Money: Gatopardism or Paradigmatic Breakdown?]* Obtenido de www.heloisaprimavera.com.ar.

Pryor, John H., Sylvia Hurtado, Victor B. Saenz, Jessica S. Korn, José Luis Santos and William S. Korn. 2006. *The American Freshman: National Norms for Fall 2006*. Higher Education Research Institute. University of California, Los Angeles (December).

Downloaded April 7, 2009 from http://www.gseis.ucla.edu/heri/PDFs/06CIRPFS_Norms_Narrative.pdf.

Putnam, Robert. 2000. *Bowling Alone: The Collapse and Renewal of American Community.* New York: Simon and Schuster.

Quijano, Anibal and Wallerstein, Immanuel. 1992. 'Americanity as a Concept, or the Americas in the Modern World-System', *Social Science Journal* 44(4): 549–557.

Quijano, Aníbal. 1977. *Imperialismo y "marginalidad" en América Latina [Imperialism and Marginality in Latin America].* La Paz: Mosca Azul Editores.

——. 2000. "Coloniality of Power, Eurocentrism, and Latin America." *Nepantla: Views from South,* 1:3. 533–580.

Razeto, Luis. 1988. *Economía de solidaridad y organización popular [The Solidarity Economy and Popular Organization].* Santiago de Chile: Edicion digital.

Rebon, Julian and Ignacio Saavedra. 2006. *Empresas recuoperadas. La autogestión de los trabajadores [Recuperated Enterprises: Workers Self-management].* Buenos Aires, Argentina: Capital Intelectual.

Rebon, Julian. 2004. *Desobedeciendo al desempleo. La experiencia de las empresas recuperadas [Disobeying Unemployment: The Experience of Recuperated Enterprises].* Buenos Aires: La Rosa Blindada / Ediciones PICASO.

Reddaway, Peter, and Dmitri Glinski. *Tragedy of Russia's Reforms: Market Bolshevism Against Democracy.* Washington, D.C.: United States Institute of Peace Press, 2001.

Reel, Monte. 2007. "Bolivia's Rural Women Are Finding Their Voice," *Washington Post,* March 6.

Reese, Ellen, Christine Petit, and David S. Meyer. 2008 "Sudden Mobilization: Movement Crossovers, Threats, and the Surprising Rise of the U.S. Anti-War Movement." *Social Movement Coalitions,* edited by Nella Van Dyke and Holly McCammon.

Reese, Ellen, Christopher Chase-Dunn, Kadambari Anantram, Gary Coyne, Matheu Kaneshiro, Ashley N. Koda, Roy Kwon, and Preeta Saxena 2008 "Place and Base: the Public Sphere in the Social Forum Process" IROWS Working Paper # 45.

Reger, Jo. 2008. "Drawing Identity Boundaries: The Creation of Contemporary Feminism." Identity Work in Social Movements, edited by J. Reger, D. J. Myers, and R. L. Einwohner. Minneapolis, MN: University of Minnesota Press: 101–120.

Reilley, Brigg, Dave Burrows, Vitalec Melnikov, Tatiana Andreeva, Murdo Bijl, Hans Veeken. "Injecting Drug Use and HIV in Moscow: Results of a Survey." *AIDS, Drugs and Society.* Ed. Anna Alexandrova. NY: International Debate Education Association, 2004: 220–238.

Reilly, Adam. 2004. "MoveOn Confronts the Future. How Does a Grassroots Power Redirect its Muscle?" Available at http://www.boston/news_features/otherstories/04302654.asp.

Reimann, Kim D. "Up to No Good? Recent Critics and Critiques of NGOs." *Subcontracting Peace: The Challenges of the NGO Peacebuilding.* Eds. Oliver P. Richmond and Henry F. Carey. Burlington, VT: Ashgate Publishing, 2005: 37–54.

Reitan, Ruth. 2007. *Global Activism.* London: Routledge.

Rendon, Laura I. 2000. "Academics of the Heart." *About Campus.* July–August: 3–5.

Renuka, Raysam. 2003. "Piqued? Make an Anti-Bush TV Spot." *The Austin American Statesman,* October 20, p. A11.

Richter, James. "Evaluating Western Assistance to Russian Women's Organizations." *The Power and Limits of NGOs.* Eds. Sarah E. Mendelson and John K. Glenn. NY: Columbia University Press, 2002: 54–90.

Rigby, Thomas H. 1991. *Political Elites in the USSR.* Brookfield, VT: Gower.

Rivkin-Fish, Michele. *Women's Health in Post-Soviet Russia: The Politics of Intervention.* Bloomington, IN: Indiana University, 2005.

"Road Map on Scaling-up Towards Universal Access to HIV/AIDS Prevention, Treatment, Care and Support in Ukraine by 2010." 2006. *UNAIDS Report* Apr. Available http://www.network.org.ua/pdf/ukraine-ua-report-eng.pdf

Rockefeller, Stuart A. 2007. "Dual Power in Bolivia: Movement and Government Since the Election of 2005." *Urban Anthropology & Studies of Cultural Systems & World Economic Development*, 36(3): 161–193.

Rodgers, Denis. 2007. "Son como una esponja. Notas antropologicas en torno de dialogos con el MTD-la Matanza" ["They are Like a Sponge: Anthropological Notes on the Dialogues with the MDT-la Matanza"]. In Toty Flores (Comp.), *Cuando con otros somos nosotros[When with Others We are Ourselves]*. Buenos Aires : Peña Lillo / Ed Continente: 125–127.

Rodriguez, Esteban. 2007. "Mas aca del Estado, en el Estado y contra el Estado. Apuntes para la definición del Poder Popular" ["Closer than the State, within the State and against the State"]. In Acha, Omar Campione y Aldo Casas, *Reflexiones sobre el poder popular [Reflections on Popular Power]*. Buenos Aires: El Colectivo: 101–128.

Rodriguez, Esteban and Mariano Pacheco. 2007. *La izquierda autonama en el laberinto: apuntes sobre el poder popular en Argentina [The Autonomous Left in the Labyrinth: Observations on Popular Power in Argentina]*. Buenos Aires: El Colectivo.

Rojas, Johnny Fernández. 2008. "La ciudad de El Alto de pie…y con la mirada en el siglo XXI" ["The City of El Alto in Struggle…and with their Sights on the Twenty-First Century"]. *La Razón*. July 16.

Romer, Nancy. 2008. "Bolivia: Latin America's Experiment with Grassroots Democracy." *New Politics*, Winter: 3–39.

Rose, Fred 2000 *Coalitions across the Class Divide: Lessons from the Labor, Peace, and Environmental Movements*. Ithaca, NY: Cornell University Press.

Rosen, Fred. 2007. "Breaking with the Past: A 40th Anniversary Conversation with Margarita López Maya." *NACLA Report on the Americas*, 40(3): 4–8.

Rubin, Jeffrey. 2006. "In the Streets or in the Institutions?" *Latin American Studies Association Forum* 37(1): 26–29.

Saenko, Y., I. Demchenko, V. Zhukov, K. Kashchenkova, V. Kostritsya, O. Lisenko, A. Marusov, Y. Privalov, and O. Trofimenko. *Monitoring Epidemii VIL/SNIDU*. [Monitoring the HIV/AIDS Epidemic] *Otsinka Efektivnosti Protidii: Social'nii Aspekt*. Kiev: Foliant, 2004.

Salamon, Lester M., and Helmut K. Anheier. "Toward a Common Definition." *Defining the Nonprofit Sector: A Cross-national Analysis*. Eds. Lester K. Salamon and Helmut Anheier. NY: Manchester University Press, 1997: 11–28.

Sandbrook, Richard, ed., 2003. *Civilizing Globalization: A Survival Guide*. Albany, NY: SUNY Press.

Santos, Boaventura de Sousa. 2006. *The Rise of the Global Left*. London: Zed Press.

Sassen, Saskia. 1998. *Globalization and its Discontent: Essays on the New Mobility of People and Money*. New York: New Press.

Scheff, Thomas J. 1994. *Bloody Revenge: Emotions, Nationalism and War*. Boulder, CO: Westview Press.

Schneider, Carol Geary. 1995. "The Drama of Diversity and Democracy." A Report for the American Commitments Initiative. Association of American Colleges and Universities.

——. 2005. "Liberal Education and the Civic Engagement Gap." (127–145) Adrianna J. Kezar, Tony C. Chambers, and John C. Burkhardt (eds.), *Higher Education for the Public Good*. San Francisco: Jossey Bass.

——. 2007. "Civic Learning in a Diverse Democracy: Education for Shared Futures." Diversity & Democracy AAC&U Vol. 10, no. 3 (Fall).

Scholte, Jan Aart. 2000. "Global Civil Society", in Ngaire Woods, ed., *The Political Economy of Globalization*. Macmillan: London.

——. 2002. "Civil Society and Democracy in Global Governance." *Global Governance*, 8: 3.

Scholte, Jan Aart. 2004. "The WTO and Civil Society", in Brian Hocking and Steven McGuire, eds., *Trade Politics: International, Domestic and Regional Perspectives.* London: Routledge.

Schönleitner, Günter. 2003 "World Social Forum: Making Another World Possible?" (127–149) John Clark (ed.): *Globalizing Civic Engagement: Civil Society and Transnational Action.* London: Earthscan.

Scott, James. 1992 *Domination and the Arts of Resistance: Hidden Transcripts.* New Haven: Yale University Press.

Secretaria de Empleo. Ministerio de Trabajo. 2007. *Guia 2007. Empresas Recuperadas por losTrabajadores [2007 Guide: Enterprises Recuperated by their Workers].* Buenos Aires, Argentina: Cooperativa de trabajadores de Artes Gráficas.

Sen, Jai and Madhuresh Kumar with Patrick Bond and Peter Waterman 2007 *A Political Programme for the World Social Forum?: Democracy, Substance and Debate in the Bamako Appeal and the Global Justice Movements.* Indian Institute for Critical Action: Centre in Movement (CACIM), New Delhi, India & the University of KwaZulu-Natal Centre for Civil Society (CCS), Durban, South Africa. http://www.cacim.net/book/home.html

Shaw, Timothy M. "Overview—Global/Local: States, Companies and Civil Societies at the End of the Twentieth Century." *Global Institutions and Local Empowerment.* Ed. Kendall Stiles. New York, NY: St. Martin's Press, 2000. 1–8.

Shelley, Louise. "Civil Society Mobilized Against Corruption: Russia and Ukraine." *Civil Society and Corruption.* Ed. Michael Johnston. Lanham, MD: University Press of America, 2005: 3–22.

Shpek, Roman V. "Priorities of Reform." *Economic Reforms in Ukraine: The Unfinished Agenda.* Eds. Anders Aslund and De Menil Georges. NY: Armonk: M. E. Sharpe, Inc., 2000: 29–48.

SIEMPRO. 2001. *Informe de la situación Social 2000–2001 [2000–2001 Report on the Social Situation].* Buenos Aires: Secretaria de Desarrollo Social / Presidencia de la Nación.

Simonson, Karin. 2003. "The Anti-war movement: Waging Peace on the Brink of War." Geneva, March Centre for Applied Studies in International Negotiations (CASIN). March.

Sitrin, Marina. 2006. *Horizontalism: Voices of Popular Power in Argentina.* Edinburgh: AK Press.

Sklair, Leslie. 2002. *The Transnational Capitalist Class.* Cambridge, MA: Blackwell.

Smith, Jackie, Karides, Marina, Becker, Marc, Brunelle, Dorval, Chase-Dunn, Christopher, della Porta, Donatella, Icaza, Rosalba, Juris, Jeffrey, Mosca, Lorenzo, Reese, Ellen, Smith, Peter and Vaszuez, Rolando. 2007. *The World Social Forum and the Challenges of Global Democracy.* Boulder, CO: Paradigm Publishers.

Smith, Jackie. 2002. "Globalizing Resistance: The Battle of Seattle and the Future of Social Movements", in Jackie Smith and Hank Johnston, eds., *Globalization and Resistance: Transnational Dimensions of Social Movements.* Lanham, MD: Rowman & Littlefield.

Spronk, Susan. 2008. "After the Water Wars in Bolivia: The Struggle for a 'Social-Public' Alternative," in *Upside Down World,* April 29.

"Srednii Dohod Zhitelya Ukrainy—200 Dollarov v Mesyats." [Average Income of a of Resident of Ukraine - 200 Dollars per Month] 2007. *Vechernii Khar'kov* 15 Mar.: Retrieval Nov. 2007 <http://www.vecherniy.kharkov.ua/news/9624/>.

Stahler-Sholk, Richard, Harry E. Vanden, and Glen David Kuecker. 2008. "Introduction," in Richard Stahler-Sholk, Harry E. Vanden, and Glen David Kuecker, eds., *Latin American Movements in the Twenty-First Century.* Lanham, MD: Rowman and Littlefield: 1–15.

Stahler-Sholk, Richard. 2005. "Time of the Snails: Autonomy and Resistance in Chiapas." *NACLA Report on the Americas* 38(5): 34–38.

———. 2007. "Resisting Neoliberal Homogenization: The Zapatista Autonomy Movement." *Latin American Perspectives*. 34 (2): 48–63.

———. 2008. "Resisting Neoliberal Homogenization: The Zapatista Autonomy Movement," in Richard Stahler-Sholk, Harry E. Vanden, and Glen David Kuecker, eds., *Latin American Movements in the Twenty-First Century*. Lanham, MD: Rowman and Littlefield: 113–130.

Starr, Amory. 2000. *Naming the Enemy: Anti-corporate Movements Confront Globalization*. London: Zed Books.

Starr, Amory and Jason Adams. 2003. "Anti-globalization: The Global Fight for Local Autonomy." *New Political Science* 25(1): 18–42.

Stedile, João Pedro. 2008. "The Class Struggles in Brazil: The MST Perspective." Interviewed by Atilio Boron. *Socialist Register 2008*: 193–216.

Stedile, João Pedro and Bernardo Mançano Fernandes. 1999. *Brava Gente: A Trajetória do MST e a Luta pela Terra no Brasil [Valient People: The Rise of the Landless People's Movement and the Struggle for Land in Brazil]*. São Paulo: Fundação Perseu Abramo.

Stefanoni, Pablo. 2005. "The MAS is of the Centre-Left: Interview with Alvaro García Linera," in *International Viewpoint Online Magazine*, IV373—December.

Stefanoni, Pablo and Ricardo Bajo. 2008. "Bolivia: Compromise and Advance." *Green Left*, November 14. www.greenleft.org/au/2008/775/39960.

Stephen, Lynn. 2002. *Zapata Lives! Histories and Cultural Politics in Southern Mexico*. Berkeley: University of California Press.

Stevenson, Seth. 2004. "Not So Amateur Night." *Slate Magazine*, January 13, p. 27.

Stieglitz, Joseph. 2002. *Globalization and its Discontents*. New York: Allen Lane/The Penguin Press.

Stirrat, R. L. "Cultures of Consultancy." *Critique of Anthropology* 20.1 (2000): 31–46.

Strata, Miguel and Fernado Mazzeo. 2007. "Introducción" ["Introduction"] Omar Acha, et al *Reflexiones sobre el poder popular [Reflections on Popular Power]*. Buenos Aires, El Colectivo: 7–15.

Sundstrom, Lisa M. *Funding civil society: Foreign assistance and NGO development in Russia*. Standford, CA: Stanford University Press. 2006.

Sztulwark, Diego. 2002. "Doce hipotesis sobre el contrapoder elaboradas desde la Argentina convulsionada" ["Twelve Hypotheses on Counter-power as Formulated in Argentina"]. *Bajo el Volcan*, 5: 47–58.

Tabera, Gabriel. 2007. "La Economía en Tiempos de Evo" ["The Economy in Times of Evo Morales"], *ECONOTICIAS*, especial para ARGENPRESS.info, Aug. 30. <www.argenpress.info/nota.asp?num=046662>.

Teichman, Judith. 2004. "The World Bank and Policy Reform in Mexico and Argentina." *Latin American Politics & Society* 46(1): 39–74.

The Economist. 2007. "An Ad Too Far." September 27, p. 17.

Tilly, Charles. 1978. *From Mobilization to Revolution*, New York: The University of Michigan, Random House.

———. 2004. *Social Movements, 1768–2004*. Boulder, Colorado: Paradigm Publishers.

Toffler, Alvin and Heidy. 1979. *La tercera ola [The Third Wave]*. Mexico: Plaza y Valdez.

Touraine, Alain. 1985a. *Social Movements and Social Change*. London: Sage.

———. 1985b. "An Introduction to the Study of Social Movements." *Social Research* 52: 749–58.

———. 1988. *The Workers' Movement*. Cambridge, MA: Cambridge University Press.

———. 2006. *Un nuevo paradigma para comprender el mundo de hoy [A New Paradigm for Understanding Today's World]*. Buenos Aires, Paidos.

Toussaint, Eric and Damien Millet. 2007. Debt: Ecuador at a Historic Turning Point, CADTM, May <www.cadmt.org/article.php3?id_article=2672>.

Treanor, Paul. 2003. "Who Controls the ESF?" *World Social Forum: Challenging Empires.* New Delhi: Viveka Foundation, http://www.choike.org/nuevo_eng/informes/1557. html.

Trofimenko, Martha B. 2003. "Law as Infrastructure: Overcoming Obstacles to Development of a Democratic State." pp 135–155 in Wsevolod W. Isajiw (ed). *Society in Transition: Social Change in Ukraine in Western Perspective.* Toronto, ON: Canadian Scholars' Press, Inc.

US Office of Management and Budget. 2006. Department of State and Other International Programs Washington, DC. Office the President of the United States of America. <http://www.whitehouse.gov/omb/budget/fy2007/state.html>.

Ukraine: Country Situation Analysis. 2007. UNAIDS. Nov. 2007 <http://www.unaids. org/en/Regions_Countries/Countries/ukraine.asp>.

US Census Bureau. 2007. *Poverty: 2006 Highlights.* Suitland: US Census Bureau. <http:// www.census.gov/hhes/www/poverty/poverty06/pov06hi.html>.

US Conference of Catholic Bishops. 2006. "Poverty USA: The Working Poor." <http:// www.usccb.org/cchd/povertyusa/about.shtml>.

USAID/Ukraine HIV/AIDS Strategy 2003–2008. 3 Oct. 2003. USAID, Kyiv, Ukraine. 27 Apr. 2007 Available http://ukraine.usaid.gov/lib/hivstrategy.zip

Utne, Leif. 2003. "MoveOn.org Holds Virtual Primary." June 23. Available at http:// www.utne.com/webwatch/2003_731/news/10655-1.html.

Uvin, Peter. "From Local Organizations to Global Governance: The Role of NGOs in International Relations." *Global Institutions and Local Empowerment.* Ed. Kendall Stiles. New York, NY: St. Martin's Press, 2000: 9–29.

Van Aelst, Peter and Stephaan Walgrave. 2003. "Open and Closed Mobilization Contexts and the Normalization of the Protester." Pp. 123–146 in *Cyberprotest: New Media, and Citizen Social Movements,* Wim Van De Donk, Brian Lad, Paul Nixon and Dieter Ructh (eds). London: Routledge.

Van Dyke, Nella 2003 "Crossing movement boundaries: Factors that facilitate coalition protest by American college students, 1930–1990." *Social Problems* 50(2): 226–50.

Vanden, Harry E. 2005. "Brazil's Landless Hold Their Ground." *NACLA Report on the Americas* 38(5): 21–26.

Vanden, Harry E. 2008. "Social Movements and New Forms of Resistance," in Richard Stahler-Sholk, Harry E. Vanden, and Glen David Kuecker, eds., *Latin American Movements in the Twenty-First Century.* Lanham, MD: Rowman and Littlefield: 39–55.

Velthuis, Olav. 2006. "Inside a world of spin: Four days at the World Trade Organization." Ethnography 7(1).

Watts, Duncan. 2003. *Six Degrees: The Science of a Connected Age.* New York: W.W. Norton.

Wainright, Hilary. 2004. "From Mumbai with Hope." Red Pepper. March. <www. redpepper.org.uk>.

Wallerstein, Immanuel. 2006. "An American Dilemma of the 21st Century" *Societies Without Borders.* Volume 1, Number 1: 7–20 (14).

Walsh, Kieron, Nicholas Deakin, Paula Smith, Peter Spurgeon and Neil Thomas. *Contracting for Change: Contracts in Health, Social Care, and Other Local Government Services.* New York: Oxford University Press, 1997.

Waterman, Peter. 2003. "World Social Forum: The Secret of Fire." World Social Forum: Challenging Empires. New Delhi: Viveka Foundation, http://www.choike .org/nuevo_eng/informes/1557.html.

Webber, Jeffery R. 2008. "Bolivia's Post-Referendum Conjuncture," *Bolivia Rising,* http://boliviarising.blogspot.com, accessed September 6, 2008.

Weber, Max. 1946. "Politics as a Vocation" in *From Max Weber: Essays in Sociology.* Translated and edited by H. H. Gerth and C. Wright Mills. New York: Oxford University Press.

Weissman, Robert. 2003. "Seattle: Global Protest Comes of Age", in Richard Sandbrook, ed., *Civilizing Globalization: A Survival Guide*. Albany, NY: SUNY Press.

Welch, Cliff. 2006. "Movement Histories: A Preliminary Historiography of Brazil's Landless Laborers' Movement (MST)." *Latin American Research Review* 41(1): 198–210.

Wellman, Barry. 2000. "Changing Connectivity: A Future History of Y2.03K." *Sociological Research Online* 4. Available at http://www.socresonline.org.uk/4/4/wellman.html.

West, Guida and Rhoda Lois Blumberg. 1990. "Reconstructing Social Protest from a Feminist Perspective." Pp. 3–406 in *Women and Social Protest*, edited by R. L. Blumberg. New York: Oxford University Press.

Wikipedia, the Free Encyclopedia. Nov. 2007. Viktor Yushchenko. <http://en.wikipedia.org/wiki/Yushchenko>.

Wilkinson, Daniel. 2008. "Chávez's Fix." *The Nation*, March 10: 31–41.

Wilkinson, Rorden. 2005. "Managing Global Civil Society: The WTO's engagement with NGOs", in Randall D. Germain and Michael Kenny, eds., *The Idea of Global Civil Society: Politics and Ethics in a Globalizing Era*. New York: Routledge.

Williams, Marc. 2005. "Civil Society and the World Trading System", in Dominic Kelly and Wyn Grant, eds., *The Politics of International Trade in the Twenty-first Century*. New York: Palgrave MacMillan.

Witte, Benjamin. 2006. "Multinational Gold Rush in Guatemala," in Vijay Prashad and Teo Ballvé, eds., *Dispatches from Latin America*. Boston: South End Press, pp. 316–325.

World Bank. 2007. *Trade Research: Migration and Remittances*. World Bank World Development Data and Research, April. <http://econ.worldbank.org/.

Wright, Angus and Wendy Wolford. 2003. *To Inherit the Earth: The Landless Movement and the Struggle for a New Brazil*. Oakland, CA: Food First Books.

Xu, Yi-chong. 2005. "Models, Templates and Currents: The World Bank and Electricity Reform." *Review of International Political Economy* 12(4): 647–673.

Yatsenko, Vladimir. 2005. "Social'noe Strahovanie i Mif o Sverhvysokih Social'nyh Nalogah V Ukraine." [Social Insurance and the Myth of Excessively High Taxes in Ukraine] *Zerkalo Nedeli* 18 Jun. Retrieval 16 Oct <http://www.zn.ua/2000/2040/50359/>.

Zavaleta Mercado, René. 1979. *El Poder Dual en América Latina [Dual Power in Latin America]*. Mexico City: Siglo XXI Ediciones.

Zhurzhenko, Tatiana. "Free Market Ideology and New Women's Identities in Post-socialist Ukraine." *The European Journal of Women's Studies* 8.1 (2001): 29–49.

——. 2005. "El Alto: A World of Difference," in *IRC Americas Special Report*, October 12.

Zibechi, Raúl. 2008. "The Revolution of 1968: When those from below said 'enough!' " Americas Program Discussion Paper, http://Americas.irc-online.org/am/5272. Washington, DC: Center for International Policy. June 3.

——. 2008. "Hacia El Fin de la Década Progresista" ["Towards the End of the Progressive Decade"] *La Jornada*, July 7.

——. 2008. "Hacia el fin de la era progresista" ["Towards the End of the Progressive Era"]. *La Jornada*, July 4.

——. 2008. "Los de abajo siguen de pie" ["Those Below Continue the Struggle"] *Rebélion*, October 21.

SUBJECT INDEX

ABONG (see Brazilian Association of Nongovernmental Organizations)
abortion, 53, 297–298
   clandestine abortions, 298
accelerated pluralism, 64, 68, 72
accountability, 31, 94–95, 99, 101, 136, 141, 164, 184, 202, 248
Action Forum, 68
ActionAid, 94, 146
activism, 4, 12–16, 30, 33, 49, 53–54, 56, 59, 61–63, 65–71, 73–75, 77, 79–81, 93, 121, 143, 159, 161, 164, 169
   activists, 15, 18, 22–23, 28, 42, 44, 46, 50, 52, 54, 57, 59–60, 66, 68–69, 75, 78–79, 83–84, 93, 95, 104–105, 107–111, 113, 121, 133, 141–143, 145–146, 150, 152, 155–156, 158, 187, 198, 238–239, 241, 262, 267, 270, 287
Addams, Jane, 15
Adolf Hitler, 80
adult education programs, 265
advocacy organization representatives, 171, 177
Africa, 1, 2, 124, 126, 129, 133
   Africans, 126
agrarian reform, 223, 284, 285
agribusiness, 268
   agrobusiness elites, 283–284, 286
agriculture, 163, 168, 173, 176, 213, 223, 236, 239, 276
Alan García, 191
ALBA, 207–208
   ALBA Bank, 208
alienation, 46, 57, 290, 295
alternative hegemonic blocks, 196
alternative media, 60, 121–122, 124, 129, 131, 133, 203–204
   alternative media/culture, 121, 122
alternative model, 136, 270, 284
alternative social power, 268
altiplano, 276, 280, 282–283
   altiplano municipalities, 280
Amazonia, 198, 287
   amazonian, 287
analytical capacity, 265
anarchism, 121, 122–124, 127, 129, 141, 149, 150–152

Andean Capitalism, 287
Andean Community of Nations (CAN), 205
Andean region, 196–197
   Andean Regional Initiative, 196
"another world is possible", 37, 57, 143, 243
anti-Americanism, 204
anti-authoritarians, 149–150, 159
anti-capitalist logic, 293
anti-corporate, 122–123, 125, 128–131
   anti-corporate/alternative globalization, 123
   anti-corporate/peace, 123
anti-terrorism policies, 196
applied sociology, 16
Argentina, 7, 156, 187, 191, 195, 198, 203, 205, 223, 235, 239, 240–241, 243–246, 250, 253–258, 260, 262, 264, 266, 269, 271
   Argentine peso, 255, 260
   Buenos Aires, 241, 258–259, 263, 265, 271
   de la rúa, Fernando, 191
   Duhalde, Eduardo, 258
   Justicialista Party, 254–256, 258–259, 264
   Kirchner Administrations (Nestor and Cristina), 191, 240, 273, 289
   Kirchner, Néstor, 191, 240
   Menem, Carlos, 254
   MNFERT (National Movement of Factories and Businesses Recuperated by the Workers), 263
   Movimiento de Trabajadores Desocupados de La Matanza (Mtd La Matanza), 257
   Partido Comunista Revolucionario (PCR), 256
   Peronism (see also Justicialista Party), 187, 244, 256, 264, 269
   Plan de Convertibilidad, 255
   Planes Jefes y Jefas de Familia (head of household subsidy program), 256
armed guerrilla movements, 266
artistic production, 142
Artists United to Win Without War, 77

NAME INDEX